The Creation of American Common Law, 1850–1880
Technology, Politics, and the Construction of Citizenship

This book is a comparative study of American legal development in the mid-nineteenth century. Focusing on Illinois and Virginia, supported by observations from six additional states, the book traces the crucial formative moment in the development of an American system of common law in northern and southern courts. The process of legal development and the form that the basic analytical categories of American law came to have are explained as the products of different responses to the challenge of new industrial technologies, particularly railroads. The nature of those responses was dictated by the ideologies that accompanied the social, political, and economic orders of the two regions. American common law, ultimately, is found to express an emerging model of citizenship, appropriate to modern conditions. As a result, the process of legal development provides an illuminating perspective on the character of American political thought in a formative period of the nation.

Howard Schweber completed his undergraduate studies at the University of Pennsylvania and received a J.D. from the University of Washington in 1989. He practiced law for several years, primarily in San Francisco, then returned to academic pursuits, earning an M.A. in history from the University of Chicago in 1994 and a Ph.D. in government from Cornell University in 1999. Since that time, he has taught in the Political Science Department at the University of Wisconsin–Madison. He is the author of *Speech, Conduct, and the First Amendment* (2003) and articles in journals such as *Law and History Review, Law and Society Review, Studies in American Political Development*, and *Science in Context*.

For my parents

The Creation of American Common Law, 1850–1880

Technology, Politics, and the Construction of Citizenship

HOWARD SCHWEBER

University of Wisconsin–Madison

PUBLISHED BY THE PRESS SYNDICATE OF THE UNIVERSITY OF CAMBRIDGE
The Pitt Building, Trumpington Street, Cambridge, United Kingdom

CAMBRIDGE UNIVERSITY PRESS
The Edinburgh Building, Cambridge CB2 2RU, UK
40 West 20th Street, New York, NY 10011-4211, USA
477 Williamstown Road, Port Melbourne, VIC 3207, Australia
Ruiz de Alarcón 13, 28014, Madrid, Spain
Dock House, The Waterfront, Cape Town 8001, South Africa

http://www.cambridge.org

First published 2004

Printed in the United States of America

Typeface Sabon 10/12 pt.   *System* LATEX 2_ε [TB]

A catalog record for this book is available from the British Library.

Library of Congress Cataloging in Publication Data

Schweber, Howard H.
The creation of American common law, 1850–1880 / Howard Schweber.
  p. cm.
Includes bibliographical references and index.
ISBN 0-521-82462-1 (hardback)
1. Common law – United States – History – 19th century.   I. Title.
KF394.S39   2001
340.5′7′0973–dc21   2003048467

ISBN 0 521 82462 1 hardback

Contents

Acknowledgments

This book is based on research that began at the University of Chicago and was continued at Cornell University and at the University of Wisconsin, supported by grants from the University of Chicago, the Mellon Foundation, and the University of Wisconsin. At all stages in the project, I benefited immensely from the guidance and critical insights of numerous scholars. In particular, I would like to thank (in alphabetical order) Greg Alexander, Richard Bensel, David Canon, Mark Graber, Isaac Kramnick, Theodore Lowi, and Steve Sheppard for their guidance, encouragement, and assistance. Portions of the research in this book appeared previously as an article in *Studies in American Political Development*; Karen Orren, Steven Skowronek, and several anonymous readers helped shape that portion of the discussion. Anonymous readers for Cambridge University Press provided thoughtful and illuminating critiques of earlier versions of the entire manuscript. Janet Donovan and Richard Parrish provided invaluable research assistance. In conducting research for this book, I was the beneficiary of the generous assistance of the reference staffs at Cornell's Olin Library, the Cornell Law School Library, the University of Chicago Law School Library, the University of Wisconsin Law School Library, the Illinois Historical Society Archives, the Virginia Supreme Court Library, the Library of Virginia, and the Virginia Historical Society. Reference librarians are the unsung heroes of the world of scholarship; certainly this book would have been impossible without them. In writing this book, I have benefited from the efforts of no fewer than three exceptionally fine editorial minds: Lewis Bateman, Andrew Saff, and Lynn Schweber. The last-mentioned of these has lived with this project since its inception, and has helped in its creation in innumerable ways, among which her keen editorial eye is perhaps the least important. Elements of the argument of this book were presented as papers at annual meetings of the American Political Science Association, the Western Political Science Association, the American Society for Legal History, and the University of Wisconsin Workshop in American Political Development, and at job talks at the University of Wisconsin's Department of Political Science and Law School. Audience members present at each of those presentations made helpful, interesting, and often provocative comments. The errors that remain are my own.

Introduction

In the decade preceding the Civil War, judges in the highest courts of
northern states created the system of American common law. The principles of tort, contract, and property liability that these judges developed
were entirely different from the inherited system of English law that they
replaced. The language and categories of pleading, the allocation and
definition of burdens of proof, the standards for the description, and the
adjudication of cases all were transformed. This was not merely a process
of revision; it was a reconfiguration of the basic reasoning process that
defined the logic of the law, its political significance, and its social function. These new, uniquely American common law principles, moreover,
remain the basic elements of American legal thought and discourse to
this day.

There was not a single, national pattern of legal development. Instead,
there were two distinct regional patterns of development, each relatively
uniform, in the North and the South. The principles of American common
law were first worked out by judges in northern courts in the 1850s.
Those principles were ultimately adopted by courts in the South in the
1870s, imported wholesale from the northern jurisdictions in which
they had been created. But the antebellum, decade-long process in which
American legal doctrines were developed and worked out was solely a
northern one. The immediate questions, then, are why was there such a
sharply bifurcated pattern in the historical development of American law,
and what are the consequences of recognizing this differential pattern
of development for our understanding of the relation between legal and
political thought and American political development in the nineteenth
century?

The American version of common law that was created and developed in northern state courts of the 1850s differed from the earlier version in a number of ways. First, where English common law had been divided into dozens of categories and subcategories, each with its own set of rules and its own approach for the analysis of cases, American common law was organized around the broad, unified categories of tort, contract, and property law that are familiar to modern lawyers. This was more than a matter of simplifying pleading practices. The new organization of legal categories meant the rationalization of the common law, such that a single set of principles would govern a vast range of different cases.

Second, the rights and duties of legal actors were similarly made uniform. In the English system, and the earlier American system, the legally enforceable obligations that one actor owed another would be determined on the basis of the status of each person and the precise relationship between the actors. In the new American system, conduct was evaluated against an objective standard rather than in terms of relational claims, and everyone was universally bound by the same duties. These duties, moreover, were not owed by one individual to another based on their relationship in a given interaction; they were owed by everybody to the world at large. That is, everyone was bound to behave in accordance with duties of care at all times because that was the obligation that the law placed on the members of American society. That obligation was not conceived in terms of the welfare of one's fellow citizens as individuals involved in transactions, but rather in terms of the collective welfare of the nation. That collective welfare, in turn, was phrased not in the traditional terms of preserving local order, but rather in terms of a vision of technology-driven progress.

Above all, the universal duty that was the hallmark of American common law in the antebellum North was the duty to avoid obstructing the wheels of progress. Technology-driven progress, exemplified by trains, defined a set of public goods that the common law would be called upon to serve. Paramount among these was the Need for Speed, the imperative demand of the emerging political economy for efficiency, regularity, and rapidity, achieved by the work of machines. The result was a universal set of duties, equally applicable to everyone regardless of his or her social position or role in a transaction, that completely reconfigured the rules for determining legal liability. Something of this idea is captured in what I will call the Duty to Get Out of the Way, an idea exemplified in new rules that made it the obligation of persons to avoid allowing themselves or their animals to be struck by trains, rather than the duty of trains to avoid hitting persons or stock. The idea also appears in the form of duties of workers to avoid injury and to ensure the diligence and efficiency of other workers, the duties of shippers of goods to avoid exposing carriers to unexpected liabilities, and the duties of railroad passengers to avoid putting themselves in positions in which they might suffer injuries. All of these were novel conceptions, and all of them were grounded in the ideas that society required the benefits of technology-driven progress, and that citizens were required to learn to behave in ways that would aid that progress.

The duty to accommodate progress swept through all areas of the law, trumping all traditionally recognized property-based rights and entirely displacing a traditional model in which legal duties arose out of the relationship between parties and could not extend beyond the relationship that defined them. This new idea of a legally enforceable duty to be part of the national mission of technology-driven progress was the solvent that dissolved the old categories of common law adjudication and made room for the new doctrines of American law.

The terms of the specific legal doctrines involved in this shift of focus will be discussed in later chapters; at the outset, what is important to recognize is that in the 1850s northern courts changed the starting point for any legal adjudication. Where previously the process of adjudication began with an analysis of relative claims of individual rights, now the focus shifted to absolute claims of universal duties. And where the earlier inquiry began with the conduct of the defendant and the harms that conduct may have caused, the initial inquiry turned instead to the conduct of the plaintiff and the question of whether such a person's claims for damages deserved to be heard. A person who failed to meet the standards of conduct demanded by the collective interest in progress would have no claim on the courts' protection.

It was in this latter sense that the new, American system of common law that emerged in the northern states in the 1850s was constructed around a model of citizenship, one that replaced private rights with public duties as its lodestone. By "citizenship" I do not mean the technical legal categories of naturalization, or eligibility for participation in the formal political process, although studies of the development of that concept in the nineteenth century have shown patterns of exclusion and inclusion that are echoed in the developments that are described here (Smith, 1997; Neuman, 1996; Kettner, 1978). In the context of the common law, the term "citizenship" refers to the qualifications that entitle a person to claim the protection of public institutions. One of the fundamental elements of nineteenth century American citizenship, as it had been in the English tradition, was the right to have one's claims heard in a court. In 1803, John Marshall stated the political proposition that made the rights of private litigants under the common law so central to English, and then American, republican thought. "The very essence of civil liberty certainly consists in the right of every individual to claim the protection of the laws, whenever he receives an injury. One of the first duties of government is to afford that protection. In Great Britain the king himself is sued in the respectful form of a petition, and he never fails to comply with the judgment of his court." (*Marbury v. Madison*, 5 U.S. 137, 163, 1803). The "essence of civil liberty" might equally have been described as "the essence of citizenship." The right of an individual to call on the powers of the state to vindicate a private claim, and the concomitant duty of the state to hear that claim, had been the sine qua non of an Englishman's full membership in the political community. In the American experience, access to courts was if anything an even more important measure of equal entitlement to the prerogatives of citizenship.

When new legal doctrines defined the characteristics of persons entitled to present their claims in a court, they defined a new, legally delimited set of standards for citizenship. The characteristics of persons entitled to bring their private claims before a court for vindication described a model of "virtues," an ideal type that defined a citizen entitled to have his or her interests heard by the institutions of public life. Parties who failed to show that their conduct had demonstrated those legally required virtues could not recover damages; the state would not vindicate such persons' claims, regardless of the conduct of the defendant. By focusing on the satisfaction of universally applicable duties, this new legal model of American citizenship went beyond the political rhetoric of "responsible individualism" (Lowi, 1986; Gold, 1990), defining to whom or what that responsibility was owed in ways that were sharply at odds with earlier models of citizens as autonomous bearers of politically guaranteed legal rights. The legal construction of American citizenship began from a rejection, rather than an affirmation, of what Leonard Levy calls "the incorrigible individualism of the common law" (Levy, 1957: 316).

The model of citizenship reflected in the new common law doctrines of the antebellum North fit neatly with a strand in nineteenth century American political philosophy that scholars have dubbed "liberal republicanism," or a theory of "liberal virtues" (Kloppenberg, 1987; Sinopoli, 1992; Dagger, 1997). Like classical republican theory, liberal republicanism demanded that citizens display certain qualities for the common good rather than solely pursuing their own interests. In the nineteenth century American version, however, these virtues were not the province solely of ruling elites, but rather belonged to everyone; concomitantly, the obligation to behave virtuously would be imposed on everyone, and the law would be the instrument for the enforcement of that obligation. In T. H. Marshall's classic formulation, citizenship implies "a kind of basic human equality associated with the concept of full membership in a community ... which is not inconsistent with the inequalities which distinguish the various economic levels in the society" (Marshall, 1964: 70). "Full membership" in the American political community includes access to courts of law. The universal duties of American common law represented the legal construction of a model of citizenship that was liberal and inclusive in its universality and its legal equality, but simultaneously republican and exclusive in its connection of the prerogatives of citizenship to the display of requisite virtues.

The liberal inclusiveness that went along with the leveling tendency of northern legal development should not be overstated. Even in northern states that rejected slavery, equality did not always extend to free blacks, a situation exemplified in the adoption by Illinois, after fierce debate, of a constitutional provision barring their settlement in the state after 1850. The construction of legal duties was also emphatically "gendered," that is, built around expectations drawn from the experiences of adult males who were presumed to define the template of public life (King, 1995; Welke, 1994, 1995; Chamallas and Kerber, 1990).[1] Northern liberal republicanism was, as its name says, a species of republicanism, a theory that contained a construction of "citizenship" in terms of qualities and virtues and extended full membership only to those persons who were deemed to possess those virtues. What was radically liberal about the system of American common law that emerged in the northern states were the very broad terms in which the population of virtuous persons was defined, and the complete rejection of any formal differentiation among classes of citizens. The experiences of blacks and women received scant attention in the formation of either the political theory or the jurisprudence in which it was articulated, but the legal model that was thus derived applied equally – and was equally unforgiving – to everyone regardless of race, gender, place of origin, or social status.

[1] A married woman, for example, could not file lawsuits in her own name in most states until the late nineteenth century. Instead, she would have to seek compensation in a suit filed by her husband or "next friend." In New York, this rule was changed in 1860; in Illinois, the rule remained in force until 1874. By the early twentieth century, most states permitted married women to sue and be sued in their own names (Bishop, 1875, vol. 2).

During the same period, the southern regional pattern was similarly uniform, and similarly reflected underlying ideas about the virtues of citizenship, but the pattern was the opposite of that observed in the North. Through the antebellum years, southern states' highest courts steadfastly resisted pressures to "reform" the common law. The political philosophy of liberal republicanism described previously was a specifically northern ideology. In the antebellum South, republicanism reigned supreme in a form uncontaminated by the intrusion of liberal ideas. Instead, southern elites' republicanism became increasingly closely tied to the hierarchical social order of slavery. In this context, political doctrines hardened around themes of preserving social order, and common law doctrines became instruments for forestalling change. These differences in dominant political cultures reflected differences in the social and political economic organizations of northern and southern society. In each case, unsurprisingly, the ideology that was reflected among judicial elites was that which provided the legitimating claims for their societies. That being the case, it may be equally unsurprising that change came to northern American common law at the same time that change came to the northern American system of political economy. In both cases, moreover, change was carried by the same vehicle: the railroads.

The differences between northern and southern legal development paralleled the differences between northern and southern attitudes about railroad development. Railroads were embraced by the same northern states that embraced legal innovation as the engine of progress toward a glorious and novel future. By contrast, slaveowning elites resisted and feared railroads, and technology generally, as potential threats, just as southern courts resisted changes to the system of common law. But the connections between railroads and the creation of American common law are much more specific than that. The cases in which the new doctrines were worked out in northern courts were railroad cases. In state after state, new doctrines were announced, tested, and developed in the context of cases involving railroads. This is an important observation for this book. It is not simply the case that railroad cases tended to feature new doctrines, it is rather the case that railroad cases were the cases – and very nearly *all* the cases – in which new principles of law first appeared. The cases from northern courts that are discussed in the chapters that follow were chosen because they are all the cases in which these states' highest courts developed new legal principles in the 1850s, and with only a very few exceptions (noted in the text), these were cases that involved railroads. Conversely, in the 1850s the southern courts whose records are examined here heard almost no railroad cases, and – sure enough – their legal doctrines underwent no revisions. And in the 1870s, when change finally came to the southern courts, it was carried, once again, by railroad cases. The cases from southern states that are discussed here are all of those in which those states' courts first announced their adoption of various principles of American common law, and once again, these were cases involving railroads.

It is not enough, however, merely to observe that modernization of the law accompanied modernization of the economy in the North, nor that resistance to legal innovation was accompanied by opposition to economic change in the South. There was nothing in the adoption of rail technology that necessarily implied radical reformation of the common law. Consider the case of England, the quintessentially modern nation of the late eighteenth and early nineteenth centuries (Alexander, 1997: 75; Hawke, 1970: 55–90). In England, railroads were treated as unwelcome intrusions by local parish elites, who responded by taxing rather than subsidizing their operations (Kostal, 1994: 364). Judicial elites resisted calls for legal reform, continuing a pattern of institutional conservatism that had been evident since the eighteenth century. The result was that the legal response to the challenges posed by the railroads was to fit them into the traditional common law system (discussed in the next chapter) (Kostal, 1994: 362–4; Hoeflich, 1989: 5). In response to injuries and damage, English lawyers created "a new field of specialized law practice" rather than attempting to unify the law into a single set of principles, while passengers and shipped goods retained the traditional protections of common carrier liability (Kostal, 1994: 365–6). Specific rules such as the fellowservant rule were adopted, but there was nothing of the kind of complete reformulation and conceptual reorganization of legal doctrine that defined the creation of a specifically American system of common law. England, for example, did not adopt a general theory of negligence until 1932, and in other matters English common law was far from uniform, with individual counties' courts adopting rules in accordance with local preference (Donnelly, 1967: 742; Friedman, 1985: 25; see generally Kostal, 1994). As Peter Karsten has observed, this fact is a challenge to any deterministic account that presents legal change as epiphenomenal to economic development (Karsten, 1997: 299). The railroads were a powerful engine for change, but the response to the railroads depended on the political environment that preceded their arrival. To understand the innovation or the absence of innovation in antebellum American law, one must first understand the political environment that preceded the

railroads, and the consequent reactions to the transformations that they
wrought.

One traditional explanation for a correlation between railroads and
legal development in America is the "subsidy thesis" associated with
Willard Hurst (Hurst, 1964; Friedman, 1985; Malone, 1986). This is
an argument that legal doctrines were nothing more than thin justifications for courts to do whatever it would take to serve the interests of the
emerging railroad industry, either because the owners of those companies
were immensely powerful or because the success of those companies was
viewed as a matter of immense importance, or some combination of these
two arguments. Other scholars have amassed considerable evidence in
favor of a similarly instrumentalist argument, but one that says that law,
and especially tort law, was developed in order to *permit* recovery from
new business enterprises (Rabin, 1981; Schwartz, 1981). Later arguments
added a level of ideological analysis; support for political economic developments, by this analysis, fit within a dominant ideology of corporate
capitalism, so that the use of law to subsidize development was merely an
expression of a greater desire to favor a system of political economy and
the legitimating ideology with which it was associated (Horwitz, 1992(a);
Wiecek, 1998).

The subsidy thesis and its variants echo earlier more-or-less deterministic theories of modernization in which legal ideas follow the necessary
courses created by economic and technological development. In Samuel
Huntington's Durkheimian formulation, the development of advanced
technologies inevitably resulted in a process of rationalization of authority, the development of specialized institutions to serve differentiated political functions, and broadening political participation (Huntington, 1968:
93–193). Theodore Lowi, similarly, describes differentiation and rationalization as the defining characteristics of the political economy of mid-
nineteenth century America. The law, in this conception, adjusted to the
demands of a changing economic order by accommodating the needs of
new classes of economic actors. Where the demands of capitalism and
the traditions of common law reasoning came into conflict, "capitalism
won out in a straight fight" (Lowi, 1979: 5). Nothing in the chapters
that follow will contradict this basic insight into what Joseph Schumpeter
called the "creative destruction" of capitalism applied to law (Schumpeter,
1975: 82).

More recently, legal historians have extended the proposition that
American law reflected American ideology still further, using the study
of the law to address the nature of American political thought and the

relationship between state and society generally (Karsten, 1997; Tomlins, 1993; Wiecek, 1998; Gordon, 1996; Kennedy, 1980). These arguments point to the idea that something called "culture" acts as an independent variable, or at a minimum as a medium of communication between different positions on the political, economic, or social spectrum. Applying this mode of analysis to nineteenth century America, Stuart Bruchey (1990) described a culture of capitalist development underlying a whole series of attitudes toward questions of law and politics. Similarly, Irwin Unger (1964) explained nineteenth century American politics in terms of competition between different value systems that had associated modes of economic activity, rather than economic systems with internally generated principles of justification. By carefully developing the intellectual threads that provided the vocabulary for nineteenth century legal discourse, legal historians have illuminated the mediated connections between legal and political concepts to show continuities and points of change in the development of common law categories (Alexander, 1997; Novak, 1996). And a growing body of work in southern American legal history has begun to examine the distinctive patterns of sectional legal development in that region of the country (Huebner, 1999; Hunt, 1998; Hunt, 1988; Ely and Bodenhamer, 1986; Finkleman, 1985). Applying arguments drawn from theories of modernization and political culture to the situation in the antebellum South, we might expect to find that powerful elites shared a dominant ideology whose legitimating claims were threatened by some aspects of railroad development. And this, too, will emerge as the case in the chapters that follow.

This book, while drawing on these works and others like them, attempts to further our understanding of nineteenth century law and politics in several ways. First, by adding a systematic comparative dimension to the analysis, this book seeks to illuminate the contours of both northern and southern legal development. Second, by focusing extensively on the connections between legal and political discourse, I have attempted to connect the development of American common law to parallel patterns in the development of regional political cultures. Both legal development and railroad expansion depended on a vocabulary that connected the dominant political economic elites with a legitimating ideology. In places where the dominant political culture was sympathetic to railroad expansion and legal modernism, both flourished. In places where the dominant political culture was hostile to both developments, neither occurred. In each case, the approach to common law development reflected the commitment of the courts to further or preserve the virtues of their societies. The values of the common law were not separate from the values of competing political cultures, they were their wellsprings. The comparative study of the development of political and legal principles can thus illuminate both, and in the process draw attention to the political commitments that are always built into any system of legal thought.

The selection of Illinois and Virginia as the key comparative cases for this study was driven by a recognition of the fact that these two states have striking similarities as well as sharp differences. Virginia, the oldest state in the Union, was from the eighteenth century through the Civil War the bastion of civic republicanism in America. Although politically Virginia was to be the leading state in the Confederacy, it was in some ways its least southern. At the outset of the Civil War, in fact, there was serious concern among southerners that Virginia might side with the Union. Virginia was also the southern state in which industrialization, and particularly railroads, had made the deepest inroads, and it was therefore the southern state in which the conflicts between traditional legal conceptions and the consequences of modernization are most clearly visible.

Illinois is in some ways the opposite case. Antebellum Illinois was an agrarian state of small towns and few cities (Howard, 1972: 146–56). Like Virginia, Illinois was politically and culturally a deeply divided state, with a southern portion whose population and outlook was predominantly southern, and a northern section settled by northerners and European immigrants. The northern part of the state, however, developed much later than the southern section. Although Illinois became a state in 1818, its entire northern section was not home to a significant number of people until the 1830s and did not become the locus of state political power until the late 1840s. Thus Illinois, and especially Chicago, represented a new state built by railroads rather than an ancient traditional society invaded by an alien force. In addition, railroads in Illinois did not develop gradually, they arrived roaring across the landscape with blinding speed. While there had been several mostly unsuccessful earlier attempts, the state's entire rail system was essentially constructed between 1850 and 1860. This meant that both the challenges and the opportunities created by new modes of transportation and communication were sharply drawn. The points of conflict between the imperatives of technological progress and the needs of traditional agrarianism were inescapable, and it was in response to those conflicts that Illinois demonstrated its political culture. As a result, in its legal development, Illinois presents an exceptionally clear case for study. Illinois' common law demonstrates the consistent pattern of legal development across the North from New England through the states of the Old Northwest, and the equally consistent relationship between law and an emerging conception of citizenship.

Virginia and Illinois do not represent the northern and southern ideological extremes, but rather points of relative convergence between two sharply separated halves of America's national culture. Nonetheless, the two states' experiences were sharply different, reflecting dominant northern and southern patterns of development. The doctrines adopted by Illinois in the 1850s were the same as those adopted in Vermont, New York, and Ohio, despite significant differences in those states' economic circumstances, while Virginia's common law followed the same path as that of Georgia, North Carolina, and Kentucky, despite the same sorts of differences in the economic and physical circumstances of those states. As in the rest of the North, in the 1850s the Illinois Supreme Court's innovations in the law defined a model of citizenship based on technological exceptionalism, an expanded conception of the public good built around an ideal of industrial progress, and the standardization of legal rights and duties, while resistance to each of those ideas was at the heart of southern legal conservatism. Later, in the 1870s and 1880s, Virginia and the other southern states adopted the new American legal doctrines in ways that evaded the conceptual commitments that had been at the heart of their original formulations.

In the chapters that follow, I will present a closer study of the arcs of political and legal development that resulted in the creation of an American system of common law. In the first chapter, I will review the differences between the political economies and political ideologies of the antebellum North and South in more detail, and spell out the ways in which the American system of common law departed from the earlier system adapted from the common law of England. In Chapters 2, 3, and 4, I will present a close study of Illinois in the 1850s as an exemplar for northern development. In Chapter 5, I will trace the similarities and differences between developments in Illinois and those of three other northern states (Ohio, Vermont, and New York). Chapters 6, 7, and 8 consider Virginia with the same kind of detailed analysis that was previously given to Illinois, and in Chapter 9 the experiences of Virginia are compared with those of three other southern states (Georgia, North Carolina, and Kentucky). Finally, Chapter 10 presents some overall observations about the significance of this study for understanding the relationships among legal, political, and social development in nineteenth century America.

The organization of the discussions of Illinois and Virginia differs slightly. The discussion of Illinois' law focuses on the decade from 1850 to 1860, during which the transformation of Illinois' common law was both begun and completed. The chapters describing that transformation are divided in the conceptual fashion of nineteenth century digests, between cases involving harms to property and those involving harms to persons, in order to show how the justices of the Illinois Supreme Court drew together these disparate elements of the old common law system into a new, unified regime. The discussion of Virginia, in contrast, is divided chronologically, to chronicle that state's resistance to change in the 1850s and the manner of its eventual wholesale adoption of new doctrines in the 1870s and 1880s. Thus Chapter 3 covers Illinois law concerning damage to property, while Chapter 4 covers harms to persons; by contrast, in the Virginia discussion, Chapter 6 considers cases involving harms to both property and persons in the 1850s, and Chapter 7 considers cases involving harms to both property and persons in the 1860s and 1870s, when the new doctrines that had appeared in the North in the antebellum years finally made their appearance in the South. These same conceptual categories are also used to organize the discussions of the other northern and southern states in Chapters 5 and 9, respectively. Finally, in the last chapter, I will return to the broader point of comparing the two cases in terms of their respective constructions of citizenship, and the lessons that may be drawn for the study of law and politics in general.

I

North and South

The term *common law* means the body of rules created over time by judges, as opposed to *positive law* – that is, statutes created by legislative enactment. Common law is developed through the accretion of precedents. There is still no better description of this process than that provided by Justice Lemuel Shaw of Massachusetts in *Norway Plains Company v. Boston & Maine Railroad*, 10 Mass. (Gray) 263, 267 (1854):

[T]he common law consists of a few broad and comprehensive principles, founded on reason, natural justice, and enlightened public policy, modified and adapted to the circumstances of all the particular cases which fall within it. These general principles of equity and policy are rendered precise, specific, and adapted to practical use, by usage, which is the proof of their general fitness and common convenience, but still more by judicial exposition.... such judicial exposition, when well settled and acquiesced in, becomes itself a precedent, and forms a rule of law for future cases, under like circumstances.

In the 1850s, therefore, it was judges who engineered the development of a new body of common law. More specifically, a handful of judges in each state, sitting on those states' highest courts, were the crucial actors in the creation and development of an American system of common law that replaced the inherited English system.

To modern eyes, the distinction between common law and statutory law appears close to the distinction that political scientists draw between "private law" and "public law." Private law rules govern the adjudication of disputes between individuals, while public law regulates conduct in the name of society at large (as in the case of criminal law) or governs the conduct of institutional actors (as in the case of constitutional law). Even today, however, the distinction is one more honored in the breach than the observance. In modern practice, legislatures (advised by committees) frequently codify rules for the adjudication of individual disputes, while private lawsuits are relied upon to enforce a range of public policies.

Conversely, in the English tradition, the authority of legislatures to draft regulations was itself drawn from common law roots, and the common law was understood to be the source for political rights and duties. Two Latin phrases captured the dual role of the common law in English tradition. The common law basis for legislative power inhered in the authority of local governments to regulate conduct in the name of the public good, found in the principle *salus populi suprema lex est* ("the good of the people is the supreme law"). Among early English settlers in North America, no one was more committed to the ideal of a society ordered by law than the Puritans of Massachusetts. It is, therefore, not surprising that within the first few years of their settlement in Massachusetts, Puritan lawmakers enacted a wide array of regulations, including wage and price controls, limits on planting and settlement, requirements for the price of beer and the size of bread loaves, and a ban on public smoking and the sale of tobacco, to name only a few (Shurtleff, 1853: vol. I, 73–145).

It would not be until the nineteenth century that America would see the development of a political ideology that posited the unregulated use of private property as the sine qua non of political liberty, an argument drawn from a mixture of theological and economic theory developed by Scottish Calvinist writers Dugald Stewart, Adam Ferguson, and Adam Smith. Through the end of the eighteenth century, and for many hundreds of years before that, one of the fundamental premises of English common law had been that *salus populi* was, indeed, *suprema lex*. As William Novak put it, "[p]ublic regulation – the power of the state to restrict individual liberty and property for the common welfare – colored all facets of early American development. It was the central component of a reigning theory and practice of governance committed to the pursuit of the people's welfare and happiness in a well-ordered society and polity" (Novak, 1996: 2).

The principle of *salus populi* pointed to the political role of English common law, captured in the phrase "the rights of Englishmen," that would be so central to the thinking of common lawyers such as John Adams. For English republicans, the common law served a constitutional function, standing outside and precedent to the particular questions of political organization or the limits of individual prerogatives. Titles of nobility might be granted or rescinded, and regimes could come and go, but the common law reflected a direct connection to claims of natural

right. In 1470 an English serjeant-at-law was confronted by a challenge to
his court's common law jurisdiction based on the claim that the defendant,
as a royal servant, could be tried only by a court of the King's Bench by
a privilege "beyond the time of memory, and as old as the common law."
In response, the magistrate declared that "common law has existed since
the creation of the world" (*Wallyng v. Meger*, 47 Selden Society 38, 1470).
And as John H. Baker observes, "it is not improbable that he believed it
literally" (Baker, 1990: 1).

By the seventeenth and eighteenth centuries, English legal writers had
moved to a different conception, one based in the recognition that common law doctrines were a collective and historical human creation. "Historical jurisprudence," as it came to be called, posited the common law as
neither divinely inspired nor created by the positive edicts of a sovereign,
but rather reflecting the wisdom of a particular historically situated community, developed over generations:

> For reason is the life of the law, nay the common law itself is nothing else but rea-
> son, which is to be understood as an artificial perfection of reason, gotten by long
> study, observation, and experience, and not of every man's natural reason.... [I]f
> all the reason that is dispersed into so many liberal heads were united into one,
> yet could he not make such a Law as the Law of England is, because by many
> successions of ages it hath been fined and refined by an infinite number of grave
> and learned men, and by long experience grown to such a perfection for the gov-
> ernment of this Realm, ... No man (out of his own private reason) ought to be
> wiser than the Law, which is the perfection of Reason (Coke, 1609: vol. I, bk. II,
> sect. 138).[1]

This meant that the common law was profoundly democratic, drawing
its legitimacy from its claim to authenticity, in sharp contrast to canon,
civil, and other forms of law. The tradition of historical jurisprudence
also recognized the capacity of the common law to evolve over time. As
generations passed, rules would be refined to more perfectly capture the
essence of the community's wisdom, or to reflect shifts in the collective
understanding of an ideal social order (Baker, 1990; Berman, 1994). Thus
by the end of the eighteenth century, the public functions of the common
law were understood to incorporate both a political theory of liberty, a
system of public order, and an understanding of history as progressive
improvement.

---

[1] Nearly three centuries later, when Oliver Wendell Holmes, Jr., said that "the life of the
law has not been logic: it has been experience," he was speaking within the tradition of
historical jurisprudence that Coke had articulated in 1609 (Holmes, 1881: 5).

The fundamental tenet of English common law for the adjudication of private disputes was *sic utere tuo ut alienum non laedas*: "use your own property so as not to harm that of another." The countervailing principle to *salus populi*, this rule declared the condition of Lockean autonomy, the equal and natural right held by all people to the ownership and control of their property, beginning with themselves.[2] The principles of *salus populi* and *sic utere* were necessarily in tension, particularly as property-based rights became the starting point for ideas of legal and political rights writ large, as Francis Hilliard explained in one of the first digests of American law:

The absolute personal rights recognized and protected by our law…may with sufficient precision be expressed as the right of personal security, and the right of private property.... The right of *private property* is that privilege, which every American citizen enjoys, to hold his possessions, lawfully acquired, against any unjustifiable interference either by the government or by individuals (Hilliard, 1835: 12).

The end result was a balance of liberty and order. To produce good social order, "police," the law was empowered to subordinate private rights to the needs of the community, while at the same time the law would dictate strict and rigid rules for the adjudication of competing claims between individuals (Tomlins, 1993: 74–96). Rights to property were an element of police, "the material foundation for creating and maintaining the proper social order, the private basis for the public good" (Alexander, 1997: 1). The traditional conception of *salus populi*, however, was defined in local terms, a point emphasized by the fact that all civil law was described under the rubric of "municipal law" (Blackstone, 1765: vol. I, 44; Novak, 1996: 10). For centuries of English legal development, then, police was the ground on which a balance was created between the ideas of private right and public good articulated in the two governing principles of the Anglo-American common law tradition.

Blackstone in America: The Reception of English Common Law and the Movement for Reform

When put into practice, the broad legitimating principles of English common law became an incomprehensibly complex system of technical practices marked by strict formal requirements, legal fictions, and an array of

---

[2] "Though the earth and all inferior creatures be common to all men, yet every man has a 'property' in his own 'person'" (Locke, 1690: 130).

overlapping, inconsistent rules that made the adjudication of an individual case a matter closer to alchemy than science.³ For Americans of the revolutionary generation, the form and content of these practices were found in the *Commentaries on the Common Law* by William Blackstone, the leading expounder of the theory of historical jurisprudence in the late eighteenth century, and the world's first university professor of common law. (Tellingly, the second such university position was held by William Wythe, appointed by Thomas Jefferson to the faculty of the College of William and Mary in 1779 [Sheppard, 1982: 749].)

As Edmund Burke famously observed, Blackstone's compilation of common law rules was more popular in America than in England. The *Commentaries* were the most widely read legal text in all parts of the country, and one of the most widely read texts of any kind (Carrington, 1990: 527–9; Klafter, 1993). And Blackstone's significance reached beyond the offices of lawyers. In American political writings published between 1760 and 1805, the three most frequently cited were, in descending order, Montesquieu, Blackstone, and Locke (Lutz, 1986: 189–97). The immense popularity of Blackstone's *Commentaries* had the interesting consequence that, from the outset, the American legal vocabulary was constructed around a much more uniform set of common law principles than anything that was prevalent in England at the same time, setting the stage for later national developments.

Blackstone imbued the common law with a political significance that reached beyond its role of legitimating the actions of local governments. He further argued that knowledge of the law was essential to good citizenship and was an element of civic virtue. "For I think it an undeniable position, that a competent knowledge of the laws of that society, in which we live, is the proper accomplishment of every gentleman and scholar; and highly useful, I had almost said essential, part of liberal and political education." A republican thinker of the first order, Blackstone connected the common law and its rules to the English ideal of political liberty. England, he wrote, was "a land, perhaps the only one in the universe, in which political or civil liberty is the very end and scope of the constitution. This liberty, rightly understood, consists in the power of doing whatever the laws permit." As a result, at a minimum it was incumbent upon every citizen "to be acquainted with those [laws] at least, with which he is immediately concerned; lest he incur the censure, as well as

---

³ For discussion of the metaphor of "legal science" and its significance in nineteenth century American thought, see Hoeflich, 1986; Berman and Reid, 1996; Schweber, 1999.

inconvenience, of living in society without knowing the obligations which it lays him under." And for those "on whom nature has bestowed more abilities and greater leisure," more was demanded. "These advantages are given them, not for the benefit of themselves only, but also of the public; and yet they cannot, in a scene of life, discharge properly their duty either to the public or themselves, without some degree of knowledge in the laws" (Blackstone, 1758: 54–5).

The common law, according to Blackstone, consisted of "general immemorial custom ... from time to time declared in the decisions of the courts of justice; which decisions are preserved among our public records, explained in our reports, and digested for general use in the authoritative writings of the venerable sages." But law was not simply the recording of custom; only customs that displayed certain qualities deserved to be treated as the basis for common law rules, or "maxims." Custom could become common law if it had "been used so long, that the memory of man runneth not to the contrary," if its use was "continued," if the recognition of the custom in the community was "peaceable, and acquiesced in; not subject to contention and dispute," and if such custom was "reasonable; or rather, taken negatively, [it] must not be unreasonable. Which is not always, as Sir Edward Coke says, to be understood of every unlearned man's reason, but of artificial and legal reason, warranted by authority of law" (Blackstone, 1765: vol. I, 73, 76–7).

Proceeding from these premises, Blackstone filled four volumes with specific common law rules. Although in comparison with actual English practice these rules were simplified, unified, and ordered, to modern eyes they retain a bewildering complexity in the categories into which different areas of the law were divided. Something of the flavor of the categories of traditional common law reasoning is captured by the divisions of Volume I, "The Rights of Persons": the chapters cover the "absolute rights of individuals," the parliament, the king, the king's family, the king's councilors, magistrates, "the people, whether aliens, denizens, or natives," the clergy, officers of the civil state, officers of the military, masters and servants, husbands and wives, parents and children, guardians and wards, and corporations.[4] Later volumes similarly defined

---

[4] The reference to corporations as persons is likely to ring familiar to modern readers aware of the rule declared in *Santa Clara County v. Southern Pacific Railroad Co.*, 118 U.S. 394 (1886), that corporations are "persons" guaranteed rights under the Fourteenth Amendment. Arguably, this apparent connection illustrates the argument that retaining a formal rule in the face of changed circumstances may be a form of radicalism rather than of conservation (see the discussion in Chapter 10). The term "corporation" meant

categories for "The Rights of Things," "Private Wrongs," and "Public Wrongs."

In the adjudication of any given case, the basic common law rule was that the rights and duties of the parties would be determined based on their specific relationship to one another. In particular, the relative rights of the parties to the use and occupation of the property on which an incident occurred would determine the rules that would apply to the case. This basic premise was laid out in a discussion by Lord Ellenborough in a case that would be frequently cited in later American cases, *Butterfield v. Forrester*, 11 East 60 (1809): "The degree of care which the plaintiff is bound to exercise will be found to depend upon the relative rights exercised or position enjoyed by the plaintiff at the time the injury complained of happened."

Butterfield, however, also pointed to a unique situation in which there was no clear relationship between the parties that could specify that one owed a duty to the other. The case involved an injury that occurred on a public thoroughfare, a unique situation in which each party had an exactly equal prerogative to the unhindered use of the property in question: "Where both parties are equally in the position of rights, which they hold independent of the favor of each other, the plaintiff is only bound to show that the injury was produced by the negligence of the defendant, and that he exercised ordinary care or diligence in endeavoring to avoid it." Except in that unique situation, however, the existence of legal duties would depend on the parties' respective rights to the use and occupancy of the property on which an injury occurred. The relationship between parties and property was one of three basic sources of legal duties in the tradition of English common law. The others were a contractual relationship, such as employment, or a special relationship recognized by the community, such as family. While there were myriad variations, property, privity, and propriety were the essential sources of legally enforceable duties in the English system. In the American common law that developed in the 1850s, property, privity, and propriety would be replaced by progress in the formulation of legal standards.

The focus on the parties' relationship to property in *Butterfield* pointed to one of the most basic ways in which railroads challenged traditional understandings. As we shall see, ambiguity about how to characterize new kinds of property associated with trains was at the heart of the problem

---

something very different in Blackstone's time from what it meant at the end of the nineteenth century.

that railroad cases posed for traditional common law doctrine. Tracks, rail yards, and the interiors of passenger cars were neither perfectly private nor perfectly public spaces. Where property-based claims of right were ambiguous, *Butterfield v. Forrester* pointed to the possibility of adjudication based on an evaluation of the plaintiff's conduct as an exception to the essentially strict liability principle of *sic utere* and the focus on "relative rights exercised or position enjoyed" by the parties. The American system of common law would result from the extension of those exceptions to the point where they entirely swallowed the original rule.

In addition to its focus on relative claims of property-based preroga- tives, the system of English common law that Blackstone described, and that American courts inherited, was based on highly formalized sets of procedures. A lawsuit could only be filed under a "writ," that is, a rem- edy available from the court. In the writ system, the starting point for the description of the case was the name of the protection that a litigant sought from the court. Thus, for example, Blackstone in his *Commen- taries* provided separate discussions of contracts as a way of obtaining a title to property and writs for contract-based remedies. Although there were contracts in 1800, there were no actions for breach of contract, only actions for "assumpsit," "covenant," or "debt." Each writ identified a specific pattern of facts that had to be alleged in order for the action to proceed. The word "tort" is an ancient one, but there was no such thing as a simple tort suit or a claim for negligence; instead there were actions for "trespass," "nuisance," "trover," "case," or "conversion." The form in which the action was brought determined the only template against which the facts in a case would be tested.

Where there was no appropriate writ, legal fictions might be employed to create a remedy. To take one classic example, consider the situation of someone who wanted to evict a squatter from his property. In England, this would have been accomplished by bringing a writ of "real action," which would entitle the owner to enter the property and forcibly retake possession. That procedure, however, was abolished in most American states because it involved granting too much power to a private litigant to enforce his own legal claims. Instead, the owner of the property would have to create a fictitious lease giving a third person the right to occupy the property; that person would then sue the trespasser in a writ of "trespass and ejectment." "The lessee," wrote Hilliard in 1835, "to sustain the ac- tion, must prove a *good title in the lessor*; and in this collateral way, the title is tried. For the purpose of dispensing with the above-mentioned forms, this action has been made substantially a *fictitious process*" (Hilliard, 1835:

258). This was the sort of reasoning that was the love of English common lawyers and the despair of nearly everyone else.

These procedures made the determination of legal prerogatives an exceedingly complex task. As Greg Alexander points out, "[f]or laypersons, the law regulating land transactions was literally incomprehensible; only the ignorant or the uninformed risk-taker would engage in even routine land transactions without legal assistance" (Alexander, 1997: 97). In practice, the strictures of writ pleading were not so extreme as they might appear. Over time, two of the writs in particular – "trespass on the case" and "nuisance" – were expanded to cover a very wide range of cases.[5] Furthermore, the writ system only described cases brought "at law"; there was an entire separate body of "equity" doctrines designed to do fairness where the law provided no specifically appropriate remedy.[6] But pleading cases in this ancient system remained a technically demanding art, mysterious to the nonlawyer and only arbitrarily connected to the experiences of the litigants. To request the wrong remedy meant to get nothing, regardless of the injury that had been suffered. In principle, even a slight deviation from the writ's terms meant that the claim could not be heard, and a claim that did not fit into any of the writs theoretically could not be heard at all. The reason was that the common law had developed piecemeal, with writs created to meet perceived needs, but without any overall program of rationalization. "To seventeenth- and eighteenth-century lawyers," observes Philip A. Hamburger, "such a division was an accurate and elegantly conceived reflection of the awkward reality" (Hamburger, 1989: 253), but to litigants it seemed simply chaotic. Blackstone's *Commentaries* were an attempt to impose some degree of

---

[5] The evolution of the action for "trespass on the case" is particularly instructive. Originally, "trespass" meant something close to what "trespassing" means in modern usage: unlawful entry onto someone else's property without their permission. Addition of the phrase "on the case" meant that not only physical invasions of real property (land) but any unauthorized invasion of any property interest could be the basis for a claim. "Hence the origin of the legal phrase – action on the case; which means an action not falling within the ancient and technical formulas, but adapted to the particular case which arises, and which otherwise would be without remedy" (Hilliard, 1859: 66). The action of trespass on the case was the ancestor of modern tort claims.

[6] A laborer who was found to be working without a valid contract, for example, could sue his employer for the value of his work (as opposed to wages set by agreement). One important role of the law of equity was to provide an avenue for women to gain legal redress for wrongs that did much to undercut the inequalities that were imposed by common law doctrines such as "coverture," the rule that a woman's property passed to her husband on marriage (Kerber, 1980: 139–40). For more general treatments of women's legal rights and prerogatives in early American society, see Ulrich, 1982; Salmon, 1986.

organization over the system, but they retained the technical complexity of writ pleading. This was the system of common law that America inherited from England and retained, essentially intact, until the middle of the nineteenth century. Before turning to an examination of why and how change occurred in the 1850s, then, a preliminary question might be why change did not occur earlier.

In the early years following separation from Britain, the common law tradition continued to be thought of as the wellspring of republican liberty. Nothing in the political discourse of revolutionary America, for example, obviously implied the rejection of England's common law. To the contrary, the American Revolution has been justly characterized as a politically radical but legally conservative event (Hartog, 1981; Zweiben, 1990).[7] Fundamentally, the grievances against the British crown were articulated in terms of prerogatives that the colonists claimed for themselves under the banner of Blackstone's common law. There were problems with the *Commentaries*, to be sure. For Antifederalists in particular, Blackstone's version of English common law was too conservative, and too infected with English monarchism to be perfectly appropriate to the American experience (Klafter, 1993: 37). This, however, could be resolved by merely excising offending passages, as St. George Tucker did in the first American edition of Blackstone's *Commentaries*, published in 1803, which immediately became the standard version for American readers.

Even with Tucker's modifications, Blackstone's common law was unsatisfactory to many Jacksonian Americans in the early 1800s. The combination of formalized, mysterious procedures and torturously complicated standards for adjudication ran against the Jacksonian preference for "liberality." This was a problem for both republicans, who looked to the common law as the seedbed of political virtue, and for liberals, who despised the idea that society's rules should be incomprehensible to anyone but a few priests (Alexander, 1997: 98). The most radical proposals for the reform of the common law called for its outright replacement by a code of positive regulations. "Codification" was a term invented by Jeremy Bentham, who viewed the legal fictions of the common law as "a syphilis which runs into every vein and carries into every part of the system the principles of rottenness" (Cook, 1981: 76). In its American

---

[7] Legacies of this legalistic heritage can be seen in numerous constitutional provisions proscribing government intervention in traditional common law activities, such as Article I, Section 9 (prohibiting interference with rights of contract or property rights) and the Seventh Amendment (guaranteeing the right to a jury trial in civil cases).

forms, this antirepublican (and emphatically anti-Whig) position itself had two distinct forms. Labor leaders such as Frederick Robinson and radical Democrats such as Robert Rantoul supported the idea of codification as a means to bring to fruition the democratic ideal of the Revolution. On the other hand, liberal elites, exemplified by Joseph Story, supported the idea that America should adopt a version of the Napoleonic Code, relying on claims of superior rationality and scientific order.[8] Perhaps the most radical suggestion of all came in 1839, when the *United States Magazine and Democratic Review* proposed to do away with all existing laws in favor of a return to pure trial by jury, "the natural progenitor of democratic government" (Cook, 1981: 162).

Until the 1840s and 1850s, however, there was little chance of significant change in the system of common law, for a number of reasons. The legacy of the Glorious Cause provided a ready language for discrediting radicals who proposed scrapping the common law system altogether or rewriting it on more democratic grounds. Lawyers were ready and able to draw on the patriotic language of revolutionary virtue in defense of their professional class. "To be eminent in *our* profession," wrote southerner Nathan Beverly Tucker, "is to hold a place among the great ones of the earth . . . to win *its* honors, and to wear them worthily, is to attain an elevation from which all other honors are accessible" (Tucker, 1834: 146).[9] In the North, Simon Greenleaf's classically republican formulation explained that lawyers would rescue the heroic tradition of the Revolution from corruption: "[I]n later days, when the integrity of that charter has been invaded, its spirit violated, and its language perverted, whether to gratify the mad ambition of one partisan, or the cupidity of many; to whom have all eyes been imploringly directed for its preservation, but to the living and honored champions and expounders of constitutional law?" (Greenleaf, 1834: 137).

---

[8] Radical discourse, too, had its elite and mass components. By the 1830s, spokespersons for the interests of wage laborers cooperated and competed for leadership with elites who argued for the extension of Napoleonic principles of rationalized governance into the American state. Regardless of class status, however, these radical voices were kept at the margins of political debate, and had little ascertainable influence on the course of legal or political development. The literature on worker ideology in the nineteenth century is voluminous. On the particular points raised here, see Wilentz, 1984a and 1984b; Kozol, 1995; Tomlins, 1993: 109; Forbath, 1991.

[9] Beverly Tucker was a southerner, and an avid, romantic devotee of the southern cause; he was one of the first prominent secessionists and boasted that none of his students left his care "without being, for the time, a Southern man in feeling and a States-rights man in conviction." This undoubtedly had something to do with the fact that his father had married the widow of John Randolph (Bryson, 1982).

There were institutional factors, as well, that strengthened the ability of the bar to resist external pressures for change. Antilawyer sentiment, and hence the popular force behind calls for dramatic reorganization of the legal system, has almost certainly been overstated (Nolan, 1976; Bloomfield, 1968). At the same time, in point of fact lawyers *did* constitute a fairly closed, or at least inward-looking, elite class, and were thus well situated to resist outside pressures for change (Gawalt, 1970: 223–32; Nash, 1965: 203–20). The period between 1800 and 1850 saw the growth of law schools, professional associations, and specialized journals, resulting in a profession that was increasingly exclusive and focused inward (Bloomfield, 1968; Ferguson, 1984). The institutional strength of the American bar meant that, short of revolution, reform would have to come from within.

There were voices for reform within the bar. The most important of these was the *American Jurist and Law Magazine*, founded in 1838 to provide a "free scope for discussion of proposed alterations in the laws" (Sumner et al., 1838: 9). Founded and edited by Charles Sumner, George Hilliard (father of Francis Hilliard, who authored several important digests of American law), and Luther Cushing, the *American Jurist* was filled with articles declaring that "the rule of law and the rule of reason are widely apart" ("Subjecting Land to the Debts of the Deceased," 1833: 457).[10] In 1830, the common law was described as "a dark forest, where the most intrepid lawyer never thinks of exploring beyond the margin," a "territory" that must be "surveyed and laid out anew . . . to let in a little light." There were as many "versions of the common law" as there were states, "each . . . essentially variant." In addition, judges within a state might disagree, "often to such a degree that it is impossible to decide the case in question without weighing the mass of precedents against each other, or recurring to first principles without regard to authority" ("Dane's Abridgement," 1830: 66; Dixon, 1835: 283–4). These expressions of concern, however, were used to justify the publication of commentaries, digests, and critical articles, not to organize a movement of lawyers committed to a political project of legal reform. "The doctrine now seems to be acquiesced in, by general consent," wrote the editors,

---

[10] The article concerns the question of whether land belonging to a debtor could be seized in satisfaction of debts if the heir to the property had not been named in the debt instrument. The emerging rule favored permitting seizure, while the old rule depended on a relationship of privity between the creditor and the new owner. The author notes that the new rule was in place "North of the Potomac," while in Virginia and in other states, the common law rule still prevailed (Ibid., 460).

"that a code must be a digest and arrangement of existing laws, [rather] than a body of enactments made *per saltum*" (Sumner et al., 1834: 344–5). By the time state courts began to hear large numbers of train cases in the 1850s, then, the idea that the system of common law needed to be modernized had been gaining force for a generation, but little change in practice or doctrine had resulted.

Long before 1850, however, there had been widespread agreement that one area in which modification of common law doctrine was required was in the all-important law of property. Traditional property rights were arguably the most central elements of the common law system for American patriots. In the traditions of both civic republicanism and Lockean liberalism, political enfranchisement flowed from the fact of property ownership (Nedelsky, 1990). Yet even such conservative legal writers as James Kent, who wept bitter tears at the abandonment of hoary legal fictions, insisted that in the American case the very untraditional preference for the free alienation of land was essential for the health of the republic.[11] Given the central place that property rights held in the analytical scheme of common law adjudication, to admit the possibility of reformulation in that area was to open the door to a wholesale reconceptualization of the idea of legal rights and duties. Why, then, were American politicians and jurists (who, after all, were often one and the same) willing to set aside their loyalty to the traditions of English law in this, the very linchpin connecting law and virtue?

The answer is that the legal conservatism of the Revolution was tempered by a thesis about which there was no disagreement among Federalists and Antifederalists – nor, later, among northern Whigs and Democrats – despite sharp conflicts over its precise terms. This was the thesis of American exceptionalism, the idea that America's history had no precedent in European experience.[12] Among republicans, it was an article

---

[11] When the New York state legislature abolished, by statute, the Rule in Shelley's Case, Kent waxed poetic in his regret: "The juridical scholar, on whom his great master, Coke, has bestowed some portion of the 'gladsome light of jurisprudence,' will scarcely be able to withhold an involuntary sigh, as he casts a retrospective glance over the piles of learning, devoted to destruction by an edict" (Kent, 1851, IV: 226, n. a.). At the same time, Kent was an eager advocate of rules that eased restrictions on economic activity, especially the alienation of land (Alexander, 1997: 127–57).

[12] Joyce Appleby argues that exceptionalism was not an important element in American political thought before the beginning of the nineteenth century. "The most that they would concede to human variety was the diversity of the physical world where different conditions prevailed" (Appleby, 1992:191). In the lexicon of eighteenth century American political theories, however, differences in physical condition were precisely what ensured

of faith that the new country would be free of the corruption of the old world. In particular, it is important to note, this meant rescuing the pure principles of timeless English virtue from the degraded state created by English monarchism (Alexander, 1997: 43–8). This provided the grounds for the argument that "discovery" of the timeless principles of English common law might actually require departure from English practice (in the North), or resistance to reforms that English jurists might embrace (in the South).[13] For laissez-faire liberals, exceptionalism was nearly eschatological. History simply began anew in 1776, as the *Democratic Review* stated in 1839: "Our national birth was the beginning of a new history ... which separates us from the past and connects us with the future *only*" (Lewis, 1955: 5).

In the early decades of the Republic, the key explanation for American exceptionalism was the availability of land. In its republican version, the argument was that the corruption of European experience would be prevented by the preservation of yeoman virtues that accompanied property ownership. "I think our governments will remain virtuous for many centuries," wrote Jefferson to James Madison in 1787, "as long as they are chiefly agricultural; and this will be as long as there shall be vacant lands in any part of America. When they get piled upon one another in large cities, as in Europe, they will become corrupt as in Europe."[14] In the liberal version, the point of free land was that there need never be "lower classes" so long as upward mobility toward eventual property ownership was the universal experience of all Americans.[15] Further, America's free land meant that it could develop a manufacturing economy in what Tench Coxe, an early proponent of technological progress,

America's historical exceptionalism, a proposition that was received in large part from the immense popularity of Montesquieu's argument in *Spirit of the Laws* and Locke's in *Two Treatises of Government.*

[13] On discovery, rather than invention, as a theme in nineteenth century judicial thought, see Karsten, 1991: 362–3. Alexander points to the pervasive legal discourse of "timelessness" as an expression of republican anxiety about the processes of modernization (Alexander, 1997: 55–9).

[14] Letter to Madison, December 20, 1787, quoted in *Great Issues in American History*, Ver Steeg and Hofstadter, eds., 1969, 2:115.

[15] Sean Wilentz, focusing on the effect that upward mobility was expected to have on the personal character of workers, calls this "free labor republicanism," which only emphasizes the difficulty of separating liberal and republican strands of early nineteenth century American thought. Wilentz: 1984a, 302–4. It is important to note that the form of ownership in question was absolute ownership in fee, as opposed to the feudal rights to occupation and use of land, which were likely to be the highest levels of ownership to which European agricultural workers might aspire (Alexander, 1997: 51–5).

called in 1786 the "middle landscape," mixing the virtues of city and countryside without the drawbacks of either.[16] Conducted in this way, industrial work could be a source for moral uplift, as Alexander Hamilton suggested in his *Report on Manufactures*: "It is worthy of particular remark that in general, women and children are rendered more useful, and the latter more early useful, by manufacturing establishments, than they would otherwise be."[17] In time, even Jefferson came to consider the possibility that American industry might retain republican virtue, so long as it was confined to small shops rather than concentrated in gigantic corporate enterprises (Licht, 1995: 16). Available land required different rules of property, precisely because the conditions of property ownership were so central to the American political condition. Therefore, paradoxically, it was precisely because Americans insisted on retaining the primacy of property as the category for legal analysis in the common law tradition that the law of property emerged early on as the one area in which significant innovation would be required.

Through the antebellum decades, the division between northern and southern political cultures increasingly centered on divergent conceptions of the exceptionalist thesis. In the North, beginning as early as the 1820s, the idea of "technological exceptionalism" defined America's future as progress, a vision of rapid, technology-driven change (Marx, 1964; Kasson, 1976; Siracusa, 1979). It was not merely that industry's harms would be ameliorated, industry was conceived as the very basis of America's exceptional claims to virtue: "The spirit of the republic . . . hails the agency of steam as the benefactor of man, and the power which stamps the character of the present age" (Lenman, 1840: 295).

Railroads, in particular, were not only the harbingers of progress but the very carriers of republican virtue: "Objects of exalted power and grandeur elevate the mind that seriously dwells on them. . . . The same will be true of our system of Rail-roads" (Caldwell, 1832: 288). In 1847, the writers of the (northern, Whig) *Scientific American* heralded the promise of a plan to bring American railroad construction to Russia: "Who knows but in a few years the now Russian serf, may stand a freeman at his own cottage door, and as he beholds the locomotive fleeting past, will take off his cap . . . and bless God that the Mechanics of Washington's land were permitted to scatter the seeds of social freedom in benighted Russia."[18]

---

[16] Quoted in Marx, 1964: 152–3, 159.
[17] Quoted in Licht, 1995: 14.
[18] "American Genius and Enterprise," *Scientific American* II (Sept. 1847).

There were skeptical voices, to be sure, both from an emerging industrial laboring class (Kozol, 1995; Wilentz, 1984b; Salvatore, 1984), and from agrarian traditionalists resistant to the rise of corporate elites (Piott, 1985; Hirschfield, 1952), but they did not often appear in the political discourse of the two main political parties in the North. Support for railroad development redefined the politics of the northern parties, as Democrats for the most part abandoned their opposition to state-chartered banks and corporate privileges, while Whigs gave up any pretense of trying to manage the rate and process of growth (Holt, 1999: 687; Shade, 1976: 145–88). When the Republican Party was formed in 1854 out of the remnants of the Whig Party and defectors from the Democrats, it, too, embraced the cause of technology and growth with unabashed fervor as the highest form of state action.

Southern conservatives, by contrast, initially rejected the idea of exceptionalism outright, then moved over time to a position that emphasized the unique virtues of southern slave-owning society. In 1850, Alexander Knox explained that both European nations and the American North had lost their way in their rejection of slavery and embrace of industrialization: "[Slavery's] existence is indispensably requisite in order to preserve the forms of Republican Government." Greece and Rome, "the cradles of liberty," had slavery; by contrast, England, the source of emancipationist thought, contained "a miserable, wretched and degraded peasantry . . . compared to whom our slaves may be regarded as occupying a most enviable condition" (Robert, 1965: 61). John Minor Botts, a delegate to Virginia's 1850 constitutional convention, went still further. "I believe," he declared, "that this Anglo-Saxon race of people in the United States of America are the only people ever formed by the hand of God, that are capable of self-government" (Bishop, 1851: 221).

The pattern of common law development paralleled these distinctions in political philosophy. In the North, the 1850s saw judges of the states' highest courts engage in the complete reworking of traditional common law rules and principles in embracing technology and progress. In the South, the 1850s saw judicial elites adamantly holding to traditional rules and, if anything, increasing the strictness with which they were applied. This is not to say that the common law in the antebellum South can be described as static. Courts made adjustments to the received doctrines of English common law that reflected the priorities of their place and time. More important, to retain old doctrines in the face of different circumstances is, itself, a choice that changes the meaning and function of a rule or decision, and the meaning and consequences of traditional common law rules that were retained by southern courts underwent considerable change by virtue of the alteration of their surrounding circumstances. But as a matter of the evolution of American law, the southern pattern of development comprised resistance to new doctrines in the 1850s, followed by the eventual adoption of a version of those doctrines in the 1870s and 1880s. To see the connections between differences in political culture and patterns of legal development, it is important to return to a consideration of the two instrumentalities that defined each region's path of economic development: respectively, railroads and slavery.

The North: Railroads, Progress, and Legal Innovation

As was noted earlier, in the North, railroads were the carriers of change. But change did not come immediately. The first great railroad construction projects, undertaken in the 1830s, were spectacular failures that bankrupted half a dozen states and launched a depression in the process. State bonds issued to underwrite speculation in rail development essentially bankrupted the governments in Illinois, Indiana, Ohio, and New York (Jones, 1989: 245–6). Even the effort to undertake such a project put strains on the system of common law in terms of describing the rights and duties of chartered corporations, the nature of "property" interests that the law would protect, and the meaning of traditional tort categories. All of these reflected the challenge that the railroads posed to the balance that was understood to exist between claims of private right and public good. But for the most part, prior to 1850 these issues were raised rather than resolved.

The railroad construction that exploded in the North in the 1850s continued, without pausing for breath or wartime, up to the economic depressions of the 1870s (Chandler, 1965: 5–11). In 1849, the only northern rail line outside of New England ran from Sandusky, Ohio, to Cincinnati. Between 1849 and 1854, twenty-two thousand miles of track were laid, while in the same period more canals were abandoned than built (Chandler, 1977: 83). By 1855 the northern rail network ran as far west as the Illinois–Iowa border. The trains of the 1850s, too, differed from those of earlier years. Trains in the 1830s had been slow-moving, limited modes of conveyance that were expensive to construct and maintain and unreliable under the best of circumstances. Running on "strap rails" that consisted of flat bands of iron bolted to wooden planks, these railroads lacked either the scale or the speed to produce a drastic increase in stranger interactions or long-distance economic activities. The new trains of the 1850s were different. These machines were fast and powerful, able to cross vast distances at a rate that shrank the country. Four-wheeled "Bogie" trucks attached to the bottoms of cars by stabilizer bars, an invention unique to American trains, enabled cars to negotiate sharp curves and steep grades. Iron T-rails replaced "strap" rails, rail gauges began to become standardized (although the northern and southern systems used different sizes), and increasingly powerful steam engines were attached to cars specially designed to haul freight or passengers (Stover, 1997: 44–5; Nock, 1979: 6–8). The result was that freight rates across the decade dropped to the point where rail rates became cheaper per mile-ton than shipment by wagon (Stover, 1997: 48; Martin, 1992: 20). As for passenger transportation, there was simply no analogue to the railroads' speed. In 1830, a trip from New York to Chicago took nearly three weeks. In 1860 the same trip took less than two days (Chandler, 1977: 85).

The result was that the railroads of the 1850s transformed the patterns of social and commercial interactions in two critical dimensions: speed and scale. Speed changed the rhythms of commerce in fundamental ways. Owners of stores did not have to take out a month every year to travel east to purchase goods, nor have to select their goods for the entire year all at once. Farmers did not have to spend weeks at a time getting their products to markets (Cronon, 1991: 76). There was a basic change in the shared experience of distance and time. Henry David Thoreau observed that even the conversational style of his neighbors seemed to have changed in response to the arrival of the rails: "Have not men improved somewhat in punctuality since the railroad was invented? Do they not talk and think faster in the depot than they did in the stage-office?" (Thoreau, 1971: 117–18). The possibilities of speed gave rise to whole new categories of professions. To operate at such speeds required highly trained workers and managers, while the growth of marketing and distribution networks led to the creation of salespeople, jobbers, warehousers, and wholesale distributors. The novelty of the machines paled in comparison to the novelty of the enterprise. The sheer scale of construction and operation necessitated the separation of management from ownership, while the scale of financing led to the public trading of securities and an entirely new version of "ownership" completely separated from the business itself (Chandler, 1977: 90–2, 209–10). The railroads created a political economy of speed.

The transformation in the scale of public life was driven by the fact that railroads were not just a medium of transportation, they were also a medium of communication. Trains carried the mail with such efficiency that postal rates dropped, resulting in dramatic increases in the volume of personal as well as business correspondence. Telegraph lines followed railroad lines in order to take advantage of their rights of way, while railroad companies utilized the telegraph system to coordinate the operation of their trains and often owned the telegraph lines themselves. The combination of transportation and communication created whole new forms of related commercial and industrial activities. Trains brought large amounts of grain to cities, so steam-powered grain elevators were invented to store it, and these, too, were often built and operated by the railroad companies. A single grain elevator, operated by the Illinois Central Railroad, could empty twelve railroad cars at a time and load ships at the mind-boggling rate of twenty-four thousand bushels per hour. The combination of trains and grain elevators, in turn, altered the very meaning of agricultural commodities. Transportation of wheat and corn by the carload rather than the sack, and storage by the ton rather than the bushel, meant the creation of standardized grades and measures (Cronon, 1991: 113). Combined with efficiencies in communication and information exchange, standardized grades provided the basis for contracts "to arrive" consummated over telegraph lines between parties hundreds of miles away, often before crops were delivered or even harvested, and a dozen different transactions could take place without any actual transfer of grain at all (Cronon, 1991: 117–20; Chandler, 1977: 195–6, 210). What William B. Cronon calls "the alchemy of the elevator receipt" created futures markets and commodities exchanges (Cronon, 1991: 264). The world of commercial interactions was standardized, rationalized, and reshaped in accordance with new forms of industrial production, transport, marketing, and management. On the eve of the Civil War, railroads employed many times as many people as the national government, and their capitalization dwarfed every other venture of the time (McGraw, 1984: 5; Chandler, 1965: 3–18). The railroads were thus not merely an event that occurred in American public space, they were the event around which a national American public space was formed.

But the expansion of the rail system did not occur without conflict. For one thing, the technology that produced speed was one-sided. Trains could go very fast, but they could not stop easily. Until the 1868 invention of the Westinghouse air brake, stopping a train required brakemen on each car to apply the brakes manually to the wheels of that car. A train moving twenty or thirty miles an hour would not be able to come to a complete stop until hundreds of yards after the command was given. As a result, trains were uniquely destructive elements in the antebellum landscape. In Lawrence

M. Friedman's evocative description, trains were "wild beasts; they roared through the countryside, killing livestock, setting fire to crops, smashing passengers and freight" (Friedman, 1985: 409). One can get a good sense of the appearance and sound of a mid-nineteenth century train in motion from testimony in an 1852 case to the effect that "the ashpan sparks from the engine can be seen at a distance of two miles," and the train could "be heard at a distance of from 2 to 4 or 6 miles depending upon weather" (*Galena & Chi. Union R.R. Co. v. Loomis*, 13 Ill. 548, 1852; ISHA file # 11999, 2, 10). The construction of rail lines running across hundreds of miles of open farmland in the West, combined with resentment over the debacle of state railroad financing, created conflicts between rail and agrarian interests to a far greater degree than had been the case in the developed states of the Northeast (Jones, 1989: 247).

Party politics offered little redress. States were in competition for markets, and the rail lines were the key to access. Railroads meant growth, and an increase in the wealth of the state. Legislators answered to the demands of investors and growing urban populations. And farmers, as a class, were not inclined to opposition. The trains promised and delivered commercial outlets for farmers' crops, which transformed farming into an industry in its own right. By the end of the 1850s, farmers as a class were primarily concerned with the rates being charged for the transportation of their crops, not with trying to prevent the construction of the rail lines. Thus for northern Democrats in particular, an argument that the "public good" would best be served by declining the services that railroads offered made little sense in the 1850s.

It is also important to realize that the northern rail construction of the 1850s was carried out by private enterprises rather than by the states, whose legislatures had become gun-shy after the failures of the 1830s. In the system of private rail construction, political conflicts were primarily a matter of competition for a share of the spoils in the form of state charters, rights of way, and other legislatively granted privileges (Holt, 1999: 686). As this description suggests, however, a political consensus in favor of the existence of a rail system exacerbated, rather than diminished, the conflicts between the railroads and those whose interests could no longer be heard in political debates. These conflicts were worked out in the state courts, as individuals brought claims of grievance forward for adjudication. *Salus populi*, after all, was a legal as well as a political concept.

The judges who sat on the highest courts in northern states were more than ready to consider a sweeping reevaluation of their governing principles. Detailed examination of cases decided by the Illinois Supreme Court in the 1850s demonstrates that time and again, justices who might have decided claims in terms of existing common law rules instead treated them as opportunities for the articulation of broad theories that connected rules of legal adjudication with political and political-economic ideological principles. This was not purely a matter of biographical happenstance. By institutional design as well as tendency, courts were more nimble than the political parties of the mid-nineteenth century. At the level of formal doctrine, control was centralized in the persons of a handful of appellate judges.[19] In addition, prior to the war, common law doctrine was much more immediately at stake in the lives of individuals, corporations, and states than were the great issues of national politics. It is therefore unsurprising that where profound political questions were at stake in the formulation of northern economic policy, they first became visible in the courts. It was at that point that political ideas about the virtues of citizens took the form of enforceable legal duties.

In the process, critical concepts in the common law tradition were profoundly altered. The ideal of *salus populi*, in particular, was expanded to fit the new understanding of speed and scale. The idea that the public good was the goal and the ultimate justification for both law and politics was an ancient one, but in the mid-nineteenth century North, the meaning of the concept underwent a profound alteration in its scale and significance for the law. The "good of the people" meant one thing when it was applied to the inhabitants of a village, town, or city, but it meant something else when applied to the public financing of railroads. From the good of a set of individuals, *salus populi* was extended to mean the future prospects of a national people, a corporate entity possessed of a collective will and a collective future that superseded any individual's interests.

The extension of the ideal of *salus populi* to large-scale corporate ventures made a crucial shift from "police" to progress, a shift from local, concrete benefits to a general, abstract good that transformed the idea of the "public" from the members of a local community to an abstract "people" that expanded to encompass the entire country. The construction of the railroads promised new markets, new conditions for social intercourse, new opportunities for greatness for the People, not just for

---

[19] The importance of this factor is suggested by the fact that at the level of trial verdicts, where such centralized control was not in place, the state of legal doctrine at any given time – and consequently the meaning of legal "change" – is much more difficult to assess. For a review of studies of jury trial outcomes in nineteenth century tort cases, see Karsten, 1997: 255–91. The difference between appellate doctrine and trial practice is the difference between law as ideology and law as social custom.

persons. With the expansion in its scale, the legal function of *salus populi* also changed. From the definition of the outer limit of private property rights that defined the regulatory authority of local government, *salus populi* became the starting point for the definition of universal rights and duties.

The reconfiguration in the concept of *salus populi* accompanied the simplification and unification of legal doctrines. A key moment in this dual process of development was the creation of a general theory of negligence. This was a mode of legal reasoning that elevated "negligence" from a descriptive term to a nearly all-encompassing category of tort actions. There were two fundamental elements to the general theory of negligence: first, the theory proceeded on the understanding that duties of care should be uniform and universal, not dependent on the specific relationships between parties; and, second, from the very beginning, the theory contained a built-in principle that made conformity to universally applicable norms of conduct a threshold requirement for recovery. In other words, the initial burden of conforming to public duties was not on the defendant, but on the plaintiff. Where earlier analyses had begun with the question, "What obligations did the defendant have toward the plaintiff?" the new scheme would begin with the question, "Has the plaintiff met his duties toward the public at large such that a court should be willing to hear his claims for relief?" It is important to recognize that in each case, the initial question was a threshold requirement, rather than simply an element of adjudication. In the older system, a plaintiff whose relationship to a defendant precluded any obligation on the part of the defendant to refrain from causing harm could not fit his claim into the terms of a recognized writ. In the new system, persons who failed to meet their universal duty to accommodate progress would be similarly barred. It was not merely that their claims would be disfavored at trial; the assertion of their interests could not be heard in a court at all.

In tort law, the development of a general theory of negligence replaced an array of different kinds of liability applicable to different situations, relationships, and legal status. Because the earlier law contained so many different categories and rules, it is difficult to describe the adoption of the general theory of negligence as a move toward greater or lesser liability; the new theory is more properly understood as containing elements of both. The general theory of negligence remains, to this day, the principle that recovery in a tort suit depends on showing that the defendant had a duty to exercise care and breached that duty, causing damage to the plaintiff.

Aside from the analytical simplification of categories that this theory implied, it was novel in a number of other ways. First, under the theory of negligence there could be no liability without fault. Some version of this "fault principle" could be found in various areas of earlier English common law (Rabin, 1981; Donnelly, 1967), but it was Lemuel Shaw of the Massachusetts Supreme Court who announced the adoption of fault as a universal tort principle in 1850: "If the act of hitting the plaintiff was unintentional... then the defendant was not liable, unless it was done in the want of exercise of due care... [T]herefore such want of due care became a part of the plaintiff's case, and the burden was on the plaintiff to establish it" (*Brown v. Kendall*, 60 Mass. 292, 297, 1850). In this way, the theory of negligence replaced a variety of writs that had made a defendant liable for all harm caused by his conduct under the rule of *sic utere*, regardless of whether he had acted with care. The focus on "duty" in negligence doctrine, moreover, opened the door to a broad reconceptualization of legal analysis when courts decided that the question was not the duty owed by a defendant to the plaintiff, but rather the duty that each actor owed to abide by general standards of conduct. This was the analytical move that turned the common law into a language for defining the universal virtues that everyone was required to display at all times.[20]

It was not only the categories of tort law that were reconfigured around the idea of public duties. In many ways, the general theory of negligence reached beyond tort law to become the template for development in other areas as well. The obligations of contract and employment and rights to property, both in the form of land and otherwise ("real" or "personal" property), were similarly brought into line with the new unified system of principles in the context of railroad cases. In the interpretation of

[20] Some legal historians challenge the characterization of the principles described here as "new." For instance, in the area of contract law, Philip A. Hamburger has argued that antecedents for the consensual theory of contract formation can be seen as early as the sixteenth century; in tort law, Robert L. Rabin and Samuel R. Donnelly have each presented evidence that the fault principle was at work long before *Brown v. Kendall*; and Karen Orren has asserted that the law of employment relations exhibited a "belated feudalism" well into the twentieth century (Hamburger, 1989; Rabin, 1981; Donnelly, 1967; Orren, 1991). Each of these hypotheses is a matter of dispute, to be sure. (See, e.g., Tomlins, 1993, arguing that labor law developed along with the rest of American common law in response to a change in the "mode of rule"; see also Montgomery, 1991, arguing that craft-based labor organizations asserted premodern legal categories in resistance to attempts by managers to implement innovations in work relations, rather than the converse.) What is clear from the historical record, however, is that regardless of whether principles such as "fault" were entirely new, they received new emphasis and took on new significance in the middle of the nineteenth century.

sales contracts, American courts moved to a "consent" theory that held that parties' contractual obligations would be determined by the duties and risks that they had intended to undertake. Included in this idea of "intent," however, was a presumed understanding and awareness of the usual conduct of business, and an implied obligation to act accordingly (Hamburger, 1989: 241–329; Atiyah, 1979). Contracts for the shipment of goods by rail, in particular, were focal points for the articulation of these expectations. Again, the pattern was one of standardization and a presumption of familiarity with modern practices, and again the development of these rules began with the railroad cases of the 1850s.

The law of property was likewise reworked in response to the move from private rights to public duties. Not only did the rise of corporations involve new kinds of property interest, but, in addition, trains posed peculiar challenges to received categories of property rights. For one thing, a railroad might be said to be simultaneously on a public turnpike (the tracks) and to be an enclosed private space (the cars). Rail yards, like other centers of industrial work, combined numerous functions, up to and including the provision of housing where employees and their families resided on railroad property. Traditions governing the use of private land, enclosure requirements, and public and private property all underwent revision when they were tested in the context of railroad cases. As had been the case for tort and contract doctrines, the governing principle in the formulation of new categories of property and new descriptions of property relations was the duty to promote progress, and the cases in which these new understandings were announced were railroad cases.

In employment law, workers seeking to sue their employers and parties seeking to hold employers vicariously liable for their employees' acts had to meet the same burden of demonstrating their conformity with the duty to promote industrial progress that had been made a precondition for asserting a claim against a stranger. Two particularly important doctrines in this area were the fellow-servant rule, which held that an employee could not recover damages from an employer for harms caused by a fellow employee, and the principle of *respondat superior*, the rule that an employer would be liable for the acts of his employee. The fellow-servant rule is a good example of a rule whose meaning changed even without the invention of a new formal doctrine. In the North, the fellow-servant rule expanded in its significance, just as "employer" changed from describing an artisan's shop to describing massive railroad corporations. In the South, the same rule had profoundly different consequences, where "employment" was construed in the context of an economy based on slave labor. The same pattern of reconceptualization without reformulation was applied to the rule of an employer's vicarious liability for the acts of employees. As we shall see, these two rules were reworked in ways that brought employment law in line with the principles that were informing new tort doctrines in the North, while the same rules were interpreted in the South in ways that suited the conditions of that region's political economy.

An important element of the duty to accommodate progress was a requirement that people be familiar with technology. This appeared most clearly in the articulation of the Duty to Get Out of the Way, mentioned earlier. It would be presumed that everyone would be familiar with trains and with railroad practices and would act accordingly at all times so as to avoid injury. This was a departure from earlier cases, which, consistent with traditional common law doctrines, had relied on the novelty of railroad technology to excuse the inattention of passersby. This was the approach of Lemuel Shaw's 1848 opinion in *Bradley v. Boston & Maine Railroad*: "[W]here a practice has long existed," he wrote, "the course which has commonly been pursued by persons of ordinary skill and care will be usually the same as that which is reasonable . . . if railroads had existed so long, etc., usual care would be a proper test; but in consideration of the recent introduction of railroads, the question of proper care . . . was for the jury to decide" (*Bradley v. Boston & Maine Railroad* 56 Mass. 539, 542–3, 1848).

As time went on, it was not merely that the toleration for ignorance faded. More importantly, the terms of the argument shifted away from custom in favor of duties to the public good. Twenty years after the fact, in *The Common Law*, Oliver Wendell Holmes articulated the point beautifully:

[W]hen men live in society, a certain average of conduct, a sacrifice of individual peculiarities going beyond a certain point, is necessary to the general welfare. . . . [O]rdinary liabilities in tort arise from failure to comply with fixed and uniform standards of external conduct, which every man is *presumed and required to know* . . . (Holmes, 1881: 86, 89, emphasis added).

The Duty to Get Out of the Way was ultimately grounded in the requirement that citizens be familiar with standards for the conduct that was required to promote progress, a goal not served by permitting one's self or one's animals to be run into by trains.

The new legal rules that were developed in the context of railroad cases quickly spread to cover the breadth of the common law. An 1856 digest of Illinois law contained no entry under "negligence," and under "torts" referred only to the possibility of choosing between a tort writ and a suit in "assumpsit." Thirty years later, a digest of Illinois law contained hundreds of cases under "negligence," covering all areas of life (Freeman, 1856; Wood and Long, 1882). The first national digest of tort law, written by Francis Hilliard, was published in 1859.[21] By the late 1860s, digests of American common law, arranged around the new, broadly defined categories that were also the basis for new curricula of legal education, were firmly in place as the third element of the familiar modern triumvirate of legal authority: statutes, cases, and treatises.

Thus the universal quality of the new duties led to the process of rationalization and unification for which reformers had been clamoring since the 1830s. Both within the various fields, and between tort, contract, and property doctrines, the rules for the determination of a party's potential liability were increasingly bound into a single, unified system of public duties. Modernization in the law followed the arrival of railroads, and the states with the most extensive rail systems were the first to modernize. The key was the imperative for standardization. Railroads not only brought the corn of a thousand different farmers together, they moved the farmers themselves, and the schoolteachers, blacksmiths, storekeepers, and barflies. The result was the same as it had been for corn, timekeeping, and the value of money. In order for society to function, there had to be a way to standardize the expectations of social conduct. For corn, standardization had been carried out by commercial practices and later by regulation. For people, new common law doctrines articulated the standardization of what everyone would be presumed and expected to know, and the conduct that the law would demand of them as a consequence. That was the regime of American common law that emerged in the antebellum North. Eventually, it would be imported to southern states as well, but not until after the Civil War and the destruction of the traditional southern social and economic order. In the 1850s, the situation in the South was entirely different from that in the North.

The South: Slavery, Reaction, and Legal Stasis

From the beginning, the position of conservative southerners was the mirroring opposite of that which dominated in the North. In the South, there

---

[21] Hilliard, 1859.

was nothing like the political economic developments that posed such a challenge to traditional modes of political and social thought in the North. Thus there was neither a welcoming ideological environment nor a powerful set of shared interests pushing the desirability of legal change. There were southern industries, to be sure, but southern industrial development lagged far behind that of the North (Kolchin, 1993: 176; Starobin, 1970b: 186–189). Southern industry took a form that was peculiarly accommodating of slavery. Robert Starobin estimates that the southern rail mileage cost one-third as much to construct as mileage in the North because of slave labor, making the relative underdevelopment of southern rail systems all the more remarkable (Starobin, 1970a: 131–2; Starobin, 1970b: 177). There was also a considerable amount of small-scale manufacturing and light industrial work on agricultural plantations (Genovese, 1974: 388). These industrial uses of slave labor were not threatening to the social order of slavery, however, because they took place outside of cities, so that slaves did not compete directly with white workers and were not separated from the oversight of their masters.

By contrast, exposing slaves to urban environments was widely considered to be dangerous. Frederick Douglass described an urban slave as "almost a freeman, compared with a slave on the plantation" (Kolchin, 1993: 177–8). In 1850 James H. Hammond, South Carolina's leading planter, agreed, writing in *DeBow's Review*, "[w]henever a slave is made a mechanic he is more than half freed, and soon becomes, as we too well know, and all history attests, with rare exceptions, the most corrupt and turbulent of his class" (Lewis, 1979: 224). "[W]e do an immense injury to the institution of negro slavery," wrote the Richmond *Examiner*, "by employing our slaves in the mechanical arts . . . and allowing them to leave the plantation in the country to congregate in towns, in factories, and in the trades" (Ashworth, 1995: 112). Furthermore, life in urban areas exposed slaves to the pernicious influences of European immigrants, who were widely believed to be closet abolitionists or, at a minimum, disloyal to the southern cause (Berlin and Gutman, 1983: 1199–1200). There were fears, too, that urban blacks engaged in miscegenation with northerners and foreigners (Ashworth, 1995: 108, n. 45; Genovese, 1974: 423–9).

Despite conservative concerns, urban manufacturers made extensive use of slave labor, creating tensions between industry and the slaveowning elite (Starobin, 1970b: 204–14). In Richmond, the most industrialized southern city, a system was developed in which once a year, at Christmas, slaves would negotiate directly with employers (primarily tobacco factories) (O'Brien, 1978: 513–14).[22] For the slaveowners, this system made it unnecessary to travel to the city or to pay commissions to hiring agents. For the employers, it was a response to a tight labor market. By the 1850s, employers were offering hired slaves cash payment for extra work, and the opportunity to make their own arrangements for room and board. The situation threatened the social relations of slave society and angered Richmond's more conservative residents. The editors of the Richmond *Daily Dispatch* warned that treating slaves as industrial employees "plants the germ of rebellion in the contract for obedience . . . " (O'Brien, 1978: 513–15). The Richmond *Examiner* called for the enactment of laws to prohibit the employment of slaves "except as house servants and agricultural laborers." Attempts to enact legislation restricting the payment of cash bonuses, however, were blocked by the powerful tobacco manufacturers, a testament to the opposition between liberal corporate capitalism and the social order of slavery (Ashworth, 1995: 111–12).

Even without the problems associated with urban life, there was tension between the interests of industry and agriculture. There was a general shortage of slave labor, reflected in consistently rising prices through the 1850s for both the purchase and hire of slaves. The utilization of slaves in southern industry put economic pressures on the plantation system in the 1850s that were only partially offset by the availability of white immigrant labor in the cities (Berlin and Gutman, 1983: 1182–1189).[23] Nor were the problems of blurring the lines between slave and free labor restricted to the cities, since it was far cheaper for industries to hire slaves than to buy them (Starobin, 1970b: 162; O'Brien, 1978: 512; Genovese, 1974: 390–2). The use of slaves as hired laborers challenged the separation of categories between slaves and freemen, particularly where slaves worked side by side – and therefore in competition – with white workers (Genovese, 1974: 389; Starobin, 1970b: 14–17). As a result, there was resistance to using slaves in industry generally, which limited industrialization by restricting the available pool of labor (Genovese, 1974: 389). The point is an important one. The use of slave labor in industry was highly profitable, and there

---

[22] Tobacco factories employed one-half of the male slave population of the city in 1860. They accounted for 69.8 percent of all workers in 1850 and 50.3 percent in 1860 (O'Brien, 1978: 511).

[23] Claudia Dale Goldin challenges the thesis that urbanization was incompatible with slavery by noting that urban slave wages continued to rise during the period (Goldin, 1975: 246). On purely economic grounds, Goldin is correct, but in the long run this evaluation overlooks the challenges – real and imagined – that urban existence posed to the social order of slavery (Genovese, 1962: 422).

was no sign in the 1850s that southern industry was on the verge of economic failure. The resistance to industrial slavery, then, demonstrates the divergence in interests between established plantation elites and a rising class of industrial entrepreneurs (Starobin, 1970a: 135–46; Lewis, 1979: 217–34).

The point, then, was not that slave labor was unsuited to industry, but rather that the success of industrial slavery challenged the specific southern model of slavery and the social order that it supported. As a result, southern elites had very good reasons to resist the most subversive of all industries, railroads. Railroads carried with them the epitome of all the threats to the slave order: urbanization, ease of travel away from plantations, exposure to outsiders, and the potential to become a huge and profitable industry capable of competing with plantation agriculture. It is therefore unsurprising that on the eve of the Civil War, throughout the South, the rail transportation network was primarily limited to connecting plantations to ports.[24]

The conflicts between industrialization and slavery in the South meant that there was no place for technological exceptionalism. Man-made technology could not be the driving force behind social development, as in the North, but instead had to be accommodated to the "natural" social and political order of slavery, a proposition explained in pseudo-scientific and theological defenses for slavery.[25] In the South, technology held no promise except insofar as it could accommodate the keeping of slaves.

As a result of the successful suppression in their states of railroad development and of industrialization generally, southern courts before the Civil War confronted few of the novel issues that were driving northern judges to reconsider the basic logic of traditional common law analysis. In addition, southern justices were far less eager to take on the role of innovators. Where southern courts confronted cases involving railroad companies, the companies appeared as traditional private property

---

[24] Starobin argues that slavery and northern-style industrialization were ultimately incompatible. He concludes, however, that the point of inconsistency between industrialization and slavery had not yet been reached by 1861. What would have been the upper limit of industrialization on the southern pattern, but for the Civil War, is an interesting matter for speculation (Starobin, 1970b: 162, 164–5).

[25] Samuel George Morton ranked races by order of abilities based on their cranial characteristics. His student, Josiah Clark Nott, proposed that the "scientific" fact of multiple divine acts of Creation demonstrated the necessary inferiority of the Negro to the Caucasian race (Morton, 1839; Nott and Gliddon, 1854). The influence of these arguments was considerable (Lurie, 1954: 227–42; Ross, 1991: 31–3).

owners seeking redress in the common law from the threat of political action. Those railroad companies faced an uphill battle, as the southern courts' guiding political norms were constructed around the conservative culture of slave society. Southern courts' stubborn retention of traditional common law doctrines expressed their rejection of new standards of citizenship as well as the political economy with which they were associated. Thus in the antebellum South as in the North, the courts and the legislatures appeared as twin articulations of a dominant political philosophy that used the language of the law to legitimate and further a vision of an ideal society. Above all, what was at stake in the legal expressions of competing political visions was a difference in the governing conceptions of public virtue.

Abraham Lincoln and the Northern Mind

The embodiment of the northern conception of legal and political virtue was Abraham Lincoln. As a state politician, Lincoln been an avid supporter of public investment in railroad construction since the 1830s, when he was a member of the state legislature that approved the grand projects of 1837. In the 1850s, when the railroads arrived in his home state in force, he avidly sought their business, describing the Alton & Sangamon Railroad Company as "a link in the great chain of railroad communication which shall unite Boston and New York with the Mississippi" (Donald, 1995: 154–5). As a lawyer, Lincoln consistently argued that both the special prerogatives of railroad corporations and the limits on those prerogatives must reflect the primacy of the public interest over private claims of right.

As a politician, Lincoln was an avid believer in the promise of technology. In an 1859 speech to the Wisconsin State Agricultural Society at Milwaukee, he clearly connected the growth of technology with the meaning of free labor and the promise of national greatness. Noting that the yield per acre from farmland in the region was far below the supposed capacity of the soil, he indicated that what was needed was research: "It is almost certain, I think, that by deeper plowing, analysis of the soils, experiments with manures and varieties of seeds, observance of seasons, and the like, these causes would be discovered and remedied." The central problem, however, was a familiar one: "locomotion." "The successful application of steam power to farm work is a desideratum," he said, and he spent several paragraphs in describing such an invention. "Our thanks, and something more substantial than thanks, are due to every man engaged in the effort to produce a successful steam plow" (Lincoln, 1859: 122–4, 126).

For Lincoln, technology was emphatically an element of American exceptionalism. In America, he declared, there were neither workers "fixed to that condition for life," nor capitalists. "A large majority belong to neither class – neither work for others nor have others working for them.... Men, with their families – wives, sons, and daughters – work for themselves... asking no favors of capital, on the one hand, nor of hirelings or slaves, on the other." That many businesses hired workers was taken to be an example of "a mixed, and not a distinct class." Lincoln drew a direct connection between the use of education to harness the powers of science – he mentioned botany, chemistry, and "[t]he mechanical branches of natural philosophy" – and political virtues. "No community whose every member possesses this art can ever be the victim of oppression in any of its forms. Such community will be alike independent of crowned kings, money kings, and land kings" (Lincoln, 1859: 126). Technology, in other words, would make free labor into a uniquely American middle class. One wonders, in 1865 did Lincoln still dream of steam engines?

Regardless, the development of a modern model of citizenship was required to be much more complete in its legal formulation than in the broad generalities of national political discourse. Declaring the supremacy of universal duties to serve the cause of national progress was a political act. Filling in the content of those public duties and enforcing them, however, was a uniquely legal undertaking. While Lincoln's speeches might demonstrate the political conceptions that drove changes in the idea of national citizenship, it was the state courts that undertook the task of defining the duties that were required of citizens in peacetime. In their creation of a body of American common law, courts undertook the articulation of universal, public duties, replacing the private, relational claims of litigants that were the sine qua non of English common law adjudication. In the next three chapters, we will explore these themes in a close examination of Lincoln's own Illinois.

2

Illinois

"We Were Determined to Have a Rail-Road"

In order to see how the development of law in Illinois reflected a response by a dominant political culture to the challenges of transformative technology, it is necessary to review some of the politics that shaped the state prior to 1850. It was not the case, in Illinois as elsewhere, that when railroads appeared they confronted a ready-made political culture set to welcome them, nor a previously identified group of interested and empowered actors poised for action. Instead, the political culture of Illinois grew in significant part around the experiences of railroad development in the 1830s and 1840s. In the process, individual actors acquired interests and became powerful by virtue of their roles in railroad development. Institutions, ranging from political parties to the state government and the courts, both guided and developed in response to the emergence of a rail-based political economic system. Interests, ideologies, and institutions were mutually constitutive elements of the environment that in 1850 would enable and encourage the Illinois Supreme Court to undertake the project of remaking the common law.

Antebellum Illinois was divided north to south into three sections, geographically, demographically, and culturally. On crucial political questions, however, the middle section itself divided, resulting in a nearly perfect bisection of the state. Reflecting the issues that divided the nation, northern and southern Illinois were split on questions of slavery, states' rights, and the role of the national government. At the same time, however, the state was united in embracing the set of conceptions that served as the linchpins for the creation of an emerging northern model of citizenship. The embrace of technological exceptionalism, an expansive conception of *salus populi* linked to industrial progress, and a conception of universal virtues equally shared by and required of everyone, were elements of a dominant political consensus that cut across divisions on other questions. In this sense, although Illinois was not by any means the most northern state in terms of its political culture, the state shared the fundamental commitments of other states of the industrializing North.

The divisions in Illinois derived from the pattern of its initial settlement. Settlement began in the south, in a line that followed the Illinois River to its junction with the Mississippi River at what would become Alton, with a second short branch of concentrated settlement running from the southern tip of the state at Cairo up to Vincennes. This line followed the contours of a fertile delta of hilly, well-watered country situated at the convergence of the Mississippi and Illinois rivers. At the time of statehood, Illinois had thirteen counties, all in this southern tip of the state, a region later known as "Egypt" because it included towns called Cairo (pronounced "Kay-ro") and Alexandria. The people of the area were southern with respect to the nation as well as the state. Settlers in that region came primarily from Kentucky, Tennessee, Georgia, and the Carolinas, and they brought their legal and political cultures with them.

The political economy of downstate Illinois was also oriented toward the American South. The key to the area's economic development was river traffic, primarily the transport of raw materials and agricultural products down the Mississippi River toward New Orleans. River commerce reached its maturity with the first of two revolutions in transportation technology, the replacement of barges by steamboats in river traffic. Steamboats were faster and carried larger loads than the barges. These purely material advantages, however, were arguably secondary to the social advantages that the steamboats brought to southern Illinois. The barges, and more particularly their crews, had created serious difficulties for settlements along the rivers. "Squadrons" of barges, each carrying thirty to forty men, would descend on a town at once, creating a riot. Steamboats, by contrast, not only carried far more cargo far more quickly, they also stopped less frequently, traveled one at a time, and generally employed a more respectable class of person (Hall, 1828: 90–1). Steamboats also carried passengers, and with their arrival a lively traffic began up and down the Mississippi River. It was only natural, then, that when southern Illinois interests looked to build a rail line, they imagined a corridor connecting themselves to the American South.

Settlement of the central prairie region was begun in the 1830s by people moving up from the South. The prairie was a vast flatland that in the summer would be covered with flowering grasses to a height of ten feet.

The fertility of the prairie soil astounded visitors. In 1819, Ferdinand Ernst, visiting Illinois looking for a place to establish a settlement, commented that in the Sangamon area farmers could grow corn to a height of ten or fifteen feet "merely by breaking sod" (i.e., without the aid of fertilizer) (Ernst, 1819: 208). William Cullen Bryant, in a letter to his wife in 1832, described the land around Alton as "the most fertile country I ever saw" (Bryant, 1850: 102, 105). Unfortunately, that same fertile soil turned to an amazingly deep and carnivorous form of black mud when the rains came in the spring and fall. This mud earned special mention by Charles Dickens on his visit to the United States in 1842. "It had no variety," he wrote, "but in depth. Now it was only half over the wheels, now it hid the axletree, and now the coach sank down in it almost to the windows" (Dickens, 1842: 234). Another traveler described the Illinois mud as "coal-black, and tenacious as tar" (Curtiss, 1852: 277). Occupied by small homestead farmers who lived lives of isolation and debilitating disease, the middle of the state had no major cities through the 1840s.

Northern Illinois was even more sparsely settled than the central region through the early 1830s, covered by heavy forests, and occupied by occasionally hostile Indians. Morris Birkbeck, traveling through Illinois in 1817 in search of a site for a town for English nonconformists (religious nonconformists accounted for a significant amount of the settlement of the area at that time), described the families of hunters whom he encountered in the heavily wooded regions west of Chicago as "incarcerated," "shut from the common air," "buried in the depth of a boundless forest" (Birkbeck, 1817: 64, 66). Settlement in northern Illinois did not begin in earnest until after the Erie Canal had opened an easy route from the east in 1825 and the Indian population was driven off in the bloody Black Hawk War of 1832 (Jordan, 1967: 584).[1] The drawing card, initially, was natural resources. Northern Illinois sat atop an incredibly rich store of lead, coal, and salt. A lead mine was established in the town of Galena, founded in 1825 with a total of four log houses; in 1826 Galena had grown to 115 houses and stores. In Gallatin, the United States Salines salt mine and processing plant were producing three hundred thousand bushels of salt annually by 1819, supporting a town of "about 80 houses, mostly

[1] Bryant described meeting troops of these militia during his travels: "Some of the settlers complained that they made war upon the pigs and chickens. They were a hard-looking set of men, unkempt and unshaved, wearing shirts of dark calico, and sometimes calico capotes." Bryant particularly enjoyed talking to a young captain named Abraham Lincoln (Bryant, 1850: 105). Treaties resulting in the removal of the last Indians from Illinois were signed in 1833.

of wood, and a wooden jail," a bank "in good repute, many stores, and several taverns" (Woods, 1822: 77).

When it came in the 1850s, the construction of a rail system not only made shipment and travel convenient, for the northern and central regions it was very nearly the case that it made them possible at all. Until then the enterprises in the northern half of the state were devoted to shipping lead, salt, coal, and timber south by river for processing, sale, and transport. So long as that remained the axis of trade, the dominance of southern Illinois remained secure. When Chicago was incorporated as a village in 1833, it had a population of only 350 (Angle, 1968: 60).

European travelers' descriptions make early Illinois society seem a veritable parody of Jacksonian vices and virtues. "[T]he American," wrote Ernst, "shows a peculiar ease which is the result of his noble freedom. Everything is done without ado and without ceremony. This manner of living, which was to me at first very strange and disagreeable, soon received my entire approval – little by little one feels himself free among free, honest people" (Ernst, 1819: 205). On the other hand, John Woods, who visited the town of Wanborough in the same year, found less desirable social attributes mixed in with the political virtues of the residents of central Illinois. For one thing, he was struck by the residents' fondness for "frolics," always accompanied by whiskey. He described them as "uniformly civil and obliging," but also as shrewd traders. Woods was also struck by the litigiousness of the residents of the town. "Most of them are well acquainted with law, and fond of it on the most trifling occasions: I have known a law-suit brought for a piggin or pail, of the value of 25 cents." Most important, for Woods, was their civic political culture. "They are a most determined set of republicans," he wrote, "well versed in politics, and thoroughly independent." At the same time, the persistence of southern racialism was also striking: "[T]hough now living in a free State, they retain many of the prejudices they imbibed in infancy, and still hold negroes in the utmost contempt" (Woods, 1822: 80, 174, 81).

Throughout the 1830s, the crucial political issues were internal improvements and banks. In 1836 the Illinois legislature, composed almost entirely of downstate Democrats, approved a series of measures to fund a statewide system of canals and railroads. The scale of the project was immense, and the benefits that were expected may be gauged by the fact that the statute provided for a payment of $200,000 to each Illinois county that was *not* to be improved, as a way to even the playing field within the state. The projects included $500,000 in state borrowing to continue the construction of the Illinois and Michigan Canal, but the centerpiece of the new system was a rail line. The 1836 plan called for a great north-south rail line running from the lead mines of Galena, through the timber- and resource-rich northern part of the state, down to Cairo, and on down the Mississippi River Valley to the port of New Orleans. The geographic focus of the plan was illustrated by the pattern of the proposed tracks. There were no east-west crossing lines in the northern part of the state, but five such lines traversed the central and southern regions. In the original 1836 plan, Chicago was barely attached to the Illinois rail system at all.

The financing for the railroad system was to be private, and sixteen private charters were issued in the first year for construction. By the end of that year, when it became clear that private financing would not be adequate for the project, the state stepped in following a special state convention held just before the commencement of the 1836–7 legislative session. In 1837 the state legislature approved a plan to raise $10 million – $3.5 million for the Illinois Central – from the profits of a new state bank.[2] Then the national Panic of 1837 hit.

The Panic of 1837 destroyed Illinois' nascent program of internal improvements at the same time that it wiped out the state's banks. The internal improvement plan of 1836 became one of the truly monumental failures in an era of large-scale failures. Of the massive proposed rail system, all that was actually constructed was part of the Northern Cross line, running from Meredosia to Springfield, with lightweight rails resting on unsecured cross ties. This line was finally made operational in 1842; in 1844 the state sold the Northern Cross at auction for $21,100, one-fortieth of the cost of its construction. In 1840–1 the legislature, having spent nearly $3 million, abandoned the internal improvement plan and closed the state banks.

In addition to financial panic, however, the year 1837 was marked by two technological innovations that heralded a change in the character of Illinois as dramatic as that caused by the completion of the Erie Canal or the introduction of steamboats. In the same year that the southern-dominated state legislature was promulgating its grand plans for a system of transportation to bring resources to the south, John Deere's "Prairie Queen" self-scouring steel plow and Cyrus McCormick's reaper went on

---

[2] In his history of Illinois, Governor Thomas Ford suggested that Lincoln and other Whigs from the Sangamon Valley supported the rail development bill as part of a logroll, in return for the transfer of the state capitol to Springfield. Robert P. Howard, however, challenges that account (Ford, 1995: 186–7; Howard, 1972: 198–9).

sale in Chicago. Deere's plow and McCormick's reaper were technologies dictated by geography, perfect examples of the way innovation occurred in places where great opportunities for economic development were blocked by local physical conditions. Together, the plow and the reaper, as much as anything else, dictated that Illinois would return to the project of railroad development.

Deere's plow solved a problem that had caused farming in the prairies to be restricted to small-scale, livestock-intensive efforts. Although the prairie soil was tremendously fertile, it was also very difficult to break. James Stuart, a Whig politician and editor, described the situation in Morgan County in the early 1830s: "The roots of the prairie grass are so firmly interwoven with the soil, that it requires all the power and steadiness of oxen to tear up the ground; but after the first ploughing with six or eight oxen, horses do the work well, and crops are raised with more ease than in any other country.... " (Stuart, 1833: 97–8). Deere's self-scouring plow solved the problem of breaking the prairie soil with its sharp, deep-cutting steel primary blade, and an additional secondary blade that shed the sticky accumulation of earth and overgrowth with each rotation of a wheel. The result was the unleashing of the tremendous potential of the rich, black soil, as farms equipped with Deere's plows were instantly able to grow far more than was needed for sustenance. Suddenly, anyone who could get to Chicago and buy one of the new plows was in the commercial farming business. In fact, for those with the land and resources to do so – especially prosperous farmers who had already invested in large amounts of draft stock – the new plow meant that if they could hire the workers, they could cultivate an area too big to be harvested – except with McCormick's new reaper. In 1847 McCormick established a reaper production plant in Chicago, and Deere moved from a small plow-making shop in Grand Detour to a larger plant in Moline. By 1857, Deere was producing ten thousand plows a year (Angle, 1968: 204).

In 1847 Bryant, returning for a second visit to central Illinois, described the changes:

[T]he road for long distances now passed between fences; the broad prairie, inclosed, was turned into immense fields of maize, oats, and wheat, and was spotted here and there with young orchards...and where the prairie remained open, it was now depastured by large herds of cattle, its herbage shortened, and its flowers less numerous (Bryant, 1850: 236).

Deere's plow and McCormick's reaper were put to good use in the north, too, where the clearing of the forests was well under way by the early 1840s. Technology had thus opened northern and central Illinois to farming on a large scale. Small farmers with herds of grazing stock were out; commercial farmers producing corn and wheat for export were on their way. Throughout the 1830s and 1840s, new settlers from New England, Germany, Ireland, and Scandinavia poured into the northern and central parts of the state, swelling the population from 157,445 in 1830 to 476,183 in 1840.[3]

The influx of immigration into the northern and north-central parts of the state, the rise of commercial farming, and the construction of canal systems linking northern Illinois with the East Coast cities produced sharp regional divisions in culture and politics, and changed the balance of economic and political power in the state. Plans for a rail system changed their orientation from the north-south axis that had defined the 1837 program to an east-west system that would direct everything through Chicago, making central Illinois a kind of gigantic suburb of the city. There were cultural as well as economic consequences. The people of southern Illinois had always thought of themselves as standing near the head of a north-south river system that led to New Orleans. The settlers of the north, by contrast, looked east for their roots and west for their futures. The issue, in other words, was whether Illinois was a southern or an Old Northwestern state. Signs of political change appeared as early as 1825, when the United States Salines Company, in the far northern part of the state, stopped using slave labor in the face of local opposition. The practice was ended throughout the state by the Constitution of 1848.[4] By the late 1840s the center of power in the state had shifted northward.

In the 1840s, Illinois was deeply divided. The lower half of the state was typically southern, entirely dominated by the Democratic Party and deeply committed to Jacksonian values and the cause of slavery. In fact, right up to the war there was serious discussion of the possibility that in the event of secession Illinois might split into two, with its southern third joining with the slave states of the South and the remainder of the

---

[3] Continuing a pattern of religious immigration, the Mormon community of Nauvoo was established in 1839. One year later it comprised between 250 and 300 brick houses, and a year later had become the largest city in the state. In 1844, however, the Mormon community was chased out of the state by their neighbors (Jordan, 1967: 584). Concerning patterns of immigration, generally, see Howard, 1972: 223–5.

[4] Slavery was abolished in Illinois by Article XIII, "Bill of Rights," § 16: "There shall be neither slavery nor involuntary servitude in this state, except as punishment for crime, whereof the party shall have been duly convicted."

state staying with the Union.[5] Upper Illinois settlers, by contrast, were predominantly Whigs and later Republicans. From early on, northern settlers were antislavery, and there was a thriving temperance movement in northern Illinois in the 1840s. Reverend J. P. Thompson of New York described Peoria as having "quite a New England aspect," and declared that Jacksonville "looks, I say, like a model New England village made to order" (quoted in Curtiss, 1852: 264).

Through the 1840s, the issues that defined the political differences between southern and northern Illinois were banks, internal improvements, slavery, and the status of free blacks. There were also party-based divisions that did not correspond neatly with geographic lines; paramount among these were the question of the franchise and the role of the state Supreme Court. Democratic legislators feared and resented the Whig-dominated court as an instrument of elite interests. In the 1840–1 session, the legislature enacted a court-packing law that abolished the circuit courts entirely, appointed five additional Supreme Court justices, and gave the Supreme Court responsibility for riding the judicial circuits of the state in addition to hearing appeals. The five additional justices appointed under the bill were Sidney Breese, Walter B. Scates, Samuel H. Treat, Stephen A. Douglas, and Lyman Trumbull. All were prominent Democrats, and Breese and Douglas had been important players in earlier controversies, involving a state government appointment and a lawsuit challenging a law restricting the voting rights of immigrants, which had given rise to the court-packing plan in the first place (Davidson and Stuve, 1877: 455–8). Thus Breese, Scates, Treat, and Trumbull, all of whom would be justices of the Illinois Supreme Court in the 1850s, took the bench having established themselves as enemies of the Whig-dominated bench and the traditional republican elitism that it was popularly understood to represent.

---

[5] An Englishman in 1860 recorded a conversation with his fellow travelers on the Illinois Central:

> One of my friends argues that as slavery is at the base of Secession, it follows that States or portions of States will be disposed to join the Confederates or the Federalists just as the climate may be favourable or adverse to the growth of slave produce. Thus in the mountainous parts of the border States of Kentucky and Tennessee, in the north-western part of Virginia, vulgarly called the pan handle, and in the pine woods of North Carolina, where white men can work at the rosin and naval store manufactories, there is a decided feeling in favour of the Union; in fact, it becomes a matter of isothermal lines.

He also mentioned his concerns for his safety when traveling through the southern part of the state (Russell, 1863: 339).

The issues of banks, internal improvements, and the status of blacks reached their apotheoses in the watershed event of antebellum Illinois politics, the Constitutional Convention of 1847. The debates in that convention articulated the clash of ideologies at work in the formulation of conflicting political positions. The meaning of the public good and the course of progress were clearly at stake in the debates over internal improvements, while what virtues were required of citizens was the issue at stake in the question of the status of free blacks. By 1847, moreover, the issues were connected. The state's role in internal improvements had everything to do with the relationship of private interest to public needs, while the matter of the status of free blacks raised the question of what limits would be placed on the equalizing tendencies of rail technology.

State-chartered banks incurred a bad reputation when they backed the canal and railroad projects of the 1830s that had ruined the state, and the system had been liquidated in 1843 (Howard, 1972: 228). Whig delegates to the Convention proposed reviving the state bank system as a way to promote development and provide a reliable, state-controlled currency. Democratic opponents asserted familiar Jacksonian arguments against the dangers of paper money. The leading figure among conservative Democrats was future Justice Scates, who "gave notice, that whenever it came to be acted upon, he should oppose and vote against *bank in every form*. . . . If we desire a valuable and reliable circulating medium, we must, as all experience shows, exclude bank paper entirely" (Cole, 1919: 87–8).

Some Whigs joined with their Democratic colleagues on the issue. James M. Davis (a central Whig from Montgomery County) described banks as unrepublican corrupters of virtue as well as instruments of financial damnation: "Many young men (indeed, all turned speculators,) threw off their jeans coats, became too proud to work upon their fathers' farms, and might be seen dressed in the finest style, looking like physicians or the greatest aristocrats. All upon credit!" Above all, Davis argued that banks were ill-suited to the particular circumstances of Illinois: "Are we not an agricultural State, and are banks necessary for us? No, sir." Scates made the same point: "Past experience has proved to us that in agricultural communities such institutions are a curse." Opposition to banks was also connected to opposition to chartered corporations, the special bête noire of Jacksonian Democrats. Horace Butler, a northern Democrat, declared that the final result of corporate charters was nothing less than tyranny, "the establishment of an aristocracy of wealth, and . . . the subjection of the many to mere dependents and servile operators" (Cole, 1919: 253–4, 88, 300).

Disputes over the desirability of a state bank and corporate charters reflected competing visions of the relationship between the state's economy and its government. The difference between the positions was the difference between a conception of the state as a single community, progressing toward a single, collective future, or as a gathering of individuals pursuing private interests. It was also the difference between the ideal of the state's political economy as an emerging industrial order versus a traditional agrarian society. The former, collectivist vision required the state to be an active participant in creating conditions for economic growth. For those who appealed to tradition, by contrast, virtue resided in those who stayed on the farms, grew crops, and avoided the temptations of capitalism and corporate enterprise. Northern Illinois delegates of all parties displayed the modern, liberal tendencies toward collectivism and universalism, while southerners clung to ideals of personal virtue and a locally defined sphere of public activities. The tensions between these different positions would become increasingly sharp as railroads spread during the 1850s.

The issue of the status of free blacks was raised in the form of a bill to exclude them from settlement in the state. The question aroused passionate rhetoric among the delegates, and on that issue geographic divisions cut cleanly across party lines. Not only southern and central Democrats but also many Whigs and future Republicans were committed to republican principles that required equality among citizens. (The usually voluble Scates, interestingly, had nothing to say on the issue.) Benjamin Bond (a southern Whig from Clinton County, and later an antiwar Democrat), who introduced the exclusionary measure, insisted that he "wanted no persons to come into the State, unless they came with rights to be our equals in all things, and as freemen." Thus free blacks should not be admitted "unless we were willing to admit them to the privilege of the ballot box, and give them all the rights of freemen and citizens of a free republic. Can we, or ought we to, do this? He would answer nay" (Cole, 1919: 202–7). Downstate Democrats made the same argument in more frankly racialist terms. Dr. James Brockman (a central Democrat from Brown County) denied the possibility that free blacks could be rights-bearing citizens: "The negroes have no rights in common with the people, they can have no rights; the distinction between the two races is so great as to preclude the possibility of their ever living together upon equal terms" (Cole, 1919: 208).

On the other side, those who favored the extension of full political rights to free blacks were uniformly northern Whigs, the same delegates who were most strongly in favor of state banks and internal improvements. Seldon M. Church (a northern Whig from Winnebago County, later a Republican) argued that an exclusionary provision would make Illinois repugnant to potential settlers from other northern states: "Would emigrants from Pennsylvania and others imbued with sentiments of humanity, come to this State, if the proposition made here in relation to blacks were to become a part of our organic law? No, sir." Jesse Olds Norton (a northern Whig from Will County, later a Republican) invoked the Privileges and Immunities Clause: "Can we say then that a citizen of Massachusetts, Vermont or New York shall be prohibited from settling in the State of Illinois, in direct violation of an article of the constitution of the United States?" And Archibald Williams (a northern Whig from Adams County) described the proposition as "more suited for the 14th than the 19th century" (Cole, 1919: 203–4, 211, 219).

The issue was divisive, indeed. Northern delegates threatened that they would not approve any constitution with the exclusionary provision, while southerners warned that they would not approve any constitution without it (Cole, 1919: 218–19). In point of fact, however, egalitarian proposals never had a serious chance of success, an outcome that had been foreordained in the early days of the Convention when a motion to strike the word "white" from a proposal to extend suffrage to all white males was defeated by a vote of 137 to 7. The argument degenerated into finger-pointing over the question of who had raised the divisive issue in the first place.

The question of the franchise and representation concerned the status of those born outside the United States. The Whigs proposed lengthy residency requirements for voting, arguing that people who had not lived for a sufficient time in America would not appreciate American political institutions. Davis warned against allowing foreign-born residents "into high and important offices, before they are sufficiently acquainted with our language to speak it plainly." He warned, "they know nothing about our institutions; they are familiar with the political governments of the land where they spent their school-boy days.... How can they form an idea of our system of government?" (Cole, 1919: 363, 370). In addition, recent immigrants would be vulnerable to manipulation. Lincoln B. Knowlton said that "[h]e had seen them led like cattle to the polls by designing demagogues." Andrew McCallen too warned that "their votes were thrown into the market, and purchased by the highest bidder." Against the nativism of the northerners there were the conservative Democrats. Scates favored a residency requirement of only twelve months: "He thought that men who came to this country as an asylum from oppression, and on account of a love for our institutions, should not be considered in the light of spies." William C. Kinney (a southern Democrat from St. Clair County, later a Republican), in favor of suffrage, connected immigration to economic development: "Is it our policy, as a state burdened with debt and sparsely settled, to restrict the right of suffrage, and thus prevent immigration to our soil?" (Cole, 1919: 516, 525).

Debates about the exclusion of free blacks from the state or the extension of the franchise to immigrants were explicitly about the meaning of citizenship and the character of desirable citizens. What kinds of persons could be participants in the political process, and whether safeguarding the future of the state required the exclusion of some kinds of persons and the extension of equality to others, were questions that forced lawmakers to confront directly their commitments to republican elitism, liberal equality, and the existing social order. Debates over a state bank and the scope of internal improvements raised similar issues in different ways, confronting Whigs and Democrats with direct challenges to their received notions of the relationship between the state and the individual, the meaning of political and social virtue, and the course of the future. In all these debates, both southern Democrats and northern Whigs were caught up in the major debates of the Jacksonian era, unable to conceive of the extent to which the issues they cared so passionately about, and the principles that they invoked, would be made irrelevant in the years to come.

In the end, the Constitution of 1848 displayed the victory of moderate Whigs and conservative Democrats, as well as some points of compromise. Slavery was formally abolished, free blacks were barred from the state, and the franchise was granted to any white male who had resided in the state for one year. There would be no state banks, no extension of state credit for projects of internal improvement, and no state bond issues in excess of $50,000. Democrats gained a provision banning special acts of incorporation "except for municipal purposes, and in cases where, in the judgment of the general assembly, the objects of the corporation can not be attained under general laws" (Article XV; Article X, § 1), but at the same time internal improvements were to be encouraged by the enactment of "liberal general laws of incorporation for that purpose" (Article X, § 6). The Supreme Court was reorganized once again. The circuit courts were reestablished, and the Supreme Court was restored to its role of hearing appeals. As for the membership of that court, recognizing the geographical divisions within the state, the new constitution provided that there should be three justices, to be elected respectively from the southern, central, and northern parts of the state (Article V, §§ 3, 30; Moses, 1892, vol. 2: 561). The victory at the Convention by moderate Democrats, and to a lesser extent conservative Whigs, reflected the beginning of a geographical shift in the center of power in the state. The positions that had the least say in the final outcome were liberal northerners and conservative southerners. Instead, the constitutional compromises set the scene for the replacement of the traditional vocabulary of Illinois politics by the new political language of an emerging consensus on a wide range of issues. The Constitutional Convention of 1847 was the last gasp of the old order in Illinois politics.

Following 1848, the Whig Party was in full retreat in Illinois, electing only one of seven members of the Illinois Congressional delegation. Democrats dominated the legislature through 1855, but party labels had increasingly little significance when compared to the geographically defined divisions in political attitudes. There were a few remaining Whigs and a good number of traditional Democrats, but there were also anti-Nebraska Democrats, Free Soil Democrats, Abolitionists, and Know-Nothings. Even as the Democratic Party established what appeared to be a hegemonic hold over the state's politics, that party was falling apart into northern and southern branches that bisected the state, and power was shifting to the north. After a reapportionment in 1852, the northern part of the state had more Congressional and state representatives than the south. In 1856, the northern-dominated Republicans were unable to carry the state for John C. Fremont against James Buchanan, but they took majorities in both houses of the state legislature and in the state's Congressional delegation in an election marred by violence and threats (Moses, 1892: 605–6).

In the midst of this intensive political party conflict, Illinois once again embarked on a program of railroad-building. The Illinois Central had first been proposed in 1835 by Sidney Breese, who remained a key supporter of the project throughout the 1840s as a United States Senator (Moses, 1892: 572). Unlike Douglas, Breese favored Congressional grants of land directly to private corporations rather than to the states, an approach that presaged the successful model for Illinois' later railroad development (Cole, 1917: 36–7). The chicanery and politics involved in these maneuverings were breath-taking. In 1843 the Great Western Railroad Company, with Breese as an incorporator and director, sought a Congressional appropriation to resume construction of the Illinois Central line abandoned after the debacles of 1837. While the proposal was being presented to Congress, a charter was being prepared in Springfield. When Senator Douglas returned to Illinois, he discovered that a clause had been "surreptitiously" inserted into the bill that had the effect of giving the company ownership of any lands granted to the State of Illinois for *any* railroad construction project. As John Moses told the story in 1892, "[u]pon being interrogated by the senator, the governor, secretary of state, and members of the legislature all denied any knowledge of the clause in the act, and it has always remained a mystery how it came to be interpolated." Douglas forced the company to release its charter by threatening to introduce legislation creating a new route and barring any existing company from participation in the construction of the line, and the episode ended (Moses, 1892: 574).

At the end of the 1840s, Congressional opposition to federal grants was based in southern states. Douglas handled this problem adroitly on a secret visit to Alabama, where he arranged for the directors of the Mobile & Ohio railroad line to support a bill to fund the completion of that route along with the Illinois Central. They in turn were able to prevail upon their representatives in Congress to set aside their scruples and support the measure, which was passed September 20, 1850, as "[a]n act granting the right of way and making a grant of land to the State of Illinois, Mississippi, and Alabama, in aid of the construction of a railroad from Chicago to Mobile." For the project, Congress granted 2,595,000 acres of federal land and 3,700 per mile of rail. The next year the State Assembly approved the creation of a railroad company to build the in-state portion of the road, to be financed by money from New York and Boston, including such notable figures as Robert Schuyler, Gouverneur Morris, and Robert Rantoul, Jr. (Moses, 1892: 577–8).

The approval of the Illinois Central charters, and the accompanying legislation, pointed to the fact that by the early 1850s many of the disputes of the 1847 Constitutional Convention were already artifacts of the past. Regardless of the position that Illinois politicians took on other issues, they were united in the desire to see Illinois have a rail system. But the extent to which the arrival of the railroads was to displace the state's political alignments and shift the center of power irrevocably northward was not yet clear. In 1850, railroads presented the last opportunity for the southern part of the state to exercise control over the process of development. The 1850 legislature adopted the "state policy" that declared that any railroad chartered by the legislature must have its terminus in a city within the State of Illinois. In combination with the Illinois Central project, the state policy envisioned a Christmas-tree system of branch lines, each ending within the state, feeding into a single interstate trunk running north to south from the northern tip of the state all the way to

New Orleans. This design clearly favored the southern part of the state, and prevented the northern areas from connecting themselves to the growing national system of rail lines. The state system remained formally in place until 1854, when a general incorporation law was adopted (updating a law adopted in 1849) that essentially made the approval of railroad charters a pro forma matter. By that time, however, the state system had already been rendered irrelevant by the growth of northern railroads. The Illinois Central, against expectations, became as much a line that fed the east–west traffic on what eventually became the Chicago, Burlington & Quincy Railroad (CB&Q), as it was a source for movement up and down the Mississippi River Valley. Above all, by the mid-1850s, Illinois was dominated by the colossus of Chicago.

Chicago was a purely artificial city, its location chosen for its access to lake barges and convenient east-west rail routes (Cronon, 1991: 23–54). It succeeded wildly. William B. Ogden acquired the 1836 charter for a railroad line to run between Galena and Chicago, hoping to make connections with Michigan lines. Unable to raise capital from eastern financiers, Ogden raised all the money he needed by selling stock to local farmers. Lines reached Elgin in 1850, Belvedere in 1852, and connected to the Illinois Central (and thence through to Galena) in 1853. By 1857 eleven main lines radiated from Chicago, comprising 3,953 miles of tracks in direct connections to the city (Howard, 1972: 242–3). Thus it was clear that, contrary to the conception of the state system, there was to be a network of lines running west and south from Chicago, but in the absence of a statewide program of public construction, no one could be sure where those lines would go. The pressure for construction of rail lines in the late 1840s, therefore, came from individual towns determined not to be passed by. Ogden's success at raising capital by selling stock locally was repeated a hundred times over as every town and village tried to get a branch line running through its territory.

The attitudes among town leaders were exemplified by Chauncey S. Colton. Colton was the leading citizen of the town of Galesburg, and a trustee of Knox College. A rail line already under construction had set a route that would miss Galesburg by three miles, an outcome that "would have virtually destroyed the town." Colton led the way in the formation of a company to build a new line, the Central Military Tract Railroad Company, to connect with pieces of other lines working their way from Chicago. In his capacity as trustee of Knox College, Colton arranged the sale of land from the college to the new railroad company, paid for in company stock. The company failed, and the stock became worthless. "But no one ever complained. We were determined to have a rail-road" (Overton, 1967: 513). Ultimately the company was revived and the plan succeeded; the Central Military Tract eventually became one of the elements of the CB&Q. The Galesburg story was typical. Between 1840 and 1850 nearly forty different local lines were begun, creating a mosaic of short pieces running from Chicago to the Mississippi River at Burlington and Quincy.

By 1854, Chicago received seventy-four trains a day and nearly twice the volume of grain that reached St. Louis (Cole, 1917: 5). The issue was no longer one of competition between St. Louis and Alton; instead, both cities saw their traffic drawn into patterns centered around Chicago. Gustavius Unonius, in 1857, described a city whose population exceeded 120,000. As impressive as the growth of the city was the growth in the city's engine, its rail system:

Chicago is the terminus of more than a dozen trunk lines from which almost twice as many branch lines extend in every direction.... While a few years ago it took eight to ten days to travel from New York to Chicago, the traveler may now make his choice among three different railroads and cover that distance in thirty to thirty-six hours. More than one hundred twenty trains, some of them consisting of up to forty fully loaded freight cars, arrive and depart each day.

Most impressive of all were the new grain elevators. Unonius delighted in figures and cited a single elevator's capacity of 750,000 bushels of grain, its ability to load two ships with 12,000 bushels each in less than an hour, and to unload, weigh, and store 3,000 bushels in ten minutes. He noted that 130 million bushels of corn and 120 million bushels of wheat were produced annually in Illinois, and that half a billion board feet of timber from Michigan passed through Chicago in one year, the forests of Illinois having long since been cleared (Unonius, 1857: 365–7). Anthony Trollope, visiting Chicago during the Civil War, called it "the favorite haunt of the American Ceres. The goddess seats herself there amid the dust of her full barns, and proclaims herself a goddess ruling over things political and philosophical as well as agricultural." Like Unonius, Trollope grasped the importance of the grain elevator as an element in the system of rails and ships:

It is so built that both railway vans and vessels come immediately under its claws, as I may call the great trunks of the elevators.... When I was at Chicago, the only limit to the rapidity of its transit was set by the amount of boat accommodation. There were not bottoms enough to take the corn away from Chicago, nor, indeed, on the railway was there a sufficiency of rolling stock or locomotive power to bring it to Chicago (Trollope, 1862, vol. 1: 158–9).

The growth of the city of Chicago as a railroad terminal not only reflected the shift in emphasis from an intrastate north-south network to an interstate east-west rail system; it is also the exemplar case of a new relationship between population and industry. Through the beginning of the 1840s, rail lines followed existing populations. Later, beginning in earnest in the mid-1850s, populations began to gather at places where rail lines crossed, or where rail lines intersected rivers, canals, and highways. Railroads viewed themselves as the engines of settlement, and so they were (Gates, 1934: 121–48).

The transformations that railroads wrought in patterns of economic activity, settlement, and the construction of towns had profound political consequences. The state system was only one of a number of political casualties of the universal desire for railroads, along with some of the organizing principles of both the Whig and Democratic parties. The provision of the 1848 Constitution prohibiting the issuance of special charters went by the wayside. Hundreds of charters were granted, most of them for the construction of rail lines, under a constitutional exception for cases where "the objects of the corporation can not be attained under general laws" (Article X, § 1). The prohibition on state banks, too, did not last long. It was only three years before the legislature, without bothering to modify the state's Constitution, voted to establish a third state bank of Illinois. The problem was that in the absence of state currency, the money in circulation all came from other states. In 1855, on a single run on the CB&Q, the conductor collected $203 in currency issued from twenty-three different banks in twelve states (Howard, 1972: 233; Moses, 1892: 569–71).[6] Currency, like everything else, had to be brought under control to keep the rail system running smoothly.

On the other hand, the Constitution of 1848 shaped the manner of rail construction in other ways. The prohibition on state investment resulted in the creation of private corporations financed by local and then interstate investment. One result was just what was intended. When a panic hit the financial sector in 1857, the state's finances remained largely unaffected. In fact, in that year Illinois resumed full payments on its old bonds, the last of which were finally paid off in 1880. By contrast, Ohio did not pay off until 1902, and Indiana, Michigan, and Pennsylvania all defaulted on portions of their internal improvement debts and repudiated their interest obligations outright (Howard, 1972: 230–1). A less obvious but equally

---

[6] A state bank would not entirely solve the problem, of course, but particularly for intrastate travelers, it would diminish the confusion considerably.

profound effect was that capital followed the rails themselves. The Illinois rail system was above all focused outward, connecting local interests to the state and then the nation both physically and economically.

The 1850s also saw the transition in public thinking from the idea of towns "owning" small local rail lines to the idea of rail lines as natural objects around which towns and cities would orient themselves. The connection of small lines together, as promised, extended the stream of commerce beyond the bounds of local experience. In the same way, the consolidation of rail lines meant that the companies' ownership and management were geographically and socially distant, from one another and from the public their companies served. Rail lines stopped being enterprises that grew out from towns, becoming instead a system that passed through towns, and finally a feature of the landscape that determined where towns should be situated in the first place.

This was the most visible reflection of the reconfiguration of thinking about *salus populi* and the meaning of progress. Traditional, local conceptions of the public good were inconsistent with a worldview that began with the assumption that long-distance rail traffic was the condition of commercial activity, the route to economic growth, and the measure of human progress. That the norms of standardization and rationalization should spill over from commercial behavior into other areas of social life was equally inevitable. What remains to be shown is the way in which this political and economic vision of a new social order defined the terms of new legal doctrines, and the special role that law was called upon to play in articulating that vision.

The Illinois Supreme Court, 1850–60

The 1848 Constitution provided that the state's Supreme Court justices would be elected by region, one each from northern, central, and southern Illinois. Across the decade, each of these regions was represented by no more than three justices: Trumbull, Scates, and Breese for the south; Treat, Onias Skinner, and Pinkney H. Walker for the central region; and John D. Caton, who represented northern Illinois without interruption from 1848 to 1861.

Many of these men had well-defined public positions with regard to the political issues that had divided the state through the 1840s. Scates and Breese were prominent moderate southern Democrats who had played important roles at the 1847 Constitutional Convention and in the formation of the Illinois Central Railroad. Breese, Scates, Treat, and Trumbull all had been among the Democratic Party loyalists appointed to the packed court in 1841. Although Caton was not prominent in party politics, he was second only to Breese as an important supporter of Illinois' internal improvements. Caton's special area of interest was not railroads, however, but rather the closely associated project of telegraph construction. In 1848, then Judge Caton was called on to preside at a meeting in Ottawa for the stockholders of the Illinois and Mississippi Telegraph Company. He became the company's largest stockholder and president, learned Morse code, and oversaw the construction of lines that would eventually become a major component of the Western Union system. In the process, Caton earned the sobriquet "the Telegraph King of the West" (Howard, 1972: 241; Cole, 1917: 31).

The bulk of the important cases discussed in the next chapter were written by two justices, Scates and Breese. Neither was solely a regional politician. Both had earlier been elected to the court in statewide elections, and Breese had been elected to the United States Senate. Moreover, there are only two substantive dissenting opinions in the cases that are reviewed in this study, and in each case the dissenting justice later joined in opinions that embraced the rule announced by the majority. Thus the creation of the new common law of Illinois in the 1850s was presided over by a handful of men who were able to reach consensus on principles that held deep implications for the meaning of economic freedom, property rights, and other fundamental political concepts.

In terms of the debates of 1847–8, these men were exemplars of the winning coalition of northern and southern moderates, but in terms of the issues that were yet to arise in the decade to come, they would prove to be modernizers of the first order. Seated on the bench of the state's Supreme Court, they were in the best possible position to recognize that the demands of the rail-driven political economy were incommensurable with the principles of either political or legal traditionalism. In time even Scates, the most conservative of the group, moved increasingly in the direction of northern-style liberalism and away from his southern republican roots when it became clear that the course of technological progress demanded an expanded conception of *salus populi* and the standardization of legal rights and obligations. In the next two chapters, we will see how these principles were worked into the formulation of abstract duties owed to the general public, and hence into an emerging legal model of political citizenship, in the Illinois court's creation of a new, American system of common law.

3

"The Memory of Man Runneth Not to the Contrary"

Cases Involving Damage to Property

In the 1850s in Illinois, the emphasis on technological progress and its associated virtues became the basis for a reconceptualization of the underlying norms of legal discourse. Between 1850 and 1860, Illinois' Supreme Court articulated a move from the traditional writ-based system of English common law to the modern categories of American legal reasoning. In the process, the judges who created the new doctrines shifted the starting point for legal analysis from private, property-based rights to public tort and tortlike duties. This shift was worked out and articulated almost entirely in railroad cases. To see how this occurred, I will first examine developments in the law governing property interests, the traditional focus of the earlier legal regime and the starting point for the American effort to create a new system of common law. In the next chapter, the same questions will be explored in the context of cases involving injuries to persons.

Clashing Property Rights: Stock Crossing Cases

It is difficult for modern readers to imagine the importance that was attached to the question of whether railroads would be required to pay damages for stock killed by locomotives in the 1850s. In southern Michigan, a "railroad war" developed over the failure of the lines to pay compensation for damage to stray cattle. Farmers tore up lines, and eventually burned the Detroit depot to the ground (Hirschfield, 1952). At state constitutional conventions in 1850 and 1851, Michigan and Ohio passed laws restricting corporations' freedom of action under their charters as a direct result of complaints from farmers over the lack of compensation. Both the central importance of stock cases as a political issue and the necessity for an explication of legal doctrine in terms of the public good were evident throughout the states of the old Northwest at the beginning of the decade.

Given the political importance of such cases, it is unsurprising that the Democrat-controlled state legislature made several attempts to intervene in favor of farmers whose stock were killed in train accidents. In 1855, the Illinois legislature enacted a law requiring railroads to erect fences along their tracks "suitable and sufficient to prevent cattle, horses, sheep and hogs from getting on to such railroad," except at crossings (Illinois Laws, 1855: Feb. 14, 1855). A general incorporation statute for railroads already required trains to blow a whistle or sound a bell when approaching a crossing, but an 1854 amendment exempted named charters from the coverage of that statute (Illinois Laws, 1854: Nov. 5, 1849; Feb. 25, 1854).

Although these statutes were decisive of the outcomes in some cases, they had little or no effect on the creation of common law doctrine. For a case to be governed by a statute, the plaintiff had to bring his case under its terms (*Terre Haute, Alton, and St. Louis Railroad Co. v. Jacob Augustus*, 22 Ill. 186, 1859, where the action was brought "in case," jury instruction relating to statutory fencing requirement was erroneous). The plaintiff would then be required to plead and prove each element of the statute including negative elements – for example, proof that the accident did not occur at a crossing, nor within a town, and the railroad company had been in business for more than six months. This last was a point of evidence that could be quite difficult to establish given the frequency with which rail companies merged, failed, or otherwise re-formed themselves as corporate entities. In one case where a railroad company had entered into a written contract specifically obliging it to fence a stretch of its line as a condition of the property deed, the plaintiff was unable to recover damages for the loss of several sheep when he was unable to prove that the corporation with which he had made the contract was identical to the corporation running the same line less than two years later (*The Joliet & Northern Indiana Railroad Co. v. Jones*, 20 Ill. 222, 1858). Thus, statutes provided the rules of decision in only a small minority of cases.

Even in cases where the statutes governed the analysis, the courts treated the legislature's efforts as little more than rules of pleading and the burdens of proof at trial, rather than rules governing liability, as Justice Sidney Breese explained in 1859: "The statute, in my judgment, does not require the railroad companies to fence their track, or impose it upon them as a duty.... The statute affects the evidence only, nothing more." *Ohio and Mississippi R.R. Co. v. Brown*, 23 Ill. 94, 96 (1859). Furthermore, the legislature also granted charters that contained immunities from these regulations, so that cases brought against these lines, too, were governed by common law rules alone. As a result, the effects of statutory enactments were to create a special class of cases exempted from traditional common law principles by positive enactment. The actions of the legislature had no effect on the adjudication of cases that, for whatever reason, remained within the scope of the common law, and it was those cases that engendered new conceptions of property rights and tort duties in this context.

The law concerning stock before railroad cases redefined the topic had been characterized by the combination of traditional common law principles and exceptionalist property rules that marked American law in the early 1800s. The rules governing adjudication of claims of this type were laid out in an 1848 case, *Seeley v. Peters*, 10 Ill. 130 (1848). Although the case is of interest primarily as a statement of the law just before the developments that are the subject of this book, it is interesting to note the ways in which, even then, the door to radical change in the law was being opened.

Samuel Seeley's hogs wandered into William Peters' field, tearing up his crops, and Peters sued for damages. In his defense, Seeley argued that Peters' fence was inadequate, and that the land adjoining the fence was public:

> Defendant then proved that the North side of said field where the hogs got in was so badly fenced, that hogs which were not breachy could go in and out of the field at pleasure... further that the North side of said field where said defective fence was, was bounded by unoccupied and unenclosed prairie and that a public road passed along said fence at least part of the way on the North side (Illinois State Historical Archives [ISHA] file # 1866, 4).

Seeley's argument was that his hogs had a right to be on the public land adjoining Peters' field, and consequently that if Peters' failed to adequately fence his land, there could be no complaint based on hogs doing what it is in their nature to do, that is, to wander about and destroy crops. Peters' argument was, simply, that Seeley's hogs had caused him harm. Seeley had failed to control his property in order to prevent that harm from occurring, so Seeley should pay damages.

The outcome of the case would depend, in part, on the rights that were implied by the word *public*, applied to property. Certainly the fact that property was public implied that everyone had a right to use it, but what happened when the use of public property resulted in damage to adjoining private property? Was it the right of private property owners to be protected against deleterious uses of public property, or was it their obligation to protect themselves? In other words, the question was whether the rights of private property owners to their property were superior or secondary to the rights of others to make free use of public land.

The trial judge delivered an instruction to the jury, requested by Peters, that put the responsibility on Seeley to control his stock: "The owner of a field is not obliged to keep up a fence around his enclosure to keep out his neighbor's cattle or hogs – but the owners of cattle permit them to run at large at their peril" (ISHA file # 1866, 4). The owner of cattle who caused damage to another's fields would be liable for damages. Furthermore, if those cattle, while running at large, should stray onto the land of another, the landowner had the right to use force to expel them, and the owner of the animals would have no claim for damages if the animals should be harmed in the process. This had been the common law rule in England since the enclosure of the common fields in the sixteenth century, a point ably and thoroughly presented by William Herndon, the lawyer for Peters (*Seeley*, 130–1).[1]

But Justice Trumbull rejected Herndon's argument out of hand as unsuited to the experience of life in Illinois, exemplifying the way that the law of property had been the locus of early legal adaptation (discussed in Chapter 1), and echoing Democratic arguments of a year before that a state bank was ill-suited to Illinois' agricultural economy (discussed in Chapter 2). The common law, wrote Trumbull, "must be understood only in cases where that law is applicable to the habits and condition of our society, and in harmony with the genius, spirit and objects of our institutions." Laws regulating the use property, in particular, had to be adjusted to the conditions of open spaces, sparse population, and free land:

Perhaps there is no principle of the Common Law so inapplicable to the condition of our country and people as the one which is sought to be enforced now for the first time since the settlement of the State. It has been the custom in Illinois so long, that *the memory of man runneth not to the contrary*, for the owners of stock to suffer

---

[1] The case also involved the construction of two statutes. One was an 1819 law requiring that enclosed fields be surrounded by adequate fences. That law was replaced by an 1835 law that added provisions making the owner of an inadequately fenced enclosure liable for injuries to trespassing animals, and requiring that the owner of an unenclosed field give notice to the owner of a trespassing animal. An additional provision in 1845 prescribed a fine for "drovers . . . who drive off any cattle, hogs, &c. of any citizen either from his own premises, or 'from the range in which the stock of any such citizen usually run.'" As Trumbull observed, "[i]t is manifest that the Legislature has all along acted upon the presumption that horses, cattle, hogs, &c., might lawfully be at large" (*Seeley*, 136–7, 144).

them to run at large. Settlers have located themselves contiguous to prairies for the very purpose of getting the benefit of the range. The right of all to pasture their cattle upon unenclosed ground is universally conceded. No man has questioned this right.... The universal understanding of all classes of the community, upon which they have acted by inclosing their crops and letting their cattle run at large, is entitled to no little consideration in determining what the law is (*Seeley*, 141–2, emphasis added).

The rule in Illinois, therefore, would be that a property owner who failed to maintain an adequate fence could not recover damages if another person's stock caused damage to the property.

While the specific rule was specifically American, the mode of reasoning was entirely English. The phrase "the memory of man runneth not to the contrary" was a quotation: it had been William Blackstone's explanation for the authority of the common law.[2] While abandoning the specific rules of English precedents, Trumbull carefully preserved the analytical approach of the *Commentaries*, grounding his opinions in three distinct elements: the conditions of development in Illinois, the customary practices in Illinois, and the "universal understanding ... of the community." None of these, however, necessarily required the retention of traditional common law rules. Trumbull's invocation of the language of timeless custom, in particular, was a bit of common law legerdemain. In the same breath with which he abolished the authority of the timeless common law rule of enclosure, Trumbull announced the discovery of a different, equally timeless order, with a parallel and equal claim to the mantle of legitimate authority.[3] Seven years later, in 1855, the "timeless" rule of the free range would itself be sacrificed in the name of a new and different rule, equally based on a claim of exceptionalism in *Great Western R.R. Co. v. Thompson*, 17 Ill. 131 (1855) discussed later in this chapter.

The more legally conservative Caton, in his seventh year on the bench, wrote a stinging twenty-one-page dissent (compared with nine pages for Trumbull's majority opinion), one of only three dissenting opinions that appear in all the cases reviewed in this study. Caton accused his colleague of sacrificing the ideal of law, expressed in the principle of *sic utere* (the

---

[2] "[I]n our law the goodness of a custom depends upon it's having been used time out of mind; or, in the solemnity of our legal phrase, time whereof the memory of man runneth not to the contrary. This it is that gives it its weight and authority; and of this nature are the maxims and customs which compose the common law, or *lex non scripta*, of this kingdom" (Blackstone, 1765: vol. I, 67).

[3] The rhetoric of discovering timeless principles, rather than crafting rules, appealed to a prevalent idea that law should be a form of science (Karsten, 1991: 362–3). As *Seeley* suggests, this process of "discovery" could involve a considerable amount of revision.

requirement that a person in using his property avoid harming that of another), for the convenience of politics:

[The] principle of the Common Law is most unquestionably the law of natural justice.... *You shall so use your own as not to injure another.* Is this maxim to be repudiated because it is not applicable to the genius of our people, and their customs and their habits? The decision of this case would seem to say so.... I have no more natural right to compel my neighbor to protect his crops against my swine, than I have his orchard against my children or myself (*Seeley*, 151).

The idea that one cannot "compel my neighbor to protect his crops" points out the importance, in traditional common law analysis, of finding particular duties owed between persons based on their relationship to one another. A property owner cannot owe a duty to me, specifically, to protect his own property, hence I cannot avoid liability for the harm to the landowner's property based on his conduct. The plaintiff's conduct, in the traditional scheme, was irrelevant in the absence of a specific duty owed to the specific defendant. This was precisely the point at which the new principles of negligence and contributory negligence would strike at the traditional system of rights and obligations. Ultimately, as we shall see, the claim of public interest in technological progress could do what a private property owner could not: impose a duty upon individuals to protect their own property from harm. In the meantime, the question of an obligation to maintain fences or a duty to control wandering stock animals began to appear in the specific context of railroad cases, with very different results.

In *Alton & Sangamon R.R. Co. v. Baugh*, 14 Ill. 211 (1852), the owner of stock hit by a train claimed that the railroad had been negligent in not erecting a fence, precisely the argument that had prevailed in *Seeley v. Peters*. As in *Seeley*, the lawyer for the railroad was Herndon, and once again the opinion was authored by Trumbull. This time, however, Herndon's arguments won the day. Justice Trumbull, paraphrasing Caton's earlier dissent, noted that his opinion in *Seeley* had not required owners of property to enclose their lands, it had only stated that if they failed to do so they could not recover for damage to their crops. Now he echoed Caton's earlier dissent: "We know of no principle of the common law, and there is certainly no statute, which compels one person or corporation to fence the land of another" (*Baugh*, 212). That is, while Peters had not been permitted to recover damages for the loss of his crops caused by Seeley's hogs, it was equally the case that Seeley could not recover damages from Peters if one of his hogs was injured while in Peters' field.

The parallel to the facts in *Seeley v. Peters* was completed by Herndon's argument, with which the court agreed, that rail lines were not really private property at all, but were rather a form of public thoroughfare:

It was never supposed, when a public highway was laid out, that the owners of lands over which it passed, would have any right to require the authority by which it was constructed, to inclose it by fences; and yet there is no distinction in principle between the obligation to fence a public highway and a railroad; and the obligation to construct cattle guards, which are a species of fence, is of the same character (*Baugh*, 212).

Describing rail lines as public highways changed the traditional duties owed between the parties. If the rail lines had been private property, then the manner of their construction and operation could have been argued to be bound by the obligation to compensate other private property owners under the principle of *sic utere*. On a public highway, however, the common law had long recognized the superiority of the principle of *salus populi*, in accordance with which private landowners could not dictate the manner of the roads' design or operation based on mere private interest.

Herndon's argument, defining railway lines as a form of public highway, situated the rail lines in an exception within the traditional system of property rights, thus avoiding the issues that railroad cases raised for the larger scheme of common law duties. That evasion, however, would not last long. During the same session, the Illinois Supreme Court announced its adoption of the principle of contributory negligence in *Aurora Branch R.R. Co. v. Grimes*, 13 Ill. 585 (1852), a case written by Caton. The rule of contributory negligence held that a plaintiff who failed to exercise adequate care would be barred from recovering damages from a defendant, regardless of the defendant's conduct. This was the logical extension of the principle in *Seeley v. Peters* that a landowner who failed to fence his land could not recover damages for harm to his crops, in that both rules contained the idea that a person who fails to avoid harms caused by the property of others has no claim for redress, a refutation of the older principle that each person was bound to use – or control – his property so as not to damage that of another. But the principle of contributory negligence went much further.

The case was not about a collision. Jacob Grimes' horse was killed when it fell through boards that had been placed over a hole on the grounds of the Batavia train terminal while Grimes was there to pick up a delivery. The testimony established that Grimes had been there before, and had taken his horse into the area of the accident in the past on the instructions of railroad personnel. A horse that steps into a hole in the ground is perhaps the quintessential fact pattern for a traditional evaluation of the rights and duties of property owners; among other places, it is specifically mentioned in the Old Testament.[4] In keeping with his dissent in *Seeley* four years earlier, Caton was at great pains to insist that he was not announcing a new principle of law, only following English precedent. This time, however, it was Caton who was being disingenuous, as his "conservative" outcome had the effect of standing property and tort principles on their heads.

Caton drew on the English case of *Butterfield v. Forrester*, discussed in Chapter 1. In that case, the English court had ruled that in the situation where plaintiff and defendant had identical rights to the use and occupation of property, a defendant could be liable for negligence so long as the plaintiff had demonstrated "ordinary care" (*Butterfield v. Forrester*, 11 East 60, 1809). "Ordinary care," said Caton, meant "that degree of care which may reasonably be expected from a person in the plaintiff's situation." The idea of contributory negligence arose in the situation where a plaintiff "is himself in the wrong, or not in the exercise of a legal right." In those cases the plaintiff "must use extraordinary care before he can complain of the negligence of another" (*Aurora v. Grimes*, 588–9, emphasis added, 591).

Caton's use of *Butterfield* demonstrates the combination of novelty and traditionalism in his approach, but to see why, it is necessary to visit the facts of *Butterfield*. That case involved a pole that had been left partially obstructing a street. A horseman, riding home from a tavern "at eight o'clock in the evening in August, when they were just beginning to light candles, but when there was light enough left to discern," collided with the pole and was injured. Lord Ellenborough ruled that there could be no recovery. The ruling was not based on the rider's lack of vigilance – for example, Ellenborough took pains to note that there was no evidence of intoxication – but on his *speed*: "[I]f the plaintiff had not been riding very hard he might have observed and avoided it; the plaintiff, however, who was riding violently, did not observe it, but rode against it" (*Butterfield*, 60–1). The question in *Butterfield*, then, was not whether the plaintiff had been careful in the process of going fast, it was whether the plaintiff had

---

[4] "When a man leaves a pit open, or when a man digs a pit and does not cover it, and an ox or an ass falls into it, the owner of the pit shall make it good; he shall give money to its owner, and the dead beast shall be his" (*Exodus* 21:33).

erred in going fast at all, on the theory that so doing turned otherwise safe conditions into hazards.

The ruling in *Aurora v. Grimes* differed from the ruling in *Butterfield* in three crucial respects. In *Butterfield*, the fault was on the party whose speed created the danger. By contrast, in *Grimes* there was no question that the boards covering the hole were dangerously inadequate, yet it was the person who failed to avoid harm who was denied recovery. In this way, *Grimes* was the first intimation of the Duty to Get Out of the Way, a duty to avoid allowing one's property to be harmed by risks created by others. The second difference was only implicit. In *Butterfield*, Ellenborough implied that the outcome should be one that encouraged persons on a public thoroughfare to travel at a slow and careful pace. In *Grimes*, Caton concluded that the operation of a rail depot could not be restricted in the name of safety. Although the case appears simply as one involving an animal killed by falling into a hole, it should not be overlooked that contributory negligence came to Illinois in a case involving a train depot, nor that trains were synonymous with speed.

The third way in which Justice Caton departed from the analysis in *Butterfield* was the basis for his announcement of a rule of contributory negligence. In *Butterfield*, the issue of "relative right" had focused on the relationship of the parties to the property on which the injury occurred. In Caton's usage, however, being "in the wrong" did not refer to unauthorized occupation of property, but rather opened the possibility of judicial evaluation of the character of the plaintiff's overall conduct. Relative rights to property became relevant only *after* a comparison of the parties' conduct:

Where a party seeks to recover damages for a loss which has been caused by negligence or misconduct, he must be able to show that his own negligence or misconduct has not concurred with that of the other party in producing the injury, and the burden of proof is upon the plaintiff to show not only negligence on the part of the defendant, but also that he exercised proper care and circumspection; or, in other words, that he was not guilty of negligence. *As to the degree of diligence or care* which the plaintiff must show himself to have exercised . . . [that] will be found to depend upon the relative rights or position of the parties in relation to the rights exercised or position enjoyed by the plaintiff at the time the injury complained of happened (*Grimes*, 587–8, emphasis added).

Thus in *Grimes* Caton announced a rule that contributory negligence would be an absolute bar to recovery, but "negligence" would be defined in terms of the level of duty that was consistent with the parties' relative rights to occupy property. In the case of the railroad depot, if Grimes had been contributorily negligent, then there would be no circumstances under which he could recover: "[I]f both used ordinary care, then the misfortune was an accident, without the fault of either, and the loss must rest where the misfortune placed it; and if neither used ordinary care, then, for the want of it, the plaintiff can not recover, even admitting that he had as much right to be upon the track as the company had to dig the well" (*Grimes,* 592). These were not, yet, universal duties of uniform application, but the analytical groundwork for that concept was being established.

The case that announced a sharp shift into a new way of thinking about negligence was *The Chicago & Mississippi R. R. Co. v. Patchin,* 16 Ill. 198 (1854). *Patchin* made three things clear: that traditional claims of rights to the occupation or use of property did not determine liability in stock crossing cases; that duties owed to the public, rather than to other parties in the case, would determine the threshold requirements for getting into court; and that the dictates of technology would determine the character of these universal public duties. The first of these moves announced the abandonment of the traditional analytical approach that had been employed in *Seeley, Baugh,* and *Grimes.* The rest of the analysis was entirely new, and made the connection between common law doctrines and standards for citizenship in terms of a universal duty to avoid impeding the wheels of progress.

Daniel Patchin was the owner of seven hogs and a cow that were killed by locomotives between June 1853 and May 1854. The hogs, according to Patchin's case brief, were "on a certain unenclosed highway" when they were struck by "certain Steam Carriages and or Locomotives, and also of divers Railway Cars attached to said Locomotives composing trains moving along said Highway." The rule in *Butterfield v. Forrester* had been that everyone has an equal right to use and occupy a highway; Patchin's lawyer, like the court in *Baugh* and Grimes' lawyer in the earlier case, was attempting to make that same characterization apply to privately owned railroad tracks.

The testimony of witnesses was that the trains never slowed their speed, and in one case actually increased it. The testimony was also that the animals could easily have walked off the tracks before being hit but did not do so (which may demonstrate that animals were as unfamiliar with trains as the local humans). Witnesses also testified that the locomotives' whistles were not sounded before the collisions (ISHA file # 2364: 1–4). The railroad called an expert of sorts, although he was not sworn in specially as such. John C. Neal testified as "an Old Railroader, familiar with their workings." Neal testified that when a train was running at full speed, checking its speed at a distance of one hundred yards would not be sufficient to save animals on the tracks, and that even at moderate speeds forty to fifty yards' distance was required to slow the train to a stop. Regarding the behavior of animals, he testified that "some cows and hogs, when familiar [with trains], will run off, and some will not." Most importantly, he testified that cattle on the tracks were a frequent occurrence, that they caused much damage to trains, and that if the trains stopped every time there was a cow on the line, they "could not make their time" (ISHA file # 2364, 4). In other words, Neal's testimony was intended to establish three points: 1) that it was in the nature of trains that they could not be stopped to avoid collisions; 2) that animals could save themselves from trains if they wanted to; and 3) that there was a need for trains to run fast.

The trial judge delivered an instruction drawn directly from the holdings in *Seeley* and *Baugh*: "There is no law that requires the Chicago & Mississippi railroad company to fence their road, nor is there any law that makes it incumbent on the owner of stock to prevent them from running at large." Animals in Illinois were permitted to roam, and "it is the duty of those having charge of the locomotives and trains, to use such care and means as may be in their power by the proper management of their trains to prevent accidents." This was an approach entirely consistent with the English rule of *Butterfield*, by which persons occupying a public highway owed no special duties to one another, still accepting the rule from *Baugh* that a rail line was a species of public highway. The trial judge rejected three jury instructions that the railroad's lawyers had requested: that if "the stock of plaintiff were... [on] unenclosed land belonging to some other person other than the plaintiff at the time they were killed, the plaintiff cannot recover"; that if "the cars of defendant at the time of killing the stock were running at the usual speed, upon the usual track, they are not liable for the stock killed"; and that "unless... the stock sued for were killed by the cars of defendant while on some of the crossings over the roads of defendant, they will find a verdict for defendants" (ISHA file # 2364, 5).

These arguments suggest that the lawyers for the railroad, too, were trying to figure out the right combination of traditional and novel arguments that would apply to their clients. The first argument was an invocation of the Illinois' "immemorial" custom of allowing animals to roam from *Seeley v. Peters*, but that argument entirely ignored the conclusion in *Baugh* that a rail line was a kind of public road. The third argument tried to explain the limit of the reach of *Baugh* by suggesting that it was only at the point of a crossing that the rail lines took on the character of a public thoroughfare.

So long as the railroad tried to argue from traditional, property-based principles, its case was likely a loser in light of the testimony. The second argument, though, that a railroad could not be liable for harms caused in the "usual" operation of their trains, was something quite different. This was an argument straight out of tort law. The idea that whatever was "usual" was therefore acceptable appealed to the same idea of community values that had supported the free range rule in *Seeley*, in an entirely new and different context. Instead of the long-established customs of a community, this argument was appealing to the brand new practices of railroad operation. In light of the contributory negligence rule announced in *Aurora v. Grimes*, the effect of this analysis was that the railroad's usual practices defined standards of conduct not only for themselves, but also for the owners of stock; failure to recognize and accommodate the fact that the usual practice of railroads was to run their trains at high speeds would constitute contributory negligence regardless of the right of stock owners to allow their animals to roam. This was the beginning of a process of redefining the norms of public conduct around the needs of railroads. The result was to turn a traditional debate over property boundaries into a contest between old and new "customary practices," a debate that turned not on relative claims of rights to use and occupy property, but on a comparison of general public duties of care, governed by the new tort doctrines announced in *Grimes*.

The argument for an outright replacement of private property rights by public, tortlike duties as the basis for the analysis of stock cases was no more than hinted at in the papers filed by the railroad's lawyers in *Patchin*, and if the case had been heard in the previous year, the resulting analysis might not have been particularly consequential. But between June 1853 and the time *Patchin* was decided in 1854, there had been a crucial change in the personnel of the Illinois Supreme Court. Justice Trumbull, ardent Democrat turned Republican, champion of free labor and free land, re-signed from the court and was replaced by Walter B. Scates. Scates, like Trumbull, was a southern Illinois Democrat who had been a prominent opponent of the Whig courts. He was a much more visionary figure than Trumbull, however, as he had demonstrated in the Constitutional Convention of 1847 (see the discussion in Chapter 2). Scates seized on the arguments of the railroad lawyers and ran with them, using *Patchin* to announce a sweepingly original view of the law governing grazing rights, enclosure, railroads, and duties of care generally.

First, Scates took pains to explain that he was not doing what all the previous cases had done, which was to evaluate the obligations that the parties had to each other. Instead, the issue in the case, and for all future cases, was determining the obligations that the parties had to society at large:

There would be but little difficulty in charging [the railroad] for willful injuries and gross negligence, if the parties to the record were alone interested.... But when we take into account and consideration the irreparable damage to life from casualties to trains from running over stock, and that the imminency of hazard to passengers is increased in proportion to the protection given to the passive negligence of stock owners in knowingly permitting their stock to frequent, stand, graze and lie upon the track, the rule becomes much more difficult of adjustment (*Patchin*, 200–1).

Regarding the argument in *Baugh* that rail lines were a species of highway, Scates declared, "I presume the right to the land upon which railroads are built, is not strictly analogous to the easement of the public in highways...but is an absolute ownership" (*Patchin*, 202).

In other words, rail lines were back to being private property, governed by the timeless rule of *Seeley*, but the consequences of that rule had changed markedly. In 1848, in *Seeley*, the rule – to which, it will be recalled, memory in Illinois ran not to the contrary – was that animals could roam on public lands, and that owners of adjoining properties had to fence their property or suffer the consequences. That outcome was unacceptable in 1854, not because it was an incorrect interpretation of private property rights but because it ran contrary to the collective interest in progress. "These roads with the mode of operating them, would become dangerous to travel, and almost useless to their owners and the communities, if the immunities of herds of wandering, loitering cattle upon them, can be put upon the footing of protected privileges" (*Patchin*, 203). The distinction between "immunity" and "privilege" turned the entire equation upside-down. The principle of free access to the range was being read as an exception to a supposition that the railroads would otherwise have been able to sue the stock owners for permitting their animals to be at large. This move could not be explained in traditional terms of community practice and usage. The railroads were recent arrivals, whose rights should have been subordinate to the timeless truths of property usage. More to the point, railroads were bound under their charters by duties to the public at large. What was the source of the farmers' duty to affirmatively prevent damage to the usefulness of trains to their owners, to prevent diminution of the value of railroads to the community, and to prevent harm from coming to railroad passengers?

Scates' concern for the safety of passengers is particularly significant. In a scheme where the duties of care between parties were determined by their relative rights to occupancy of the property, passengers could not even figure in the equation. Passengers held no property rights to the tracks at all. There was no contractual relationship between stock owners and passengers, and there certainly could be no issue of the relative obligation of passengers to construct fences. Furthermore, traditional common law tort principles could have no application in a case where passengers had not in fact been injured and to which they were not parties. The argument in *Baugh*, that rail lines were a type of highway, would have meant that rail passengers and cattle had equal duties of care toward one another, which would have returned the question to why the passengers (i.e., the train) did not avoid running into cows and horses. As for traditional nuisance principles, if the tracks were to be viewed as private property, then that analysis should have turned on an analysis of whether hogs or locomotives were inherently more dangerous, which would seem to favor the claims of the farmer for compensation. Why, then, did farmers owe a duty to *passengers* to keep livestock off the tracks?

The answer was that they did not. Scates was introducing the idea of a duty owed not to other named parties but to the public at large:

Speed in the transit, and punctuality in arrivals and connections, are desirable, are required in this mode of conveyance. They are lawful. Speed may be regulated by the companies, to suit the times and the places. Trains running at high speed, cannot be suddenly stopped; nor will the same means effect it, within the same distance. It must depend more or less upon the condition of the rail, the grade, the weight of train, and rate of speed. A casual spectator may possess little knowledge of the adequacy of the means, in particular cases. When such obstructions, as cattle, which may be thrown from the track, are discovered too near to avoid collision by stopping the train, it has been said, and with a high degree of probability, that the greater the speed, the greater the safety to the train in the collision (*Patchin*, 204).

This was the source of the stock owners' obligation to avoid discomfiting passengers whom they had never met. The passengers were part of the larger society of Illinois, and the people of Illinois had a Need for Speed. The very quality that in *Butterfield v. Forrester* had been the source of risk, the plaintiff's speed, was now invoked as the positive good that everyone had a mutual duty to promote, or at least to avoid impeding. The rail companies, providers of speed, were the only ones who could know or decide how to deliver this public necessity. The interests of private property owners were not an element of the equation, a point emphasized by the characterization of stray cattle; not even trespassers anymore, they were now simply "obstructions." And what constituted "ordinary care" was a question that could be answered only by an expert in railroad operations: the "Old Railroader, familiar with their workings" who testified in the trial.

Based on these considerations, the court in *Patchin* remanded the case and recommended new jury instructions. The fact that farmers were in breach of their duty owed to the public at large did not completely bar recovery, but it meant that railroads could be found liable only on the basis of conduct that was "wanton, or willful, and gross negligence" (*Patchin*, 204). To some extent, this rule still reflects an extension of traditional principles rather than a completely new form of analysis, suggesting that Scates himself may not have grasped, or been ready to announce, the implications of his argument. The analysis in *Patchin* continued to be based on the idea that duties were relative, but the trigger for an adjustment to the parties' relative obligations had changed. The comparative element in *Butterfield* had been triggered by a plaintiff's lack of any particular right to occupy public property; in *Grimes*, Caton had extended that principle to hold that standards would be altered to disfavor parties guilty of contributory negligence generally; now, in *Patchin*, Scates further extended the principle to find that the balance of legal duties would be altered to disfavor plaintiffs who failed to prevent their property from becoming an impediment to the community's Need for Speed.

Even under the court's announced standard, however, one might have thought that a train that gave no alarm, and in fact sped up as it approached a standing cow, might have been found to have engaged in willful conduct. "Willful" conduct, after all, only connoted deliberate rather than negligent actions, without any necessary imputation of evil motive. Deliberate conduct by the train operators seems clearly present in the facts cited by Scates at the beginning of his opinion:

Nothing hindered the engineers from seeing the stock, and . . . no alarm was given by whistle, the speed of train was not checked, nor does it appear that any attempt or effort was made to do so. Stock was killed at different times, by different trains, all in daytime. Witnesses thought the freight train that killed the cow, rather than slowing, increased speed. Such is the case.

In fact, this last point had been contested in the testimony of witnesses, but Scates was going out of his way to establish a rule of law that did not depend on particular facts. It would follow, *a fortiori*, that in any less egregious fact situation the rule would be the same. Scates proposed that the increase in speed might be interpreted in two ways: "as care for the safety of the train, for which the highest degree of care was required, or as evidence of wantonness or willfulness" (*Patchin*, 200). Scates, predictably, chose the former interpretation. Now the question was not simply one of the relative duties of the stock owners and train operators toward one another, it was also one of the duties of the train operators to their passengers. The railroad had a duty *not* to avoid causing damage to property whose owners failed to prevent it from becoming at risk. Railroads, stock owners, and passengers alike were part of a single web supported by the public's right to the benefits of technology.

The reference to the railroads' duties to their passengers pointed to yet another sense in which the technology of transportation had blurred legal categories. In running a train, a railroad company engaged simultaneously in a dozen different kinds of action: property owner, common carrier, operator of a dangerous machine, holder of a corporate charter, and provider of a public service, just to name a few. The multiplicity of relationships created a parallel multiplicity of duties that could easily conflict with one another. Duties might run from railroad to stock owner, from stock owner to passengers, from railroads to passengers, from passengers to railroads.[5] There was no analogue to this situation in the private property rules of *Seeley*, nor in the experiences of other common carriers such as carriage companies and canal barge operators. Scates was pointing to a project of unifying the scheme of tort duties into a single system that would define standards for all these different actors. Ultimately, nothing less than a unified system of tort law could accommodate a political economy built on rails.

The project of unification was carried forward in 1855, in *Great Western R.R. Co. v. Thompson*, 17 Ill. 131 (1855). Another change had occurred in the personnel of the court: Samuel H. Treat, Scates' Democratic ally, had resigned and been replaced by Onias C. Skinner, who leaned much more toward the conservative traditionalism of Caton. In *Seeley*, Caton had dissented forcefully, protesting the sacrifice of timeless legal principle in the name of local custom. In *Thompson*, Skinner took on the same role. This

---

[5] Presumably, in an appropriate fact setting, the court might have discovered duties flowing from passengers to the owners of wandering stock (e.g., if passengers were engaged in throwing sharp objects out the windows of moving trains), although no case of this type appears in the record.

time, ironically, what Skinner was protesting was the abandonment of the rule of *Seeley* in the name of a new and different claim of public interest – precisely the development that Caton had foreseen in his earlier dissent. This was the second of three dissents that appears in the cases reviewed here, and it was as futile an effort as the first one.

Thompson involved a horse that was struck and killed while running over tracks in a culvert, down a steep and curving grade. There was testimony from a defense witness that "at the ordinary rail road speed down such a grade, the cars would run down near half a mile after the brakes were applied before they could be stopped." Presented with these facts, the lawyer for Thompson presented an argument couched purely in the property rights language of *Seeley* plus a dash of nuisance reasoning, alleging a duty to maintain fences based on common law principles rather than statute: "The company, not regarding their duty in this behalf, had not enclosed, and did not enclose the said pieces or parcel of land over which said dangerous machines were running as aforesaid, with a good and sufficient fence or enclosure, as they were bound to do." Thompson's lawyer relied on the old idea that the horse had a right to be in the place where he was killed; the animal – not its owner – was described in the complaint as "a free commoner and at large." The defense requested a jury instruction to the effect that there could be no recovery if the death of the horse had been the result of "unavoidable accident." The judge modified the instruction by adding the phrase "and that they used all the diligence in their power to prevent it" (ISHA file # 2333: 10, 7, 2, 14). At the request of Thompson, the judge also delivered a separate instruction stating that the railroad was liable if its employees "did not use all the means in their power to prevent the damage to the horse" (*Thompson*, 117).

Scates, now chief justice, took the opportunity to continue the process of defining universal public duties. Farmers, as much as railroad engineers, were citizens of Illinois, and citizens of Illinois were expected to accommodate the community's Need for Speed. But Scates went even further, announcing a consideration of public policy that went beyond the public interest in speed to something entirely different: "A common impression that railroads are under the liabilities of insurance for persons they carry, and for the highest possible degree of care towards all persons and animals consorting about the track and trains, leads to a greater degree of carelessness in others than is compatible with their own safety or the interest of the roads" (*Thompson*, 134). The traditional rules were undesirable because they did not do enough to inculcate virtues – care in avoiding harms caused by railroads – on the part of members of the general public.

Three years later, this would be the argument used to explain the creation of the fellow-servant rule (discussed in the next chapter),[6] but *Thompson* demonstrates the roots of that rule of employment law in a more general set of principles governing the conduct of property owners. The idea that law should inculcate desirable behaviors in the populace at large moved beyond the idea of public policy to the beginnings of a legal model of citizenship. This was the beginning of the process of reconceiving common law rules as mechanisms to direct, rather than reflect, customary patterns of public behavior. Scates was turning the courts into mechanisms for the creation as well as the articulation of communal norms.

Skinner's dissent in *Thompson* articulated the frustration experienced by lawyers and judges who tried to make sense of the flurry of new doctrines in traditional common law terms: "By the settled law of this State stock may *lawfully* run and range upon unenclosed lands, and I can find no satisfactory reason for distinguishing, in this respect, unenclosed railroads from common highways and open prairies and woodlands. The law must be the same in either case" (*Thompson*, 134). But Skinner stood alone in his dissent, and his argument was not heard in the opinions of the Illinois Supreme Court thereafter. In an 1856 case involving a collision between a train and a steer, Justice Caton both reiterated the public duties of stock owners and defined the special role of the courts:

The defendant's train was rightfully on the track, and could go nowhere else. The plaintiff's steer was there wrongfully. . . . His being there, was not only dangerous to the steer, but to the property of the company and the lives of those upon the train, and courts and juries should not strain the law to encourage the owners of stock, to allow it to run into danger, which exposes not only their own property, but the lives and property of others" (*Ill. Central R.R. Co. v. Reedy* 17 Ill. 580, 582–3, 1856).

Together, *Patchin* and *Thompson* signaled the complete jettisoning of the old, property rights–based analysis of duties with regard to property. The new scheme would emphasize the duty to accommodate the public's need for technological advancement by inculcating desirable patterns of behavior among members of the community. As for specific rules, in stock crossing cases the rail line was obliged to use no more than ordinary care, and would be liable only for willful actions, while the contributory negligence of the owners of the stock could be raised as a defense.

---

[6] *Illinois Central R.R. Co. v. Cox*, 20 Ill. 21 (1858), opinion by Sidney Breese. See discussion in Chapter 4.

Overturning verdicts and remanding cases, however, did little to specify the precise contours of the new doctrines. What were the standards of care, from what body of law – new or old – would they be drawn, and how would they work in operation? In 1856, Scates would make his most complete effort to address and resolve these questions in *Central Military Tract R.R. Co. v. Rockafellow*, 17 Ill. 541 (1856). The case involved an ox that was struck and killed by a train. Rockafellow's lawyer, as usual, stated his client's case in terms that were utterly traditional, utterly acceptable to the trial court, and, by 1856, utterly irrelevant. Rockafellow said that at the time of the accident his ox "lawfully running at large then and there lawfully came and was upon said Rail Road." The railroad lawyers, by now, knew better. They bypassed considerations of property rights altogether, and went straight to a recitation of contributory negligence: "[Rockafellow] knowingly, negligently and carelessly suffered and permitted the ox . . . to wander and stray upon and about the defendant's rail road" (ISHA file # 12278: 5–6).

In his analysis, Scates made it clear that the issue of who was rightfully where was utterly irrelevant to the case. He also made it clear, as he had done in *Thompson*, that the "ordinary and reasonable care" standard would not apply to a train that ran into wandering cattle. He went further, however, and took the opportunity to specify the precise duties of care that would apply in this very important class of cases. Earlier, Scates had made a great point of differentiating the relationship of railroads to passengers and the community – to whom they owed "the highest duty of care" – from their relationship to owners of stock (and, by extension, land) over which trains might happen to run. Now he took the opportunity to unify the standards of care for railroads, running from liability to passengers to stock crossing cases, using a single, tripartite scheme. His source for this new scheme was neither property nor tort law, but rather the specialized contract principles of the law of bailments.

Bailments is the body of law that governs situations where one party has entrusted property to another, a situation that describes a variety of the business activities of a railroad company. Then as now, there were varying classes of "bailees," running from bailees for hire (subject to strict liability for property damage) to inadvertent bailees. Scates wrote as though it were a given and obvious fact that the various categories of bailees governed *all* the conflicts that might arise out of the operation of a train: "The degrees of care or diligence are three, and are well defined and illustrated in Story on Bailments . . . " (*Rockafellow*, 549).

The equation of negligence with the law of bailments blurred any distinctions between claims based on rights to property and claims based on a duty of care. What makes this transformation particularly striking is that it occurred in a context in which there was no privity of contract. In other words, a set of standards that had been developed to govern competing rights in a special contractual relationship was taken out of its context and applied as general duties of care in all situations. The duties to respect others' property interests in a true bailments situation were turned into an exceptional case in which the railroad owed something more than the usual, general duties that applied all the rest of the time.

This was the process of articulating uniform duties, applicable to everyone at all times, that defined "citizenship" in the sense of the model of a person entitled to the protection of the law. The key criterion remained the characterization of the activities of the parties, but not in order to determine the duties that applied between the parties. Instead, the initial question would be whether the plaintiff had demonstrated that he had acted as a respectable public citizen entitled to assert a claim:

Counsel in arguing these questions, seem frequently to forget all distinction between goods on freight, and trespassing stock on the road-bed – between walking or driving upon it from idle curiosity or business calls, and taking passage on the cars. Every farmer, mechanic, laborer and citizen, in the pursuit of his ordinary occupation or calling, though not as dangerous and unmanageable as railroad trains, is yet equally liable with railroads for damage done to his neighbor's stock or property of this description (*Rockafellow*, 551).

Scates made sure that future readers would understand that none of the traditional bases for distinguishing between the applicability of one rule or another would survive. The location in which an event took place made no difference to the calculation of these uniform duties: "The degrees of care and negligence are the same, while pursuing it upon his own premises, and would be the same if transferred to or done upon the common highways." Nor was it the case, as it had been in *Baugh*, that railroads were some kind of a quasipublic environment: "Railroads are not common highways, in the sense of public wagon roads, upon which every one may transact his own business with his own means of conveyance, but only in the sense of being compelled to accept of each and all . . . " (*Rockafellow*, 551).

Turning to the lower court's jury instructions, Scates stated that the judge had described an unduly strict standard by stating that the railroad would be liable for a want of ordinary care rather than solely for willful conduct. Scates could have made this point in a single sentence merely by citing his own earlier opinion in *Patchin*. He was not yet finished, however, declaring the end of the property rights regime in cases involving damage to property:

> Although we might not interpret [the instructions] as making railroads insurers, as they are for freights, yet we cannot well stop short of all the care and liabilities of a bailee for reward. The relation of the parties to each other, and that of plaintiff to the property, is wholly misconceived. There are no such relations as bailment or carrier creates – and no such liabilities imposed. *Sic utere tuo, ut alienum non laedas*, has more application, and may be violated by a reckless, wanton, or grossly negligent injury, as we have said in 16 Ill. R. 198 [*Patchin*] (*Rockafellow*, 551).

The turn away from a property rights regime was thus complete. Where owners of animals carelessly permitted them to be at risk of harm, a railroad could be liable for harm to them only in the event that it exhibited willful misconduct. And such misconduct could not inhere in the ordinary operation of trains, defined by the railroads' usual practices: "We may reasonably doubt the legal right of owners of wandering stock to question the size and heft of trains, and the power or inability of attached engines, as passengers and freighters might do in cases of delay or damage from such cause" (*Rockafellow*, 551–2). The principle of *salus populi suprema lex est* had become the basis for the creation of an entire new system of common law analysis in which all parties would be judged in terms of their accommodation of the public need for railroads, a standard that the law imposed on "every farmer, mechanic, laborer and citizen."

The laws governing access to property had not been changed. Neither *Seeley* nor the statutes discussed therein were overruled. Instead, those principles had simply been made irrelevant by the introduction of an entirely new way of talking and thinking about the responsibilities of property owners to the public good. These responsibilities gave rise to specific duties of care in private suits deductively, as particular expressions of a general rule. Earlier cases had begun with the question of the relationship between the parties and their relative rights to occupy property. That inquiry, in turn, required careful consideration of the nature of the property on which an event occurred. Railroads presented a problematic case for this kind of analysis. What kind of property did a rail line comprise? Private land? A public highway? Something in between the two?

The new approach dispensed with the question altogether. In Scates' unified scheme of adjudication, the specific relationships between the individual parties were irrelevant; a court's job was to consider the nature of their activities in the abstract, and then to apply a single, uniform scale of tort duties. The principles of bailment liability were to be applied analogically, to determine the kinds of duties that might inhere between plaintiffs, defendants, and other persons who were neither parties to the suit nor in any particular relationship with those who were. That was how the language of contractual obligation led to the discovery of duties that stock owners owed to passengers and train operators owed to the residents of distant towns. The political economy of speed had transfigured the notion of *salus populi* around the ideal of technological progress, and now the law would define the universal duties that every farmer, mechanic, and citizen owed to the furtherance of that ideal. The opinions examined in this section demonstrate the project of consolidating the rules governing the adjudication of competing property interests around these duties.

Caton and Scates did not complete the project, however. Stock crossing cases were not the most difficult places at which to challenge traditional claims of legal right. If there were to be a complete and coherent system of public duties that would govern the determination of rights to recovery based on rights to property, that system would have to be applied in *all* cases. In *Rockafellow*, Scates had taken pains to mention that he was not addressing situations in which carriers were "insurers, as they are for freights," that is, when contractual duties between parties bound in privity were involved. The basic duty of stock owners was described earlier as the Duty to Get Out of the Way. What sort of responsibility to avoid obstructing the wheels of progress might be invoked in the face of a formal contract between a railroad and shippers of freight and baggage? Would these most respectable of citizens, like farmers, be called upon to demonstrate the virtues of citizenship in the railroad republic?

Common Carrier Liability and the Creation of Extracontractual Duties of Care

In 1857 Justice Scates resigned and was replaced by the man who would complete the transformation of Illinois' common law, Sidney Breese. Breese picked up where Scates had left off in *Rockafellow* by rewriting the duties of common carriers. Revisions in the rules governing common carriers struck at the heart of the laws governing corporations and the idea of public duties generally. Common carriers were a common law version of a public corporation before the formal institution existed. A business classified as a "common carrier" was required to deal with all customers equally, charge a single set of rates, and would be strictly liable for damage to property that occurred in the course of its business.

The reason was simple, and singularly applicable to railroads: common carriers operated businesses that were essential to society.

In 1851 Justice Caton, the Whig traditionalist, described the traditional understanding of the duties of a common carrier:

> He is the *absolute insurer* of the property against all losses, except those occasioned by the cause above specified. . . . As he is supposed to be better qualified, than even the owner himself, to take care of the property while in transit, he has the absolute control over it, and can make such disposition of it as he sees proper, and he must see to it that he carries it safely (*Fisher v. Clisbee*, 12 Ill. 344, 351, 1851, emphasis in the original).

This is a classic statement of property rights doctrine. During transit, the carrier was permitted to usurp the owner's property rights by exercising dominion and control over the goods being shipped. In return, the carrier, a bailee for hire, became strictly liable for any damage to that property in recognition of the fact that the property was not his, but was merely entrusted to him.

A year later, the rule was reiterated in *Woods v. Devin*, 13 Ill. 746 (1852). In *Woods*, a passenger on a steamboat sued for the value of goods that were lost in a carpet bag he was carrying with him. The carrier argued that it was in the business of transporting passengers, not freight, but the court ruled that a passenger could be expected to carry baggage. The carrier then argued that it should not be responsible for the cost of two valuable pistols that were in the luggage, but again the court referred to the essentially strict liability of common carriers: "The moment it was received on board the defendant became responsible for its safe delivery" (*Woods*, 748–9, 751).

Breese ended the reign of that traditional view of the duties of common carriers in 1858, with *Chicago & Aurora R.R. Co. v. Thompson*, 19 Ill. 578 (1858). The case involved a wooden box that James Thompson shipped by rail from Illinois to Pennsylvania. Inside the box there were "[o]ne new suit of broadcloth clothes, one small trunk, three fine shirts, three pairs of woolen stockings, seven hundred and fifty dollars in bank bills, fifty dollars in silver money, and one rifle." During transit, the box broke open. The clothes and rifle were damaged and the money disappeared. The lawyers for the rail line, like the lawyers in *Woods*, argued that they had not expressly contracted to transport goods for the defendant. They then argued that there had also been no implied contract relating to the bank bills, on two grounds: that transporting bank bills was not part of the railroad's business as a common carrier; and (somewhat in contradiction of the first argument) that "[i]t is not proved that the appellant was either paid, or was to be paid, by the appellee *its certain, or its usual, or its reasonable reward* for the transportation of said bank bills" (ISHA file # 2991: 1, emphasis in original). Finally, in a single sentence, the lawyers mentioned the principle of contributory negligence as a defense to a contractual claim: "[I]f the negligence or improper conduct of the plaintiff below contributed to the loss of these bills, he cannot recover" (ISHA file # 2991: 3–4).

Confronted by these arguments, Justice Breese might simply have decided to accept them, and thereby rule in favor of the railroad. Instead, he took the case as an opportunity to declare an entirely new way of thinking about common carriers, the scope of tort-based duties, and contracts generally. Reviewing English precedents, Breese first concluded that money was, in fact, included in the phrase "goods and chattels." Then, however, Breese concluded that bank bills were not money. Turning to a review of insurance law, Breese again found that "money, bullion, or jewelry" were included under the general term "goods," but then again found a way to except bank bills from this classification, in a three-page exercise in legal deconstruction based on the extension of rules governing the interpretation of specially defined terms in insurance contracts to the general language of the common law (*Thompson*, 585–7).

This, however, was not the end of the analysis, but only the beginning. The railroad, after all, was not an insurance company except by analogy, no insurance contract was present in the case to be interpreted, and the timeless authority of custom was unlikely to be located in the practices of the insurance industry. What did the exegesis of "bank bills" have to do with the tradition of strict liability of common carriers for damage to property entrusted to them? At this point, Breese connected the idea of insurance coverage to the duties of common carriers in a new way. First, in a sentence borrowed nearly verbatim from the railroad's brief, he reiterated the point that the rail line was not specifically a common carrier of bank bills: "If the bank bills, when out of the box, were not 'goods' in the ordinary acceptation of that term, concealing them in a box would not make them so, nor would they thereby lose the distinctive character *the whole community accords* to them" (*Thompson*, 587). Here was a reference to the timeless authority of custom, but the custom in question would be defined by the practices of a community consisting of railroads and their insurers. The reference to the expectations of "the whole community" provided the bridge to a wholesale conversion of a traditional analysis of contract/property rights into tortlike duties, by way of the startling idea that a contract for common carriage was actually a species of implicit insurance contract, not merely by analogy but in strict legal fact: "The company is the insurer, the owner or party freighting, the insured, and the premium is the price paid for transportation.... Now, to make a contract of insurance valid and binding, there must be good faith on the part of the insured..." (*Thompson*, 589).

"Good faith"! One can envision the lawyer for Thompson, reading along, reaching this last phrase, and feeling the ground suddenly shift under his feet. His client had approached this case from one of the strongest positions known in the canon of traditional contract law, that of a property owner who has entrusted a bailment to a common carrier. In such a case, the attention of the court ought to have been focused exclusively on the railroad. Was it a common carrier? Did it accept goods, as bailees, for transport? Did it fail to deliver those goods safely? Were there extreme extenuating circumstances that made delivery impossible? Instead, by the wholesale importation of a separate and distinct body of law, the court was turning its attention to the plaintiff, and asking, did *he* act in good faith? Did he act as the community would want people in his position to act? Did he create a situation for the railroad where there was unexpected risk? To do so, to act in a way that the community did not expect, to hide a treasure in a pigskin, would be fraud. "[C]oncealment, or the suppression of any fact or circumstance material to the risk, is fatal to the contract... it is a species of fraud" (*Thompson*, 589). Just as the law of bailments had been imported into the analysis of rights of real property usage in *Patchin*, now defenses to insurance coverage were being introduced into the warp and woof of common carrier liability. In both cases, the point was not to bring a case within the narrow ambit of a technical rule, but to expand a rule specific to the experience of railroads to cover everyone else.

Breese's conclusion did not entirely lack precedent, but to find support he had to reach back into the archives, where he found support in a New York case from 1827[7] and an English case from 1769.[8] The difference between those earlier cases and *Thompson* was the effort that Breese made

---

[7] Companies "incorporated for the transportation of goods... are not common carriers of packages of bank bills" (*Allen v. Sewall*, 2 New York 327, 1827, quoted at *Thompson*, 588).

[8] In *Gibbon v. Paynton*, 4 Burrow's 2298 (1769), where a coach passenger hid money inside a mail bag, the coach line was not responsible when the bag arrived with the money gone, based in part on the fact that the company had advertised that it was not responsible for money, jewels, or other valuables unless the coachman was specifically advised of their presence.

to turn the case into a revision of an entire body of law. Breese observed with regard to the English precedent, "[t]he court here did not, as distinctly as we have attempted to do, judge this case upon the principles of insurance, but all their arguments lead to it. . . . [t]he whole bearing of the case is on fraud and deceit" (*Thompson*, 591). The reference to "fraud," in this case, was not an invocation of the specific rules of that civil offense, it was rather a way of pointing to Thompson's failure to live up to his duty to avoid exposing the railroad to unexpected risks. No less than derailment or delay, financial loss was an impediment to the railroads' public purpose. Like a cow appearing on the tracks too close to permit the train to be stopped in time, Thompson's bank bills imperiled the railroad enterprise in ways that violated community standards.

Here, then, was a statement of the unified scheme of tort duties, anticipated by Caton, initiated by Scates, and completed by Breese. Everyone, in all their dealings, was bound by a duty to be the kind of prudent citizen whose existence furthers the progress of the community, by living up to the community's expectations so as to provide railroads with a predictable, rational system of risk analysis. These duties were not owed to other parties in a lawsuit, they were owed to everyone, to society at large. These universal duties were uniform, and would be enforced in the courts by uniform standards of care. Everyone was equally an agent of the public good, and everyone was equally required to display the same set of virtues conducive to progress.

In an important sense, the famous rhetoric of "responsible individualism" was a myth. What emerges most strongly from this review of cases involving interests in property is the theme of a corporatist conception of citizenship. This theme has been identified in the politics of Illinois in a somewhat later period (Einhorn, 1991), but in these cases we can see its genesis in the creation of new property law doctrines in the 1850s. The reworking of legal principles around a system of political economy both required and articulated a new idea of "citizenship" – full membership in the society and entitlement to the protection of one's interests by its laws – grounded in universal duties owed to the public good. What was of crucial import in this transition was not the specific outcomes of cases, nor the particular standards of care that were imposed, but the conceptual shift in the vocabulary of thinking about the law and the responsibilities of citizenship.

Some of the specific rules announced in *Patchin*, *Thompson*, and *Rockafellow* were overruled some years later in *I.C. R.R.Co. v. Middlesworth*, 43 Ill. 64 (1867) (where stock is killed by a railroad company at a place where no fence is required by law, the company is liable for simple negligence regardless of the contributory negligence on the part of the owner). But this was merely an adjustment, of which there would be many, to the balance between private rights and public duties. The vocabulary by which property rights could be asserted, and property interests protected, had been irrevocably reconstructed around a model of citizenship designed to accommodate the fact of railroads and the changes that they represented. This model of citizenship was grounded in the standardization of property, as the old distinctions between corporate and private property, public thoroughfares and private lots, and vested rights and the public usage lost their significance. The supremacy of the principle of *salus populi*, and the huge expansion in the reach of that principle, was reflected in the creation of common law duties to use one's property in ways that would serve the general interests of an abstract collectivity. Across the range of cases concerning claims of damage to property, the 1850s saw the creation of a reasoning process that began with the assertion of a universal duty to use property in the service of an ideal of technological progress.

These connections between the organizing concepts of this discussion and the doctrines of American common law appear, if anything, more strongly in the cases discussed in the next chapter. These were cases that involved harms to persons, and in the application of the idea of universal duties to those cases, the courts explicitly engaged in the construction of a model of citizenship.

4

"Intelligent Beings"

Cases Involving Injuries to Persons

Cattle were not the only things with which trains collided. Persons could be injured or killed when trains ran into them at road crossings, or when trains derailed, or in the always perilous process of getting on or off. In addition, the treatment of passengers could cause injuries to the dignity of respectable persons, as when a passenger was ejected for lacking a proper ticket. And of course, persons working on the railroads were injured or killed with monotonous regularity. When trains caused injuries to people, the same issues that gave rise to the idea of a public duty to avoid harm in the context of property were drawn with greater urgency. The outcome, however, was the same. Persons had a duty to govern their own conduct, as well as that of their property, in accordance with the standards of legal citizenship.

Injuries to Strangers: Crossing Cases

Collisions with people usually occurred at crossings, places where the traditional prerogative of mutual access to public highways collided with the realities of railroad operation. The Illinois legislature enacted a law in 1849 that required trains to give notice of their approach, by bell or whistle, and to keep a lookout on approaching a crossing. But by the rule of contributory negligence that was announced in *Aurora v. Grimes* (see the discussion in Chapter 3), the negligence of the plaintiff would stand as an absolute bar to recovery. This reasoning drew from the logic of property law that a landowner owed no duty of care to trespassers, since such persons had no right to be where they were in the first place. The rule against recovery by a trespasser was a logical corollary of the traditional common law approach that began in each case by comparing the rights of the parties to occupy the place – the property – in which injury was suffered. In the case of stock, this rule was what had made it so important before the 1850s to determine who had a duty to maintain fences, since in the traditional scheme the answer to that question defined the status of the animals as trespassers or, like the horse in one of the cases discussed in Chapter 3, "a free commoner and at large" (*Great Western R.R. Co. v. Thompson*, 17 Ill. 131, 1855).

The rule of contributory negligence as it was discussed in the previous chapter was not so much a matter of measuring the fault of the plaintiff as it was a "clean hands" rule that required the plaintiff to demonstrate his own innocence as a threshold matter of proving his entitlement to assert a claim. That remained the character of the rule as it applied to pleading requirements; plaintiffs who failed to "aver the negative" would not be permitted access to the court. The problem was that this understanding of contributory negligence made a hash of the idea of pervasive and universally applicable public duties. Railroads had always had public duties as chartered corporations, and if that concept was to be extended to private citizens, then its meaning for both corporations and individuals would require adjustment.

Sure enough, through the 1850s, in the context of injuries to persons, the rule of contributory negligence that had been announced in *Aurora v. Grimes* gave way, through a characteristic process of trial and error, to a more nuanced doctrine. The eventual outcome of this process of development was that the term *contributory negligence* came to mean a version of what would later be called comparative negligence. The test had nothing to do with the private rights of property owners and the definition of trespass. The analysis of the duties that railroads and travelers owed to one another would begin with an evaluation of the degree to which each had deviated from their public duties.

The shift from contributory to comparative negligence was announced in the 1858 case of *The Galena & Chicago Union R.R. Co. v. Jacobs*, 20 Ill. 478 (1858). The four-and-a-half-year-old son of Jacobs, a local baker and storekeeper, was visiting friends among the workers' families who occupied shanties inside a rail yard. The boy was struck and killed by a train while crossing the track.[1] At trial, the bulk of the testimony was

---

[1] Accidents were not uncommon along these tracks. One of the witnesses mentioned, purely in passing, that one of her own children had been killed when "[t]he express train cut off its [sic] feet after the accident to Jacobs' children" (ISHA file # 12514, 21).

devoted to defining the status of the child with relation to the property of the railroad, and to determining whether there had been negligence on the part of the child or his parents. The judge delivered a traditional jury instruction, requested by the plaintiff, that connected the railroad's duty of care to its relationship to the child and the parties' relative rights to use of the property: "If . . . the Plaintiff was by the express or implied permission of the defendant at the place where the injury occurred then it was the duty of the defendant to use due care and diligence in running their trains over the place in question."[2] At the same time, an instruction imputing contributory negligence to the parents was delivered at the request of the railroad, again with modifications by the judge: "[If] the plaintiff or his parents knew that there was a railroad at the place where the injury occurred . . . and that notwithstanding the plaintiff was permitted negligently to wander thereon, then plaintiff was on the railroad of the defendant at his own peril" (ISHA file # 12514: 10–21, 22–4). Despite the latter instruction, the jury returned a judgment for the Jacobs family in the amount of $2,000.

On appeal, the railroad argued that the child had been a trespasser and therefore that it owed him no duty of care. In response, Jacobs' lawyer attempted to make two points. First, he argued that running a train without a lookout in a place where people were known to walk constituted a lack of "proper care" regardless of the parties' relative rights to be on the property. Furthermore, he pointed out, "[i]n this instance more than ordinary care was required," since there had been testimony that the train had no brakes. Jacobs' lawyer also painted the case as one that raised the risk of destabilizing the happy confluence of interests between classes that was so central to the idea of America technological exceptionalism:

The circumstances that her house was a poor one, and she a person in humble life, can make no difference. . . . If this mother was negligent, no families that are poor or in moderate circumstances, can reside any where in the neighborhood of a railroad, for each child would need an attendant. To charter a railroad would be in effect to depopulate the country through which it would pass. The whole route would have to be abandoned to the company and its agents. . . .

Above all, the lawyer argued that the rules governing mere property should not apply in cases involving human life: "Human beings are not to be placed on the same level with sheep and cattle. Children are not to

[2] These kinds of distinctions were retained in the law governing homeowners' liability in all American jurisdictions until the late 1960s, and persist in some jurisdictions to this day.

be run over with impunity, either on highways or on railroads" (ISHA file # 12514: 25–6, 27–9).

Jacobs' lawyer had missed a crucial point. The emerging scheme of public duties was based on the formalistic equalitarianism of antebellum liberalism. The idea that a particular class of (free white) citizens might need special protections against the costs of progress was incommensurate with the language of legal standardization. Similarly, the idea that there should be different standards for property and tort law ran afoul of the project of unification, rationalization, and standardization that drove the reconceptualization of political and legal language. In the new way of thinking, children were *precisely* on par with cattle insofar as their parents had a duty to prevent them from obstructing the progress of trains and thereby coming to harm. The exceptional product of American technology, after all, was not upward mobility, it was progress.

Justice Sidney Breese lost no time in disposing of the argument that the plaintiff's child had a right to be on the tracks. Whatever implied permission might have been granted to the workers who lived within the enclosure of the rail yard did not extend to others. The plaintiff's argument, however, was not so much weak as it was simply irrelevant. The relationships between the parties, in the new way of thinking, did not determined the parties' duties of care:

Railroads may not omit all care, prudence, or skill, and ground themselves upon an immunity from all responsibility because they are lawfully pursuing their own business upon their own land.... [T]hey may not with impunity, wantonly or willfully, nor with such total or gross negligence as evidences willfulness, run upon and injure persons or stock trespassing upon the road (*Jacobs*, 489).

The last point demonstrated Breese's departure from the language of common law reasoning. In the case of wandering stock, the idea that the railroads owed a duty to avoid "wanton or willful" injury had at least a connection to a property law doctrine: the *Seeley* principle that in Illinois the owners of stock were entitled to allow them to roam free on public range, and landowners who did not maintain adequate fences would have no claim for damages caused by such animals. The idea of a duty of care owed to trespassers, however, announced the creation of a different kind of law, a common law doctrine that served the public good in the manner of a legislatively enacted regulation.

In this new scheme, there were two paramount duties: the railroad's duty to avoid posing unnecessary risks to the public, and the public's Duty to Get Out of the Way. Ultimately, these two public duties would have to be brought into some kind of balance. Citing language from *Great Western v. Thompson, Rockafellow* and *Patchin*, as well as *Grimes* (see discussion in Chapter 3), Breese launched into a ten-page analysis of the rule of contributory negligence, at the end of which he arrived at an astonishing conclusion:

> [A]ll care or negligence is at best but relative.... The true doctrine...is, that in proportion to the negligence of the defendant, would be measured the degree of care required of the plaintiff – that is to say...wherever it shall appear that the plaintiff's negligence is comparatively slight, and that of the defendant gross, he shall not be deprived of his action (*Jacobs*, 497).

This new "gross/slight" rule was not that a plaintiff would recover any time he or she had been less negligent than the defendant. But, the principle of contributory negligence would cease to apply when the defendant's negligence outweighed that of the plaintiff by a sufficient degree. In *Aurora v. Grimes*, the fact that the plaintiff's horse was a trespasser had implied that he "must use extraordinary care before he can complain of the negligence of another" (*Grimes*, 591). Here, the act of trespassing would be treated as a form of negligence and balanced against the carelessness of the property owner. This is the language of law in flux, written by a judge who is consciously engaged in the difficult task of translating political principles into new legal doctrines. Having reinterpreted a central element of the new tort doctrine that he himself had done so much to create, Breese did what judges frequently do in such circumstances: he asserted that he was merely following precedent. "Although these [earlier] cases do not distinctly avow this doctrine in terms, there is a vein of it very perceptible, running through very many of them" (*Jacobs*, 497).

The comparative version of the contributory negligence rule was further developed the next year by Justice Pinkney H. Walker, in *Galena & Chicago Union R.R. Co. v. Dill*, 22 Ill. 265 (1859). John Dill and a female companion were riding in a top buggy when they approached a railroad crossing. There was a warning sign at the crossing, reading "Railroad crossing – Look out for the cars while the bell rings or the whistle sounds." According to his passenger, Dill sped up as he approached the crossing, apparently trying to beat the train. If that was his aim, he did not succeed. The impact "threw Dill fifty feet in height from the buggy, from which height he fell upon the cars attached, upon which he was carried forty rods...whereby he was greatly injured..." (*Dill*, 266–7). The jury awarded Dill damages of $15,500. On the railroad's motion for a new trial, the trial court reduced the amount of the judgment by $3,000 but refused to set aside the verdict, and the railroad appealed.

The Galena line was exempt from the 1854 statute requiring trains to give notice, so on appeal the issue was entirely one of common law duties of care.[3] The railroad argued that Dill's own negligence had caused his injuries: "Dill was himself the author of his injury.... he hastened his horses by whipping them, and rushed carelessly into the danger." The railroad also added a new twist to the theory of contributory negligence. According to its argument, the duty to prevent a collision should rest on Dill as the party most easily able to avoid accident, rather than on the helpless railway train: "The cars cannot deviate from the track; other vehicles can. One is bound by an iron rule to a single direction; the other can move in any direction, at the pleasure of the party driving. Ordinary vehicles can halt almost instantly; a rail road train cannot" (ISHA file # 12784: 30–1). The lawyer for the railroad company was groping toward something that was to become a crucial element of American law. The statement that "it is presumed" that a person will avoid injury included the presumption that such a person would be aware of the limitations on a train's ability to stop or change direction. As Oliver Wendell Holmes would put the matter thirty years later, these were things "everyone was presumed and required to know" (Holmes, 1881: 259).

Dill's lawyer similarly focused on the nature of locomotives and the difficulty of controlling them, but he tried to make the opposite case:

The motive power of a railway train being steam and that of a highway traveler being either leg, horse, or ox power, and the steam power being comparatively uncontrollable must use a more extraordinary degree of diligence than the highway traveler.... If the Railway is in law entitled to the precedence the extraordinary motive power by means of a superior locomotion becomes an engine of infamy (ISHA file # 12784: 6–7).

Dill's lawyer was asserting the traditional principle of *sic utere*, while the railroad company was appealing to an as yet unnamed duty, shared

[3] The fact of the Galena line's exemption was described by Dill's lawyers:

> "[I]t happens that a short time prior to this particular collision, by some hocus-pocus lobby legislation a special act was passed on the day of [illegible] which is inserted among the private session laws of that year exempting the appellant from the operation of that general rule – thus making that railway company the special pet of the legislative power of this state. To my astonishment this *private act* was paraded before the court and jury upon the trial of this cause" (ISHA file # 127884: 11, emphasis in original).

One of Dill's arguments on appeal was that the special statutory exemption was unconstitutional (*Dill*, 270).

by Dill and the railroad company alike, for everyone to exercise his or her abilities to prevent accidents from occurring.

Justice Walker, in his opinion, attempted to fit the new rules into old language by describing the case as a double exception. Not only statutory obligations but also claims of superior property rights did not apply in this case because the collision took place at a highway crossing. "When the public highway became established, every person became possessed of the right to travel over it at all times.... This right is not superior to, but is only co-extensive with the rights of others." In this pure negligence situation, railroads were neither more nor less responsible than other persons for avoiding accidents:

Their locomotives and trains being heavy and less under their control than that of vehicles employed on common highways, they cannot be held to have them as completely in their power to prevent injury, as persons may have theirs who travel on highways. But this should not excuse efforts to foresee and prevent collisions, at the crossings of public highways. On the other hand, persons using the highway must be held to the use of all reasonable efforts on their part, in like manner to foresee and avoid danger. A want of proper circumspection on their part is liable to produce disastrous consequences to railroad travelers, as well as to themselves (*Dill,* 270–1).[4]

Here was the same unequally weighted gross/slight comparative negligence standard that had been established in *Jacobs,* but this time specifically connected to general duties owed to the public ("railroad travelers") and a specific consideration of the requirements of technology. Most important, railroads and passersby had the same duties. In the end, the verdict was overturned because Dill was presumed not only to be familiar with trains, but also with top buggies. Knowing that he could not see out to the side, said Walker, Dill should have stopped and gotten out to see whether there were approaching trains.

It is perhaps not surprising that traditional principles failed to illuminate the court's reasoning in crossing cases. Since by traditional rules each party had an equal right to occupy a highway crossing, by those rules neither owed it to the other to exert any particular efforts to avoid injury, and of course traditional law had no place for duties owed to third parties such as travelers. Thus in this instance the introduction of public tort

---

[4] Walker also took pains to observe that the fact of a legislative enactment did not dictate any policy preferences to which the courts were required to pay heed: "Where such acts are not required by legislative enactment, their omission does not raise a legal inference that the injury resulted from a want of their performance" (*Dill,* 272). The courts, not the legislature, would determine common law duties of care.

concepts appears as the creation of new legal duties, filling what had come to be perceived to be a gap in the law by extending the idea of contributory negligence into new and different areas. The situation was different, however, when the cases involved injuries to passengers and employees. These were persons who were in contractual privity with railroad companies, and therefore were each already covered by a defined set of duties of care. The introduction of public tort duties in cases involving passengers and employees involved the outright replacement of an existing scheme of private contract rights by a new set of tort-based principles of public duty.

Passengers

Breese's opinion in *Rockafellow* (discussed in the previous chapter) had answered crucial questions about railroads' duties as common carriers of goods, and their rights to expect passengers and shippers to comport themselves to the customary practices of the "community," defined as the railroad company and its customers. Those same themes were central to the analysis in a remarkable series of cases arising out of a single train derailment in 1852. The derailment resulted in three published opinions of the Illinois Supreme Court: *Galena & Chicago Union R.R. Co. v. Lewis H. Yarwood ("Yarwood I")*, 15 Ill. 468 (1854); *Galena & Chicago. Union R.R. Co. v. Fay*, 16 Ill. 558 (1855); and *Galena & Chicago. Union R.R. Co. v. Yarwood ("Yarwood II")*, 17 Ill. 509 (1856). All the opinions were authored by Justice Walter B. Scates, and all but one were unanimous.[5] Through his analyses in these cases, Scates began to define the duties of railroad companies and passengers, to each other and to the cause of progress.

   Lewis Yarwood, Albert Fay, and Samuel C. Jones boarded a train at Elgin, Illinois, bound for Clinton, on August 2, 1852. According to Jones' testimony, when they were ready to board, the conductor told them, "they had better go into the Baggage car, as the passenger car was full" (ISHA file # 12293, 29).[6] The train, typically, consisted of a locomotive followed by the tender, baggage car, second-class car, and first-class car. It was a warm day. Once the three men, along with some railroad employees, were

---

[5] Onias Skinner wrote a one-sentence dissent to the second opinion that read, "I am unable to concur in all the conclusions and reasoning of the foregoing opinion" (*Fay*, 571).

[6] The identity of the conductor might have been thought far from trivial; Wiggins was Lewis Yarwood's uncle. That fact, however, is not mentioned in any of the court's opinions.

in the baggage car, they removed their coats. Playfully, Yarwood pulled out Fay's shirttail, and Fay returned suit. The three young men, chasing each other, ran out of the baggage car and back along the train. Then the train derailed.

Just as trains had trouble stopping quickly, they also had trouble staying on the tracks even under the best of circumstances. The most common cause, and the one at work in the *Yarwood* and *Fay* cases, was a "snake-head," a place at the joining of two rails where one had buckled, causing its end to rise up enough to jostle a wheel loose from the track. The quality and construction of the rails themselves had a lot to do with the problem. Scarce funds, stiff competition, and the desire to maximize profit all induced line directors to use second-hand track or second-grade materials and designs. In *Yarwood I* there was testimony that the first portion of the line coming out of Elgin had been "T" track (similar to modern steel rails), which then changed to much less secure "strap" track, essentially flat strips of metal nailed to planks.

When the locomotive hit the snake-head, the rear wheels of the second-class car and the front wheels of the first-class car came off the track, and the entire train rocked violently. Yarwood and Fay, however, were the only passengers who jumped off the train, and they were the only passengers who were injured. Fay suffered a badly broken leg, and Yarwood a broken leg and sprained ankle, "and his body [was] otherwise severely bruised and injured" (ISHA file # 12293: 28). At the initial trials, Fay was awarded $10,000 in damages, including pain and suffering, and Yarwood was awarded $1,000. The facts in these trials were not primarily the point of dispute, although there was conflicting testimony about whether the train had slowed adequately when it passed from the T rails to the less secure strap rails. It was undisputed that the rails had been checked that morning, but also that snake-heads could easily arise between one traversing train and another. There was no conflict in the testimony describing the experiences of the passengers – that the cars rocked violently, that the experience was a frightening one – nor that the cars ran for two hundred yards after leaving the tracks, gouging deep ruts in the earth.[7]

The trial judge in the first *Yarwood* case delivered two instructions requested by Yarwood over the objections of the railroad, and declined

---

[7] E. B. Wells, a first-class passenger traveling with his daughter, testified that when the cars went off the tracks, "there was a general rising of passengers and catching hold of seats and of one another.... there was a general screaming of the ladies asking what they could do" (ISHA file # 12215: 15–16).

to deliver an instruction that the railroad requested. These three instructions, unsurprisingly, were those that defined the levels of care required of the parties. Regarding the duty of the railroad company, the instruction that the company had asked for read, in part, "that the defendant... as a common carrier of passengers, is not an insurer of personal safety against all accidents, but is liable only for the want of such care and diligence as is characteristic of cautious persons." Scates wrote that this instruction was properly rejected, as it failed to describe the full degree of the responsibility of a common carrier, which he derived from a review of English authorities: "[T]he uniform current of authorities in both England and the United States is uniform as to their liability for slight negligence, and in holding them to the utmost prudence and caution" (*Yarwood I*, 474, 469).

In addition, the jury instructions contained a well-recognized rule of general application that when a passenger jumped from a moving coach, that action could not be taken as a bar to recovery "[if] the plaintiff had reasonable grounds to believe, and did believe, that his life or limbs were in danger." As for the passengers' conduct before the accident, in light of the near-strict liability of a carrier of passengers, only a direct causal connection between the plaintiff's conduct and his injuries would suffice to establish the defense, "unless the jury further believe that such scuffling and playing contributed to produce this injury" (*Yarwood I*, 469–70). In these instructions, the trial judge raised the idea of contributory negligence, but he did so in an essentially incoherent fashion, grafting the rule onto a set of principles based on the contractual duties of common carriers. As in the case of damage to stock, Scates set out to fashion a single, unified set of standards that would accommodate both the ideas that common carriers had duties of care and that passengers could lose the protection of those duties by their actions.

First, Scates explained the relevance of the idea of contributory negligence cases involving injuries to passengers:

These companies operate with a powerful and dangerous agent, and must be held to a strict liability for care, skill, caution and diligence. But at the same time we must expect a *proportionate degree* of prudent discretion in the traveling public, according to the degree of danger in this mode of conveyance, so that this liability of companies may not be unnecessarily increased (*Yarwood I*, 473–4).

The idea of a "strict liability" limited by a countervailing "proportionate degree of prudent discretion" demonstrates the slippage that was under way in the system. But what was truly novel was the duty of passengers to exercise a "proportionate degree" of care so that the "liability of companies may not be unnecessarily increased." This was a theory with no precedent in the traditional rules of recovery for common carriers, and no basis in contract law.

Scates turned to the idea of the contractual relationship between railroad and passenger, and then used it to define a set of entirely extracontractual obligations that moved the idea of common carrier liability out of the vocabulary of private rights and into the realm of public, tortlike duties. This was precisely the move that Breese made with regard to property rights, using the law of bailments as his model, in *Chicago & Aurora R.R. Co. v. Thompson* (see the discussion in the previous chapter):

When passengers take their seats, they are entitled to occupy as against the carrier and subsequent passengers. While this right is recognized and protected to them, they are required to conduct themselves with propriety, not violating any reasonable regulation of the train; nor have they a right to interfere with the seats and accommodations possessed and secured by other passengers; they are not entitled to make the length and breadth of the train a common possession; nor should they disturb the quiet and convenience of others, or interfere with the management of the train by passing from car to car, unless for reasonable refreshment and other reasonable purposes (*Yarwood I*, 472).

Initially, this litany contains a complete statement of the rights and duties of passengers conceived in the traditional language of contract/ property rights. A passenger takes his or her seat with a right to occupy that property. This right can be asserted against the former owner of the property (the carrier) and parties asserting subsequently vested rights to the occupation and use of that property ("subsequent passengers"). These rights, however, are bound within a broader contract of passage, and are restricted by the railroad's "reasonable regulations."

There are other elements at work, however. A passenger has no right to "make the length and breadth of the train a common possession" nor to pass between cars "unless for...reasonable purposes." The source of these restrictions was entirely mysterious as a matter of traditional contract or property law. The passageways, whether conceived of as property held in common or as property to which the railroad had granted access, should have been equally open to all in the absence of a contrary regulation, and there had been no mention of any such regulations in the case, as Scates implicitly acknowledged.[8] More important, there was no obvious

---

[8] In the second trial, the brakeman from the train testified that he believed there was a rule prohibiting passengers from standing on the platforms between cars, but "could not say

basis for the distinction between reasonable and unreasonable conduct as a legal matter. Property owners had the right to make use of their property in any way not injurious to others, not only in a fashion determined by a court to be "reasonable." The standard had been imported directly from tort law.

The requirement that passengers act with "propriety" was a purely implicit standard, found neither in the parties' relative property rights nor in the terms of their contract. But it was the violation of that standard that constituted the contributory negligence. "Had the plaintiff below remained in the car in which he engaged his passage . . . the necessity for leaping would not have arisen even in the mind of a timid person. But he, with the others taking passage in the same car with him, got into a play and scuffle" (*Yarwood I*, 472–3). The phrase "play and scuffle" is evocative of the underlying point, which was not that Yarwood and Fay were in breach of their contract, but that their conduct was not "reasonable."

Scates got a second crack at trying to form a unified system of super-contractual duties in the appeal from Fay's lawsuit, *Galena & Chi. Union R.R. Co. v. Fay*. The jury instructions in Fay's trial were essentially similar to those in Yarwood's, with a few additions. One instruction requested by the railroad said that if Fay had jumped from the train "under a rush and under apprehension of danger when in reality there was no danger," then he could not recover. The trial judge rejected another requested instruction that described the company as bound to protect passengers "as far as human care, foresight and skill can possibly go," in favor of a standard calling for "the utmost care foresight and diligence" (ISHA file # 12215: 26, 28–9).

Referring to his own earlier opinion in *Yarwood I*, Scates first proposed that the degree of care required from both carriers and passengers depended on the technologies of transportation involved in the case:

The care, vigilance and skill must be adapted to the motive power and means. A servant well qualified to steer a boat or manage a team, might be totally unfit to manage steam, or regulate the running of a boat or locomotive . . . we can see no propriety or justice in relaxing from a proportionate care on the part of passengers, according to the increased hazards of the mode of transportation adopted by them (*Fay*, 568).

That a person trained to handle a team of horses might not be qualified to operate a train seems fairly self-evident. What was far from self-evident

whether [there were] any printed rules to that effect on that train or not" (ISHA file # 12293: 31).

was the proposition that a person might be *unfit to be a passenger* on a particular form of conveyance. The implicit secondary claim in the preceding
quotation is that an element of the role of train passenger was to know
the risks involved, to know the level of precaution that the passenger had
a right to expect from the railroad, and to act accordingly.

The analysis in *Fay* still did not easily fit the simple model of the case of
a farmer who pulled his cart onto railroad tracks in the face of an oncoming locomotive. The problem was timing. In his earlier opinion, Scates
had relied on an idea of the right to occupy property to connect Fay's
"inappropriate" conduct with the injury that followed when he leaped
from a derailed train. Now he made the connection a direct one, ignoring
issues of where Fay had a right to be in favor of a general unwillingness
to let a "play and scuffle" create the conditions for a compensable injury:

> Suppose he had carelessly placed articles upon the platforms of the cars, li-
> able to be shaken off and across the track, and they were carelessly suffered
> by the servants of the company to remain until thrown under the wheels, and
> the cars to be thrown off the track thereby, would a justifiable leap, after the
> necessity occurred, exculpate his previous carelessness, although he might show
> theirs?

The Duty to Get Out of the Way, unnamed in contract and unknown in
property, had become the touchstone for the creation of an entire new
class of duties to avoid allowing harm to be caused as a result of the
negligence of a common carrier in the operation of machinery at any point
in the future. The duties of carriers of passengers were "qualified . . . by
the reciprocal duty of the passenger, that his want of ordinary care does
not cause or contribute to produce the injury" (*Fay*, 569–70).

The third opinion was delivered on the appeal from the retrial of
Yarwood's claims, in *Yarwood II*. Scates took one more stab at tying the
system of legal doctrine together into a single set of categories. As it had
been before, the issue was contributory negligence and the problems that
arose from applying that broad tort doctrine to the detriment of the contractual obligations of common carriers. This time, Scates approached the
matter as a question of pleading and trial practice:

> There is, doubtless, a sensible distinction between persons receiving an injury
> while sustaining this relationship to the wrong doer, and those who do not. . . .
> Where the plaintiff in the action does not sustain that relation to the defendant, he
> must, in addition to the accident and his own injury, affirmatively show his own
> freedom from carelessness or negligence in causing or contributing to produce it
> (*Yarwood II*, 518).

Far from imposing near-strict standards of liability on the railroad, Yarwood's status as a paying passenger merely meant that his case was an exception to this general rule of pleading. But for that contractual relationship, an injured person would be required to show affirmatively his or her worthiness to be heard before the claim against the railroad could be brought into court at all.

The focus on pleading and the creation of strong threshold requirements for getting one's claims to adjudication gives Scates' argument a powerful formalistic tenor. At the same time, however, Scates emphasized that the jury was to determine whether any particular course of conduct actually constituted contributory negligence: "Negligence is a question of fact and not of law; and the court had no right to determine it" (*Yarwood II*, 518, 520). This deference to the jury contrasts markedly with Scates' earlier search for an authoritative legal standard. Here, however, jurors were being asked not to evaluate the conduct of railroads, but the conduct of their fellow citizens, and the standards they were being asked to impose were community standards of respectability, prudence, and competence. The legal formulation focused that question on the plaintiff's mental state ("rashly") and the degree of familiarity with railroads and their hazards that he displayed ("an undue apprehension"). The continued reliance on local, community standards to define prudence was the limiting factor in Scates' analysis. As in the case of property damage claims, the project of modernization was taken up and completed by Sidney Breese after Scates' retirement in 1857.

Breese put the finishing touches on the project that Scates had begun with *Chicago, Burlington & Quincy Railroad Co. v. Erastus Hazzard*, 26 Ill. 373 (1861). *Hazzard* involved a passenger who was riding on the caboose of a freight train, rather than a regular passenger train. When the freight train pulled into the station at Galesburg, it stopped for a moment before reaching the platform. The conductor informed Erastus Hazzard that "'up-town people,' or business-men," usually got off at that point, in order to be closer to the main part of town (*Hazzard*, 383). Hazzard stepped out to the platform of the caboose, at which point the train suddenly jerked forward, spilling him off of the car. Hazzard suffered a dislocated ankle and a fractured leg, along with various bruises, for which he was awarded $11,000, including damages for pain and suffering and interruption of his business.[9] His business, in fact, may have been the element

---

[9] When his case reached the Illinois Supreme Court, Hazzard was far from healed. In a pathetic handwritten addendum to his printed brief, he wrote, "I have been advised by

that made this case an important opportunity for working out comparative negligence doctrines. Hazzard was, in Breese's words, "an eminent attorney and counselor, skilled in drafting bills in chancery, special pleas, and in the preparation of able and voluminous briefs in important cases, and in arguing from them" (*Hazzard*, 390).

The fact that Hazzard was a lawyer set the stage for the peculiar setting of the published opinion. It appears (the record is incomplete) that the railroad's appeal, based on predictable claims of contributory negligence plus an argument that the damage award had been excessive, was initially granted without a published opinion.[10] The railroad had argued that whatever duties it might have owed to passengers riding in a passenger car, it had a lesser obligation to ensure the safety of a passenger who chose to ride in a freight train's caboose. Hazzard, the skilled preparer of "able and voluminous briefs," filed a Petition for Rehearing, the source for the quotations in the preceding paragraph, and it was in response to that petition that the court published its opinion. The case thus appears as an unusually direct dialogue between the justices of the court and a lawyer requesting that they reconsider and clarify their own previous opinion.

There were three bases for Hazzard's appeal. The first was that the train had been subjected to an excessively violent jerking motion:

It cannot be denied that the *violent* jerking of a train of cars is not only injurious to the train itself, but it is also dangerous to the employees and passengers riding upon the train.... [T]he question before the jury covered the broad ground as to whether the jerking at that particular time and place, under the circumstances...*was necessary* and *unavoidable* or whether it was occasioned by the negligence and carelessness of the Engineer (ISHA file # 13586: 2).

Second, Hazzard argued that the absence of a guard chain across the back of the caboose constituted negligence on the part of the railroad company. The trial judge had issued a jury instruction that the absence of the chain ought not to be considered evidence of negligence, reading "it is not *usual* to place a chain across the back end of a '*caboose car*,' and the omission

eminent surgeons to have my limb amputated, as being preferable to going lame through life, but I cannot *make up my mind to it.* I think I can satisfy the Court on argument, the damages are not too high" (ISHA file # 13586: 7, unnumbered pages). Many of the briefs filed by the railroads' lawyers were printed, but this was quite unusual for a plaintiff's brief.

[10] No copy of that opinion or its associated papers appears in the archive, and its author is unknown. The record does include a copy of Hazzard's original "Brief of Authorities," but the arguments are entirely duplicative of those that appear in a more developed form in the Petition for Rehearing.

to do so is not negligence." Hazzard asked the supreme court to rule that this instruction had been in error: "Your petitioner thinks the Court on reflection will . . . say that the defendant is equally bound to furnish a *safe* car for their passengers to ride in, and that if a *guard chain* is essential and necessary to render the cars *safe*, that the defendant was bound to use such *guard chain*, no matter whether such *guard chain* was in *common use* or not" (ISHA file # 13586: 2, 5). Third, Hazzard asserted that the train's conductor had been negligent in instructing him to alight at a point before the train had reached a full stop at the platform.

All three of Hazzard's claims rested on the contractual duties of the railroad as a common carrier. He had asked the conductor whether there was a car "that carried passengers," was told there was, purchased "a ticket of *the same kind usually* sold to passengers," paid "*the usual fee*," and was received on the train "as *a passenger*, not as *freight*" (ISHA file # 13586: 8). As for the railroad's defense of contributory negligence, Hazzard pushed the issue at exactly the point where Scates had focused, on the question of pleading. Hazzard challenged the idea that a plaintiff should be required to plead his own lack of contributory negligence: "Every man is presumed to be innocent until the contrary is proven. Every man is presumed to have discharged his duty until the contrary is shown; and why this rule should be changed, at this late day and especially to favor corporations, is a matter marvelous in the eyes of your petitioner" (ISHA file # 13586: 1).[11]

The last point, about pleading requirements, demonstrates that Hazzard had not grasped the profound change that had occurred in the nature of the Illinois Supreme Court's conception of the role of common law courts in society. For Hazzard, the court remained an arena in which private parties' interests were contested in terms of rights derived from the ownership of property. Hazzard was correct that the requirement of pleading the negative made no sense from this perspective, as it seems to be designed solely to give an unreasonable advantage to defendants and to deny the premise of equal entitlement to be heard. The problem, as Breese explained in his opinion, was that the threshold showing of fitness had nothing to do with the interests of plaintiff and defendant, but

[11] Hazzard was also apparently angry over the conduct of the appeals by the railroad's attorneys. Referring to the original abstract of record attached to the railroad's appeal, he wrote, "through the ingenuity of the counsels who prepared the record of the case, it is so changed by omissions and alterations as to give it an unwarrantable color in favor of the defendant" (ISHA file # 13586: 3). Hazzard's complaint contains a cautionary observation for researchers concerning the reliability of factual accounts in an appellate record.

was entirely a question of the parties' duties to the public at large. The railroads' duty to the public good was to run trains and thereby provide progress; the passengers' was to avoid interfering with that progress. The nature of the showing that was required to demonstrate one's entitlement to be heard in the common law courts thus demonstrated the contours of a new, legalistic concept of citizenship.

Before returning to the theme of contributory negligence, however, Breese went through each of the plaintiff's claims, in each case saying much more than he had to, and in the process mapped out the reasoning process required in cases of injuries to passengers. The question of whether the train had been improperly jerked provoked a three-page disquisition in the published text regarding the techniques of stopping a moving train. At the end of this treatment, Breese replied to Hazzard's argument that a skilled driver would not have produced so great a jerk in the cars: "It is unimportant how many witnesses may swear, that an engine driver, of competent skill, can always regulate the exact amount of steam to let on. He may put on just as little or just as much steam as he pleases.... *His duty is, to put on enough*. Jerking then is inevitable" (*Hazzard*, 379, emphasis added). The reference to the driver's duty to get the train into the station makes no sense if the issue is the driver's duty of care in connection with Hazzard's claim of negligence. The driver, as the agent of the railroad, was bound by its duty of care toward Hazzard, to which his duties to his employer were irrelevant. Breese's language, however, is perfectly sensible if one recognizes that the driver owed a duty to the public at large, not only to his employer, to put on enough steam to get the train to the station, since this obligation could not be limited by any claim of a countervailing duty of care toward Hazzard.

Moving to the absence of a chain on the back of the caboose, Breese argued that such chains are not commonly present on freight trains. Of course, this did not answer Hazzard's argument about the duties of common carriers, as Breese conceded: "It was the practice to permit passengers to ride in it, for which the usual passenger fare was demanded, so that it is not for the defendant to deny his liability as a carrier of passengers." That did not mean, however, that the duties of the railroad were the same in both situations. Instead, those duties were tempered by the presumption of the passenger's awareness of the conditions of his particular mode of travel:

The public are not invited to occupy the caboose; they are permitted to do so if the urgency of business, or other motive, forbids delaying to wait for the regular passenger train. The passenger takes the car as he finds it, and must put up with all its deficiencies and inconveniences, and wants of safeguards; the company being responsible only for the care and vigilance, and skill and proper management of those having it in charge, *such as it is*, and that it is not defective in any essential particulars. The plaintiff knew all about this car when he got into it.... The only obligation, then, upon the defendant, was to carry the plaintiff safely in the caboose *as it was. He took it as it was.*

Breese cited the statement in *Fay* that "a passenger takes all the risks incident to the mode of travel, and the character of the means of conveyance which he selects," while the carrier was only required "to adapt the proper care, vigilance and skill to that particular means" (*Hazzard*, 379–80, 381 [emphasis added], 382). In *Fay*, of course, the Court had only observed that rail passengers are expected to recognize that trains pose different dangers from those encountered on boats or horse-drawn wagons. Breese had drawn that principle into the proposition that passengers would be assumed to be familiar with trains and their tendency to jerk on reaccelerating; the differences between passenger and freight trains, ordinary cars and cabooses; and the dangers associated with getting off each at a point prior to the platform. In each situation, a passenger "took it as it was," assuming the risk and therefore the responsibility for avoiding injury.

The most interesting discussion of all concerned Hazzard's claim that the conductor had put him at risk by suggesting that he might alight before the train had reached the platform. Certainly the conductor had the authority to order a passenger to leave by a particular manner. In this case, however, the testimony had been only that the conductor had informed Hazzard that he might alight at that point, and that such was the custom of "uptown people." Breese concludes that Hazzard had no right to rely on the conductor, but rather that "of the whole matter the plaintiff was his own adviser":

Suppose the plaintiff knew without being informed by the conductor, that "uptown people," or business-men, usually got off at that place, and had attempted to get off there, and an accident happened, would the defendant have been liable? Should the fact then, that the conductor gave the plaintiff this information, be held to be a direction, or order to him, to get off there, so as to throw the risk on the defendant? We look upon it as mere information given to the plaintiff (*Hazzard*, 382–3).

This statement, taken on its own, seems to make the railroad immune from liability for any act that it does not actually compel a passenger to undertake.

The real import of the reasoning, however, came in the comments that followed, in which Breese shifted his attention from a characterization of the conductor's statements to a description of Hazzard himself:

He was of mature age, sharp understanding, and familiar with the hazards attendant on traveling by a railroad.... It is a standing precaution, known to every man, woman and child above the age of puberty, who has ever traveled on a railroad, that it is full of danger to leap or step from a car when in motion, and *none do it, but those who by practice, know how to regulate and dispose of their own momentum*.... He knew, though the train was for the moment slacked up by shutting off the steam, that the slack was subject to be taken up suddenly, and his own experience told him when it is so taken up it is always with a jerk, affecting the rear car more sensibly, or in a greater degree than any other.

Lest a reader assume that he was making a specific argument about Hazzard, rather than announcing a generally applicable standard, Breese forthrightly declared the model of rational actor whom he had in mind: "Had the conductor made such remarks as he did to an ignorant boy, or to an inexperienced woman, and they had acted upon them and been injured, carelessness and negligence might be properly chargeable; but the plaintiff was familiar with railroad traveling and had full knowledge of the risks he ran, and was acting upon his own design" (*Hazzard*, 384–5).

Here, finally, was a clear and complete statement of the unifying principle that Scates had been groping for in his earlier decisions, and that Breese had built up to by first carefully delineating the kind of knowledge that a plaintiff should be expected to have. An adult male was someone who followed only his own counsel, who by legal presumption would not undertake a dangerous action unless he was competent to do so, and who understood the ways of trains. Anyone who did not fit those criteria was outside the scope of the railroad's required cognizance, and had no right to recover for injuries.

From this perspective, Breese was able to make short work of Hazzard's claim that the pleading requirements relating to contributory negligence were improper:

In the case of Yarwood and Fay, it was held that passengers took the risks incident to the mode of travel, and the character of the means of conveyance which they select, the party furnishing the means being bound only to adapt the necessary care, vigilance and skill to those means, *the carrier and passenger owing reciprocal duties each to the other* (*Hazzard*, 387).

But for the last, emphasized phrase, Hazzard's argument that contributory negligence was a defense, and therefore could not require the plaintiff to plead the negative, would have been perfectly sensible. The idea that the passenger owed a duty to the carrier, however, changed the picture. The passenger's duty was not based on contractual obligation or competing property rights, which would have to be proven by the defendant; it was an independent tort duty that preceded and superseded the contractual relationship. The duties were "reciprocal" because both railroads and plaintiffs were members of a larger public. A plaintiff who could not plead facts to show that he had abided by his duty as a member of the public was in no position to complain of a railroad that had breached its lesser, private duties to him.

From reading the review of preceding cases, one might be forgiven for concluding that the idea of a largely unstated concept of common law public tort duties operated solely to protect railroads from liability. In fact this was not the case. In *Hazzard*, the only public duty assigned to the railroad was to get the train to the station, when Breese declared that it was the duty of the engineer to use "sufficient" steam (in a case, it should be noted, that involved no questions of the duties of the engineer as an employee). In other cases where the railroad clearly violated its duties to the public, however, the Illinois Supreme Court did not hesitate to uphold verdicts favoring injured plaintiffs. For instance, in *Chicago, Burlington & Quincy R.R. Co. v. George*, 19 Ill. 510 (1858), a passenger was injured in a collision between two trains. One of the trains was "wild," meaning it was several hours off of its schedule. In that case, Justice Walker had no difficulty in defining the duty that the railroad owed to the public, and thereby upholding the recovery by the plaintiff: "The evidence shows that the defendants' train was running several hours out of time when the collision occurred. They, in doing so, must have known the hazard they ran, and that the other train, without a mere chance, would be on the road at the time and place where the collision occurred" (*George*, 517). Similarly, railroads had a public duty to charge consistent rates, and would be forced to pay compensation for a breach of that duty (*Galena & Chicago Union R.R. Co. v. Rae*, 18 Ill. 488, 1857).

Conversely, there were a series of cases that involved no obvious public duty on the part of passengers, and in which railroads did not gain the favor of legal protections from the justices. These were cases in which passengers, found not to have valid tickets in hand, were set off of trains between stations. Where respectable passengers such as Benjamin Parks, a lawyer, or Samuel Vanatta, a minister, were put off trains in this manner, the Illinois Supreme Court had no hesitation in upholding verdicts in favor of the plaintiffs, although in each case verdicts of $1,000 were found to be excessive.[12] These ejectment cases cannot be described simply in terms of economic interests or business philosophy. Instead, they stand for the proposition that the universal standards of the law were standards of respectability. That is, persons would be required to meet standards of conduct, but in return they would be considered to be entitled to respectful treatment. The railroads had a public duty to avoid giving offense to persons of good character even when they exercised their private contractual rights to demand payment for their services.

Passenger ejectment cases reflect the leveling, inclusive aspect to the otherwise demanding, exclusive effects of new legal doctrines. As in the case of trains that failed to stay on schedule, these cases also demonstrate that new duties were imposed on railroads as well as on passengers. According to traditional legal principles, after all, the railroads could owe no duties whatever to passengers who lacked tickets, since there could be no privity of contract between them. Under the new tort-based concept of universal duties, however, railroads had duties to behave decently to anyone who did not violate a universal duty of care in his or her own conduct. Passengers quietly occupying their seats had not violated any of the extracontractual duties that they owed to the railroads and their fellow passengers. Consequently, the railroads would not be relieved of an extracontractual duty owed to those passengers. Railroads were entitled to the benefit of duties that passengers owed to the public; they were not a new elite entitled to run roughshod over the dignity of citizens. Railroad employees, in particular, were not to be thought of as holding any personal authority by virtue of their positions:

[A]mong the great multitude of conductors necessarily employed throughout the state, with the utmost caution on the part of the companies, it is almost inevitable that some will want discretion, while others may be influenced by passion, or, worse still, an exaggerated notion of their authority, and a morbid ambition to display (*Parks*, 18 Ill. 468).

These passenger were respectable not because they occupied a differentiated stratum of society, but precisely because they had behaved in accordance with universally applicable standards. And, railroad employees owed them a duty to behave decently not on the basis of any specific relationship, but as a matter of those same universally applicable standards of conduct. Ticketless passengers were undoubtedly in the wrong, but they

[12] *Chicago, Burlington & Quincy R.R. Co. v. Parks*, 18 Ill. 460 (1857); *Terre Haute, Alton and St. Louis Railroad Co. v. Vanatta*, 21 Ill. 188 (1859).

were not standing in the way of progress, so progress had no right to run them over.

As was the case concerning harms to property, the question remained: how would the new theories of universal public duties and uniform expectations work out in connection to relationships bound by formal contracts? The answer appeared most powerfully in the radical reworking of the common law governing employment.

Employees: The Illinois Fellow-Servant Rule

The 1850s saw the beginning of modern employment law in Illinois with the announcement of the fellow-servant rule in 1858. The fellow-servant rule stated that where an employee was injured as the result of the negligence of a fellow employee, the employer could not be liable. Labor law is often described as a separate body of legal doctrine with its own arc of historical development, and there is some truth to that characterization (Orren, 1991; Forbath, 1991). Certainly the brief discussion of a single case that follows is not intended to examine the complex and arguably independent developments in labor law in the period, only to point to a few crucial points of continuity between the treatment of cases involving injuries to employees and the other types of cases that have been discussed in this and the preceding chapter. In particular, the 1858 formulation of the fellow-servant rule in *Illinois Central R.R. Co. v. Cox*, 20 Ill. 21 (1858), demonstrates the same idea of pervasive duties to the public good, and the same pattern of a body of law shaped around new conditions dictated by technological change that has previously been seen in the contexts of property, contract, and tort claims generally.

In February 1855, the Illinois Central Railroad contracted with a company called Bennett & Scott to supply them with firewood. Bennett & Scott were to use the railroad's cars, under the direction of the railroad's conductor, engineer, and fireman, to deliver the wood. Othneille Cox was one of the workers hired to load and unload the firewood. On February 9, he and his fellow workers loaded a train in such a way that some of the pieces were sticking out to the side. As the train progressed down the track, the protruding pieces hit a car sitting idle on a parallel track and were thrown back along the train on which Cox was riding. He was knocked off the car and killed, and his widow sued (ISHA file # 8732: 2–3).

There were two important legal issues to be resolved in the case. First, who was "operating" the train the day Cox was killed? We have already seen problems that arose when it became difficult to connect a corporation that constructed a rail line with another corporation that operated cars along that line, but here the issue was purely a formal one. Bennett testified that he and his partner "had charge of the train, and the men on the same had to obey our orders" (ISHA file # 8732: 2). By traditional rules, Bennett & Scott might have been treated as an entirely separate entity from the railroad. The problem with this reasoning was that it would turn the operation of a railroad corporation into a gigantic amalgamation of separate enterprises, as independent contractors were used for everything from supplying water and constructing rail lines to building rail cars. In addition, railroad companies frequently leased their lines or cars to other companies, making it difficult for prospective plaintiffs to ascertain the legal owner of a train or stretch of track. The reality, of course, was that these arrangements merely reflected the new form of business organization that characterized industrial corporations. The fact, as in *Cox*, was that the railroad company effectively maintained control over what happened on its lines regardless of the formal arrangements.

In point of fact, had the court accepted the argument that the rail line was separate from its subcontractor, there might have been a benefit to Cox's estate in the particular case, but a whole range of other kinds of claims would have been made vastly more difficult to prosecute. It is evident from the requested jury instructions that Cox's lawyer was not thinking of the possibility that the fellow-servant rule would be invoked. Instead, his concern was to establish that Bennett & Scott and the Illinois Central Railroad were the *same* entity for purposes of the lawsuit: "If the jury believe from the evidence, that Bennett and Scott were but the employees, agents of the defendant, to haul in the wood of company, or have it hauled in, and not contractors, then they are but their servants, and not contractors in the sense in which it is used in the instructions for defendant" (ISHA file # 8732: 3).

The railroad did, indeed, request instructions suggesting that it should not be responsible for the actions of Bennett & Scott's employees on the grounds that the relationship of contractor to principal did not make Bennett & Scott "the agents or servants of such company, in such manner as to charge them, the said company, with any injury that might occur to a servant of Bennett and Scott...." The railroad's lawyers, however, also included a whole string of instructions declaring the fellow-servant rule. That rule stated that as an employer, Illinois Central Railroad was only responsible for hiring "competent servants." If Cox's fellow servants were in fact competent, then he (or his estate) could not recover damages for any injury that resulted from "the carelessness, negligence or unskillfulness of fellow servants, while acting in the same service, without their [the employer's] knowledge or sanction." Cox, according to these instructions, "virtually undertook to run all the ordinary risks incident to his employment," including the "unskillfulness or negligence of his fellow servants," and it was "presumed in law that his wages were commensurate with the hazard to which he was exposed" (ISHA file # 8742: 3, 4). The requested instructions were given, the jury awarded Cox's estate $1,000 in damages, and the railroad appealed.

The judge's instructions articulated the fellow-servant rule quite clearly, and it seems beyond dispute that the jury's verdict was, in fact, contrary to those instructions. That ground, alone, would have been sufficient for reversal of the verdict, but once again Breese took the case as an opportunity to clarify the legitimating principles at work in the legal doctrine. The railroad's argument had grounded the rule entirely on the contractual obligations of master and servant, but Breese went much further:

It is right and proper that one servant should not recover against the common master for the carelessness of his fellow-servant, provided competent servants have been selected by the master. It is important to all concerned that each servant should have an interest in seeing that all his co-servants do their duty with proper care and fidelity, and who will take care to report the negligent and unskillful by whom their lives may be endangered, to their principal. This will make them all prompt and vigilant, and their master's interest be closely interwoven with their own, and all properly regarded. *Independent of this*, it must be understood that each servant, when he engages in a particular service, calculates the hazards incident to it, and contracts accordingly. This we see every day – dangerous service generally receiving higher compensation than a service unattended with danger or any considerable risk of life or limb (*Cox*, 26–7, emphasis added).[13]

The emphasized words are the key to the analysis: the issue of implicit contractual undertaking was *independent* of the real justification of the rule.

Breese's formulation had no cognizable parallel in traditional contract or property rights, nor in the older version of tort duties that derived from the evaluation of those rights. The idea that a servant had a duty to be vigilant of the actions of his fellows arguably reached back to ancient notions of employment where an apprentice became a part of a household,

---

[13] Breese asserted that the rule had been adopted previously. As had been the case in *Hazzard*, however, Breese was being disingenuous. The earlier case, *Honner v. Illinois Central Railroad Company*, 15 Ill. 550 (1854), did not, in fact, contain a clear statement of the fellow-servant rule.

but it had no obvious root in contract rights claims. The idea that it was "important" that employers' and employees' interests be "closely interwoven," moreover, had no such precedent. Breese was alluding to an idea of an economy as an integrated system, one that required that all participants play their roles appropriately. This was the employment version of the public tort duty to contribute to a technologically dictated vision of progress. "If this were not so," he concluded, "no great enterprises could be safely undertaken and carried on, nor would there exist that vigilance and care on the part of the employed, which is so vital to their success" (*Cox*, 27). The "great enterprise" of which Breese spoke was not merely a railroad line, it was the entire political economy of speed that the rails were bringing to Illinois.

The connection of employment law with the rest of the system of public tort duties is suggested in *Cox*. It would be stated with force when the fellow-servant rule was reiterated the next year, in *Moss v. Johnson*, 22 Ill. 633 (1859). John M. Johnson, a carpenter, was riding to his work site on a train belonging to his employer, as was apparently the custom. The train derailed, he was thrown off, and both legs were broken. Johnson's lawyer argued that he had been aboard the train in the role of a passenger, and that the railroad should therefore be held to the duties of a common carrier. At trial, the judge delivered two key instructions requested by Johnson's lawyer: "[W]hether the plaintiff was or was not in the employment of the company (unless he had some control over the train or road) they were bound if they undertook to transport him upon their cars to have a safe road, well built of sufficient materials, and to use ordinary care skill and diligence in transporting him." The railroad requested an instruction that was rejected, which read:

[If] the Plaintiff ... was a hand employed by the defendants upon the Road as a carpenter and was riding in the construction of the same and ... he got voluntarily upon the cars without paying any fare or assuming to pay any, without any request from the defendants and ... the accident occurred without the gross fault or negligence of the defendants ... then there could be no recovery (ISHA file # 12850: 12, 21).

The reference to the slight/gross comparative version of contributory negligence strikingly suggests that the railroad's lawyers, as well as Johnson's, were unaware of the potentially preemptive effect of the fellow-servant rule as it had been announced in *Cox*. The jury awarded Johnson $1,000 in damages and the railroad appealed, focusing on the three previously quoted instructions.

On appeal, Johnson's lawyer argued that the fellow-servant rule did not apply. He did so by challenging the premise that common employment created a valid presumption of familiarity with the conditions of work:

He had no control over the engine or cars, and no authority on the train. The freight cars, being open box cars, were placed behind the passenger car. They were loaded, two of them with iron and two of them with ties. This was clearly wrong and unusual. The passenger car should have been placed behind the loaded cars, but Johnson could not direct as to this. He was in the defendant's employment, just as an attorney would have been. He was in their employment, just as a book keeper would have been. He was not employed to run the hazards incident to a negligent running of the cars.

The reference to an attorney and a bookkeeper was a pointed reminder that railroads had become massive business corporations hardly analogous to the model of field hands sharing the back of a wagon on the way to a field. The lawyer returned to his theme in the closing section of his brief:

The ground upon which the exemption to liability lies is that the employee had skill in the employment he engaged in and could know whether or not the service was properly or improperly performed and took the risk not only of the employment but of the skill and faithfulness of his colaborers. . . . This is the only ground upon which such exception ever could rightly be made. But does a carpenter or attorney of a road have any such knowledge or skill or can they be more than a stranger or at all interfere with the running of the train? (ISHA file # 12850, 28, 38).

Johnson's case, in other words, turned on the idea that there were not such things as generic "workers," but rather specific relationships between a particular worker's job description and the operation of the business in question.

In his opinion for the court, Breese first dispensed with Johnson's argument on the facts:

[T]he defendant in error was in a condition to know the condition of the road, passing over it as he did daily, in carrying out his contract with the company as one of its employees, and he must be presumed to have contracted in view of all the hazards to which he was exposed, by an insecure and imperfect road – making up trains upon it – as well as the negligence of his co-employees.

That restatement of the rule in *Cox* would have been sufficient, but, as always, Breese ventured beyond the arguments that had been presented by the lawyers to further his project of identifying the unifying conceptual bases to the principles of tort liability. Uncharacteristically citing to authority from Scotland rather than the United States or England, he made his theme freedom, and his hypothetical counterargument, slavery:

There is manifest propriety in distinguishing between the two classes of cases, involving free persons on the one hand and slaves on the other.... A slave may not with impunity remind and urge a free white person, who is a co-employee, to a discharge of his duties, or reprimand him for his carelessness or neglect; nor may he, with impunity, desert his post at discretion, when danger is impending; nor quit his employment on account of the unskillfulness, bad management, inattention or neglect of others of the crew.

By contrast, "[t]he defendant in error was his own master, fettered by nothing but considerations of his own interests, and they prompted him to incur the hazards which have been so injurious to him" (*Moss*, 642).

The equation was complete. A free person – any free person, regardless of the status of employment – had a *duty* to pursue his own interests, a duty which included the exercise of vigilance over his fellow workers, familiarity with the conditions of his work and its technology, and the requirements of public progress. The admixture of traditional republican and liberal principles here is remarkable. The public good required that free citizens display virtues. Those virtues were defined as the rational and sensible pursuit of one's own interests in a manner that would not conflict with technologically driven progress. The common law would enforce that public duty by making a demonstration of its fulfillment a prerequisite to any recovery for harms to private interests. Workers, no less than farmers, mechanics, shippers, and passengers, owed a duty to the public good to conduct themselves in a way that demonstrated the level of knowledge and awareness that, in Holmes' words, "everyone is presumed and required" to possess.

The specific application of the fellow-servant rule was later limited in 1870 when it was ruled not to apply in a case where the employee had no alternative but to make use of the dangerously inadequate equipment supplied by an employer.[14] Five years after that, the rule was further held to have no application in cases of "gross" negligence by a fellow employee (*Toledo, W. & W. Railway Co. v. O'Connor*, 77 Ill. 391, 1875). The harshness of the ruling in *Jacobs* was modified to a considerable extent in 1871, when the court upheld an award of damages with the observation

---

[14] In *Perry v. Ricketts*, 55 Ill. 234 (1870), a mine employee was entitled to recovery for injury suffered when a rope that had previously been spliced and patched failed, despite evidence that coworkers had warned the employee that he risked injury working in that mine.

that the standards of negligent supervision by parents should not be the same for those "who work for a living" as it was for "those who are able to hire servants to give constant attention and care" to children in their charge (*Chicago & Alton Railroad Co. v. Gregory*, 58 Ill. 226, 230, 1871). Similarly, as noted in the previous chapter, the rules governing liability for damage to stock were revised in 1867 in *Illinois Central Railroad Co. v. Middlesworth*, 43 Ill. 64 (1867).

All of these later cases demonstrate that the balance between competing claims of private right and public duty were not worked out at once, and indeed the process of adjustment continued unabated through the end of the nineteenth century and into the modern era. These revisions, however, were undertaken in terms of the vocabulary of American common law, which remains a permanent part of the legal landscape to this day. What is important about the cases from the 1850s is that they contained the first articulation of that vocabulary, and the model of public citizenship around which the rules of private litigation were designed.

Far from a model of "responsible individualism," what emerges in the shift from property rights to tort duties is a corporatist model. Individual citizens have become akin to chartered corporations, bound by duties to the public, at the same time that the "public" itself has come to have a corporate existence and interests of its own. The model of the citizen thus became that of a kind of shareholder, obliged to support the collective effort to enhance the value of the general "stock" in the industrialized society. Such a shareholder would be entitled to complain to the rule-makers in the corporation only so long as their own stock certificates were in good order, and entitled to recover damages only when the public goal of the corporation – not merely the private rights of the shareholder – had been imperiled by the actions of others.

In this model, railroad companies were "citizens" just as much as their passengers or employees. The difference was that railroad corporations had special jobs to do, and the duty of everyone else was to accommodate them in their work. This was the Duty to Get Out of the Way – out of the way of moving trains, out of the way of the organization of the railroad business, out of the way of the rumbling wheels of progress. These duties applied to everyone, everywhere, at every time. They defined not the great virtue that would drive national progress, but the minimum virtues that would be required to permit progress to occur. These were not the subjects of aspiration to be bred in political rhetoric, they were legal obligations that were imposed as threshold requirements for the protection of the law in public life.

5

The North

Ohio, Vermont, and New York

The system of common law rules that emerged in Illinois in the 1850s was part of a larger, regional pattern of northern legal development. The states of the antebellum North did not develop their laws in lock-step, to be sure. Each state's path of legal development was specific to its own conditions, its politics, and the actors who played key roles both on and off the bench. But despite these variations, there were core aspects to the development of new legal concepts in the 1850s that were reflected across the breadth of the northern states. Throughout the region, the traditional focus on competing individual property rights was replaced by a focus on collective duties, and the meaning of *salus populi* was transformed from a statement about the maintenance of an established set of practices to an embrace of technology-driven progress. The outcome, across the North as in Illinois, was that access to the courts was both liberalized and constrained: liberalized by the unification and simplification of legal doctrines, and constrained by the imposition of requirements that litigants demonstrate their compliance with politically desirable traits of citizens before they could be heard. The process of development that was observed in Illinois, too, was echoed in other northern states in the decade before the Civil War. Initially, legally conservative judges attempted to fit new situations into established common law doctrines, then eventually, through a process of trial and error, revision, and adaptation, the states' highest courts settled on versions of the new, American system of common law.

To see these consistencies, as well as some of the variations, between Illinois and other northern states, consider the development of common law doctrines in the 1850s in Ohio, Vermont, and New York. These states were chosen as examples of, respectively: a fellow state of the Old Northwest; a small New England state whose political economy and physical geography were almost entirely unlike those of Illinois; and one of the oldest, most established, and most developed states of the North.

Space does not permit the kind of close examination that the last three chapters undertook in the case of Illinois, but the extent to which Illinois exemplified a broader pattern of northern development in the 1850s can be seen in a review of three basic areas of doctrinal development: the rights and duties of landowners, reflected in stock cases; the general duties of care owed between strangers, seen most clearly in crossing cases; and the reconsideration of the legal duties owed under private contracts, exemplified in cases involving injuries to passengers and employees. In all three categories, these northern states demonstrate a pattern of working from traditional strict rules based on private property rights toward the articulation of broadly conceived tort and tortlike duties owed to the public at large and consonant with the quest for technology-driven progress. In all three states, the new rules were worked out almost entirely in the context of cases involving railroads. In addition, in all three of these states, as in Illinois, it is entirely inadequate to describe these principles simply in terms of a "subsidy" to industry. The outcomes of the cases, measured in that narrowly instrumental sense, are widely divergent. The very same principles of public duties that shielded railroads from liability in New York were employed to subject railroads to liability in Vermont and Ohio. What is consistent across the states is that the analytical vocabulary in terms of which adjudications were carried out came to converge around political models of citizenship articulated in legal doctrines, despite the variations in the particular outcomes that these doctrines were used to support.

Ohio

Ohio's Supreme Court approached its consideration of railroad cases in the 1850s from a tradition of Jacksonian populism. No one exemplified this tradition better than Justice Rufus Ranney, who in the state's 1851 constitutional convention stated his conception of the prerogatives of corporations this way: "If the exercise of corporate power promotes the public good, continue it: if it does not, take it away" (Jones, 1989: 249). Other Ohio justices shared Ranney's feelings. In an 1851 case, Justice Rufus P. Spalding argued, in a dissenting opinion, that counties should not be allowed to impose taxes to support rail development projects. "It need not be denied," he wrote, "that railroads are, in many instances, public improvements of great usefulness. But . . . it will not do to say that they are such a public use that private property may be taken, without the consent of the owner, to construct them" (*Griffith v. The Commissioners of Crawford County and the Ohio & Indiana R.R. Co.,* 20 Ohio 609, 622–3, 1851).

Early stock cases were analyzed entirely in terms of traditional property and contract principles, as in an 1854 case involving horses struck by a train that adjoined an unfenced pasture (*The Cincinnati, Hamilton & Dayton R.R. Co. v. Waterson,* 4 Ohio St. 424, 1854). Ranney began by observing that railroads had no special rights as landowners: "They hold them as other proprietors do, and if they see fit to leave them unfenced, they can no more treat the intrusion of domestic animals as a trespass, than other proprietors can." The railroad's lease required it to defray the costs of building fences, but required Waterson to undertake their construction. As a result, "he could not, over the breach of his contract, suffer his animals to go upon the road without being liable for their trespasses" (*Waterson,* 435).

Later that same year, however, the Ohio Supreme Court began to modernize its treatment of stock cases in *Kerwhaker v. The Cleveland, Columbus and Cincinnati R.R. Co.,* 3 Ohio 172 (1854). A group of hogs wandered from an unenclosed field onto the tracks and were killed. Justice Thomas W. Bartley noted that Ohio, like Illinois, rejected the English rule requiring the owners of stock to keep them fenced in or be liable for damages they caused, on the grounds that such a rule was "inapplicable to the circumstances and condition of the people of this State, [and] inconsistent with the habits, the interests, necessities and understanding of the people."[1] The difficulty lay in determining the applicability of traditional rules to railroad cases:

Railroad companies have become important and useful public agents, affording vast facilities for trade and travel, and producing extensive results upon the social condition, as well as the business of the country. . . . [T]he application of this injunction to railroad companies in their peculiar business, so widely differing from the ordinary pursuits of persons, must frequently become a matter of no inconsiderable difficulty (*Kerwhaker,* 176–7).

[1] Among the cases from other jurisdictions that Bartley cited were *Seeley v. Peters* from Illinois in support of his ruling, and *The Tonawanda R.R. Co. v. Munger* from New York (discussed later in this chapter) in opposition. The different rules suited the different environments. A rule requiring enclosure might be "suitable to an old and highly cultivated country . . . [but] it has no suitable and proper application in Ohio" (*Kerwhaker,* 179, 182).

Had the railroad chosen to fence its line, it might be able to sue the stock owner for trespass, but as neither party had acted to prevent the unfortunate meeting of hogs and locomotive, neither had a claim in property law (*Kerwhaker*, 185). The question, therefore, was purely one of negligence, and the determination of the proper standard of care. Bartley used the case to announce Ohio's adoption of a rule of contributory negligence, but subject to a raft of exceptions: owners of dangerous instrumentalities had special duties to keep them under control; the rule would not bar recovery where the exercise of ordinary care by a plaintiff would not have prevented the damage from occurring; a plaintiff who put his property in a position of danger might be precluded from recovering in cases of accident, but would retain the right to recover damages in cases of actual negligence; and the negligence of a plaintiff would preclude recovery only where it was a proximate, rather than remote, cause of the injury – the latter principle grounded in its application to unfenced rail lines by quotations from two Vermont cases, *Trow v. The Vermont Central Railroad Company* and *Quimby v. The Vermont Central Railroad Company* (both discussed later in this chapter). In the end, Bartley ruled that there was no negligence in either the railroad's or the farmer's failure to restrain the stock by a fence, so the only question was whether the train had been operated negligently, and the case was remanded on that basis (*Kerwhaker*, 198, 200).

The *Kerwhaker* rule was reaffirmed the next year in *The Cleveland, Columbus and Cincinnati R.R. Co. v. Elliott*, 4 Ohio 474 (1855), which also cited the two Vermont cases that had been cited in *Kerwhaker, Trow*, and *Quimby*. In *Elliott*, Justice Allen G. Thurman made causation the key to applying the principle of contributory negligence: "The remote negligence of the plaintiff will not prevent his recovering for an injury to his property, immediately caused by the negligence of the defendant. The negligence of the plaintiff that defeats a recovery, must be a proximate cause of the injury." The immediate negligence in case of a collision, he said, was that of the conductor of the train, whose "paramount duty ... is to watch over the safety of the persons and property in his charge; subject to which, it is his duty to use reasonable care to avoid unnecessary injury to animals straying upon the road" (*Elliott*, 477). This was a different version of Illinois' gross/slight rule, with the same tendency toward a comparative evaluation of the parties' performance of their duties, including a railroad's duties to passengers and the general public as well as toward farmers' wandering stock. This was also, obviously, a sharp departure from the traditional idea that a property owner owed no duties toward trespassers seen in *Waterson*, in favor of an idea that railroad operators owed duties to everyone, and everyone's property, that might happen to cross their path.

In 1859, the issue was revisited under different circumstances. In *The Bellefontaine & Indiana R.R. Co. v. Schruyhart*, 10 Ohio 116 (1859), a train ran into some cattle around twilight. The engineer testified that he might have been able to see the cattle in time to slow down, but that his vision had been impaired by the presence of a headlight at the front of the train. The question was whether a railroad should be found negligent in having a headlight on board, in light of testimony that such a light decreased the risk of collision with persons and other trains but increased the likelihood of collisions with animals because of its effects on the engineer's vision. The answer of the Ohio Supreme Court was that the railroad had duties that trumped its obligations to use its property so as to avoid harm to that of others. The railroad had an "unqualified right... to carry a head-light on its train at night, when necessary for the safety of the train and strangers":

> If it be shown that the carrying of a head-light, in the night season, be necessary or even conducive to the safety of the lives and property embarked upon the train, it is the right and duty of the company to see to it, that such light be then carried, however much it may increase the danger of cattle suffered to stray upon the road of the company (*Schruyhart*, 119, 120).

The reference to a duty of avoiding harm to strangers, as well as passengers, points to the multiple relationships that collided in the operation of a train. Railroads stood in the center of a web of relations through which connections were drawn to everybody and from everybody in a way impossible to articulate in terms of privity of contract or private duties.

The Ohio Supreme Court's consideration of crossing cases began in 1858, leading to further development of the principles of contributory negligence in *The Cleveland, Columbus & Cincinnati R.R. Co. v. Terry*, 8 Ohio St. 570 (1858). The basic rule, as Justice William V. Peck explained, was that each side was obliged to demonstrate "ordinary care." Lawyers for the railroad argued for a "clean hands" version of the rule, such that any negligence by the plaintiff would bar recovery: "So inflexible is this rule of law, and of such general application, that even children of such tender age as to be incapable of taking any care of themselves, and even lunatics, are said to be subject to its requirements." Justice Peck was not sure: "[T]he ordinary care required by the rule, has not only an absolute, but also a relative signification. It is to be such care as prudent persons are accustomed to exercise, under the peculiar circumstances of each case.... The circumstances, then, are to be regarded in determining whether ordinary care has been exercised" (*Terry*, 578).

The question was the degree to which the individual characteristics of the parties in the case were cognizable "circumstances." Terry, the plaintiff, was partially deaf and hence could not easily hear the signal of an oncoming train, but on the other hand she was aware of her infirmity and had further restricted her ability to see and hear by wearing a veil. "Would persons of ordinary prudence and capacity, partially deaf, but conscious of that infirmity, and with her head so muffled as to prevent her seeing with accuracy, attempt to cross the track at the time, and under the circumstances, when she made the attempt?" The answer was no, and hence Terry had breached her duty to behave prudently. But that argument only went as far as to apply to persons who could be called upon to conform with community norms. The railroad's absolute version of the rule would not apply:

In the case of a person of unsound mind, or of tender years, the recovery is allowed because, not being possessed of capacity and intelligence to properly apprehend the peril and adopt measures to avoid it, negligence cannot justly be imputed to them; while Mrs. Terry was of mature age, and, for aught that appears in the bill of exceptions, in the full possession of all her mental faculties.... The reason, then, which authorized the exception in the one case, does not arise in the other (*Terry*, 578).

There were no other important crossing cases in Ohio in the 1850s, but the contours of the principles of contributory negligence were complete; everyone would be required to show ordinary care, which would be defined as meeting generally understood standards for prudent conduct under the circumstances, and breach of that duty would relieve a defendant of liability except in extreme circumstances. The Ohio Supreme Court's most detailed exploration of the new principles of American common law occurred in the context of employment, specifically the fellow-servant rule. The treatment of the rule perfectly reflected the control of legal conservatives in the first half of the decade, the gradual accession of principles of universal duties to promote technological progress thereafter, and the ultimate displacement of the vocabulary of property-based private rights in favor of tortlike public duties.

The fellow-servant rule was initially rejected outright in 1851, in *The Little Miami R.R. Co. v. Stevens*, 20 Ohio 415 (1851). To suggest, said Justice William P. Caldwell, that an employee assumed the risk of a fellow employee's negligence was a perversion of contract principle: "So far as an implied contract, in reference to the business, will be presumed, it will be on the hypothesis that the business is to be properly managed. He can not be presumed to have contracted in reference to injuries inflicted on him by negligence – by wrongful acts." As for the argument from public policy, Caldwell was equally unimpressed: "It is a matter of universal observation, that in any extensive business, where many persons are employed, the care and prudence of the employer is the surest guaranty against mismanagement of any kind." If anything, said Caldwell, the fact of the employment relationship increased the liability of employers for injuries to their workers caused by other workers' negligence: "Indeed, we think that those who have others in their employ are under peculiar obligations to them to provide for their safety and comfort, and we think they should at least be held legally responsible to them as much as to a stranger" (*Stevens*, 423, 435).

Previously, Justice Spalding had dissented in *Griffith* on the grounds that the railroad was not so "public" an entity as to warrant its support through taxation. Now he dissented again, this time on the contrary basis that the courts should recognize the primacy of the public good in the operation of railroads: "The agents of railroad companies are intrusted with the care of the lives and property of individuals. Any principle which may encourage negligence endangering these, is fatal to all the great interests of society, and subversive of its order and well-being." The danger, he argued, was that workers would allow themselves to be injured in the hope of recovering damages, and in so doing place the general public in peril: "[A] bribe is held out to him to incur personal risks, which he may have facilities to render partially harmless to him, but which may carry destruction to a hundred homes, and make widows and orphans throughout the land, by a reckless waste of human life. '*Salus populi suprema lex*'" (*Stevens*, 447, 450–1).

Three years later, the fellow-servant rule was adopted, but with the caveat that it would be held not to apply where the negligent employee was the supervisor of the injured worker (a limitation that would have excluded the application of the rule in *Stevens*). The opinion was written by Ranney in *The Cleveland, Columbus & Cincinnati R.R. Co. v. Keary*, 3 Ohio St. 201 (1854). Ranney, the Old Jacksonian, began by observing the universal applicability of duties of care: "In the complicated relations of civilized society, no force can be employed, no business pursued, which is not likely to result in injury to others, unless it is controlled and directed by an intelligent will, conscientiously and carefully employed to prevent it."

As a result, the law would require that everyone who employed a "force" should "skillfully and carefully control it, and with a skill and care proportioned to the power of the person he thus employs." The measure of the duty of control, moreover, was to be found in the consequences of the actions taken: "The skill and care must be reasonable, and it is not reasonable when it does not furnish at least ordinary security against injury to others" (*Keary*, 206). The focus, in line with the traditional common law rule of *sic loedas*, was on the outcome rather than the conduct; an ordinary level of security was the test, not conformity to ordinary expectations for behavior. This was a way of thinking that was well on its way to being displaced by the idea of ordinary course of business, and the testimony of experts on the proper and customary operation of railroads.[2]

Ranney then launched into a twelve-page review of cases from England, Scotland, Massachusetts, and Illinois, before finally declaring the matter of the fellow-servant rule to be a question of contractual interpretation: "Our plain duty is to endeavor to ascertain the true nature of the relation between the parties, and the inherent elements of the contract on which it is founded, and from them deduce the principle that ought to govern." This was, again, the old language in which the contractual relations between the parties would determine their respective duties:

> It is the duty of the servants to obey the orders of the superior thus placed over them, and to perform as he shall direct. . . . But they cannot be made to bear losses arising from carelessness in conducting the train, over which their employer gave them no power or control until we are prepared to say that justice and public policy require the consequences of duty omitted by one party to be visited upon the other, although stripped of all power to prevent such consequences (*Keary*, 217–18).

Unless, in other words, the courts were willing to redefine the traditional contractual duties of private parties, the fellow-servant rule could not be applied in cases such as *Keary*.

Justice Robert B. Warden, concurring, would have gone even further and rejected the fellow-servant rule altogether. As a contractual matter, he said, the argument of assumption of risk was a myth. Furthermore, the supposed social advantages of the rule seemed to him equally unpersuasive, because it encouraged unvirtuous behavior: "In the instance of an equal, such watchfulness would be fruitless unless it were accompanied

---

[2] *The Bellefontaine & Indiana R.R. Co. v. Bailey*, 11 Ohio 333 (1860).

by tale-bearing; and what an equal would disdain to do, an inferior would not dare to attempt – while no officer in command would submit to such conduct in an inferior" (*Keary*, 225). There is considerable charm in the idea that an industrial employer would be unwilling to have in his employ workers who would "bear tales" against one another, and the analogy to a military company speaks volumes about the antiquated republicanism that motivated Warden's view of the world. Caldwell, Ranney, Peter Hitchcock, and Warden all assailed the fellow-servant rule on the grounds that, in their view, it did not comport with traditional understandings of what constituted a virtuous worker and a rights-bearing citizen. Spalding, in his dissent, challenged the Ohio Supreme Court to join with other common law courts in embracing the new principle and the conception of the universal duty to further a broadly defined public good on which it rested.

In 1856, Chief Justice Bartley distinguished the *Stevens/Keary* rule – that the fellow-servant doctrine would not apply to employees injured by the negligence of their superiors – from a case involving a train conductor injured due to a defect in a brake chain. The conductor not only was not injured by the negligence of a superior, he was injured by a defect of which it was his duty to be aware. As a result, he assumed the specific risk of a defective brake chain as an element of his employment. The company, therefore, could not be liable unless it had been guilty of breaching its duty of "reasonable and ordinary care and diligence":

And this neglect, in order to create a liability on the part of the company, must be the wrongful act of the company as distinguished from the neglect of a mere operative or agent of the company. For . . . it appears to be settled, both in England and in this country, that the company is not liable to an operative or agent in its employ, for injuries resulting from the carelessness of another operative or agent, when both are engaged in a common service, and no power or control is exercised by the one over the other (*The Mad River & Lake Erie R.R. Co. v. Barber*, 5 Ohio 541, 560–1, 1856).

Moreover, if an employee were aware of an unsafe condition and nonetheless continued in his employment, then he might be deemed to have waived his right to sue the company for injuries thereby sustained.

Keary and *Barber* thus defined an exception to the fellow-servant rule based on whether the justification of encouraging vigilance in employees made sense in the context of a particular case. In *Whaalan v. The Mad River and Lake Erie R.R. Co.*, 8 Ohio 249 (1858) and *Manville v. The Cleveland & Toledo R.R. Co.*, 11 Ohio St. 417 (1860), the meaning of the fellow-servant rule was entirely reconsidered. The question in each case was whether two employees, neither of whom was the supervisor of the other, counted as "fellow servants" if their work was entirely unrelated. Thus the question was not one of the negligence of a superior, but rather of the definition of "common employment." In *Whaalan*, a construction worker employed by the railroad was struck and injured by a piece of wood that was thrown or fell from a passing train. To be sure, both the workman and the negligent operators (or loaders) were mutually employed by a single railroad corporation, but did that make them fellow servants?

Applying the logic of *Keary* and *Barber*, the answer should have been no; just as a subordinate cannot exercise vigilance over his superior, so too a worker cannot exercise vigilance to ensure the adequacy of the performance of employees involved in unrelated activities. Such a rule, in fact, had been announced in Indiana.[3] Justice Jacob Brinkerhoff, however, turned to a New York case, *Coon v. Syracuse and Utica R.R. Co.* (discussed later in this chapter) for his inspiration, and concluded that "if we admit that there may be departments of duty in the business of a common employer, so distinct from each other as to require an exception to be made to the application of the general rule, still, we must hold, on the authority of well considered adjudications, that this is not a case to create such exception" (*Whaalan*, 256).

The ruling in *Whaalan* still left the door open for an exception to the fellow-servant rule to be worked out in some subsequent case. That door was slammed shut with finality in 1860. *Manville* involved a railroad employee who was injured when the train he was riding on to get to his work site was involved in a collision. Chief Justice William Sutliff explained that the phrase "common service" took on special meaning in the context of railroad corporations: "The employees of the company are necessarily numerous, and their respective duties diversified, and the departments in which the duties of the employees are discharged, in many instances disconnected." Sutliff therefore made a distinction between two sets of railroad employees: "[C]ertain of the employees, the contractors, financial agents, legal advisers . . . can not be considered as the servants of the company, in the sense implied by the rule referred to" (*Manville*, 424). Financial agents and lawyers, after all, could hardly be considered "fellow servants" of engineers and workers. But the explanation for the distinction was not the logic of *Keary*, which required asking the uncomfortable question of whether employees were actually in a position to exercise

---

[3] *Gillenwater v. Madison & Indianapolis Railroad Co.*, 5 Ind. 339 (1854), and *Fitzpatrick v. New Albany & Salem Railroad Co.*, 7 Ind. 436 (1856).

the mutual vigilance that the rule was supposed to encourage. By that logic, after all, even employees on a single train might not be fellow servants: "The respective duties of those assigned to different positions upon the train, will be found, to a great extent, necessarily independent of each other.... And yet the most limited application of the rule must necessarily embrace such cases." The new test for common employment, then, was not one that related to the policy or contract theories that had justified the formulation of the fellow-servant rule. Instead, the rule would be defined in terms of the *goals* of the employment: "[I]n this sense those employed in facilitating the running of the trains, by ballasting the track, removing obstructions, or keeping guard to prevent obstructions, and those employed at stations, attending to switches ... as well as those upon the trains, operating, may all be well regarded as fellow servants in the common service" (*Manville*, 425–6). In other words, a rule invented in the context of railroads was being given a concededly artificial construction lest it be revealed to be utterly inapplicable to railroads. Instead, the justifying principles that legitimated the rule were reformulated to fit the special claims that railroads made on public policy and the law.

Finally, like the Supreme Court of Illinois, during the years leading up to the Civil War, the Supreme Court of Ohio redefined the duties of railroads as common carriers of freight and baggage. These cases, however, were quite different in their outcomes from their Illinois counterparts. For one thing, the Ohio court was much more likely to protect shippers and passengers against the negligence of the railroad than to require them to conform to the railroad's standards. In an early case of this type, *The Mad River & Lake Erie R.R. Co. v. Fulton*, 20 Ohio 318 (1851), a passenger was permitted to testify as to the value of her lost baggage, over the objection of the railroad company. On appeal, Justice Caldwell dismissed the railroad's concerns of fraud out of hand:

> If the person be known in the community where the suit is brought, it will not be difficult to rebut any exorbitant claim that he might set up for the value of his wardrobe. The character of an individual's wardrobe is generally about as well known among his acquaintances as that of any other part of his property. And if the party should be a stranger, a great deal of evidence could, in most cases, be obtained, that would enable a sensible jury, from their knowledge of men and things, to detect any attempted extortion (*Fulton*, 326).

Eight years later, in a case involving the loss of cattle being transported to market, the court similarly ruled against the railroad defendant, but the reasoning of the opinion was markedly different from *Fulton's* emphasis on traditional community understandings and familiarity with local personalities. In *Welsh v. The Pittsburg, Fort Wayne, and Chicago R.R. Co.,* 10 Ohio 65 (1859), a shipper was told by a railroad agent that a train's cattle cars had two defective doors that could not be relied upon to remain closed, and nonetheless contracted to ship his cows. Sure enough, the doors failed, and twelve cows escaped the train en route. By straightforward contract reasoning, the shipper's explicit contractual assumption of risk might have been the end of the matter – "if the contract be valid, it is equally clear that the plaintiffs have no legal ground of complaint" – but Justice Josiah Scott was after a larger principle. Just as it had in Illinois, although with different results, the peculiar public role of the railroads would redefine the rules governing the liability of common carriers in Ohio:

In this state, at least, railroad companies are rapidly becoming almost the exclusive carriers both of passengers and goods. In consequence of the public character and agency which they have voluntarily assumed, the most important powers and privileges have been granted to them by the state.... [I]t is but reasonable that they should employ a degree of care and diligence, proportioned to the magnitude of the interests with which they are intrusted (*Welsh*, 75).

The fact that the shipper had been warned of the defect in the car doors was made irrelevant by the fact that the railroad was the only game in town, which called into question the "morality and public policy" of the contract itself: "The defendant could, under the circumstances, and therefore did, impose upon them such conditions of risk as were alike inconsistent with the previous understanding of the parties, and with the duty resulting from the public employment in which the defendant was engaged" (*Welsh*, 76–7). This very early statement of what would eventually become known as the doctrine of unconscionability in contracts demonstrates the force of the point, made here repeatedly, that the creation of universal duties owed to the public good was not a process that translated simply into support for one side or the other. Rather, as these Ohio cases demonstrate, what was at work was not only the creation of new bodies of legal rules but also the reworking of existing systems of traditional principles that cut across common law categories and ushered in the modern American system of common law. The same principles had resulted in different outcomes in Illinois, and would do so again when they were adopted by the Supreme Court of Vermont.

Vermont

As noted in the preceding section, the Ohio Supreme Court drew heavily on the law as it had developed in Vermont. In the Vermont Supreme Court, the dominant figure in the 1850s (and beyond) was unquestionably Isaac Redfield, later the author of such treatises as *The Law of Railroads*. Redfield, as his literary efforts implied, tended to see the law as it related to railroads as a discrete and separate category of common law doctrine. The principles that he and his colleagues announced in railroad cases in the 1850s, however, reached far beyond their original setting.

The key stock cases from Vermont, cited in Ohio opinions, were *Quimby v. Vermont Central R.R. Co.*, 23 Vt. 387 (1851) and *Trow v. The Vermont Central R.R.* 24 Vt. 487 (1852). The facts in *Quimby* were simple. A railroad had neglected to fence its track, horses had strayed onto the track, and a collision had occurred. Redfield noted that the common law rule in Vermont required landowners to fence their parcels. But he concluded that the railroad was not entitled to the benefit of this rule because under the terms of its charter, it was not the outright owner "in fee" of land that it acquired by condemnation. The question of whether the horses were trespassers therefore did not apply, while the issue of negligence on the part of their owner was irrelevant because under terms of the condemnation, the railroad was required to construct fences: "[U]ntil the company had either built the fence, or paid the land owner for doing it . . . we do not think, that the mere fact, that cattle get upon the road from the lots adjoining, is any ground of imputing negligence to the owners of the cattle" (*Quimby*, 393–4).

The decision in *Quimby* was thus grounded entirely in traditional categories of contract and property law. The Vermont Supreme Court began the move toward the eventual dissolution of those categories the following year in *Trow*. In *Trow*, a horse was hit at a crossing where there were no cattle guards. Animals were accustomed to wander in the area, and there was no evidence of negligence in the operation of the train. At trial there was a verdict for the owner of the horse. Since there was no claim of negligence in the operation of the train, the issue on appeal was the scope of the railroad's *Quimby* duty of maintaining fences.

Justice Pierpoint Isham observed that the strength of the railroad's duty depended on the circumstances:

In places thickly settled, and where animals for domestic use and purposes are necessary, much greater diligence and care is required of a Railroad corporation, in the construction of their fences and guards than would be required in places thinly settled or remote from individual habitations, as the danger of injuries from such causes is proportionably diminished. That would be considered gross negligence in the one place, which would not be so considered in the other.

In this particular case, there was little to choose between the parties. If the railroad had been negligent in failing to maintain adequate fences, "the plaintiff is chargeable at least with the same degree of neglect, in permitting his horse to run upon the highway." Nor was there any difference between the proximity of the causation that linked the two parties' negligence with the loss of the horse: "If either of the parties had done their duty, and conformed to the requirements of the law, the injury would not have been sustained. In such case, no action can be sustained by either of the parties . . ." (*Trow*, 494, 496). The case, then, stood for the proposition that in evaluating the conduct of property owners, the question was not simply one of who was a trespasser and who rightfully the occupier of the space where the incident occurred, but rather a proximate/remote causation comparison similar to the gross/slight rule seen earlier; the contributory negligence of a stock owner would prevent recovery unless the railroad's negligence had been significantly greater.

Two years later, in 1854, a new element came into play. *Thorpe v. The Rutland & Burlington R.R. Co.*, 27 Vt. 140 (1854) was the first case to apply Vermont's General Railroad Act of 1849, which required railroads to construct cattle guards at crossings. This pointed to one of the differences between Vermont and Illinois. In Vermont, tensions in the law were played out in significant part in terms of the relationship between statutory enactments and common law doctrines of private rights to a far greater extent than was the case in Illinois. The court in *Thorpe* began by citing the proposition that while a corporation's charter constituted a contract, so that a legislature could not defeat the purpose of that contract by subsequent enactment, the corporation remained subject to laws passed for the general welfare like any other private actor. When the court turned its attention to the fencing statute in particular, however, an interesting additional distinction arose. The railroad argued that the fencing statute created only private duties, that is, a right to sue that belonged exclusively to the owners of adjoining properties rather than a standard of care applicable in all claims arising out of the operation of the rail lines.

Redfield, responding to the railroad's argument, proposed an interpretation of the law that retrospectively altered the meaning of the older divisional fencing statutes as well as the law applicable to railroads:

> If it professes to regulate a matter of public concern, and is in its terms general, applying equally to all persons or property coming within its provisions, it makes no difference in regard to its character or validity, whether it will be likely to reach one case or ten thousand. Slaughter-houses, powder-mills, or houses for keeping powder, unhealthy manufactories, the keeping of wild animals, and even domestic animals, dangerous to persons or property, have always been regarded as under the control of the legislature.... I do not now perceive any just ground to question the right of the legislature to make railways liable for all cattle killed by their trains (*Thorpe*, 153–4).

Railroads were inherently public undertakings by virtue of the risks that they posed to the public, and therefore fell under the traditional principle of *salus populi*. That authority not only empowered legislatures to create statutes, but also empowered courts to turn those statutory rules into principles for the adjudication of private claims. This was a perfect example of the invocation of public duties in the context of private claims that blurred the distinction between public and private law. It made no difference that only the owners of adjoining properties were immediately at risk, nor that the common law of Vermont made it the duty of those landowners to maintain fences to control their stock. The railroads' public duties derived from the character of the enterprise, not from their relationship with the other party to a lawsuit.

The use of common law to impose public duties on railroads depended, however, on the peculiar nature of their business. Up to this point, in Vermont, there was not yet a statement of the idea that *everyone*'s conduct was a matter of "public concern." That principle arrived in 1858, in *Holden v. The Rutland & Burlington R.R. Co.*, 30 Vt. 297 (1858). In *Holden*, Justice Asa O. Aldis applied the proximate/remote causation, but gave it a new twist, turning the question into one of foreseeability:

> If the defendants, in the exercise of such care and judgment as a prudent owner of the horse would have used, ought to have foreseen, that the horse escaping might reasonably be expected to get into such pasture and so get injured, then they would be liable; but if the probability of an injury from such causes was so remote as not to be reasonably expected by any one in the exercise of such prudence, then they would not be liable (*Holden*, 304).

The case is unremarkable except for this last quoted sentence, but that formulation deserves consideration. The earliest versions of the formulation of the duties of property owners was a "clean hands" principle that said, simply, that if a person or a person's property was trespassing, then the owner of the property on which the trespass occurred owed no particular duties of care whatsoever. That became the strict contributory negligence rule, which continued the tradition that a plaintiff who had acted wrongfully was not entitled to recover regardless of the conduct of the defendant. The gross/slight and proximate/remote rules were modifications of the principle that pointed the way toward a comparison of the conduct of both parties, implying mutual duties to avoid causing harms unrelated to the prerogatives of property ownership. Now, in *Holden*, the Vermont Supreme Court had given that mutual duty a name in terms of a universally applicable standard of judgment. Everyone was required to foresee the reasonable risks of harm related to their conduct, and to act accordingly. This duty had nothing to do with particular relationships between the parties, nor rights and duties connected to the ownership of a particular piece of real property. Instead it was a general statement of a universal requirement of prudence that the courts would enforce.

When it came to cases involving injuries to persons, Vermont recognized a version of the rule of contributory negligence as early as 1849. In *Cassedy v. Town of Stockbridge*, 21 Vt. 391 (1849), the township was sued for injuries suffered by Cassedy when his wagon overturned. Cassedy claimed the reason for the accident was that the road was too narrow, but the defendants introduced evidence that Cassedy was intoxicated on the night of the event. The trial judge instructed the jury that if the plaintiff "was wanting in ordinary care and prudence, and that... this want of ordinary care had contributed in any, the slightest, degree, to produce the injury complained of, the plaintiff was not entitled to recover." This instruction was upheld, despite the defense's objections that the requirement that the plaintiff's want of care "had contributed... to produce the injury" was uncalled for. "There are different degrees of intoxication," wrote Justice Loyal C. Kellogg, "and people may differ widely in their views of what constitutes intoxication. Different individuals may be very differently affected by the use of the same quantity of intoxicating drink. Hence it became proper for the court to explain to the jury what degree, or amount, of intoxication was necessary to deprive the plaintiff of his remedy against the town" (*Cassedy*, 398–9).

The next year, in 1850, Vermont's Supreme Court began its consideration of the meaning of contributory negligence in earnest. *Robinson v. Cone*, 22 Vt. 213 (1850), was a case about a three-and-a-half-year-old boy who overshot the end of the hill on which he was sledding and ended up in the road. He was only three feet from the edge of the roadway, which was more than twenty feet wide. Nonetheless, a sleigh, being driven "with great force down the hill upon a smart trot," ran over the boy. His left leg had to be amputated, his right shoulder was dislocated, and he suffered "other injuries received." The instructions to the jury were complex; if the boy was not "in the exercise of ordinary care and prudence, at the time of the injury, and . . . the injury would not have happened, but for the want of such care and prudence on his part, it would be their duty to render their verdict for the defendant, whether he was in the use of such care and prudence, or not" (*Robinson*, 218).

This, despite *Cassedy*, was the basic "clean hands" version of contributory negligence. The obvious complicating factor was the age of the plaintiff. The jury was instructed that "in determining the amount of care and prudence to be required of the plaintiff, they need not measure it by the rule, that would be applicable to an adult, but might consider, that he was a child, about four years of age," so that the degree of care required was only that with which "a child of his age and capacity would be expected to act." The jury was also instructed that "if the boy were of so tender years, as to be absolutely incapable of observing and avoiding travellers, it might be gross negligence in the parents to permit him to be in the street – and in such case the defendant would not be liable, unless he were also guilty of gross negligence." In other words, like Mrs. Terry, in *The Cleveland, Columbus and Cincinnati RR. Co. v. Terry*, 8 Ohio 570 (1858), discussed earlier in this chapter, the child was not entitled to consideration based on his personal capacities, but also like Mrs. Terry, he was required to live up to the Duty to Get Out of the Way in the sense and to the degree appropriate to the standards for citizens of his *type*.

Justice Redfield began with the familiar citation to the English rule of *Butterfield v. Forrester*: "Two things must concur to support this action . . . fault of the defendant, and no want of ordinary care to avoid it, on the part of the plaintiff. This is substantially the formula, which, since that time, has been followed, in charging juries in road cases. . . . " That basic rule, however, was only the starting point. In addition, Redfield concluded, there were two critical principles at stake. First, concerning the possibility of negligence on the part of the parents, he observed that a defendant was obliged to exercise the care required based on assumptions about the capacities of the persons whom they encountered:

[A]lthough a child, or idiot, or lunatic, may, to some extent, have escaped into the highway through the fault or negligence of his keeper, and so be improperly there, yet if he is hurt by the negligence of the defendant, he is not precluded from his redress. If one knows, that such a person is in the highway, or on a railway, he is bound to a proportionate degree of watchfulness, and what would be but ordinary neglect, in regard to one whom the defendant supposed a person of full age and capacity, would be gross neglect as to a child, or one known to be incapable of escaping danger.

Second, the degree of care required of a plaintiff was that which the defendant could reasonably expect from a person of that type:

One might possibly injure a deaf or blind man, without fault, through ignorance of his infirmity, expecting him to conduct differently from what he did. But in the case of a child four years old, there could be no doubt, the defendant was bound to the utmost circumspection, and to see to it, that he did not allow his team to acquire such impetus, after he saw the child, that he could not check them, or avoid injury to the child (*Robinson*, 224–6).

The one case for which Redfield had particular disrespect was a New York case, *Hartfield v. Roper*, 21 N.Y. 619 (1839), whose application of a strict version of contributory negligence he described as "far less sound in its principles, and infinitely less satisfactory to the instinctive sense of reason and justice" than the rule he had just announced. This kind of dialogue between state courts was the basis for the emergence of a regional, and later a national, system of common law, and no one was more active in the process than Redfield. Vermont's Supreme Court did not revisit the general issue of contributory negligence in crossing cases again before the Civil War, but the basic elements of a modern rule were in place. The issue would turn on a comparative evaluation of the parties' negligence, and the standards of care in each case would be those expected of parties of that type, and each party would be entitled to act in accordance with what those standards implied they had a right to expect from the other.

Throughout the 1850s, the formulation of railroads' contractual duties forced the Vermont Supreme Court to wrestle with the problem of defining the kind of entity that railroad corporations represented. In 1850, the Court held that so long as a corporation was acting within its charter, any damages caused by its actions were subject to being ascertained by court-appointed referees under the state's condemnation statute. "Beyond that," wrote Redfield, "if they incur liabilities, either for torts, or by way of contract, they are liable like other persons" (*Vermont Central R.R. Co. v. Baxter*, 22 Vt. 365, 1850). Workers employed by a contractor doing work for the railroad had entered onto the plaintiff's property and engaged in blasting and hauling stone for construction of the rail line. The issue was whether the actions of the contractor's employees bound the railroad company. By traditional principles of agency, the answer would be no, but that was not sufficient for the case at hand: "The power conferred upon railroad corporations, to take the land and other materials adjoining the line of the road for the purpose of constructing the road, is one in derogation of the ordinary rights of land owners, and one which could only be conferred by the legislature.... [W]hether the corporation construct their road themselves, or by contract with others, is unimportant" (*Baxter*, 371–2). The exceptional liability of a railroad for acts of its agents, contrary to traditional principles of agency, was also at issue in a case upholding a statute entitling the employees of railroad corporations' subcontractors to proceed directly against the railroad for their wages in the event of nonpayment against a challenge under the state constitution's Takings Clause (*Branin v. The Connecticut & Passumpsic Rivers R.R Co.*, 31 Vt. 214, 1858). The public powers granted to a railroad corporation, then, altered its relationships to contractors and the balance of common law rights and obligations between itself and others.

In 1856, the Vermont Supreme Court considered the case of an engineer injured when a defective firebox exploded. The court used the case to express its conception of the fellow-servant rule, and then to extend both that rule and its exceptions to the question of the duties owed between master and servant generally. In brief, the Vermont rule was that an employer was liable for using defective materials just as he would be liable for employing unsuitable fellow employees:

[W]hatever may be the agent which the master brings into his service, whether animate or inanimate, the master is bound to exercise care and prudence that those in his employment be not exposed to unreasonable risks and dangers.... It is only such injuries as have arisen after the exercise of that diligence and care on the part of the master, that can properly be termed accidents or casualties, which the servant has impliedly agreed to risk, and for which the master is not liable (*Noyes v. Smith*, 28 Vt. 59, 64, 1856).

The employer had been found to be negligent in that its agent, the conductor and master mechanic at the rail yard, had failed to inspect the train adequately. Although these fellow servants were not themselves unsuitable, the consequence of their negligence was to render the equipment unsuitable; the intervention of the machine rendered the fellow-servant rule inapplicable.

New York: Learned Hand

New York's treatment of stock cases was in some ways similar to that of Vermont. Both states began with the English common law rule that required landowners to maintain fences, rather than allowing their stock to run free. In New York, as in Vermont, the cases involved the interpretation of statutes as well as the application of common law doctrines. And when those statutes got into the hands of New York's Court of Appeals, its members immediately turned to the very same modernizing principles that were seen driving the course of legal development in other northern states. As for the outcomes of the cases, in sharp contrast to Vermont and Ohio, but similar to Illinois, in New York the application of new legal principles heavily favored the railroads.

The first New York case to tackle the conflicts between the traditional rights of property owners and the railroads was *The Tonawanda R.R. Co. v. Munger*, 5 N.Y. 255 (1848) (mentioned earlier in the Ohio Supreme Court's discussion of *Kerwhaker*). The case arose when cattle broke through the fence around a pasture, wandered from there onto an adjoining roadway, and from the roadway entered onto railroad tracks, where they were struck and killed. Unlike Illinois or Ohio, New York did not have a tradition of permitting stock to wander freely. Instead, Justice Samuel Beardsley held to the old English enclosure rule:

It is a general rule of the common law that the owner of cattle is bound, at his peril, to keep them off the land of other persons, and he can not justify or excuse such an entry by showing that the land was unfenced. Fences were designed to keep one's own cattle at home, and not to guard against the intrusion of those belonging to other people (*Munger*, 259).

Then there were the various fencing statutes. New York had a statute that required owners of property to keep fences between their land and adjoining properties, but that rule did not apply to the case because Munger's property adjoined a highway. There was also a catch-all state statute that provided that towns could establish rules for fencing requirements, and that "any person who shall thereafter neglect to keep a fence according to such rule or regulation, shall be precluded from recovering compensation in any manner, for damages done by any beast, lawfully going at large on the highways, that may enter on any lands of such person." The Town of Gates, where the collision took place, had a statute dating back to 1838 that required fences around all property, and said further that cattle "might run at large" (*Munger*, 261). Acting under authorization of the state statute, the Town of Gates had thus put in place something very close to the common law system familiar from Illinois, possibly reflecting the division that persists to this day between the interests of rural upstate New York and the more populous downstate counties.

At this point, a straightforward application of the laws might have led to the conclusion that Munger's cattle were at large as they had a right to be, and that the railroad had violated its statutory duty of maintaining a fence. The complaint was not that the cattle had caused damage to the railroad's fields, after all, it was that the cattle had themselves been killed. If the law did not require Munger to keep his cattle fenced in, then he had not contributed by his negligence to their deaths; however, the railroad's failure to fence established its own negligence, and thus presumably the railroad was liable under a theory of trespass against Munger's property. But this was not the analysis.

To begin with, the New York Court of Appeals held that the town's statutory fencing requirements could not possibly apply to railroads: "It would be absurd to require fences to be made at such places, and the mere general terms of a town regulation should receive a more rational interpretation." More important, the authorizing state statute was itself inapplicable to the case of a railroad, because a contrary reading would prevent the satisfaction of New York's Need for Speed: "It is not too much to say that this would be wholly impracticable without entirely defeating the great object, accelerated speed, for which railroads are allowed to be constructed." The statutes, therefore, did "nothing to change the rule of the common law" (*Munger*, 263). Since the town's fencing and at-large rules did not apply to railroads, Munger was bound by his common law duty to maintain fences to keep his cattle in, and the railroad was not bound to maintain fences or cattle guards to keep Munger's cattle out. Therefore, the cattle were trespassers, and the railroad owed them no duty of care.

But Justice Beardsley did not stop there. Instead, he took the opportunity to explore the principle of contributory negligence. Beardsley began with the property rule: "[a] man is under no obligation to be cautious and circumspect towards a wrongdoer." The application of the rule of contributory negligence was thus bound up in the property law doctrines of trespass, an indication of the unformed state of the law of negligence: "It would be a new feature in the law of trespass, if the owner of cattle could escape responsibility for their trespasses by showing he had used 'ordinary,' or even extraordinary 'care and prudence' to keep them from doing mischief." The cattle, finally, were trespassers because railroad tracks remained private property: "Railroads, although designed to subserve the public interest and convenience, are still not highways, but in strictness mere private property, and no town has any right to authorize cattle to enter on them." The judge invited the state legislature to enact appropriate statutes – "I am strongly inclined to the opinion that further legislation would be proper to guard against the entry of cattle on land used for the tracks of railways" – but in the meantime, the common law principles of trespass would permit no recovery (*Munger*, 266–7, 268).

In two important ways, *Munger* is similar to the early Illinois cases. First, the language of the analysis is traditional, property rights–based common law, defined in writs (here, "trespass"). In New York in 1848, there was no independent body of general negligence principles to be balanced and evaluated, only the ancient rule that a property owner owed no duty of care to a trespasser. At the same time, we can see the beginning of new ways of thinking prompted by the differences between railroads and other forms of property, in the reference to the public's "great object, accelerated speed." New York, like Illinois, had a Need for Speed.

The New York Court of Appeals advanced its analysis of stock/fencing cases into a full-fledged articulation of modern American common law principles in *Corwin v. The New-York and Erie Railroad Company*, 13 N.Y. 42 (1855). The case turned on the effect of an 1848 law that required railroad corporations to "erect and maintain fences on the sides of their road . . . and also construct and maintain cattle guards at all road crossings," and provided that in the absence of fences and cattle guards, "the corporation . . . shall be liable for all damages which shall be done by their agents or engines, to cattle, horses or other animals thereon" (*Corwin*, 46). The outcome of the case could have been determined merely by referring to the specific terms of the statute, but Justice Richard P. Marvin took the opportunity to explain that the new law was based on the inadequacy of the older common law principles:

[A] new state of things has arisen: a power, but recently discovered and applied to the uses of man, has been appropriated as a motive power to the moving of large and heavy bodies at a velocity before unknown, acquiring a momentum and speed endangering the lives of all animals coming in contact with the moving mass, whether locomotive or cars, and at the same time putting in jeopardy the lives and limbs of all those who are connected with the train (*Corwin*, 47).

The railroad did to New York common law the same thing that it had done to Illinois common law: it disrupted the system of determining relative duties of care based on the relationships of the parties by binding a whole set of disparate parties into a web of interrelated dangers and interests.

The new statute was also quite different from the old fencing statute. The old law had merely determined duties between private parties; the new law declared a duty owed to the public at large. The key was the railroads' duty to passengers: "The danger to passengers . . . is great and imminent whenever the locomotive or cars in their rapid movement come in collision with any substance disturbing the regularity of the motion or speed acquired." But the railroads also had duties to stock owners, and to the public at large: "The general duty of erecting and maintaining fences on the sides of their roads is now imposed upon the railroad corporations; this duty is to be performed for the public benefit and security and also for the benefit of the owners of cattle generally." Hiram Denio wrote separately to emphasize the point: "I am of opinion that the statute imposes a public duty upon the railroad corporations, for a violation of which they are subject to indictment, whether individual interests are affected or not" (*Corwin*, 47–8, 53–4).

The specific outcome is different from that most often seen in Illinois, in that the railroad rather than the farmer is the party upon whom the public duty falls most heavily at this stage of development. The vocabulary is that of universal public duties, but in *Corwin* those duties have not been extended beyond the corporations to reach the construction of a universal model of legal citizenship. That extension would come with the discovery that the statutory requirement gave way to the rule of contributory negligence, which occurred in 1857 in *Poler v. The New-York Central R.R. Company*, 16 N.Y. 476 (1857). Poler, the owner of some cattle, discovered that the gate erected by the railroad to secure his field was defective. He propped the gate closed with a pole, which was blown over by the wind, permitting his cows to wander onto the track where they were killed. In such a case, ruled Justice Samuel L. Selden, there could be no recovery, because Poler had breached a duty to the railroad that was an implicit complement to the railroad's statutory duty to the public:

There is no doubt that although the statute imposes upon the railroad company the absolute duty of maintaining fences, gates, &c., yet a duty in this respect also devolves upon the proprietors along the road. They have no right quietly to fold their arms and voluntarily to permit their cattle to stray upon the railroad track, through the known insufficiency of the fences which the corporation are bound to maintain (*Poler*, 481).

As elsewhere, crossing cases provided the context for the New York Court of Appeals' further development of the principles of contributory negligence. The basic rule announced in *Hartfield* as early as 1839 was spelled out in *Brown v. Maxwell*, 6 N.Y. 592 (1844). *Brown* merely announced the existence of the "clean hands" version of the rule, however, and did not attempt to make the rule a basis for a reconsideration of the system of common law duties. The development of a more sophisticated rule of contributory negligence began, inevitably, in cases involving railroads. In *O'Mara v. The Hudson River Railroad Company*, 38 N.Y. 445 (1858), the principle that contributory negligence would bar recovery to an infant or lunatic was abandoned. The case involved an eleven-year-old boy struck by a train while crossing a street. Chief Justice Ward Hunt ruled that the question of contributory negligence had to be left to a jury to be decided on its facts, and that, moreover, the duty of the railroad varied with the character of its potential victims:

The old, the lame and the infirm are entitled to the use of the streets, and more care must be exercised toward them by engineers than toward those who have better powers of motion. The young are entitled to the same rights, and cannot be required to exercise as great foresight and vigilance as those of maturer years. More care toward them is required than toward others. In the case of a child but two or three years of age, no knowledge or foresight could be expected. This an engineer is bound to know, and if the child is within his view, to act accordingly. In a case like the present, that of a boy eleven and a half years of age, the jury were not bound to require the same demureness and caution as in the case of an older person (*O'Mara*, 449).

The rule remained in place, but now it had taken on the air of a comparative evaluation of the parties' negligence rather than a "clean hands" rule, just as it did in Illinois.

The further development of negligence doctrines in New York in the 1850s was carried by railroad cases involving contractual obligations, beginning with *Holbrook v. The Utica and Schenectady Railroad Company*, 12 N.Y. 236 (1855). The train on which Mrs. Holbrook (the suit was filed by her husband) was traveling passed so close to another that she was struck and suffered a severe injury to her elbow, which was resting on the window sill and thus protruding out of the passenger car. The railroad argued that its contractual obligation was only to carry Mrs. Holbrook safely *within* the car, and that if her elbow had been protruding beyond the sill of the window, then that constituted contributory negligence in the strict form that we have seen in trespass cases. Instead, the court concluded that Mrs. Holbrook should be barred from recovery only if her conduct constituted "negligence or want of ordinary care... [that] contributed in any degree to the result" (*Holbrook*, 244). The inclusion of a causation requirement took the rule out of the "clean hands"/trespasser category and into the modern idea of negligence contributing to the harm suffered.

Throughout the decade, the New York Court of Appeals continued to elaborate on the idea that railroad corporations owed generalized duties to the public at large, rather than simply private duties of the kind recognizable under ancient common law principles. Thus a verdict against a railroad for injuries suffered by an employee whose ticket had been procured by his employer (thus precluding any direct privity of contract between passenger and railroad) was upheld on the grounds that railroads' duties to their passengers did not rest on contract doctrines but on more abstract duties to the common weal, as Justice Selden explained:

The duty arises in such cases, I apprehend, entirely independent of any contract, either expressed or implied. The principle upon which a party is held responsible for its violation does not differ very essentially, in its nature, from that which imposes a liability upon the owner of a dangerous animal... in these cases, the duty is to the public, while in the present case, if it exists at all, it is to the individual; but the basis of the liability is the same in both cases" (*Nolton v. The Western Railroad Corporation*, 15 N.Y. 444, 448–9, 1857).

A similar fact pattern resulted in an even more potent formulation of the railroads' duties to the public in *Smith v. The New York and Harlem Railroad Company*, 19 N.Y. 127 (1859). That case, too, involved an employee traveling on a ticket obtained by his employer. In *Smith*, the employee was injured when the train ran off the tracks due to a defective switch. In upholding a verdict against the railroad and in favor of Smith, Justice Martin Grover upheld a jury instruction to the effect that the railroad could be found liable for failing to incorporate the latest improvements in its equipment. "The safety of the public will be promoted by adopting such a rule," declared Grover. "Such liability tends to promote caution in these transactions of such vast importance to the public. A contrary rule will induce carelessness and negligence. There was no error in that portion of the charge relating to the duty of the defendant to adopt new improvements, by which the danger of accidents would be materially diminished." Justice Selden wrote a separate concurrence to emphasize his agreement as to the central point of the decision: "A stronger case for the application of the rule than is here presented could scarcely arise. The improvement related to a part of the apparatus of the road which is the source of numerous accidents. Its utility was undoubted and the expense trifling" (*Smith*, 130–1, 133–4).

The emphasis on the traditional idea of the public duties of corporations, translated into new forms, makes sense given the differences between New York and Illinois. New York was already heavily settled, with well-established economic and political interests, by the time large-scale railroad construction got under way. Thus it is not surprising that there was less of the sense of a state whose future rode on its railways than in Illinois. This difference, however, did not prevent railroad cases from pointing in the direction of uniform, universal standards applicable to persons as well as to corporations. At the same time that the New York Court of Appeals was defining a new set of public duties applicable to railroads, it was also extending this novel concept of duty to individuals, and working out the parameters of those duties by trial and error. The continuing development of the rules of contributory negligence after *Corwin* and the adoption and modification of the fellow-servant rule are key illustrations.

Like the rule of contributory negligence, the fellow-servant rule was initially adopted in New York as a strict bar to recovery. The rule had been mentioned in 1844 in *Brown v. Maxwell* (discussed previously), but it was formally announced and adopted in New York in *Coon v. The Syracuse and Utica R.R. Co.*, 5 N.Y. 492 (1851). Coon was employed to ride along the track in a handcar and look for defects such as breaks in the line or "snake-heads." On this occasion, he was run over by a train running without lights, off its schedule, and without any notice to Coon that such an extra train was to be expected. On these grounds, a finding of negligence against the railroad would have been an easy call. Instead, Justice Samuel A. Foote cited three cases, from England, Massachusetts, and South Carolina. "They all concur," wrote Foote, "in sanctioning the principle, and I fully acquiesce in their judgment.... It must now be considered as settled, and hereafter to form a part of the common law of the country" (*Coon*, 496).

This was lawmaking in the style that would be seen in the postbellum South, the outright importation of complete doctrines from other jurisdictions (see the discussion in Chapters 8 and 9), but it was not to last long in New York. The New York Court of Appeals revisited the issue in *Keegan v. The Western Railroad Corporation*, 8 N.Y. 175 (1853). A railroad employee was injured when a defective boiler exploded. The testimony showed that the defect in the boiler had been brought to the attention of the railroad, which had failed to remedy the defect. The fellow-servant rule, said Chief Justice Charles Ruggles, did not apply in such a case: "They are applicable only where the injury complained of happened without any actual fault or misconduct of the principle.... Whenever the injury results from the actual negligence or misfeasance of the principal, he is liable as well in the case of one of his servants as in any other." On the other hand, the rule remained in place where the negligence in question was one of a fellow agent of the principal. In such a case, "the fault will not be imputed to the principal . . . as it will where the injury falls on a third person, as for instance on a passenger on a rail road. In the case of a passenger the actual fault of the agent is imputed to the principal on grounds of public policy; in the case of a servant it is not" (*Keegan*, 180–1). In a neat reversal of the usual reasoning, the fellow-servant rule was presented not as an exception to *respondat superior* (the vicarious liability of employers for the acts of employees) justified by concerns of public policy, but rather as a background principle that remained in force because the public policy required to justify the doctrine of *respondat superior* was found inapplicable to the case. The rule remained the same, but the starting point for analyses had moved from a statement about private rights to an invocation of public duties.

New York's freight cases, too, reflected the sense that railroads had broken the common law mold. In *Clarke v. The Rochester and Syracuse Railroad Company*, 14 N.Y. 570 (1856), the Court of Appeals relaxed the old rule of strict liability for common carriers where the goods to be transported were animals – in this case, horses:

A bale of goods or other inanimate chattel may be so stowed as that absolute safety may be attained. . . . But the carrier of animals, by a mode of conveyance opposed to their habits and instincts, has no such means of securing absolute safety. They may die of fright, or by refusing to eat, or they may, notwithstanding every precaution, destroy themselves in attempting to break away from the fastenings . . . or they may kill each other.

Demonstrating that the boundary between North and South was not a formal, impermeable bar to communication, Justice Denio drew on a U.S. Supreme Court case authored by John Marshall and analogized horses to slaves. Marshall had explained that a common carrier engaged in the transport of slaves "was not an insurer of their safety, but was liable only for ordinary neglect; and this was put mainly upon the ground that he could not have the same absolute control over them that he has over inanimate matter." By extension, the same rule would apply to horses. On the other hand, where "the cause of the damage for which recompense is sought is unconnected with the conduct or propensities of the animal undertaken to be carried," as in the case of a collision or derailment, then traditional liability rules would remain in force (*Clarke*, 573–4).

The analogy to slaves demonstrated Denio's recognition that, in the South, slaves constituted an intermediate category between person and object. The difference, of course, was that extending that intermediate status to horses did nothing to preclude the articulation of universal standards of care. The role of railroads as common carriers was further considered in two cases involving delays in transportation, *Wilbert v. The New-York and Erie Railroad Company*, 12 N.Y. 245 (1855), and *Weed v. The Panama Railroad Company*, 17 N.Y. 362 (1858). The outcomes of the two cases were different, calling attention to the issues of public interest that motivated the Court of Appeal's different analyses of the two situations. In *Wilbert*, the plaintiff's complaint was that the rail line had delayed getting perishable goods to market due to an "an unusual demand for transportation at that time," with consequent losses to the shipper. Chief Justice Denio declined to impose the strict liability of common carriers in such a situation: "If, under such circumstances, a railroad company would be liable on account of a tardy delivery, the business would be quite too hazardous to be followed by prudent men." A dissenting opinion was written by a noted judicial conservative, New York Justice Learned Hand. Hand objected to the abandonment of the traditional common law rules in the name of enticing "prudent men" to enter the railroad business: "No one will contend that a railroad company would be justified in leaving a passenger midway on his journey because they had not sufficient cars; and the same principle applies to freight, though the absurdity of the proposition is not so striking" (*Wilbert*, 249–50, 252–3).

Hand's hypothetical case became concrete three years later, in *Weed*. On a trip across western New York state, four hundred passengers were left stranded overnight in a train that stopped at a crossing where there was no lodging, on a stormy night. The case was tried as a claim for breach of contract, in which the railroad company was liable for the actions of the conductor, who ordered the train stopped under the principle of *respondat superior*. The railroad argued that it should not be liable for a willful act by its agent because such an act was outside the scope of his proper employment. The Court of Appeals reviewed a number of cases in which a servant or employee willfully damaged the property of another, but found the present situation to pose a different set of concerns by virtue of the contractual relationship between passenger and rail line as common carrier: "In the present case, by means of the wrongful, willful detention by the conductor, the obligation assumed by the defendants to carry the wife with proper speed to her destination . . . was broken. . . . The obligation to be performed was that of the master, and delay in performance, from intentional violation of duty by an agent, is the negligence of the master" (*Weed*, 368–9).

New York, then, did not go as far as Illinois in redefining the contractual obligations of common carriers, drawing a limit at the point where harm to passengers, rather than a loss of property, occurred as the result of intentional conduct. This is a distinction in the point at which the outer limit of the new system of common law duties was drawn, however, not a basic difference between the systems of common law that the two states adopted. In New York as in Illinois, by the end of the 1850s, traditional writ pleadings and rules that defined duties in terms of privity or the parties' respective property rights had given way to new, broadly defined categories of public obligation worked out in the adjudication of cases involving railroads.

Conclusion

This review of cases from Ohio, New York, and Vermont demonstrates variations in the particular rules adopted among northern states. At the same time, however, all three of these northern states were consistent with Illinois in the 1850s in three crucial ways: they reconfigured their system of common law rules to further the progress of trains and the new forms of business that ran them; they adopted an expansive and abstract conception of *salus populi* defined in terms of a common duty to further technological progress; and they unified the different areas of their law around central legitimating conceptions of duties, owed by everyone to the public at large, that defined the virtues required of all citizens.

In the next chapters, we will turn our attention to Virginia and then to other southern states, where we will see that in the decade before the Civil War, the premises that underlay the emerging system of American common law were incommensurate with the political culture of those states' dominant, conservative elites. As a result, unsurprisingly, we will see that the pattern of antebellum southern legal development was entirely different from that in the North.

6

Virginia through the 1850s

The Last Days of Planter Rule

When compared to the experience of Illinois, the story of antebellum Virginia law is the story of what did *not* happen, and why. At the point of intersection between law and politics, the conflictual relationship between the different parts of the state translated into the complete rejection of the emerging system of American common law. As before, the explanation lies in the interaction of ideology, interests, and institutions. In its political philosophy, Virginia's elite adamantly rejected the appeal to an expanded and abstract concept of *salus populi* and the ideal of standardization; in its political economy, Virginia was dominated by an established set of interests opposed to the transformative power of railroad expansion, independent capital markets, and the growth of interstate trade; and in its courts, where Illinois' highest judges had imposed change on a professional core of lawyers frequently slow to catch on, the justices of Virginia's Supreme Court[1] made it their role to resist pressures from below to modernize the state's legal doctrines.

There were significant similarities between Illinois and Virginia in the 1850s. Both states, for example, could be divided into three sections, and in both cases those geographical divisions defined the lines of political conflict. Rather than being divided north to south, however, Virginia was divided east to west, between the western Trans-Allegheny (itself separable into the northwest and southwest regions on the basis of patterns in settlement and economic activity), the central Shenandoah Valley region,

---

[1] At different times, Virginia's highest court was variously referred to as the Virginia Court of Appeals, the Virginia Supreme Court of Appeals, or the Virginia Supreme Court. For convenience, "Virginia Supreme Court" is used throughout this and upcoming chapters.

and the eastern region comprising the Tidewater and Piedmont.[2] These regions were separated by natural obstacles, the Blue Ridge and Allegheny Mountain ranges. East of the Blue Ridge Mountains, the Tidewater and Piedmont comprised lowland plains and rolling upland hills. Between the two mountain ranges was the Valley, a mixed terrain containing both fertile bottom land and rocky, mountainous areas. The western Trans-Allegheny region consisted of narrow valleys separated by spurs jutting out from the Allegheny Mountains. Despite its difficult terrain, the western region contained much fertile land and extremely rich deposits of minerals including coal, iron, and salt (Freehling, 1982: 12–14).

Politically, from the early 1800s through the Civil War, Virginia was fundamentally bifurcated into east and west, as the central region tended to split down its middle over the most important political decisions (Shade, 1996: 119–20). As in Illinois, these divisions were directly connected to competing ideologies centered around the meaning of citizenship and the political function of law. What separates Virginia from Illinois, in these terms, was that in Virginia there never was the kind of shift in power to new geographical centers and new ideological forces that took place in Illinois. At its heart, the politics of antebellum Virginia was a story of the continuing domination of the state's governing institutions by conservative eastern interests, a situation that made Virginia's appellate court almost impervious to the forces of change.

Virginia: East and West

Virginia in the years following the Revolution had been marked by the prominence of its lawyers. Writing in 1813, St. George Tucker, himself one of the most eminent legal writers and educators in early America, described the eminence of the Virginia bar in eloquent terms: "Socrates himself would pass unnoticed and forgotten in Virginia, if he were not a public character, and some of his speeches preserved in a newspaper: the latter might keep his memory alive for a year or two but not much longer"[3] (Warren, 1966: 49). Eighty years later, Henry Adams, writing in his *History of the United States*, would look back on the same era and observe that "[l]aw and politics were the only objects of Virginia thought, but within

---

[2] The 1782 Equalization Act had divided the state into four regions for purposes of determining property tax rates: Trans-Allegheny, Valley, Piedmont, and Tidewater.
[3] Among other accomplishments, Tucker produced the first American edition of William Blackstone's *Commentaries* and served on Virginia's highest court from 1804 to 1811. His son, Henry St. George Tucker, served on the same court from 1831 to 1841.

these bounds the Virginians achieved triumphs" (Dabney, 1971: 135). The first American university professorship in law was established by Thomas Jefferson at the College of William and Mary. Jefferson appointed his own teacher, George Wythe, to the position, making Wythe the second university professor of common law in the world after William Blackstone at Oxford.

Economically, Virginia in the late 1700s was entirely dominated by tobacco planters, as John Randolph explained during the debates over taxation during the 1829 Constitutional Convention: "Virginia was then not only throughout, a slave-holding, but a tobacco-planting Commonwealth.... [T]obacco was, in fact, the currency, as well as staple of the State. We paid our clerks' fees in tobacco: verdicts were given in tobacco: and bonds were executed payable in tobacco" (Shepherd, 1830: 315). The population of the state was concentrated in the east. In 1790, 72 percent of the white population of 442,000 resided in the Tidewater and Piedmont, another 20 percent resided in the central Valley region, and less than 8 percent lived in the Trans-Allegheny (Freehling, 1982: 285).

The population of Virginia did not undergo anything like the transformation that was experienced in newly settled Illinois in the antebellum period. In the 1820s, a pattern of dramatic growth in counties west of the Alleghenys – the counties that would later become the State of West Virginia – contrasted with static or declining populations in the east. From 1820 to 1830, the population of the western counties grew 36 percent while the east grew by approximately 2 percent (Bruce, 1982: 2). Thereafter, the populations of both regions stabilized. In 1830, a little more than half the white population of the state (54 percent) lived in the Tidewater and Piedmont, a fifth (20 percent) in the Valley, and a little more than a quarter (26 percent) in the Trans-Allegheny west. In 1830, according to U.S. Census figures, the white population of the state was distributed as shown in Table 6.1.

TABLE 6.1. *Distribution of Virginia White Population by Region, 1830*

Total state population	694,302
Tidewater and Piedmont	375,657 (54.1%)
Valley	134,791 (19.4%)
Trans-Allegheny	183,854 (26.5%)

Source: Freehling, 1982: 286.

TABLE 6.2. *Distribution of Virginia White Population by Region*

	1850	1860
Total state population	849,800	1,047,411
Tidewater and Piedmont	401,259 (44.8%)	447,248 (42.7%)
Valley	162,550 (18.2%)	172,960 (16.5%)
Trans-Allegheny	330,991 (37.0%)	427,203 (40.8%)

Source: U.S. Census figures, at Freehling, 1982: 286.

TABLE 6.3. *Slaves as Proportion of Total Population, by Region*

	1850	1860
Tidewater	44.5%	41.9%
Piedmont	50.5%	50.2%
Valley	18.8%	17.1%
Trans-Allegheny	6.8%	5.7%

Source: U.S. Census figures, at Freehling, 1982: 287.

From 1840 to 1850, the total regional populations were almost perfectly static. The eastern population declined from 1,055,083 to 1,054,358, while the western population declined from 314,484 to 313,500 (Shade, 1996: 22). From then on, the only significant change was the continuing growth of the populations in the western counties. Overall, from 1820 to 1850 the state's population went from approximately 1 million to 1.3 million, with a relatively consistent ratio of whites to blacks (ranging from 57:40 in 1820 to 63:33 in 1850) and a small population of free blacks (ranging from 3.5 to 4 percent of the state's population). Table 6.2 shows the regional distribution of Virginia's white population from 1850 to 1860.

Comparing the distribution of slave and white populations between eastern and western regions paints a picture of startling difference. There were 469,755 slaves in Virginia in 1830, of whom 88.6 percent were in the Tidewater and Piedmont regions. That number increased slightly to 475,528 in 1850, of whom 86.6 percent were in eastern counties; in 1860, the figure was 490,865, of whom 87.2 percent were in the east. To see the effects of this distribution, consider the figures in Table 6.3, reflecting the proportion of the population that was made up of slaves in each of the different regions in the years following 1850.

Detailed figures are even more revealing. In 1850, seventeen out of thirty-eight counties in the Tidewater region and eighteen out of thirty-one counties in the Piedmont region had populations that were over 50 percent slave. For the Tidewater region, these figures become even more extreme when one excludes the three most urban counties of Richmond, Norfolk, and Alexandria; with slave populations of 31.5, 35.3, and 13.8 percent, these counties ranked thirty-fifth, thirty-sixth, and thirty-eighth, respectively.[4] In the western regions, no county had a population that was 50 percent slave; in the Trans-Allegheny region, in nine out of forty-nine counties for which data is available, slaves comprised less than 1 percent of the population. Ten years later, the pattern was even more distinct. In the Tidewater and Piedmont regions, fifteen out of thirty-eight and seventeen out of thirty-one counties, respectively, were more than 50 percent slave. In the Trans-Allegheny region, the number of counties whose population was less than 1 percent slave had risen to sixteen out of sixty. (These figures are compiled from U.S. Census figures at Freehling, 1982: 279–86.)[5]

Although the total population was stable, there nevertheless were changes in the character of Virginia's citizenry in the east. In 1860, more than one-third of free workers in Richmond were foreign-born, almost all of whom had arrived in the preceding ten years. Old Virginia elites did not welcome the new populations any more than did the elites of New England, a common attitude expressed by Frederick Law Olmstead's 1852 description of people he saw on a visit to Richmond: "Very dirty German Jews, especially, abound, and their characteristic shops (with their characteristic smells quite as bad as Cologne) are thickly set in the narrowest and meanest streets, which seem to be otherwise inhabited mainly by negroes" (Shade, 1996: 22; see also Berlin and Gutman, 1983: 1190). The new populations exercised little if any political power, at least partly because old elites succeeded in preserving restrictions on franchise and representation (as described later in this chapter) that gave them disproportionate power right up to the Civil War.

In terms of party politics, Virginia was Democratic territory. In all but five of the seventeen years from 1835 to 1851, Democrats held majorities in

---

[4] The other was Accomack County, with 29.3 percent. Accomack was an "Eastern Shore" county, separated from the rest of the state by Chesapeake Bay and Maryland. Its economy was almost entirely maritime, making it unsuited to widespread use of slave labor (Freehling, 1982: 13–14).

[5] Only two western counties in 1860 had slave populations over 20 percent, and one of these was the anomalous Montgomery County. This county was the residence of Gordon Lloyd, who used slaves as cowhands on his 3,000-acre ranch, a situation quite different from that of slaves and slaveowners in the plantation east (Shade, 1996: 73).

the House of Delegates that ranged from 53 to 63 percent (the exceptional years were 1838–41, when Whigs held narrow majorities). Democrats held the Senate every year in the period (Shade, 1996: 169, 172, 178). But party identification was not a significant indicator of either interest or ideology. The votes for Whigs and Democrats were geographically incon-sistent across time and did not break down into neat patterns.[6] On crucial issues – the ratification of the 1830 Constitution, the antislavery vote of 1832, secession – regional patterns consistently trumped party affiliation. Furthermore, when Virginians took positions in national politics, it ap-pears that these were extensions of positions developed within their state, rather than the converse. Thus if one wants to understand the politics of Virginia's dominant eastern elites, in particular, an understanding of the meaning of the division between east and west must be the analytical starting point.

Recent historical writers have attempted to create a more complex account of antebellum Virginia society (Shade, 1996: 18). A textured and detailed understanding of any historical event is always desirable, but the preceding facts demonstrate a stark truth. In antebellum Virginia, "eastern" and "slavery" were coextensional concepts, and the conflicts that shaped the state were the conflicts between east and west. This was never more clear than at the Constitutional Convention of 1829.

Virginia's Constitutional Convention of 1829 was in many ways the completion of the debates between Federalists and Antifederalists of the late eighteenth century, the "last gasp," as one historian has called it, "of Jeffersonian America's passion for political disputation" (Peterson, 1966: 271). Among the participants in the 1829 Convention were James Madison, James Monroe, John Randolph, and John Marshall. Of these, however, only Randolph played a significant role in the debates. The Con-vention was led on both sides by prominent figures belonging to the next generation: for the east, Abel Upshur and Benjamin Watkins Leigh, and for the west, Chapman Johnson. While there were numerous specific is-sues, including the election of judges, there were three that overshadowed all others: the basis for the franchise and representation, internal improve-ments, and slavery.

In 1829, the right to vote and the calculation of populations for repre-sentation both depended on freehold ownership of property, a system that

---

[6] One exception was the election of 1840, in which the divisions matched almost perfectly, with all western and half the central counties voting Whig, and the other half of the state voting Democrat (Shade, 1996: 98).

according to one estimate disenfranchised three-quarters of white males in the state[7] (Chandler, 1901: 22). A proposal was brought forward that would have extended the franchise to all white males. John R. Cooke, supporting the proposal, cited Locke, Sydney, and Milton, and invoked "principles deep-seated in the nature of man," that "a *majority of the community* possessed, by the law of nature and necessity a right to control its concerns." In response, Leigh called the idea of white male suffrage "new at least in our State, if not new throughout the world," and called sarcastically upon those who supported the idea to explain themselves. "He hoped the friends of these new propositions ... would give ... some better reasons than that such principles were unknown to our English ancestors, from whom we have derived our institutions." Leigh's statement contained the essential elements of early nineteenth century southern conservativism: antiexceptionalism, a preference for tradition over innovation, and above all a commitment to the preservation of traditional legal rights over the assertions of "abstract" political theory. "[N]o rational man," said Randolph, "ever did govern himself by abstractions and universals" (Shepherd, 1830: 53–4, 316).

The rejection of abstraction was not a uniquely southern position by any means, but rather the traditional language of conservative republicanism.[8] Within this conception, the functions of law and government were grounded in individuals' property rights; the business of government, for Upshur, was to direct "the property concerns of the partnership." That reasoning demanded that citizenship be limited to property owners, since to permit non-property-holders to have political influence would grant them control over the property of others (Shepherd, 1830: 73). Protection from the threat of chaos was to be found in the tradition of the common law, as James Arbour explained: "Give me liberty in the English sense – liberty founded upon *law*, and protected by *law*.... I want no French liberty – none; a liberty which first attacked property, then the lives of its foes, then those of its friends." And Randolph, as always defiant, joined the chorus: "Do you think that we shall tamely submit, and

---

[7] This estimate has been criticized as unduly high (Bruce, 1982: xiv), but the general point that the property qualification denied the vote to large numbers of white males is not in doubt.

[8] James Kent, the exemplar of the conservative northern Whig, drew the connection between republicanism, property, and anti-exceptionalism in an 1821 address opposing the idea of universal suffrage: "That extreme democratic principle wherever tried has terminated disastrously. Dare we flatter ourselves that we are a peculiar people; exempt from the passions which have disturbed and corrupted the rest of mankind?" (Johnson, 1918: 42).

let you deprive us of our *vested rights*, and reduce us to bondage?" This was Burkean conservatism, and western delegate Lucas Thompson complained that "Burke, Filmer, and Hobbes, judging from their arguments, have become the textbooks of our statemen" (Shepherd, 1830: 157, 318, 411, emphasis in the original).

Eastern conservatives argued that the connection between property and republican virtue was universal and timeless. In his diary of the convention, Hugh Blair Grigsby, a young delegate and a perfect easterner, recorded a dialogue in which William Fitzhugh Gordon, a western reformer, waxed eloquent on the idea that the basis of all value was labor. In response, William Daniel said that "the only state of man in which society did not exist, was the interval between the creation of Adam and the creation of Eve, in this interval Adam held property, and this might show that the right of property was prior to the foundation of society" (Grigsby, 1829: 50–1). The prerogatives of property preceded all political theorizing and even the law itself. This was the point at which the conservative position became an attack on the claim of American exceptionalism, as Leigh explained: "All the Republics in the world have died this death. In the pursuit of a wild impracticable liberty, the people have first become disgusted with all regular Government, then violated the security of property which regular Government alone can defend, and been glad at last to find a master." To bestow political power on those without property was to invite the corruption of all the virtues of citizenship:

But extend the right of Suffrage to every man dependent, as well as independent, and you immediately open the flood-gates of corruption. You will undermine the public and private virtue of your people, and this your boasted Republic... will share the fate of all those which have preceded it, whose gradual decline, and final extinction, it has been the melancholy task of history to record (Shepherd, 1830: 157, 367).

In the end, none of these theoretical arguments mattered as much as the assertion that Virginia's slavery was a special case. "I have thus endeavored to prove," said Upshur, "that whether it be right as a general principle or not, that the property should possess an influence in Government, it is certainly right as to us. It is right because *our* property, so far as slaves are concerned, is *peculiar*" (Shepherd, 1830: 75). The peculiarity of the institution pointed to a move away from both American exceptionalism and republican universalism to *southern* exceptionalism, a creed that had nothing in common with the political vocabulary of the North.

The discussions of the connections between property and virtue underscored the incommensurability of eastern conservatism with the idea of universal standards. Persons – even free white males – were not the same, and therefore could not be entrusted with the same political authority. As Upshur pointed out, once one started down the road of natural equality, there was no telling where the issue would end:

In point of rights, nature does not own any distinction of age or sex. Infancy has equal rights with mature age; and surely it does not consist with the gallantry of the present day, to say that the ladies are not at least the equals of ourselves. Nay, more Sir, nature as strongly disowns all invidious distinctions in complexion: in her eye, there is no difference between jet and vermilion. A distinction does indeed prevail here, Sir, and a wide one it is. But the same rule of taste would not answer in Africa: for the African paints the devil white. According to your rule of numbers, all these various classes and descriptions of persons must count (Shepherd, 1830: 67).

Westerners protested indignantly that they had no designs on the institution of slavery, but conservatives could not be dissuaded from drawing the connection (Bruce, 1982: 175). This, ultimately, was the crux of all the conservative arguments against extending the franchise, that the principles invoked to justify that step could not be easily restrained from attacking their peculiar institution. Abraham Lincoln initially opposed slavery because it implied inequality among white laborers. Twenty years earlier, Virginia's conservatives opposed equality among whites because it would undermine the legitimating logic of slavery.

In 1829, there was no real sentiment for abolition in the Convention nor, for that matter, in Virginia at large. Instead, the immediate fear of slaveowners was that their property would be taxed to fund internal improvements designed to benefit the west. Johnson, leader of the western faction, urged the conservatives to expand their idea of self-interest beyond the local good of their own district and the present state of their economic interests: "Enlightened and liberal expediency, which looks to consequences immediate and remote . . . and regards all interests, partial and general, which in short has the lasting public good for its object . . . lies at the foundation of moral and political law, and is the true test of moral and political propriety" (Shepherd, 1830: 75, 264). There was one eastern representative who agreed. Robert B. Taylor, of Norfolk, was the lone eastern delegate to support a bill that would have provided that taxing and spending bills should be voted on in proportion to the amount of tax revenue collected in each district the previous year, a reform that would have favored western projects. On November 6, Taylor – branded a "traitor to the East" in Grigsby's journal (Grigsby, 1829: 29) – rose to defend himself. "I came here, Sir, as a Virginian; prepared to promote the interest of Virginia: fully believing that the petty and temporary interests of my district are as nothing, in comparison to the interest it has, in the general prosperity of the State" (Shepherd, 1830: 223). His eastern colleagues were unimpressed; five days later he was forced to resign, replaced by the twenty-four-year-old Grigsby, whose only obvious qualifications were his availability and his unswerving devotion to the interests of the eastern slaveowning class.

The ousting of Taylor may have been nothing more than a power play by an autocratic leadership unwilling to brook dissent. On the other hand, eastern elites understood that Taylor's appeal to the common good of Virginia over and above the interests of his particular district threatened to stake a claim to legitimacy incommensurate with their sectional preference for a peculiar institution. In addition, traditional republicanism was above all conservative, a theory that defined virtue as conduct tending toward the preservation of the existing social order. Taylor, by speaking in favor of railroad development in the western part of the state, was attempting to connect the language of republicanism to the prospect of industrialization and political economic change; in other words, Taylor's was a northern version of republicanism that had no place among southern elites. Finally, the appeal to the duties of a "Virginian" implied a uniformity among persons of that description that contradicted the fundamental premise that different classes of persons defined incommensurately separate categories of citizenship. In other words, the same division between traditional and novel interpretations of *salus populi* that was observed in northern legal development similarly appears in the political discourse of antebellum Virginia.

The outcome of the 1829 Convention was never in doubt. Although there were a number of close votes, the Virginia Constitution of 1830 was in nearly every respect a blueprint for the continuation of eastern control. The state government would consist of a lower House of Delegates with 134 members, of whom seventy-eight would come from the Tidewater and Piedmont (Article III, § 2). There was also to be a thirty-two member Senate, with nineteen drawn from the eastern counties (Article III, § 3). These numbers were fixed, regardless of subsequent changes in the size or distribution of the state's population. As a result, as the (free, white) population of the western districts increased, its voice in government remained limited to that which had been granted in 1829. The Constitution was ratified as it had been written, on a close vote that divided the state in two (Shade, 1996: 53; Sutton, 1989: 106).

Through the 1830s, the rhetorical divide between east and west became more and more pronounced. In 1832, Thomas Jefferson Randolph proposed the abolition of slavery in Virginia. In response, Daniel raised the specter of separation: "The people of the East regard the continual agitation of this question, even if it is not finally carried, as far more injurious and destructive than a division, and if the subject is again brought before the House next session it will be the signal for a proposition at once to divide" (*Virginia Law Register*, 1901: 5). Intensifying regional divisions accompanied the production of pro- and antislavery pamphlets through the 1830s, as the connections between representation, financing for internal improvements, and the sanctity of slavery were cemented once and for all (Shade, 1996: 69, 203; Genovese, 1992).

One concession to the west, did come out of the legislative session of 1832. The House of Delegates approved funding for the creation of the James River and Kanawha Company, and subscribed $100,000 of its stock. This company was charged with connecting Richmond with the Ohio River, either by canals, railways, or both. But the west got little benefit from this concession. Under the guidance of Joseph C. Cabell, president of the company and uncle of Justice William Cabell, the company decided to continue the James River canal to Lynchburg, to make the Kanawha navigable, and to connect the two waterways with a short railroad (Moger, 1952: 423). No trans-Virginia rail plan would be undertaken so long as the eastern river ports and canal interests had anything to say about it, lest the profitability of their own projects be jeopardized (Wertenbaker, 1962: 174–6).

Even if the canal plan had succeeded, it would have created a slow system of transportation that would ship western goods exclusively to eastern Virginia river ports. This was almost certainly part of the plan for the James and Kanawha. Conservatives looked askance at the idea of "foreign"– that is, northern – corporations doing business in their state, and most especially at the idea of intrusion by foreign railroads. In 1836 the B&O's rail lines reached Harper's Ferry and began drawing goods away from the James River. Then the company requested a charter to construct a line to Wheeling. An editorial in Thomas Ritchie's Democratic Richmond *Enquirer* stated the eastern position:

Baltimore is spreading her arm around us, and is not only endeavoring to secure the trade of the west by obtaining an avenue through our territory, which she flatters herself she will be able to secure through our sectional jealousies and our want of enterprise, but is taking from us even the trade which we have hitherto enjoyed. A large portion of the trade of the Valley of Virginia, which formerly came to Richmond, now goes to Baltimore upon the macadamized road down the valley (Wertenbaker, 1962: 176–7).

The proposed interstate railroad, to Virginian conservatives, was nothing less than a plan for encirclement of the slaveholding East by her philosophical enemies and economic rivals. The canal plan was designed to forestall that possibility.

The second problem with the James and Kanawha Canal program was that it was a failure. There had been efforts to construct a canal to connect the James and Kanawha rivers since the late 1700s. The new company received state and municipal support, but unlike the Erie Canal project, which crossed the Allegheny divide at an elevation of 650 feet, the Virginia project faced elevations of 2,200 feet, and the costs of such construction were prohibitive. Although building continued through the 1850s, the James-Kanawha project failed to breach the mountains or attract significant western trade.

For Wheeling and the west, the failure of the James and Kanawha project and the refusal of the legislature to undertake rail development – which was obviously a better alternative for crossing the high Allegheny passes – were crushing disappointments. The lack of connections to ports via rail was a devastating limitation on development in the western counties. Ultimately, in fact, the conflict over railroad development and its connection to the issues of slavery and political representation would lead to the secession of West Virginia from the rest of the state. To see why, it is necessary to step back and look at the development of western Virginia.

In 1816, Congress had designated Wheeling to be the western terminus of the Cumberland Road. The road was completed in 1818, and the effects were immediate. Mail service from the east went from a weekly post carried on horseback to daily stage deliveries. By 1822, five thousand wagons from the east arrived annually at Wheeling merchant houses, and hundreds more passed through going east or west. The constant flow produced the kinds of middleman enterprises characteristic of growing capital markets: commission merchants, warehouses, and manufacturers, as well as hotels and stores. An excellent point of embarkation for navigation of the Ohio, particularly in light of uncleared river obstacles to the north, Wheeling boatyards produced flatboats, keelboats, and even steamboats. By the end of the decade, the only rival for Wheeling in the Ohio Valley was Pittsburgh.

Through the 1820s, however, Wheeling's fortunes relative to Pittsburgh declined. The waterway from Pittsburgh to Wheeling was cleared of obstacles, but the federal road fell into disrepair. An 1827 War Department report found it in "shocking condition" and concluded that at least one bridge "would not stand a twelvemonth" (Monroe, 1992). By this time, there was an obvious alternative. In February, 1827, a group of twenty-five prominent Baltimore citizens met to discuss the possibility of constructing a rail line 380 miles long, running from Baltimore to the Ohio River. O. S. Nock nicely captures the grandeur of the project and the dizzying speed of its adoption:

British railway promoters faced with opposition on every hand, and wearied by long and acrimonious struggles in Parliamentary committees, might well have rubbed their eyes in wonder when following the first meeting of the projectors on 19 February, an Act of Incorporation by the State of Maryland was granted on 28 February, and confirmed by the State of Virginia on 8 March – *seventeen days* from the first meeting to the final "go-ahead" (Nock, 1979: 2).

When the B&O's first subscription of a then-staggering $4 million was announced in 1827, it was oversold in a matter of months, and later capital was raised in New York, Philadelphia, and even from the good people of Wheeling, who had despaired of getting any help from their own state government.

During this same period, there were few efforts at railroad construction in Virginia. In 1838, a nine-mile stretch of track was constructed to the James River from Petersburg, but the next project was not completed until 1854, and it would not be until 1873 that the Ohio River was finally connected by rail to the Chesapeake.[9] That extraordinary fact can only partly be explained by competition between sectional economic interests. Virginia had no shortage of eastern seaports, yet the dominant eastern elites – their control over the legislature guaranteed by the outcome of the Constitutional Convention of 1829 – adamantly resisted every attempt at the construction of rail lines to connect the cities and resources of the west with those ports.

Moreover, the manner in which the few rail construction projects that went forward were undertaken showed sharp differences from the approach that we have seen in the case of Illinois' railroads, and characterized the difference in outlook between Richmond and Wheeling on questions of political economy. As early as 1816, even before James Madison's

---

[9] This was the South Side Rail Road running west from Petersburg to Lynchburg (about one hundred miles). In 1856, the Virginia and Tennessee was constructed from Lynchburg west to Bristol, and in 1858, the Norfolk and Petersburg went east to Chesapeake Bay and to the Chesapeake & Ohio Railway port at Newport News (Nock, 1979: 42–3).

veto of the Bonus Bill and the effective end to federal attempts at internal improvement for twenty years (until 1838), Virginia established the pattern for transportation development that it would employ throughout the antebellum period. In a series of charters for toll roads and bridges, the state legislature adopted a "mixed enterprise" approach of state subsidies, state bonds, and state guarantees for privately subscribed bond issues, all in return for partial state ownership of the lines as well as various systems of repayment with interest. These were the financing provisions contained in the charter of the Richmond & Danville Railroad Company in 1858, for example, just as they had been in charters granted in 1816 (*An Act of the General Assembly Concerning the Richmond and Danville Railroad Company*, 1858: 6–12).

These elements of Virginia's approach to railroad financing were consistent with railroad and other transportation development schemes throughout the antebellum South, where corporate control over railroads was kept carefully within each state and development was a state-run operation, partly to ward off the intrusion of northern investment capital (Gordon, 1996: 16, 39–40). From 1830 to 1860, approximately $45 million was spent on railroad construction in Virginia; of this amount, $24 million was in the form of state funds, and $6 million came from towns and counties. The state held three-fifths of all the railroad stock issued before the Civil War (Moger, 1952: 425–6). This approach was in marked contrast to the private and local financing that characterized Illinois' railroad-building efforts after the 1830s.

State control was only one aspect of a broader difference in the conception of industrial development that drove northern and southern patterns of development. Wheeling, like the northern states, looked outward, to interstate commerce carried by rail. Its hoped-for connection to points east was to make it a southern Chicago, a point through which the great body of east-west traffic from the southern Ohio Valley would pass. In Illinois, the outward-looking aspect of railroad development was further emphasized by the separation of capital from industrial operations, something that Illinois' railroad boosters actively sought in the form of financing from New York and Boston. Richmond, by contrast, looked to protect intrastate commercial interactions and to keep both operations and capital under its own control. The emphasis on canals, importantly, not only suited those business interests, they also prevented the incursion of outside – read "northern" – forces and capital.

In 1845, the B & O submitted a second application for a charter, along with petitions for its approval from all the western counties. The House of Delegates, with its permanent eastern majority, rejected the proposal, although it permitted the company to construct a line to skirt southern Pennsylvania and then descend to Wheeling. This would not prevent Wheeling from having connections to the north and south, but it would prevent that commerce from reaching eastward, and it would leave eastern Virginia unobstructed access to the remainder of western Virginia in the event of the completion of the James River and Kanawha system.

Westerners were enraged. A convention of thirteen counties was held at Clarksburg. The delegates approved a statement, reported in the Niles *National Register*, that included the following:

We deny that any line of improvement is entitled to exclusive privileges to the injury of others, or that the northwest must be deprived of an outlet to its natural market, because it might abridge the trade of the James River and Kanawha Company. We are determined that our claims shall not be treated as though we were a mere colonial dependency, and in future will vote against all appropriations for railways and canals in other parts of the State until our rights have been recognized (Wertenbaker, 1962: 255).

The reference to "a mere colonial dependency" accurately identified a discrepancy between the eastern and western views of the state's economic system. From the perspective of Richmond, the west was a classic periphery that would supply materials and products to be brought east for sale or for shipment out of the state's Fall Line river ports. In an interesting parallel to Illinois, this focus on an east–west axis of interaction challenged the reality that for Wheeling and the west, the future was, and had long been, to the north and south. In 1846, when the idea of railroads could hardly be considered unduly speculative, eastern interests again defeated a bill to invest $4.8 million in a Central Virginia rail line to run from Richmond to Wheeling (Wertenbaker, 1962: 174–5).

Thus it was that eastern domination of the legislature in 1832, and the foreordained failure of the James and Kanawha project, left western Virginia isolated throughout the 1830s and 1840s. By the end of the 1840s, the issue of internal improvements had reached the point of destabilizing the state. Representation of persons rather than property, abolition of slavery, and the construction of railroads continued to be the rallying cries of the west and the *bêtes noires* of the east throughout the 1840s. In 1850, a second Constitutional Convention was called.

The Constitutional Convention of 1850

Once again, easterners were able to use their guaranteed dominance in the House of Delegates to ensure that voting for delegates would be on a "mixed" basis that included a property-ownership qualification, thus guaranteeing to themselves a dominant position at the convention. The ratio of eastern to western (Trans-Allegheny) delegates would be seventy-six to fifty-nine, giving the east a majority even larger than the one it enjoyed in the House of Delegates. Had a "white basis" been used to determine representation, the west would have had a majority of seventy-four to sixty-one. William A. Cabell, past justice of the Virginia Supreme Court, wrote to his uncle, Joseph C. Cabell, that the west was coming to Richmond angry: "They are much injured by the Superior influences which [the bill for a convention] gives the east" (Sutton, 1989: 116, 117). Western papers said the issue was "Wealth against Men," and that the westerners were "slaves" of eastern masters (Shade, 1996: 266). Nonetheless, the delegates to the 1850 convention were different from those who had gathered in 1829. The proportion of delegates who owned more than twenty slaves dropped from 50 to 21 percent; the proportion who owned none at all rose from 7 to 40 percent. In 1829, 57 percent of delegates were planters; in 1850 that number was only 29 percent.

There were a variety of issues on the table. There was widespread support among both westerners and easterners for reforming the "oligarchy" of the county court system that gave local power to prominent individuals appointed by their powerful peers. Westerners also sought the election of the governor and the expansion of executive powers to act as a check on the legislature, and supported a scheme for publicly supported education. But the fundamental issues in 1850 were the same as they had been in 1829. The questions of the property qualification for the franchise, the qualifications of representatives, and state expenditures on railroad development dominated the discussions. Attitudes about these issues had, if anything, hardened since the 1830s. "Many Whigs are ultra and many Democrats conservative," observed the *Whig*, the term "ultra" referring to southern Whigs who set sectional loyalty above party affiliation (Shade, 1996: 273, 118–22, 267). In addition, easterners continued to fear western abolitionism, a fear that was exacerbated by a popular 1847 pamphlet written by Henry Ruffner that called on westerners to insist on universal white franchise to "insure success" of the "equally momentous ... cause" of abolition (Freehling, 1982: 232).

By this time, there was no question that if the franchise were extended to all free whites, the west would have a dominating majority: "Its operation will be to transfer, at once, the legislative control of the State to the western division," said Robert E. Scott, a leading easterner.[10] There was equally no doubt that linking the franchise to property favored the east. John Chambliss explained that the mixed basis was required to ensure the representation of property interests: "[W]e find that while there is a majority of population of ninety thousands beyond the mountains; we find in the east a minority possessing two-thirds of the property.... I came here to protect that property; I came here to protect the slaves of my district as well as the persons"[11] (Bishop, 1851: 292, 293). The rhetoric of the western argument, by this time, had reached the level of rebellion. "We are not here," said William Smith of Greenbriar, "to complain of the want of kindness or liberality on the part of the eastern people, in the actual administration of the government. We are here for a very different purpose. We are here to deny their right to govern us at all"[12] (Bishop, 1851: 287, 290). John S. Carlile accused the east of being in league with South Carolina, the only state that used the mixed basis for voting favored by easterners. Making an argument that was repeated by several speakers, Carlile accused the east of harboring hidden ambitions to restrict all government to slaveowners: "They have evidently organized their government for the protection and the protection alone, of that portion of the people that may be possessed of this property, of which we have heard so much during our session here"[13] (Bishop, 1851: 374–5).

[10] Scott was a prominent Democrat from Fauquier County. The son of Judge John Scott, Jr., who had served in the 1829 Convention, Scott was a lawyer, a member of the House of Delegates in 1835–42 and 1845–52, attended the 1861 Secession Convention, and was a member of the Provisional Congress of the Confederacy from July 1861 until its adjournment in February 1862. He was killed in a skirmish with deserting Southern soldiers near the end of the war. Biographical material throughout, unless otherwise noted, is taken from Tyler, ed., 1915; Brown, ed., 1903; Malone, ed., 1934; and the *National Cyclopaedia of American Biography*, 1904.

[11] John Randolph Chambliss was a Greensville County lawyer, a governor's aide in 1856–61, and a brigadier general in Virginia's militia during the Civil War. He was killed in battle in 1864.

[12] Smith was a farmer who never learned to read or write. He was a Henry Clay supporter, and a member of the House of Delegates in 1819–20 and 1828–9, then a justice of the peace in Mercer County in 1837–49.

[13] Carlile came from Barbour County. He was a member of the State Senate, 1847–51, and a member of the U.S. Congress, 1855–7. Carlile was a spokesman against secession. He attended the 1861 Secession Convention and voted against secession, then led the call for the Wheeling Convention. He was elected to Congress from "loyal" Virginia, and then elected to the U. S. Senate from West Virginia, where he served until 1865.

Arguments of reformers that power should be equally distributed once again gave rise to cries of alarm that the natural distinctions between persons that underlay the social order were under attack, as in this statement by James Barbour:

[W]hy do gentlemen content themselves with claiming upon this principle an equality of political power? . . .Gentlemen impressed with this view should not stop at a re-organization of our political system, then should re-organize the social system; they should lift their view still higher, and address their morning and evening supplications to high heaven that the system of nature itself should be organized on a principle different from that applied to it by infinite wisdom[14] (Bishop, 1851: 367).

The negative model of choice was French despotism, as Willis P. Bocock explained: "[T]hey discarded every thing that was of old. They were infinite radicals, for they dethroned the God of Heaven, and erected a Goddess of Reason, and worshipped her. They were infinite radicals, and the only ones that I ever knew of, until the gentleman from Accomack declared himself" (Bishop, 1851: 226).[15]

The fear of radicalism, as always, was accompanied by the traditional republican fear of political power elevated above property rights. Bocock and Barbour warned of the corrupting seduction of power unchecked by property (Bishop, 1851: 230, 371). And the agent of corruption, said Scott, would be the lure of the railroads: "[T]he source of the danger is in the boundless wants of the west for internal improvements." James M. Whittle spoke of "a spirit of internal improvement... by which the interests and passions of men were to be more aroused, than from any cause which had ever been in operation among us"[16] (Bishop, 1851: 344, 478).

---

[14] Barbour, a lawyer from Culpeper County, served five nonconsecutive terms in the House of Delegates. He attended the Secession Convention in 1861, and served as a Confederate officer in the war but resigned due to ill health.

[15] The "gentleman from Accomack" was Henry Wise, a rare pro-reform delegate from the east (see footnote 4, earlier in this chapter).

[16] Whittle was a Pittsylvania County lawyer, and a state senator, 1861–3. In general, following eighteenth century convention, eastern conservatives used "public" as a synonym for "political," as when Barbour, speaking of claims to political equality, denied that there were "prerogative powers" at stake, and said, "I do not use the word prerogative in the narrow sense of the English common law, but in the more enlarged meaning ascribed to it by public writers" (Bishop, 1851: 221, 368). On the other hand, Henry A. Wise employed a more modern conception of the term "public" when he responded to an argument about the corruptibility of governors: "The gentleman, instead of addressing himself to public reasons, addresses himself to private reasons. Instead of addressing himself to the reasons of public good, he addresses himself to the motives which might govern a particular person in office" (Bishop, 1851: 93).

Richard L. T. Beale said those who favored a "majority of mere numbers" would "plunder" the state treasury for internal improvements, and pronounced railroads "unnatural" when compared to the "rivers God has placed upon this earth" (Shade, 1996: 277).[17]

The North was a looming presence on the eastern side of the debates. Future Virginia Supreme Court Justice Richard C. L. Moncure, in one of the very few substantive comments that he made during the debates, asserted the compact theory of the U.S. Constitution, and defined Virginia as an "absolute sovereign."[18] In a debate over the conditions under which the governor should have the authority to call up the state militia, John Minor Botts raised an ominous hypothetical question: "[S]uppose the Congress, in the exercise of usurped power, were to undertake to abolish slavery in the States – and suppose the southern States of this confederacy were in convention, convened for the purpose of determining what action it was proper and necessary to take." A rebellion against the national government, Botts assured his listeners, would do nothing to alter the relationship between citizens and the government of the state: "Our relations to the federal government are changed but there stands our State constitution, by which [the governor] is bound in all respects as much as he was before" (Bishop, 1851: 253).

The threat of secession and the constant references to the hostility and fear of the North translated directly into an argument against railroad development for eastern delegates. The western part of the state saw its future in the development of a national economy, drew on themes of an expansive conception of the public good, and conceived of the state as an instrument of progress. Easterners, in turn, sought to protect their economic system against the threat of outside interference, appealed to traditional principles that defined *salus populi* in terms of specific local conditions and the preservation of social order, and conceived of the state as a shield to preserve the order of things against the threat of change. Westerners appealed to commercial development, interstate commerce, and the benefits of American progress, while easterners spoke for a static

[17] Beale was a lawyer and planter from Westmoreland County. He served in the United States Congress, 1847–9 and the Virginia Senate, 1857–61. During the Civil War, he became a brigadier general in the Confederate army, and returned to Congress in 1879–87.
[18] "The constitution of Virginia was framed before the constitution of the United States.... The constitution of 1829 gave to the government of Virginia all the powers of an absolute sovereign – powers which shall permit her and enable her to carry on the important purposes and objects of the State, whether she be in or out of this confederacy" (Bishop, 1851: 252, 259).

natural social order, the perfection of which was attested by old tradition and new knowledge alike.

Given these profound differences, it is hardly surprising that the Convention was extraordinarily bitter, requiring six ballots merely to elect a clerk on the first day. On the key questions of suffrage and representation, voting split perfectly along geographic lines that divided both parties, and after months there was no sign of any resolution. Western strength of population and economic resources was too great to ignore completely, as was the evident risk of outright division between the two halves of the state. Nonetheless, easterners used their superior numbers, ensured by the political advantages that had been built into the Constitution of 1830, to limit changes in the mixed basis system. At the last minute, a pure compromise of interests was proposed and accepted: the freehold property requirement would be removed from the franchise, but the east would retain a permanent ten-vote majority in the Senate. In return, slaves would be taxed at a fixed value equivalent to $300 worth of land, far below their market value (Virginia Constitution of 1851, Article III, Article IV, § 23). Other, less fundamental, issues were resolved quickly. Article VI, covering the judiciary, reorganized the manner in which judges were selected. Echoing the construction of the Illinois Supreme Court, the justices of Virginia's Supreme Court would be elected from each of five geographically defined districts for twelve-year terms.

As welcome as these political reforms may have been, the Reform Constitution of 1851 did not change very much in terms of the economic development of the state. The eastern and western halves of the state were by this time on irrevocably separate tracks, participating in irrevocably separated systems of political economy. The difference was not simply one of industrial versus agrarian economies. There was industry in eastern Virginia, exemplified by Richmond's famous Tredegar Iron Works and an important locomotive factory in Alexandria (Quenzel, 1954: 181–9). These industries, in fact, increasingly posed legal and political problems because of the unanticipated issues that arose in their utilization of leased slave labor.[19] Far from providing the kind of unifying consensus that was emerging in Illinois, however, industry in Virginia was a focal point for the conflicts between the interests and ideologies that divided the state.

[19] See the discussion in Chapter 1. For a discussion of particular problems that the use of slave labor posed for the development of employment law doctrines, see Wertheim, 1986; Lewis, 1979. For discussions of the role of slave labor in railroad construction and operation, see Licht, 1983: 67; Starobin, 1970a, 132–3.

The justices of Virginia's high court in the 1850s represented the most conservative, most traditionalist elements in the society. In Illinois, the courts had defined the rights of private individuals in terms of public duties. Virginia's justices, by contrast, would define even public entities in terms of their private interests. Southern republicanism was based on a duty to promote the public good, but in the southern version that concept retained its traditional, local meaning rather than taking on the expanded, abstract quality that appeared in the courts of northern states. The political function of the law, too, was different. In Virginia, the common law retained its function of safeguarding a social order and legitimating a political economy based on slavery and the agricultural plantation. As a result, through the 1850s Virginia's Supreme Court clung to the traditional common law conception of legal rights and duties that depended on the differentiations between categories of persons and the particular relationships between actors. Although the specific rules were modified to suit their society, the analytical process, categories of pleading, and basic principles of adjudication that the Virginia courts relied upon in 1860 would have been familiar to Blackstone a century before.

7

The Common Law of Antebellum Virginia

The Preservation of Status

In reviewing the appellate cases from Virginia in the 1850s, the picture that emerges is one of great intellectual efforts invested in the project of stasis. Where Illinois moved boldly to articulate a new, American system, Virginia's high court dug in its heels and became, if anything, more traditionally English than the English themselves.[1] This was not because Virginians were unaware of developments elsewhere. To the contrary, the highly advanced state of Virginia legal education gave the state the potential to be a center for modernization. Furthermore, in the cases before the high court, lawyers repeatedly attempted to introduce new modes of analysis, but the judges would have none of it. Where Illinois was a story of judges crafting and imposing a new system on the legal community, Virginia was a story of judges preventing the legal community from adjusting the regime of rights and duties to accord with modern requirements. And where Illinois was a story of railroad cases providing the setting for working out and defining new legal doctrines, Virginia was a story in which the handling of controversies involving railroads provided the clearest articulations of judicial resistance to change. The antebellum Virginia Supreme Court chose the traditional path of analysis on each of the crucial points around which the Illinois court had constructed its new model. In Virginia, the adjudication of cases would continue to take as its starting point a comparative evaluation of private property-based rights, treating *salus populi* as a local phenomenon, and conceiving of economic activities – whether carried out by business corporations, towns,

---

[1] For instance, Virginia adopted some but not all of the reforms in lower-court jurisdiction initiated in English courts in 1850 (*Quarterly Law Journal*, 1856: 6–10).

or individuals – as exercises in private interest rather than as instruments bound to the pursuit of public good.

Until 1788, Virginia had a "double-headed court system," one for appeals in criminal cases and another for appeals in civil cases. In 1788 a unified supreme court was established, to consist of five justices "chosen by joint ballot of both houses of the legislature," and with it a firm principle of judicial review. This system was changed after a Constitutional Convention in 1851, in one of the few steps that had widespread support from both western and eastern delegates. Thereafter, the state was divided into five judicial sections, each of which would elect one justice to the Virginia Supreme Court for a term of twelve years. One circuit judge for each of twenty-one judicial circuits was also to be elected by the voters for an eight-year term. The election of judges was an element of a sweeping democratization of Virginia's state political system, including the introduction of the popular election of the governor, the lieutenant governor, and the attorney general (Morris, 1975: 8–11, 17–19).

The traditional dominance of a few elite families over Virginia's judiciary, however, was not altered by the new provisions. Between 1850 and 1861 there were a total of six justices on the state's highest court. Among them, William J. Daniel, Jr., and Richard C. L. Moncure were clearly the dominant figures. In the cases that tested new doctrines, they account for nearly all the opinions, the vast majority of them written for a unanimous court. Daniel was the son of a General Court justice, the son-in-law of Justice William H. Cabell, and the nephew of Justice Briscoe G. Baldwin. Cabell, in turn, was the nephew of Virginia Supreme Court Justice Paul Carrington. At one point, Daniel sat on the bench with his future father-in-law (Cabell) and his uncle (Baldwin). Daniel's successor, Wood Bouldin, married Daniel's sister (Martha Daniel). Moncure's connections were to the legislature. He was the son of a state representative, all three of his brothers served in Virginia's House, and one of them also sat in the Senate. Of five justices elected in 1852, three were already appointed members of the court (Daniel, Moncure, and John J. Allen). The other two were Green B. Samuels and George Lee. The only other election held under the Constitution of 1851 was in 1859, when William Robertson was elected to replace the deceased Samuels (Morris, 1975: 30–2).

Virginia's justices were also notable for their attachment to the southern cause. At their deaths, Daniel and Moncure were each remembered for their ardent "patriotism" above any other characteristic. Daniel joined the court in 1847 after serving four terms in the House of Delegates, where his devotion to the east caused Thomas Ritchie to dub him "the Leonidas of the Western Pass." He was replaced by the Alexandria government in 1865, "driven from the bench by the hand of tyrannic power – not by Virginians – simply because he was too pure, too patriotic and too incorruptible to unite with the invaders and enemies of his native State" (Halsey, 1901: 5, 7, 9). Daniel then returned to private practice with his son and son-in-law, and established the most successful appellate practice in the state. Nor is it the case that judges with Confederate sympathy disappeared from Virginia's highest court after the war. Moncure, too, was known and remembered for his devotion to the cause of the South and his later sympathy for claims brought by Confederate veterans, but he sat on the Virginia Supreme Court from 1851 through 1880 without interruption, through several rather radical changes of government[2] (Ould, 1883: 4; J.C.L., 1885: 449–52). For that matter, Edward Burks, who joined the court in 1877 under the post-Alexandria political regime, had been a prominent member of the Confederate legislature during the Civil War (Christian, 1897: 323–36).

The democratization of the judiciary thus had little effect on the dominance of eastern conservatives over the appellate bench. The conservatives' hold over the state's Senate also meant that there was little conflict between legislature and bench. During the period of the popular election of justices, the Virginia Supreme Court did not strike down any statutes (Morris, 1975: 20–1, 31). Given these facts, it is perhaps not surprising that, when compared with the experience of Illinois, the outstanding feature of Virginia's common law in the antebellum period was the near-total absence of substantive change. In this, however, there is a striking difference between the circuit courts and the state supreme court. By the end of the 1850s, there were no cases reported at the circuit court level under theories of "assumpsit" or "trespass on the case"; instead, cases are listed in the modern manner, under headings of "negligence" and "contract." In the records of the Virginia Supreme Court, by contrast, through the 1870s and 1880s, cases continued to be commonly filed under forms of "trespass on the case," "trover," and "assumpsit,"

---

[2] Moncure was a member of the Reform Convention in 1851, then was elected by the General Assembly to fill a vacant seat on the Virginia Supreme Court. After adoption of the 1851 Constitution, he was elected again, this time by popular vote. In 1866, Moncure was nominated to return to the high court (following the adoption of the 1864 Constitution) by Governor Francis Pierpont and elected by the legislature. He returned to private practice in 1869, then was elected to another twelve-year term on the court by the General Assembly, under the 1870 Constitution.

as well as under "negligence" and "breach of contract."[3] It was not, in fact, until the 1890s that Virginia's high court finally abolished the old forms of action (Bryson, 1983: 273–84). The first case filed in Virginia's highest court under a general theory of negligence was *Union Steamship Co. v. Nottingham* in 1866; in indices of reported cases from the circuit court, the first such case appears eight years earlier.[4]

When it came to the substance of legal doctrines, the Virginia Supreme Court's resistance to innovation became nearly absolute, an attitude that presented the law as an impediment to the success of new forms of economic activity rather than as its spur. The absence of emergent legal doctrines was partly the result of an absence of cases to carry them. Throughout the decade, the court simply refused to hear railroad cases, and consequently avoided many of the prominent issues arising across the country as a result of railroad development. When Virginia's justices announced legal doctrines, they used nonrailroad cases, and used them to follow the general southern trend of preserving traditional modes of analysis. The lack of railroad-related precedents produced frustration among Virginia's bar, as in an unsigned 1856 article in the state's preeminent law journal: "No case, involving the liability of Railroad Companies in this State, for accidentally killing or injuring animals on railroads, by the locomotives or cars, has yet been decided in our Courts; and the decisions in other States are very conflicting, so that the question of the extent of such liability in this State must be matter of doubt." The author called on the state's courts to adopt the rule of contributory negligence, citing the Illinois Supreme Court's analysis in *Aurora v. Grimes* (see the discussion in Chapter 3) as his model (*Quarterly Law Journal*, 1856: 295). An 1861 article made the same complaint about the Virginia Supreme Court's failure to announce any rules concerning the fellow-servant rule and other issues of employment-based liability[5] (*Quarterly Law Review*, 1861: 1–9).

---

[3] For example, *Baltimore & Ohio R.R. Co. v. Whittington's adm'r*, 30 Vir. 805 (1878), was appealed to the Virginia Supreme Court under a theory of trespass on the case. As late as 1886, the great legal reformer David Dudley Field reported that premodern forms of common law pleading persisted among southern states (Field and Dillon, 1885: 594).

[4] *Union Steamship Co. v. Nottingham*, 17 Vir. 115 (1866); *Hawley v. Baltimore & Ohio R.R. Co.*, 3 *Quarterly Law Journal* 89 (Circuit Court, Wheeling, 1857).

[5] The rules for permissive or mandatory review of cases on appeal in Virginia remained unsettled in this period. In an 1818 case, the Virginia Supreme Court had held that a case could not be reviewed unless its transcript on appeal included both a "viva voce" record of oral testimony and conclusions of fact reached by the jury, a burdensome transcript requirement that would have kept the vast majority of cases out of the high court. On the other hand, it appears to be the case that the Virginia Supreme Court could, if it chose

As noted earlier, the Virginia high court's adamant resistance to change had nothing to do with any ignorance of the system of American common law that was being developed in the North. Its legal journals were full of reports of cases from states around the country and nations abroad, and by the 1840s complete volumes of reported cases were freely available, and citations to those reports were common. Nor is it sufficient to rest with a simple instrumentalist explanation to the effect that Virginia's justices disliked corporations generally, or railroads in particular, because they themselves were invested (literally and figuratively) in the plantation interests. Instead, just as the formation of legal doctrines in Illinois served the project of constructing a new model of mass citizenship, the preservation of old rules in Virginia served the goal of maintaining an existing social order and the philosophical commitments that provided its conceptual underpinnings.

Slavery required Virginia's resistance to doctrinal change, just as railroads drove Illinois' innovation. The key points of that resistance were the negative versions of those that were driving the project of legal modernization in Illinois: the rejection of technology-driven progress, preservation of a local sense of *salus populi*, and the insistence that legal duties continue to be defined by the relationships between private parties, rather than reflecting public, universally applicable obligations. The Virginia Supreme Court likewise rejected the move away from a conceptual regime grounded in private property rights to the idea of abstract tortlike duties. The ultimate effect of the Virginia high court's resistance to change was to forestall the project of using private law to construct a new model of public citizenship.

The Challenge of Corporations

One of the contexts in which Virginia's traditionalism was most pronounced was in the treatment of corporations. Corporations, in Virginia, were entities designed for the pursuit of private interests, lacking both the special prerogatives and the duties that northern corporations assumed by virtue of their public purposes. Like other private citizens, Virginia's corporations were entitled to the ownership and use of property, subject

---

to, hear cases that lacked such extensive documentation. As late as 1885, a writer could only say that "while this case has never been expressly overruled, it has been essentially qualified in its application...." (*Virginia Law Journal*, 1885: 258–9). The absence of clear rules of appellate procedure makes it difficult to evaluate adequately the justices' exercise of discretion in taking or declining cases on appeal.

only to countervailing property- and contract-based legal claims. Strikingly, this vocabulary extended not only to corporate businesses, but to municipal corporations as well. Both were equated with the standard legal model of the citizen as a self-interested, rights-bearing property owner. The preservation of the public good, in other words, did not require the creation of new public duties specific to these novel economic entities, but rather the assimilation of new forms into the existing system of private rights.

In 1834 the City of Richmond gave the Richmond, Fredericksburg, and Potomac Railroad Company (RF&P) a piece of property for its Richmond terminus, and the right to construct and operate a rail line running along Broad Street (then called H Street) in the heart of the city's center.[6] Almost from the first day of operations, there were complaints by residents about the hazards and inconveniences presented by the operation of these trains. In 1839, the city's Common Council reached an agreement with the railroad whereby it paid for paving a section of the road and agreed to restrict the speed at which its trains would run in the city. In 1845, the city's Common Council enacted regulations to limit the operations of trains, at least partly on the theory that the regulations were required to abate a public nuisance. These events did not occur in the context of courtroom proceedings. In three written reports prepared in 1839, however, the railroad company and a specially formed committee of the Richmond Common Council (which produced both majority and minority reports) filed "briefs" relating to the controversy. Their arguments laid out competing conceptions of the nature of commercial and municipal corporations and the meaning of *salus populi*.

The railroad company began with a traditional analysis, basing its case on the idea that RF&P was an entity possessed of contract rights, to whom the city owed contractual duties: "The right given by its charter . . . cannot lawfully be diverted." The argument turned to an expansive, collective idea of progress as the ultimate public good, however, in responding

---

[6] The Richmond, Fredericksburg, and Potomac Railroad was incorporated in 1834. Language in the charter provided:

> [The] president and directors are "invested with all the rights and powers necessary for the construction, repair and maintaining of a railroad" (§7) "located as aforesaid." Especially are they empowered (§24) "to purchase, with the funds of the said company, and place on the railroad constructed by them under this act, all *machines*, wagons, vehicles, carriages and teams of any description whatsoever, which they may deem necessary or proper for the purposes of transportation" ("Brief of Railroad Company," 1874: 1–2).

to the claim that the operation of trains constituted a public nuisance: "[T]here is nothing unreasonable or inconsistent in supposing that the legislature intended that the part of the public which should use the highway should sustain some inconvenience for the sake of the greater good to be obtained by other parts of the public in the more speedy traveling and conveyance of merchandise" (Letter of Con. Robinson, president of RF&P, to Richmond Common Council, 1838, "Brief of Railroad Company," 1874: 40–1). The argument by the railroad pointed to the conception of *salus populi* as collective progress that northern courts would routinely employ to reject claims of nuisance or interference with property rights raised against railroad and tram companies. (Technically, in fact, the argument was entirely unnecessary, since an activity authorized by state charter could not be a "nuisance" by definition [Hilliard, 1859, vol. 2: 67–8].) The lawyers for RF&P, in other words, were trying to make an analytical bridge from traditional private claims to a principle that would vastly expand the prerogatives of their corporation.

In 1839, however, the City of Richmond could draw on an argument that to modern ears sounds rather peculiar: the city, a chartered municipal corporation, had its own private rights of property ownership derived from its contractual relationship with the State of Virginia. In other words, the City of Richmond was the precise equivalent of a railroad company:

We think the question whether the steam engines of the railroad company shall be excluded now, or twelve months hence, or even in five years, as altogether an unimportant one when compared with the question of *power*. . . . [W]e deny that [the legislature] could recall our chartered rights by piecemeal, or authorize a private company to violate and trample upon those rights at pleasure ("Committee Majority Report," 1839: 44–5).

The competition, in this view, was not between public and private interests, but between two sets of private rights, each created by charter and each exerting a claim upon an external public authority. The City of Richmond was the owner in fee (outright) of its soil. It followed that the only right that RF&P could have obtained from the legislature was a right of way: "They obtained no property in the soil, and they paid no equivalent in money even for the use of the street." The city's superior claim to ownership of its property – and nothing else – provided it with the authority to regulate the running of locomotives ("Committee Majority Report," 1839: 46, 50). As far as the committee majority was concerned, the argument that the City of Richmond had a duty to promote the public good in the form of railroads was a red herring. The authority of a city to enact regulations was itself the byproduct of the city's possession of vested property rights. The principle at work was not *salus populi suprema lex est* (the good of the people is the supreme law), but rather *sic utere tuo ut alienum non laedus* (use your own property so as not to injure another).

In the 1840s, the controversy between Richmond and the RF&P was settled on political rather than legal grounds by a series of compromises on both sides. The case would arise again in the 1870s, at which time it would appear before the Virginia Supreme Court and, ultimately, the United States Supreme Court (see the discussion in Chapter 8). In the meantime, the question of competition between private rights and public duties in the context of corporate rights came before the court in 1855 in *Slaughter v. The Commonwealth*, 13 Vir. 767 (1855).[7] A Connecticut insurance company brought a constitutional challenge to a state statute that imposed special taxes and licensing requirements on foreign corporations (Code of Virginia, ch. 38, § 25, p. 210). The case directly challenged the state's ability to prevent the incursion of northern capital, a point of central importance for the construction of the railroad system. The Connecticut company argued that the statute violated its constitutional rights under the Privileges and Immunities Clause (Article IV, §2, clause 1) by treating the company differently from domestic insurance companies.

The Virginia Supreme Court was not impressed. Corporations, they ruled, held no constitutional rights because they were not "citizens." In its comments, the court struck at the heart of the connection between the status of corporations, encroaching modernity, and the defense of the southern social order:

The privileges and immunities guaranteed to them [the citizens of Connecticut] are annexed to their *status* of citizenship. They are personal, and may not be assigned or imparted by them, or any of them, to any other person, natural or artificial. If it were otherwise, and these citizens could impart their right to others, the limitation of the guaranty to "citizens" would be without practical effect; the right might be imparted to classes, and for purposes in contravention of our policy and laws; and thus our welfare or even our safety be endangered (*Slaughter*, 771).

This was a perfect statement of the ancient republican conception of citizenship and its limits. Corporations could not be citizens because to make them so would be to admit the possibility that the classification was one subject to being opened to new members. Worse, not only elite individuals but whole classes of persons might be considered "citizens." Furthermore, although the point is never mentioned in the case, if prerogatives granted

---

[7] Citations are to *Gratton's Virginia Reports* unless otherwise indicated.

to a corporation – an "artificial person" – in one state could demand observance in another, then the same might be true of citizens generally. It was obviously the case that there were "classes" of citizens in, say, Massachusetts whose rights must never be entitled to the protection of the Virginia courts:[8] "[W]e do not recognize the authority of Connecticut to confer on her own citizens privileges or immunities in Virginia, which we have not given to our own citizens within the state" (*Slaughter*, 771–2).

Stock Cases

As in other states, a second area in which the Virginia Supreme Court faced challenges to traditional order was in claims arising from collisions between trains and stock. Although the court did not announce rules governing the adjudication of stock collision cases in the antebellum period, at the circuit court level, Virginia's judges were beginning to fashion a body of legal doctrine. These opinions, of course, did not have precedential authority outside their circuits. Nonetheless, the reasoning displayed in these cases demonstrates the conservative reactions of judges confronted by the challenges of railroad technology, while the absence of any effort by the appellate court to revise the outcomes may indicate satisfaction on the part of the justices.

In *Hunter v. Baltimore & Ohio R.R. Company*, 2 *Quarterly Law Journal* 253 (Circuit Court of Marshall County, 1857), the owner of several cows hit by a train sued a railroad company for his loss. The judge pointed out that in the absence of any legislative pronouncements, the issue was purely one of common law duties.[9] Railroads, like any other party, were obliged to exercise reasonable care and diligence to avoid causing harm to the property of others. The parameters of that duty, however, were extremely fluid, "taking into consideration the time, place, and the proper mode of running, management, use and employment of the engine as determined and settled by experience and skill in railroad running, and . . . a knowledge of the habits of each particular class of animals straying at large on the line of the railroad, and as such habits are affected and influenced by such railroad running" (*Hunter*, 255).

---

[8] Commentators have pointed out that a strong reading of the Privileges and Immunities Clause would have made slavery itself unconstitutional, since blacks in Southern states were denied rights they would have had elsewhere. (See, e.g., Ely, 1980: 22–23.)

[9] "There is nothing in the laws of Virginia compelling persons to keep their stock enclosed or from straying about; nor is there anything in its laws compelling railroad companies to enclose their roads and erect cattle-guards" (*Hunter*, 253).

In the next year, another judge made a more detailed analysis in *The Richmond and Petersburg Rail Road Co. v. Martha J. Jones, 3 Quarterly Law Journal* 84 (Chesterfield Circuit Court, 1857). The evidence did not establish the precise point at which Jones' cow had been struck and killed. The judge therefore considered two distinct possibilities: that the cow had been struck while standing on a point where the tracks crossed a public thoroughfare, or that the cow had been struck on a portion of the line that was the railroad company's private property. In the former case, traditional modes of analysis would apply, an approach emphasized in the treatment of the cow as a rights-bearing "citizen":

In that case, the cow was passing upon a public highway where she had a legal right to travel. . . . If the collision occurred there, does it not present the familiar case of two individuals, who have a common right to travel on the same road, and which imposes upon each the duty of so exercising that right, as not to injure the rights of others. The maxim *sic utere tuo ut alienum non laedas* here emphatically applies (*Jones*, 87).

Here are the familiar elements of the tradition that the Illinois courts were in the process of jettisoning: the analysis that begins with an evaluation of relative rights to occupation of property, the description of an animal as a rights-bearing entity on the theory that the rights inhere in property, and the description of legal duties as the effect of a relationship between parties.

Interestingly, if the incident were determined to have occurred on a portion of the rail line that did not coincide with a public thoroughfare, then the same traditional property rights analysis led the same judge to recognize an early version of the general theory of contributory negligence. This was not the rule that, in the North, had resulted in a general reconceptualization of legal duties. Instead, the principle remained one grounded in the specific duties owed by one party to another, analyzed in terms of relative rights to the use and occupation of property.

First, without citation to any precedent, the judge of the Chesterfield County Circuit Court, for the first time in Virginia, announced the general rule of negligence: no liability without fault. From there, he moved to the conclusion that sometimes cattle would be hit by trains, and there was simply nothing to be done about it:

[I]f a man is engaged in the prosecution of his lawful business and an *accident* occurs, by which another is injured, without negligence or misconduct on his part, he is not responsible for it. . . . If cattle thus turned out to graze at large upon the uninclosed lands of the neighborhood, should stray upon the track of a Railroad, the utmost obligations upon the Railroad Company, would be to use all proper care and caution to avoid an injury to them. But if by *inevitable accident* they are killed, it is the misfortune of the owner, and he must bear the loss (*Jones*, 86, 88).

The plaintiff failed to make "even a colourable case." This was a reference to pleading requirements that meant not simply that the owner of stock would lose at trial, but that his claim could not be heard in court at all. In that case, the destruction of the stock by the trains was "the misfortune of the owner," and "inevitable." Trains, apparently, were part of the landscape, so that collisions with trains were events like floods or encounters with poisonous snakes.

Another circuit court judge in 1859 declared that "a railroad company is under no obligation to enclose its line of works...in this respect it occupies the position only of an ordinary land-holder. If, therefore, the stock of a coterminous land-holder goes upon the railway and is killed without the negligence or default of the Company, the owner must bear the loss."[10] This argument, too, pointed to the challenge that the facts of railroad operation posed to traditional tort and property law doctrines. These were mere hints, however. Without a high court interested in the generation of new rules and principles, cases such as this one remained curiosities for journal authors.

In the 1856 *Quarterly Law Journal* article on the subject of railroad liability mentioned earlier, the author urged the adoption of a rule absolving railroads from liability. The same issue, however, contained a review of the state of cases across the South prepared by "an able railroad counsel." This unnamed lawyer, contradicting the journal's editor, observed with apparent approval that southern judges followed a path different from that of their northern brethren. Northern decisions "generally are opposed to the liability of the Companies," while in the South, "decisions generally are in favor of such liability, unless the *Company* can show that the damage was entirely accidental and happened notwithstanding every care and precaution were taken by its agents to avoid the accident" ("Liability of Railroad Companies," 1856: 295).

In addition to providing his legal analysis, the railroad lawyer also mentioned justifications for his conclusions that read as a warning to railroad companies about the political context of railroad development in Virginia.

---

[10] *Clark v. Virginia and Tennessee Railroad Co.*, 4 *Quarterly Law Journal* 280, 282 (Circuit Court of Washington County, 1859).

First, he asserted that a presumption of liability for damage to stock was essential to keeping the costs of condemnation assessments low, a neat reference to southern railroads' fear of unfriendly assessors, a fear that was generally absent in Illinois where local authorities were the most enthusiastic boosters of railroad development. Second, he expressed concern about the consequences of a public perception that railroad companies were not assuming responsibility for the harms that they caused: "Besides the consideration mentioned above, it is probable that the refusal of a Company to pay for such damages, would occasion a clamor against it, more detrimental to its interests than the value of all such damages would be likely to amount to" (*Clark v. Virginia and Tennessee Railroad Co.*, 4 *Quarterly Law Journal* 280, 298, Circuit Court of Washington County, 1859).

Thus what had appeared as a lingering and marginal voice of early populist resentment in the North appeared to this lawyer to be politically necessary and legally well established in the South. As a result, he concluded, the southern rule was that railroad companies should be held liable unless "every care and precaution were taken by the agents of the Company to avoid the accident, or that it was occasioned by the carelessness, folly, or wrong of the owner of the animal... the burden of proof, avoiding, excusing or mitigating the damage, being on the Company, not on the owners." That rule, however, had one crucial exception: "It is not intended to include slaves in this designation; who being sentient beings are considered capable of understanding and avoiding the danger, and as to whom, therefore, a different rule of law would apply" (*Clark*, 296–7).

The final comment directs our attention to the special influence that slavery had on Virginia's legal development. Railroads exercised pressure toward standardization, and Illinois courts used the law to extend that theme to the requirements of citizenship. The existence of slaves, however, was inimical to standardization at every level. As the justices of Virginia's high court recognized, the real threat posed by the arrival of railroads was not the pressure for the standardization of commercial grades of grain, but the pressure that they created for uniform and universal rights and duties. The justices of the Virginia Supreme Court recognized that the standards of conduct that were becoming prevalent in Illinois threatened the basic distinction between citizens and slaves. This was not an obvious issue in cases involving contract and property rights, but it was an immediate point of concern when the issue turned to questions of liability for injuries to persons.

Injuries to Persons

The connection between slavery and the formulation of legal standards of conduct was made clear in *Farish & Co. v. Reigle*, 11 Vir. 697 (1854). *Farish* was a classic example of a case involving an injury to a passenger, except that the conveyance in question was not a train, but a stagecoach. Justice Daniel's opinion in the case, however, was about railroads and slaves, even though he never mentioned either.

In *Farish*, the plaintiff suffered severe and lasting injury when the stagecoach in which he was riding overturned. The evidence showed that the defendant's stage was a good one, the horses steady, and the driver competent. The one aspect of the driver's conduct at issue was his examination of the brakes before setting out. There was a technological dimension to the question. The horses' harnesses had not been equipped for "breeching" (forcibly slowing) the horses; testimony from witnesses differed on the question of whether the invention of block brakes (wooden brakes operating directly on the wheels) had rendered breeching equipment superfluous (*Farish*, 698–700).

Jury instructions requested by the plaintiff included the statement that "passenger carriers are liable for injuries resulting even from the slightest negligence," and "if the jury further believe that such running off of the horses might have been prevented if the horses had been properly harnessed . . . then the defendants are liable in damages." The latter instruction was delivered with a modification: "that in speaking of the horses being 'properly harnessed,' the court must not be understood to express any opinion whether the horses should have breeching or not," a question left to the jury. The state of the art, in other words, was not a matter for legal rules or expert testimony, but rather a question of communal sense. The jury returned a judgment for the plaintiff in the amount of $9,000 (*Farish*, 701–2).

On appeal, the stagecoach company's counsel borrowed a leaf from the book of the northern bar, arguing that the company's duties to passengers should be based not on the traditional strict liability of common carriers, but on the property-based law of bailments: "[T]he principle applicable to carriers of passengers is that applicable to bailees for hire; and therefore they are responsible for only ordinary negligence" (*Farish*, 703). To support their argument, they appealed to a U.S. Supreme Court case out of Kentucky, decided in 1829, called *Boyce v. Anderson*, 2 U.S. (Peters) 150. This citation introduced the element that had been entirely missing in Illinois: *Boyce v. Anderson* was a case about the transport of slaves.

In *Boyce*, Chief Justice John Marshall had ruled that the responsibility of the carrier should be measured by the law governing liability for injuries to passengers rather than the strict liability principles covering damage to goods, and that the rule regarding the carriage of passengers was "that the carrier was answerable for injury sustained in consequence of his negligence or want of skill, but no further." The lawyers for the stagecoach company in *Farish* added an argument from the perspective of public policy: "The counsel took up the question upon principle, and insisted that as it was an open question in this state, sound principle and sound policy forbade the adoption of the very harsh rule . . . which seemed to look upon carriers of passengers as criminals to be punished, not as useful citizens to be encouraged and protected" (*Farish*, 703–5). The language of the argument is striking for what it does not include. There is no reference to an assertion that carriers serve a function essential to the public good, or the corollary argument that passengers must behave in a way calculated to facilitate the provision of that public function. In answer to the presentation of traditional concepts of the near-strict liability of common carriers, the company had raised the argument that it was a respectable citizen entitled to the protection of its traditional interests as a property owner.

In the most important paragraph in his opinion, Justice Daniel rejected the description of the stagecoach company as the preserver of traditional values. As a transportation company, he insisted, they were agents of change, and hence to be treated with mistrust – a clear reference to the railroad corporations who were not in court but who were undoubtedly watching the case with intense interest:

[A]t a period when the facilities for travel are so rapidly multiplying, and the amount of travel is so constantly on the increase, I feel no disposition to relax any of the rules which hold the carrier to a strict accountability. When so many causes are conspiring to engender and foster a love for the excitement of rapid traveling, which is daily betraying the managers and conductors of every species of conveyance into a fatal disregard of all the precautions essential to the preservation of the limbs and lives of those committed to their charge, I do not think that the law should slacken the reins by which to some extent at least, it holds them in check. On the contrary, policy, humanity and reason all seem to require from the courts a stern adherence to the principles which tend to insure the greatest care on the part of the carrier, and the least danger to the passenger (*Farish*, 718–19).

"Every species of conveyance" made the true target of his comments plain. Illinois might have a Need for Speed, but Virginia's citizens would be protected against such devices by the traditional strictures of the common law.

But what of the precedent on which the stagecoach line had relied? Here Justice Daniel, who had once suggested that private property preceded the creation of Eve, identified the tangled connections between property, slavery, and technology in antebellum Virginia. Daniel cited *Stokes v. Saltonstall*, 13 U.S. (Peters) 181 (1839), a case following *Boyce* that limited that precedent to cases involving slaves. Therefore, as to free passengers, carriers remained liable for any want of care whatsoever. Justice Daniel quoted the crucial passage from *Stokes* to demonstrate the point:

> The Court [in *Boyce*] distinguished slaves, being human beings, from goods; and held, that the doctrine as to the liability of common carriers for mere goods, did not apply to them, but that in respect of them, the carrier was liable only for ordinary neglect. The Court seem to have considered that case as being a sort of *intermediate one between goods and passengers.* We think, therefore, that any thing said in that case, in the reasoning of the Court, must be confined in its application to that case; and does not affect the principle which we have laid down (*Farish*, 712; *Stokes*, 192).

The identification of slaves as "an intermediate form" between person and property defines the obstacle to the modernization of Virginia's tort doctrines. To see why, it is necessary to turn our attention for a moment to the broader question of the relationship between slave law and the development of common law doctrines in general.

The very phrase "slave law" implies that there was an analytically separate category of legal reasoning unique to cases involving slaves. This has been an operating assumption in analyses that posit slavery as both a modernizing and a reactionary force in southern legal development. For example, some scholars argue that slavery was a modernizing force in southern commercial law (Wahl, 1998: 28). The old rule of *caveat emptor*, after all, was ill-suited to the trade in slaves, which often took place at a distance, by way of agents. Instead, slave sellers had an affirmative obligation to inform buyers of defects. On the other hand, in one case where the buyer was himself a professional trader, he was expected to be able to tell for himself whether a slave had dropsy, and in the absence of an affirmative misrepresentation by the seller was unable to collect damages for breach of warranty.[11] In this argument, the conditions of slavetrading had something in common with the Chicago grain trade, and similarly

---

[11] *Brugh v. Shanks*, 5 Vir. 598 (1833); *Wilson v. Shackleford*, 4 Vir. 5 (1826); see Wahl, 1998: 36.

resulted in the creation of balanced doctrines of liability in sales suited to a modern system of extended markets.

It is hardly surprising that slave transactions should have figured prominently in the development of the southern law of commercial sales. Across the South, the huge portion of the total wealth that was contained in slaves made it inevitable that the economics of slavery would drive the development of commercial law.[12] On closer inspection, however, there are profound differences between slavery and the market in grain. The key characterizing feature of the new forms of commercial interactions that arrived with the railroads was standardization. By contrast, slaves were the most inherently nonstandardizable commodity imaginable, and the slave market was ill-suited to capital investment or speculation (Tushnet, 1981: 158–69; Wahl, 1998: 199, n. 44). Rules for slave purchases carried few implications for general commercial practices, let alone a broad preconception of public relationships, because the market had no parallels in other economic sectors. Furthermore, the political dominance of slaveowners created a barrier to change at the point where slaveowning interests might have suffered. As a result, developments in the law of slave transactions did not spill over into other areas of the law.[13] As we saw in the case of Illinois, one of the fundamental pressures in the modernization of the common law was pressure toward rationalization within the system of laws. Thus, at a minimum one would have to distinguish between the path of modernization in northern and southern legal development.

Conversely, turning to the area of tort law, an argument holds that "slave law" was a separate and unique area of southern jurisprudence that retained its ancient form while the rest of the legal system was modernized around it. This argument, not at all coincidentally, is the parallel of arguments that have been made about the development of northern labor law (Orren, 1991). Both southern slavery and northern labor, according to these analyses, represented exceptional islands of ancient practice in a system generally moving toward modernity (Tushnet, 1981: 8). The

---

[12] Roger L. Ransom and Richard Sutch estimate that slaves constituted 60 percent of southern agricultural wealth in the five cotton states, and that the average slaveholder had two-thirds of his wealth in slaves (Ransom and Sutch, 1977: 52–3). See also Wright, 1978.

[13] Jenny Bourne Wahl, for example, finds that patterns in the law relating to slave transactions did not lead to changes in rules governing livestock sales, and concludes that "the common law of slave sales...stands alone" (Wahl, 1998: 193–4, n.2). For a thorough catalogue and discussion of slave cases across the South, and the relationships between slave law and property law generally, see Morris, 1996: 61–80.

problem was that the system of slave law was incommensurable with an emergent, liberal conception of property as "the expression of individual will, subject to regulation only for the most pressing social goals" (Tushnet, 1981: 213; Oakes, 1990: 159). By contrast, slaves were the most republican form of southern property. Slaveowners were therefore more, not less, subject to the demands of *salus populi* than owners of other kinds of property. Applying that principle, the Virginia Supreme Court issued a series of rulings that prohibited slaveowners from incorporating provisions into their wills giving slaves the option of being freed (Tushnet, 1981: 228; Morris, 1996: 430). The right to emancipate slaves was subject to "general principles of public policy regulating the transmission and acquisition of property" (*Wood v. Humphrey*, 12 Vir. 339, 1853). The crucial question, always, was the definition of the concept of "public good" that was involved. The public good of Virginia would be served by insisting that elite actors display the virtues of property owners, not by removing the distinctions between classes of persons in the name of furthering technological progress. Slavery was the most politically important form of property ownership, so it was the locus of the greatest attention in the courts' construction of citizenship, but analytically the law governing the disposition of slaves was of a piece with the larger project of preserving the traditional common law system.

There are other reasons to question the idea that slave law could have remained a separate regime within a larger system of common law development. A separate system of slave law would have had to encompass more than the legal rules governing slave–master relationships and commercial transactions in slaves. A separate category of slave law implies a set of rules governing all situations in which slaves might become participants. In *United States v. Amy*, 4 *Quarterly Law Journal* 163 (1859), for example, the Fourth Circuit Court of Appeals in Virginia, Supreme Court Chief Justice Roger Brooke Taney presiding, confronted the question of whether a slave was a "person" for purposes of a criminal statute that provided that if "any person shall steal a letter from the mail," the penalty was to be a prison sentence of two to ten years. Counsel for the slaveowner, in a position which he conceded to be radical, argued that the federal government's prosecution "confounds the legal character and attributes of the African slaves in the United States, who are purely *chattel slaves* – with their character and attributes as *natural persons*." To prosecute a slave for a crime, went the argument, would "subject the slave to . . . the civil or legal responsibilities of the citizen. . . . A slave has no such rights to exercise or claim, and no such responsibilities can be thrust upon him."

Ultimately, this lawyer was asserting the claim that slaves' separate status did, at least in criminal cases, require that they be governed by a separate body of law: "Accordingly we shall find that in each slave-holding State of the Union, there is virtually a separate code of penal laws for slaves" (*Amy*, 170–1, 168, 171–2).

Much of the slaveowner's argument was based on appeals to the ruling in *Dred Scott*. Taney was hardly unfamiliar with that case, but he rejected the argument, pointing to the dangers inherent in separating slaves from citizens in the context of criminal punishments:

The offenses were as likely to be committed by slaves as by freemen, and the mischief is equally great whether committed by the one or the other. And if a slave is not within the law, it would be in the power of the evil disposed to train and tutor him for these depredations on the mails and post offices, and as the slaves could not be a witness, the culprit, who was the real instigator of the crime, would not be brought to punishment (*Amy*, 199).

Taney's comments point to the crucial fact that the law of slavery governed the conduct of slaveowners as well as that of slaves. This issue arose not only in the context of crimes and *in futuro* manumission, but also in growing problems of competition between hired slaves and free workers. Such competition, as noted earlier, was a point of tension between slavery and the industrial order; it was a problem that would be exacerbated, rather than relieved, by the creation of a separate body of slave law.

Finally, and perhaps most important, the maintenance of a separate category of slave law would have undermined the presumption of a scale, running from chattel to citizen, that was the justifying ontology for slave society in the first instance. Justice Daniel made the point clear in a ruling in 1858:

No man is allowed to introduce anomalies into the ranks under which the population of the state is ranged and classified by its constitution and laws. It is for the master to determine whether to continue to treat his slaves as property, as chattels, or, in the mode prescribed by law, to manumit them.... But he cannot impart to his slaves, as such, for any period, the rights of freedmen. He cannot endow, with powers of such import as are claimed for the slaves here, persons whose *status* or condition, in legal definition and intendment, exists in the denial to them of the attributes of any social or civil capacity whatever (*Bailey v. Poindexter*, 55 Vir. 132, 210, 1858).

Taney might find a universal and equal obligation to refrain from the commission of crimes, but Virginia was not going to abandon its ideal of an ordered, graded set of "ranks under which the population of the state is ranged and classified."

Daniel's appeal was to political as well as formal legal principles. The debates in the constitutional conventions of 1829 and 1851 made it clear that "categories" were not unique to slave law, they were the grounding concept for southern traditionalism in law, politics, and society. Eastern conservatives warned over and over for example, that extending the franchise to nonpropertied whites would lead to social egalitarianism that would extend to free blacks and ultimately to slaves themselves. The political justification of slavery rested on religious and "scientific" claims about human nature that extended to free blacks and whites, and therefore drew the connection between slave law and broader patterns of common law development, just as in the discussion of Illinois the development of the fellow-servant rule was seen to be a part of a larger pattern of imposing universal social duties. Ordinary chattels and real property,[14] slaves, free blacks, children, women, white males who did not own property, and citizens each occupied a separate rung in a ladder of status and prerogative that articulated the basic justification for the social order and the political and legal systems. The existence of slaves as a middle category between person and property linked the laws of persons and the laws of property into a single, graduated system.

Virginia's courts, in adjudicating slave cases, were confronted by the same issues of constructing a model of citizenship that Illinois' courts faced in the context of railroad accidents. In Illinois, the progression had been from a regime based on the equation, "I own property, therefore I have rights," to one based on the sequence, "I have duties, therefore I must control my property." The Duty to Get Out of the Way was based on the possibility, and hence the obligation, to exercise control over one's property. But slaves ultimately could not be controlled. This was the fear, and the realization, that had gripped Virginia politics since the Nat Turner uprising of 1831, and that had been so powerfully reflected in the revisions to its constitution in 1851. Slaveowners could not guarantee that their property would not attempt escape or suicide during transit, nor that their property would not cause problems for the shipper. Slaveowners needed the help of the transportation industry, above all others, to preserve their control over this most valuable and important of all forms of property.

In 1836, Virginia passed a statute imposing a $100 fine on anyone who transported slaves without permission, and additional laws extended

---

[14] One expression of the difficulty that southern courts had in defining the precise nature of slave property appeared in the periodic treatment of slaves as akin to real property rather than as chattels (Morris, 1996: 61–80; Tushnet, 1981: 164).

the fine to the operators of ferries and bridges in 1839. An 1855 statute required all ship masters to allow their ships to be searched for runaways before embarking from Virginia ports. What was true of ships was equally true of railroads. As Jenny Bourne Wahl observes, "[s]tates with the most railroad miles or the most miles per slave . . . were the first to codify and clarify their laws regarding railroads and slaves. As railroads grew in importance, so did the specificity of the common law concerning liability for aiding slaves to escape" (Wahl, 1998: 95, 97–98, 99). The railroads arrived at just the time when the fragility of the slaveowners' control was uppermost in their minds, exacerbating the conflict between the demands of slave society and those of rail-driven technological progress.

The alternative, to concede that slaves had intelligence and will, came perilously close to admitting that potentially rights-bearing persons were being held as property, an admission that would utterly subvert the conservatives' careful construction of a formal identity between slaveowners' property rights and the political rights of persons. This was the truly subversive effect of any move toward uniform and universal standards of conduct: the erasure of essential differences between categories of persons. This also identifies the crucial mistake in the argument of the stagecoach line in *Farish* when it embraced the proposition that the traditional duties of a carrier to its passengers should be replaced by a new system drawn from the law of bailments. In making this argument, the lawyers for the line unforgivably attempted to extend a rule about the treatment of property, such as slaves, to define the treatment that was required for citizens. The "intermediate" category to which slaves were assigned did more than keep them in a state of legal limbo, it created a barrier between personal and property rights that prevented the kind of conceptual unification that was at the heart of Illinois' legal experimentation.

It is critical to recognize that slaves were "intermediate" only metaphysically. In terms of the railroads' duties of care, slaves were a uniquely *disfavored* form of property. Railroads, as bailees for hire and common carriers, faced strict or near-strict liability for harms to baggage as well as passengers under traditional principles. With regard to slaves, uniquely, the obligation of the transporter was only to avoid negligence. This was the kind of low standard of care that was applied to everybody in the North, under the principle of contributory negligence and the fellow-servant rule. The treatment of those rules in antebellum Virginia is the next topic for consideration.

Contributory Negligence and the Fellow-Servant Rule

The special case of slaves does a great deal to explain the very high duties of care that railroads were required to satisfy toward all other persons and their other property. The maintenance of the highest possible standards of care toward citizens emphasized the vast distance between themselves and lower, intermediate forms of life. Concerning the obligation to employ advanced technology, for example, Daniel was entirely unwilling to give credence to the idea of an established industry standard:

If the proposition contended for by the plaintiff in error is to be received as the law, viz: that he undertakes only that his coaches, harness and fixtures shall be sound and complete of the kind used on his line, it follows that he may be excused from liability in the face of the amplest proof to show that owing to their style or kind, they were positively dangerous. In no case that I have seen can any warrant be found for such a rule (*Farish*, 716).

Once again, this is in sharp contrast to the willingness of the Illinois court to acknowledge the existence of a railroad-based community, possessed of customary modes of interaction and collective standards for knowledge and judgment.

Another distinction was the burden that passengers were expected to assume concerning their own safety. When Erastus Hazzard chose to ride in a caboose, the Illinois Supreme Court held that he assumed the risks incident to his mode of travel, including the absence of a restraining chain at the end of the car.[15] Justice Daniel, by contrast, was quite specific in his refusal to place a burden on passengers to be familiar with the technology of transportation:

Such a rule seems to me to alter the relative rights and duties of the carrier and passenger. The passenger, instead of relying on the carrier to use the proper care and judgment in the selection of the coach, harness, &c. with a view to its safety, would have to use the utmost diligence, whenever about to take passage, in enquiring into the style and fashion of the coach used on the line, and then to determine for himself whether or not a stage constructed after such style or fashion, would or would not, probably, be safe. The law, I think, imposes no such duty on the passenger (*Farish*, 717–18).

The references to assumption of risk and presumed standards of expertise demonstrate the same connection that was seen in the Illinois cases between general rules of contributory negligence and the fellow-servant

---

[15] *Chicago, Burlington & Quincy Railroad Co. v. Hazzard*, 26 Ill. 373 (1861), discussed in Chapter 4.

rule. In fact, Virginia's version of the fellow-servant rule was different from that which we have seen in operation in Illinois. The Virginia Supreme Court did not rule on the question of the fellow-servant rule in the 1850s, but in 1857 the circuit court in Wheeling – the city most invested in railroad development in the state – weighed in on the matter.

The case, *Hawley v. Baltimore and Ohio Railroad Co.*, 3 *Quarterly Law Journal* 89 (1857), involved a conductor who was injured in a collision that occurred when another employee, Connor, inadvertently left a side-switch open, which sent Hawley's train off the track. This was precisely the scenario that had given rise to the strict version of the fellow-servant rule in New York, which had been so eloquently defended by the Illinois Supreme Court as necessary both to protect the public and to preserve the "freedom" of the worker to assume risks. The rule adopted in *Hawley* was only slightly different from that adopted in Illinois, but the language of its articulation was completely different.

The fellow-servant rule as it was announced in *Hawley* had very large loopholes designed to protect employees against the artificial presumption of a free assumption of risk that was so important to the Illinois justices. The company would escape liability only if the incompetence of Connor and the relevant conduct by the railroad had been personally known *to* Hawley. That is, the fellow-servant rule would be treated as a special case of assumption of risk, not as an independent bar to recovery:

> If the company used due care in selecting Connor and had no notice of such carelessness, if such existed; or, if he was careless of that duty, so assigned him, and this carelessness was known to the plaintiff and he continued in his employment; or, if only during their common employment Connor became careless, and his superior officer as aforesaid was informed thereof and neglected to remove him, and the plaintiff with notice thereof continued his employment...he must be presumed to have adopted such employment with such risk... (*Hawley*, 90–1).

The shift in focus, from the state of the railroad's knowledge to the state of the plaintiff's knowledge, made all the difference in the allocation of the burden of proof. The assumption of risk by the employee would have to be affirmatively proved by the employer, rather than being presumed from the nature of the labor market or the inherent nature of "free" workers.

The Illinois Supreme Court had emphasized that its fellow-servant rule defined the difference between free workers and slaves. Virginia's rule did the same, but of course Virginia had real slaves against which to compare its treatment of free white workers. Virginia, raising the protection of free workers above that of slaves, also raised the level of their protection above that granted to the interests of the railroad company. This reflected the southern assertion that northern workers were caught in something truly unthinkable: slavery unjustified by racial difference. This outcome also, however, reflected the complete absence of the totalizing language of an abstract "public" whose interests the railroad could be presumed to serve. Once again, the existence of the "intermediate category" meant the impossibility of moving toward a regime of universal duties. Virginia's courts would stand as a bulwark against the threats of rationalization and standardization by preserving the traditional common law rights of private property owners.

One of the few cases heard by the Virginia Supreme Court that dealt with claims brought by railroad passengers was *Virginia Central R.R. Co. v. Sanger*, 15 Vir. 230 (1859). In *Sanger*, a passenger was injured when a train derailed due to the fact that a large rock that had been stacked next to the tracks during blasting came under the train's wheels. The Virginia Supreme Court, confronted by a claim involving parties bound by privity of contract, made no effort to find limiting principles or countervailing extracontractual duties: "The duties which a carrier of passengers owed to his passengers, and the duties which he owes to other persons, between whom and himself the relation of carrier and passenger does not exist, are essentially distinct." Daniel went further, however, and reasoned that the duties owed to passengers by railroads were conceived to be broader even than those that had been at issue in *Farish*:

> [T]he sphere of such duties is, in the case of the rail road company, generally of a much broader extent than that which usually limits the office and duty of a carrier of passengers by stage coaches or other like means of public conveyance.... Combining in themselves the ownership as well of the road as of the cars and locomotives, they are bound to the most exact care and diligence not only in the management of the trains and cars, but also in the structure and care of the track, and in all the subsidiary arrangements necessary to the safety of passengers.

In addition, Daniel ruled that the fact that the rocks in question had been left close to the tracks by employees of a contractor, rather than railroad employees, was irrelevant "if the company, by its officers charged with the duty of guarding the track against obstructions, saw or might, by the exercise of proper vigilance, have seen" the danger (*Sanger*, 242, 236, 240).

Daniel's ruling on the last point imposed a general duty of watchfulness on railroad employees. This was the converse of the emphasis on vigilance in Illinois' doctrines of contributory negligence and the fellow-servant rule. In the North, the law imposed a universal duty on everyone to vigilantly avoid being in harm's way, lest they obstruct the forward progress of trains. This duty derived from no traditional, private, property-based relationship, but from a new conception of duties owed to the abstract conception of a collective good unalterably tied to the promise of technology. In Virginia, the duty of vigilance fell on railroad companies by virtue of their contractual relationship to passengers. Once again, the development of a rule relatively unfriendly to corporations resulted from the focus on private relationships as the wellsprings of legally enforceable duties, and the very high degree of care that mere artificial persons were required to demonstrate for the benefit of free Virginians.

The fellow-servant rule, however, was no more than implicitly involved in *Sanger*, and up to the Civil War, Virginia's Supreme Court never announced a doctrinal position on this crucial question, just as it never addressed the relative duties of rail, stock, and agricultural property owners. This silence, and the principles implicit in Daniel's ruling, continued to draw complaints from Virginian legal writers who looked to join the modern, American trend in common law development. An 1861 article in the *Quarterly Law Review* addressed the problems of employer and fellow-servant liability, and recommended a kind of blend of southern and northern principles as a resolution. The author recommended adoption of the fellow-servant rule "in the case of a white or free servant injured by the negligence of another servant in the same service or employment," based on the employees' assumption of the risks incident to employment. Recognizing that the issue had not been resolved in Virginia, the author predicted a limited application of the fellow-servant rule would be applied: "When it arises...the exception in favor of the master will probably not be extended beyond the cases, when it is the duty of the servant to prevent the injury, or when his act or omission concurs to produce it" (R.B.H., 1861: 1–2, 4).

The problem for the author of the article, as Daniel recognized perhaps more clearly than anyone, was that the importation of rules modifying the traditional relationships of employment and liability created huge conceptual conflicts when applied in a system that prominently featured slave labor. A slaveowner could not be sued by his slave, of course, but by the late 1850s, the Virginia economy increasingly featured the practice of leasing slaves out to industrial and other urban employers.[16] The questions that this practice raised for the fellow-servant rule had to do with injuries to free workers caused by slaves, and injuries to slaves caused by the

[16] See the discussion in Chapter 1. On the decline of urban slavery, see Goldin, 1991.

negligence of free workers. The difficulty, once again, was posed by the position of slaves as intermediate beings between human and chattel. If slaves were mere animals, then they could not be expected to exercise vigilance, and the employer who hired them from their owner should be strictly liable for any harms they suffered. Conversely, if slaves were persons capable of vigilance – well, the end of that road was clear.

The *Quarterly Law Journal* author tried to avoid the problem with a paternalistic argument that equated slavery to minority or, for women, marriage: "The slave . . . is hampered and restrained by his legal incapacity. His condition is founded to some extent upon the opinion, that his true interests require that he shall have a master." The writer also went further, observing that slaves were inherently unreliable, and that employers who hired them owed a duty to the interests of the general public to exercise vigilance over their actions: "Both humanity to the slave and the public security, where he is employed in a service involving the public safety, would seem to require that no contract should be implied, whereby the hirer should be relieved of his obligation to exercise the most active supervision over the slave" (R.B.H., 1861: 6–7, citing cites cases from Georgia, South Carolina, and Florida, and a contrary case from North Carolina). So the rule would be one that disadvantaged the employer, especially the industrial employer, *vis-à-vis* both the public and the slaveowner. Common carriers had fewer duties to safeguard slaves than any other kind of property, but employers would be required to exercise greater vigilance over slaves than over any other class of workers.

As a straightforward matter of balancing interests, both legal and economic, the attempt to preserve a slave system in the midst of modern tort duties meant at every point that slavery trumped modernization.[17] The question of relative interests, however, was only part of the problem. The philosophical justification for the fellow-servant doctrine was the idea that "free labor" entered the marketplace with the same latitude, judgment, and ability to exercise vigilance as railway passengers and corporate investors. The analytical starting point for the determination of the duties owed between parties was this presumption of standard, universal duties

---

[17] Frederick Wertheim argues that the fellow-servant rule produced the anomalous result that hirers had a higher duty of care toward slaves, under bailment law, than they had toward free workers under the laws governing employment. Wertheim proposes that this outcome demonstrates a general tension between slavery and industrial labor (Wertheim, 1986: 1114–15, 1136). This tension, between the protection of private property and the lesser protections provided to free labor, was the conflict that required the Virginia courts to subordinate the interests of industrial employers to those of slaveowners.

that applied to standard, universal persons. That idea, above all other aspects of northern modernization, was liberal anathema to the republican categorization of persons that created the language of legitimation for the society of eastern Virginia.

There is one other important motivation that may have driven Virginia's justices in clinging to the political ontology that justified the law of slavery. There is no reason to believe that Daniel, Moncure, and their colleagues were personally cruel men, and indeed Daniel was remembered as a kindly master to his own slaves. Yet the law that defined slaves as an intermediate category of property protected an immensely brutal system, and judges hearing cases could not avoid confronting that brutality. At the risk of engaging in psychological speculation, it seems reasonable to suppose that to be a participant in a system of laws that supported the evident cruelties of the slave system required jealous preservation of the principle of difference between social categories. Daniel and his fellows were the guardians of that legitimating principle of difference. This alone may be a sufficient explanation for resistance to the kind of integration of contract, tort, and property doctrines into the single regime of universal duties that was observed in Illinois. The philosophical justifications for slavery and the universal duties of American common law were ultimately and irreducibly incommensurable.

8

Virginia's Version of American Common Law

Old Wine in New Bottles

The immediate postwar period in Virginia, as in the South generally, was a period of military rule, economic chaos, and the threat of social upheaval. A new constitution, written by Virginian Republicans while the war was still raging, became the basis for the "Restored" government. This document was little more than a military edict; the statewide recorded vote for ratification was an improbable five hundred to zero (Van Schreeven, 1967: 10). Once again, the key provision related to the franchise, but this time it was Confederates who were not allowed to vote. Under this system, Thaddeus Stevens' Radical Party was elected to power in 1866 with sixty-five of one hundred seats in the legislature; of those sixty-five seats, twenty-six were filled by northerners (Wertenbaker, 1962: 236). In 1867, Congress passed the Reconstruction Act, imposing a draconian form of reconstruction that put control over elections in the hands of the military. In Virginia, the military governor called a constitutional convention chaired by John Underwood, a federal judge from New York who had presided over the trial of Jefferson Davis. With Underwood as chair, the new convention produced a draft constitution that contained two clauses disenfranchising most men who had served in the Confederacy. At the personal intervention of President Ulysses S. Grant, these two clauses were presented to the voters for ratification separately from the rest of the text. Those clauses were defeated, but the remainder of the 1870 Constitution was adopted, and remained in force until 1902. Despite the defeat of the two disenfranchising clauses, the 1870 Constitution was despised by Virginia's conservatives. In 1874, in his message to the legislature, Governor James L. Kemper called it "odious to the people" and "mischievous in operation" (Van Schreeven, 1967: 11–13, 14).

After 1867, control over the national government's southern policy was in the hands of moderate, business Republicans who had little interest in radically reshaping southern society (Foner, 1988: 315–16). It quickly became clear that the South would largely be left to reconstruct itself, which meant the discouragement of democratic participation by freed blacks and the reappearance of traditional elites. The enactment of restrictive Black Codes, beginning in 1865, was the harbinger of the process of the reassertion of the economic and political hegemony of conservative elites[1] (Foner: 1995, 346–7). By 1868, the revolution was effectively over in Virginia. In that year's elections, the new Conservative Party swept state government in a vote heavily divided on racial lines. The pattern of Virginian elections for the next three decades was set in this contest, with conservative white candidates running and winning on platforms that emphasized the threat that black political power posed to the social order. The rhetoric, moreover, remained the same that it had been in 1829 and 1850. In an 1870 mayoral election in Norfolk, Conservatives warned that victory by the Radical Party would mean "subordination of property, intelligence, and industry to pauperism, ignorance, and of Anglo-Saxon enterprise. . . . negro magistrates on your bench, negro policemen on your streets, negro legislators in your councils . . . negro commissioners in your schools" (Wertenbaker, 1962: 243, 245).

Nonetheless, the relationship between Virginia's conservative elites and their state's political culture was fundamentally changed. In the absence of slavery, conservatives could no longer draw on the vocabulary of republican constitutionalism to argue that modernizing trends were incommensurable with Virginia's unique political genius. It was also no longer the case that industrialization could be realistically stopped at the state's borders. The secession of West Virginia meant that the east had to reach beyond its borders to obtain raw materials and to reach markets, while the continuing development of the northern rail system had reached a point where "natural" market relationships were those connected by railroads. To remain outside the national rail system no longer meant that Virginia could exercise control over the flow of commerce, but rather implied that commerce simply flowed around it. In the absence of a well-developed rail system, for example, it would be far simpler for Wheeling

---

[1] As noted earlier, similar codes had been established in Richmond in the 1850s, in response to the presence of large numbers of slaves circulating in the city. The postbellum codes reflected the continuation of a mindset that survived the abolition of slavery intact.

to ship its goods through Pennsylvania than through the now separate state of Virginia. There was, then, no longer the conjunction between interests and ideology that had characterized the inward-turning focus of eastern Virginian conservatism. The old economic order was gone, and with it the argument that the state's well-being depended on resisting the encroachments of the national economy.

The economy of Virginia showed a similar mixture of continuity and change. On the one hand, the proposition that a "New South" appeared following the Civil War is challenged by a number of facts. The postbellum South was marked by a racial caste system enforced by laws, a party system divided between white Democrats and black Republicans – which increasingly meant a single-party system dominated by old elites – and a rural economy based on a form of agriculture that mimicked key economic relationships of the earlier plantation system[2] (Oakes, 1990: 202; Schwartz, 1979: 8; see also Foner, 1988: 596–7; Kolchin, 1993: 224). In many ways, indeed, the "New South" looked a great deal like the Old South.

On the other hand, there was a new power arising in Virginia. An emphasis on the similarities in social structure between plantation and tenant farming, for example, overlooks a crucial shift in ownership toward a class of merchants, who held the liens in the crop lien system (Goodwyn, 1976: 28–31, 118–19; Kolchin, 1993: 195–7). Furthermore, while industrialization in Virginia was not widespread, industrial interests nonetheless had the favor of Republicans and unique access to northern investment capital (Foner, 1988: 380–81). Nor were there any longer serious arguments against the proposition that rail expansion was the key to economic development, despite the persistence of public debate. But there was a considerable amount of common interest between ruling elites and the rising industrial and non-planter classes. From the beginning of Reconstruction, race and the fear of black power and an undiminished social conservatism among white elites kept economic competition from translating into the kind of genuine political opposition that had existed between east and west in the 1850s.[3]

[2] For a detailed description of the crop lien system and tenant farming practices in general, see Orser, 1988.
[3] As Richard Bensel points out, at the beginning of the Reconstruction period there were two fundamental alternative tracks toward Southern industrialization:

> "One was expensive, state-centered reorganization of the southern political economy with consequent constraints on national economic growth.... The other alternative was an accommodation with the southern plantation elite that

The translation of this new political order into the personnel of the Virginia Supreme Court proceeded through the de-democratization of the selection process. Replacing the popular elections of the 1850s, the 1870 Constitution restored the system of legislative election to twelve-year terms, with one justice to be chosen from each of three regions. This meant that conservative domination of the state government in the 1870s translated into complete domination of the high court, and to a lesser extent of the circuit courts as well. Politically prominent families continued to provide the bulk of justices: seven out of thirteen justices elected between 1866 and 1894 had at least one immediate family member who had previously served in the legislature or on the bench (Morris, 1975: 29).

Two of the three justices who played important roles in defining Virginia's new common law doctrines, elected to the bench in 1870, were Richard Moncure and William T. Joynes. The third was Edward C. Burks, who joined the court in 1877. Burks had been a prominent member of the Confederate legislature, and was famous for his fervor for the southern cause. He was also a legal conservative who would later become a noted critic of codification and the incursion by legislators onto the traditional areas of common law authority[4] (Christian, 1897: 323–36). These three justices, decidedly southern in ideology and sympathy, crafted Virginia's version of modern American common law between 1867 and 1878. The changes in the rules of adjudication were quite dramatic, as William Daniel discovered in several unsuccessful appearances before his erstwhile court and, in the case of Moncure, his colleague. This reconfiguration of Virginia's common law doctrines, however, was very different from that which had taken place in Illinois in the 1850s.

First and most important, Virginia's transition was abrupt, showing none of the pattern of trial and error, gradual development, and reliance on in-state precedent that characterized Illinois' legal development. When

would enable efficient northern exploitation of the southern export economy during…industrialization (Bensel, 1990: 8; see also Schwartz, 1979: 11–12).

[4] "Our legislation seems to be getting looser and looser – each succeeding legislative session furnishing much nutritious food for hungry lawyers, and not a little poison for the people. As for the Code, a work of three years and more of careful labor, it is pretty well 'done for'.... This is an object lesson to all who advocate a codification of the common law." The "Code" to which Burks referred was an 1887 codification of the state's statutory laws produced by a committee comprising Burks, former Justice Walter R. Staples, and future Justice John W. Riley (Christian, 1897: 334, quoting *Lacy v. Palmer*, 2 *Virginia's Law Register* 96, 1896).

new rules were adopted in the 1870s, they were adopted wholesale from national digests, a pattern common to other states trying to catch up with the development of modern legal doctrines in the industrial North (Friedman, 1985: 347, 364). By far the most commonly cited sources in the cases discussed in this chapter were two digests, Vermont Supreme Court Justice Isaac Redfield's *Law of Railways* and Thomas G. Sherman and Amansa Redfield's *Sherman and Redfield on Negligence* (Redfield, 1867; Sherman and Redfield, 1869). Nor did the Virginia justices display the independent creativity that had been the hallmark of the 1850s Illinois opinions. Far from straying afield from the arguments before them, the Virginia decisions nearly always reproduced the arguments of the lawyers almost verbatim.

Paradoxically, perhaps, the imposition of legal rules from an established national model did less to strike at the heart of traditional modes of analysis than the gradual development of doctrines in northern states. The absence of an analytical process that gradually resolved contradictions and filled lacunae in legal doctrines meant that the tensions between new and old ways of thinking were never worked through. Virginia simply imposed a new system of rules for adjudication on top of a preexisting and arguably incommensurate conceptual framework. Virginia's common law, as a result, was neither internally coherent nor as modern as its formal set of rules suggested. The new rules dictated different outcomes, but the essential process of analysis, and the legitimating norms that it incorporated, remained the same. In particular, the hierarchy of preferences among rights claims remained what it had been before: property rights first, followed by contractual rights and obligations (as in corporate charters), followed by a strictly limited conception of general rights and duties. As a result, the introduction of the language of public interest meant that, in conflict with private property claims, corporations had more responsibilities and fewer rights than in the North. Conversely, tort-based claims by individuals were subject to stringent restrictions that protected the property rights of corporations.

Virginia's common law also retained other important aspects of its earlier analytical framework. Despite the adoption of modern pleading, for example, there was no conceptual unification of doctrines. Essentially, "negligence" remained the special plea of trespass on the case, albeit with a new name. Just as under the old writ, negligence law would require case-by-case evaluation of particular circumstances, with no set of general standards that defined a starting point extraneous and precedent to the relationships between the parties. Thus categories of citizenship appeared in the law as elements of the circumstances of a private dispute rather than as superlegal articulations of a political ideal or unifying conceptual underpinnings to the system of legal reasoning. There was no uniform set of public virtues around which a coherent system of standards might be established, nor pressure for their discovery. In this way, Virginia's private law essentially remained private. Its highest court imported the new American legal doctrines, but it refused to adopt an expanded, abstract notion of public good, the existence of extracontractual public duties, or the equation of technology with progress.

Virginia's adoption of modern rules turned their meaning upside down. Initially, at least, corporate employers rather than employees were burdened with a duty of vigilance. In the cases where property rights gave way to public duties, it was so that corporate interests could be subordinated to claims of political sovereignty, rather than the converse, and railroads were required to recognize and accommodate differences between social classes. Once again, the preservation of the idea of classes of citizenry, in overt opposition to the universalizing tendencies of northern modernism, dictated much of the form that the new rules took through the 1870s.

As these observations suggest, in many cases, Virginia common law favored individuals over corporations. But the outcome was not always simple. Just as northern courts imposed duties of care on railroads at the point where their conduct threatened an idealized model of public citizenship, Virginia's justices favored railroads where plaintiffs stepped out of their private roles. One way to conceive of the difference is in terms of the relative importance of categories of legal actors. In both Illinois and Virginia, the categories of legal actors could be divided into persons, corporations, and governmental entities. In the Illinois version of this division, corporations and governments had a great deal in common, and persons were called upon to accommodate themselves to the needs of those public entities. In Virginia, conversely, corporations and persons were essentially interchangeable – and so, too, were governments, unless they were acting in a specifically sovereign capacity. Virginia law was an instrument for the accommodation of a traditional model of private citizenship to the reality of modernization. As a result, finally, Virginia also shows nothing of a shift in the political function of the law that was seen in the North. Ultimately, like its politics, Virginia's common law was old wine in new bottles.

Damage to Property

In 1866, in office for only a few months and while federal troops still patrolled the streets of the capital, the Virginia Supreme Court announced its adoption of the northern principle of contributory negligence in *Union Steamship Co. v. Nottingham*, 17 Vir. 115 (1866). Not coincidentally, the justices did so in a context that simultaneously announced the expanded range of the common law. The case rose out of a collision between a schooner, the *Amazon*, and a steamship called *The City of Richmond* on the James River in 1855. The testimony showed that it had been a dark and foggy night, and that the schooner had carried inadequate lights. As for the steamer, there was insufficient testimony, according to the trial judge, to find its crew guilty of any negligence.

The judge at trial entered a ruling in accordance with a rule of admiralty law: that in a case of a collision in which fault could not be determined, the damages of the parties should be split evenly between them. Justice Joynes declined to apply the rule of admiralty, instead using the case to announce a general common law rule of contributory negligence:

> [T]he admiralty rule adopted by the court below, by which the loss in such a case is divided equally between the parties, does not prevail in the courts of common law, and is inconsistent with common law principles. When the negligence or fault of the injured vessel contributed to produce the injury, so that the injury results directly from the negligence or fault of both vessels, the common law does not undertake to say how much of it is due to one and how much to the other, and leaves the loss where it falls (*Nottingham*, 123, citing three English cases).

The Virginia rule, therefore, appeared as the "clean hands" requirement that barred any recovery for a plaintiff who was in any degree negligent, with nothing of the gross/slight allocations of fault and the subsequent development of comparative negligence standards characteristic of northern law. This is the first example of the pattern of postbellum legal development in Virginia. New rules were adopted in their entirety and in formulaic, sterile edicts. The announcement here of the rule of contributory negligence shows nothing of the process of working out, experimentation, and adjustment that led northern courts to develop their various versions of the rule over a ten-year period. Nor did Joynes choose to adopt one of the northern states' comparative negligence principles. England had no general theory of negligence, and hence no general principle of contributory negligence. The English cases that Justice Joynes cited were specific cases involving boats, nothing more.

A few years later, the rule of contributory negligence received further amplification when the Virginia Supreme Court finally issued a ruling on the troublesome question of collisions between trains and wandering stock in *Trout v. Virginia and Tennessee Rail Road Co.*, 24 Vir. 619 (1873). Justice Moncure, like Justice Joynes in *Nottingham*, decided the issue by the adoption of English rules. Moncure's analysis started with a comparative evaluation of parties' property rights, and ended with a comparison of duties owed to various categories of actors that maintained the strict distinction between public and private duties. Most importantly, there was nothing of the move toward doctrinal unification that this same category of case had brought to the fore in Illinois twenty years earlier.

An 1860 statute provided that where railroad tracks crossed private property, the lines were required to provide "proper wagon ways across the road from one part of the said land to the other," which in the Court's opinion included "efficient cattle guards"[5] (Vir. Code ch. 56 §§ 22 (1860), at *Trout*, 632). The cattle-guards at the wagon crossing on Trout's land were left up. Some horses wandered onto the tracks, became trapped by the adjoining fences, and were struck and killed. Trout's lawyers first argued that this meant that his horses were rightfully on the railroad track at the time of the collision: "The common law rule binding every owner to restrain his own cattle being reversed by the Statute of Virginia," they argued, the horses "were not trespassers, but were 'rightfully' there, and being injured by the defendant's negligence, plaintiff is entitled to recover." This language echoed the argument that an Illinois lawyer had made twenty-one years earlier, in 1852, when he described a horse as a "free commoner and at large" (*Aurora Branch R.R. Co. v. Grimes*, 13 Ill. 585, 1852). But that had been a losing argument, and by 1873 the appearance of language describing an animal in this way would have been absurd in an Illinois court.

Having established that his horses had a property right in the use of the tracks, Trout's lawyers asserted that the railroad's negligence derived from the failure of the driver to ascertain that the cattle-guards were down: "[H]e neglected to ascertain if they had escaped through the drawbars, *nay, he did not even look to see if the drawbars were down.* . . . " Had the engineer looked to see that the drawbars were down, said Trout's lawyers, he could

---

[5] The same statute provided that railroad tracks could not be constructed within an incorporated town without the permission of the town's government, a provision that suggests that the issues raised in the negotiations between the RF&P and Richmond (discussed in the previous chapter) had remained unresolved in other cases.

have stopped the train in a distance of forty feet (Virginia Supreme Court Library [VSCL] file #137: 2–3, 3). The claim that the train could have been stopped within a distance of forty feet was the subject of a good deal of conflicting testimony. William C. Hooper, the locomotive engineer, testified that "he could not have stopped the engine under 600 feet," as at the time the first animal was struck the engine was running at a speed of eight miles an hour. Hooper also testified that "there is great danger of throwing the trains off the track when the engine runs over a horse, and the danger is increased when the train is running slowly." Other witnesses' testimony produced various estimates of the stopping distance of the train that ranged from thirty feet to one hundred fifty yards. Robert Mitchell, division-master for the train company, estimated that "[f]rom the bridge to where the first horse was killed he thinks a mail train running at full speed, say 17 or 18 miles an hour could not be stopped under 800 or 900 feet" (VSCL file #137: 18, 13–14, 15, 20, 21).

The observation that stock collisions posed dangers to trains opened the door to the main argument of the railroad's brief, an argument drawn almost entirely from citations to Isaac Redfield's digest:

In determining the question of negligence, the duties due from the Railroad Company to the passengers upon its trains, and as carriers of the U.S. mail, should be considered. It would be impossible for the Company to properly perform these duties if the running of its trains is to be constantly interrupted by vagrant, trespassing animals, and the Company is to be punished in damages when such animals are accidentally killed or damaged by its trains in the regular and lawful performance of their obligations to the public (*Trout*, 635).

In support of this argument, the brief quoted from *Railroad Co. v. Skinner*, 19 Penn. State Rep. 298 (1852) as the case was referenced in Redfield's *American Railroad Cases*: "A train must make the time necessary to fulfil its engagements with the post-office and the passengers; and it must be allowed to fulfil them at the sacrifice of secondary interests put in its way; else it could not fulfil them at all. The maxim, *salus populi*, would be inverted, and the paramount affairs of the public would be postponed to the petty concerns of individuals" (*Trout*, 646). The characterization of the horses as "trespassers," of course, reflected the retention of some of the older language of property rights. The same language appeared in the railroad's argument. Trout's failure to close the gate leading from his property was "contributive negligence . . . and his horses were trespassers upon the property of the appellee."

In response to these arguments, Trout's lawyers appealed for preservation of ancient traditions. The opinion in *Skinner*, they argued, "is ... expressly declared by Judge Redfield not to be the law in any coun-try where prevails the maxim, '*Sic utere tuo ut non laedas alienum*' "[6] (*Trout*, 628–9, 634). These arguments perfectly illustrated the conflict between the new and the old versions of common law discourse. On the one side, a reconceived notion of *salus populi* drove the modernization of the com-mon law with its invention of a duty to promote technological progress, while against that argument common law traditionalists appealed to *sic utere*, the rights of private property owners, as the bedrock of traditional legal discourse. The railroad quoted authorities from Vermont and Pennsylvania. Trout's lawyers, perhaps feeling that citation to cases from the days of slavery would not be politic, quoted English precedents.

The court, clinging to its conservative traditions, sided entirely with Trout. Justice Moncure described the issues in the case in terms of the railroad's private obligations under contract and property law principles:

Railroads are of great public utility, and indeed are now indispensable, as means of travel and of commerce.... They are charged with the duty of carrying safely, the passengers whose lives are entrusted to their care; and as they are held by law to a strict accountability for the faithful discharge of this duty.... But subject to this paramount duty of taking care of the passengers under their charge, it is also their duty to be careful to avoid injury to stock which may happen to be upon their road; at least when there without the fault of the owner of such stock. Fortunately for all parties concerned, the means proper to be used to avoid injury to such stock, are generally the best means that can be used for the safety of the passengers.

Significantly, Moncure showed no willingness to accept the statement of the train engineer that in a collision with stock, speed equaled safety. Above all, the outcome turned on Moncure's reiteration of the attitudes that had been expressed in *Farish & Co. v. Reigle*, 11 Vir. 697 (1854). *Farish* was the stagecoach case in which Justice Daniel had declared his concern that "at a period when the facilities for travel are so rapidly multiplying, and the amount of travel is so constantly on the increase.... I do not think that the law should slacken the reins by which to some extent at least, it holds [carriers] in check." In 1873, Virginia's high court would still recognize no Need for Speed, nor accommodate those who sought to use the demands of technology as the measuring standard for public conduct.

---

[6] Redfield, speaking of the Pennsylvania court's opinion in *Skinner*, wrote, "These views have sometimes been adopted in the jury trials in other States. But they are certainly not maintained to the full extent in any country where the maxim *sic utere tuo, ut alienum non laedas* prevails *even to the limited extent recognized in the common law in England*'" (*Trout*, 648, emphasis added).

As for the question of contributory negligence, Moncure accepted the
recent adoption of the rule in Virginia, but he denied that it was at issue
in the case (*Trout*, 649–51).

Thus by the early 1870s, Virginia's high court had accomplished the
move that is characterized here by the phrase "old wine in new bottles."
New rules were adopted, but they were almost completely divorced from
the philosophical principles that had justified their creation in the first
instance. The rule of contributory negligence would apply in stock collision cases after 1873, but not on the basis of any universal duties owed
by stock owners to promote the political economy of speed, nor on any
acceptance of the idea that technology-driven progress would benefit everyone in the long run. The fundamental ideological elements of antebellum southern legal thought remained the same: suspicion of technology
and innovation, preservation of individual property rights and traditional
English common law categories, and focus on the relationships between
the parties as the basis for defining duties of care. It was in the context of
injuries to persons, however, that the Virginia Supreme Court most clearly
demonstrated its approach to modernization of the law.

Injuries to Strangers

Norfolk & Petersburg R.R. Co. v. Ormsby, 27 Vir. 455 (1876) involved a
toddler, Charles Ormsby, who was terribly injured when a railroad flatcar
ran over his arm. The flatcar had been standing stationary on its tracks
in the middle of a residential street all day. When it came time to couple
the car to a train, every precaution was taken: the engineer slowed the
locomotive down to the minimum sustainable speed, there were no fewer
than three lookouts, and the train's bell was rung continuously. But the
coupling pin had been removed from the flatcar during the day, and the
lookouts did not see the small child (VSCL file #1212: 3). As a result,
instead of jolting back a mere two or three feet, the flatcar was sent
rolling backward more than ten feet, running over the boy. The child's
arm was terribly mangled and had to be amputated at the shoulder. The
jury awarded a judgment of $8,000 for the Ormsbys (they had asked
for $30,000), and the railroad appealed. On appeal, there were three
critical questions: had the railroad employees been negligent? Had the
child been contributorily negligent? Had the parents been negligent in
failing to supervise the child, and, if so, was that a bar to recovery?

Additional facts were developed in the testimony. Earlier in the day,
a railroad employee had seen a small boy playing on the tracks behind

the stationary flat car "in a *very dangerous* position, and drove him away from the car in the direction of his mother's residence," which was 180 feet away. Mrs. Ormsby had given birth four days earlier and was bedridden, and her husband was away at work. At 3:30 P.M., Mrs. Ormsby told her servant to wash Charles' face, upon which he ran out the door onto the tracks, where he was run over. Neither the lookouts nor any of three men who were watching the attempt to couple the flat car to the train saw the child until after his arm had been run over (VSCL file #1212: 3–4, emphasis in original).

The railroad's brief was a straightforward statement of the modern doctrines of contributory negligence that had developed in northern jurisdictions in the 1850s: "The appellant was in pursuit of its lawful business. It was employing all usual and necessary precautions to prevent accident. The injury complained of was occasioned by the plaintiff suddenly throwing himself in the way of a moving train of cars, thus being run over before the agents of the appellant in charge of the train could prevent." The railroad's lawyers quoted the company's corporate charter and the city's statute authorizing construction of the railroad, and argued that the railroad had employed all customary and reasonable efforts to avoid accident: "[I]t would be unjust to hold it accountable for an unavoidable accident which it could not possibly have foreseen." Finally, the railroad invoked the Illinois-style rule of pleading that placed the burden on the Ormsbys to "prove the negative," that is, to establish the absence of any contributory negligence on their part as a prerequisite to consideration of their claims against the railroad. This doctrine "is founded in reason and common sense," because of the special status of a child: "So far as third persons are concerned, the acts of the parents are the acts of the infant. The negligence of the parent is the negligence of the infant." Thus the railroad, like the child, appeared as the victim of the Ormsby parents' negligence, and could not reasonably be blamed: "The law makes no unreasonable demands. It does not require from corporations or individuals the exercise of superhuman wisdom or foresight" (VSCL file #1212: 1, 5, 7, 9).

In response, the Ormsbys' lawyers filed an extraordinary forty-three-page brief. They agreed that in "extreme cases" the question of negligence was a question of law, to be decided by a judge, but that in the great majority of "intermediate cases" the discretion of the jury should be left undisturbed:

It is this class of cases and those akin to it that the law commits to the decision of a jury. Twelve men of the average of the community, comprising men of education and men of little education, men of learning and men whose learning consists only in what they have themselves seen and heard, the merchant, the mechanic, the farmer, the labourer; these sit together, consult, apply their separate experience of the affairs of life to the facts proven, and draw a unanimous conclusion. This average judgment thus given it is the great effort of the law to obtain.... In no class of cases can this practical experience be more wisely applied than in that we are considering (VSCL file #1212: 8–9).

The reliance on the jury, rather than on abstract legal rules, emphasized the case-by-case form of consideration of all relevant circumstances that was the hallmark of the premodern system.

Turning to the question of contributory negligence, however, the argument turned away from the older vocabulary of property rights and instead imported an abstract duty of care. Citing an 1857 Connecticut case involving an injury to a three-year-old-girl, the lawyer for Ormsby made the question one of blameworthiness rather than status: "If she was a trespasser, she was only technically so, and under the charge the jury must have found that she was moved only by the *impulse of childish instinct*, and was not old enough to be charged with fault or blame for being in a place of danger" (VSCL file #1212: 19, emphasis in original). Ormsby's lawyer acknowledged Virginia's adoption of the "clean hands" rule: "A is injured by the negligence of B, but A contributed to the injury by his own negligence, and, therefore, cannot maintain an action against B." A child, however, was incapable of negligence because he was incapable of exercising caution: "[I]f he has no remedy against B, it is not because B is guiltless, or has done him no wrong, but because the wrong co-operated with the wrong done him by his parents. We cannot see how a result so monstrous can flow from the doctrine that an infant is not *sui juris*, unless that doctrine be, that he *in fact belongs* to another and has *no* rights, which others are bound to respect" (VSCL file #1212, 28, emphasis in original).

The railroad, in other words, was asking the court to treat the child like a slave: "There is a very high sense in which an infant belongs to his parents, and, too, an equally high sense in which the care of his person is exclusively confided to them. But this is an arrangement of divine and of human law for the benefit of the infant, and it is a perversion of this law to hold that no other persons owe him any duty" (VSCL file #1212, 29, 30). In the antebellum years, southern writers had insisted that northern industrial workers were no better than slaves; the Ormsbys' lawyer was not willing to see the ruthless rules of modern, northern tort law similarly reduce the status of Virginia's citizens to a single mass category of prestige and protection. The one position that the lawyer urged the court to eschew absolutely was one that would have treated children of respectable families (the Ormsbys, after all, employed a servant) as something less than persons.

The remaining issue was the conduct of the parents. In Illinois law, contributory negligence meant that a plaintiff had breached a duty owed to the public at large. Since children could not be burdened with public duties, the question of contributory negligence in cases involving children in Illinois turned on the degree to which the parents had met or failed to meet their public duties. The Ormsbys' lawyer's argument was entirely different in kind. If the parents had failed in a duty, it could only have been a private duty owed to the child, since the parents only had a relationship with the child. The remedy would be, then, not to let the railroad off the hook for its failure to fulfill its own duty to the child, but to recognize a separate claim by the child against his parents: "[T]he discretion of parents in this respect may be abused, and its abuse is a wrong to the child.... But on what just principle can the proposition be worked out, that such a wrong will excuse a farther wrong done by a third person, if it so happen that both wrongs co-operate in doing injury to helpless and unoffending infancy?" (VSCL file #1212: 30).

Justice Moncure's opinion was short on legal citation and long on factual analysis, and the structure of his narrative followed the brief of the Ormsbys' lawyer to the letter. The railroad had been negligent in failing to ensure the presence of a coupling pin: "Why was not such a probable danger guarded against by fastening the pin to the flat?" Too, the railroad employees were negligent in failing to look for a child beneath the wheels of the stationary flat car, which he described as a kind of attractive nuisance: "Was it strange or extraordinary that the plaintiff, a child only two years and ten months old, should have been found on the track under or near the car then standing just in front of his mother's door, and only forty feet therefrom? A flat left nearly all day in the street might naturally be expected to be a play place for the neighboring children." Moncure dismissed the idea of a child's contributory negligence without reference to a single authority.

Regarding the duties of the parents, he first reviewed the facts in a manner as sympathetic as possible to Mrs. Ormsby and found that she had not been negligent. And on the legal questions, he simply deferred to the lawyers: "[T]here appears to be much conflict in the cases, many, and perhaps most of which were cited in the arguments of the learned counsel.... [W]e concur in the principle ... that the neglect of parents and guardians is not imputable to infant children and wards in such cases" (*Ormsby,*

474–6). In other words, the negligence of the parents (if any) could not be a factor in the case because the parents had not, themselves, had any dealings with the railroad. The parents had no contractual relationship with the railroad, and had made no use of the railroad's property; hence the parents had no duties in the case.

Once again, the Virginia Supreme Court held fast to the idea that duties of care could arise only from particular relationships between parties, relationships that were themselves defined in terms of contractual obligations and rights to the use and occupation of property. It is important, though, to recognize that the outcome on the question of imputed negligence did not break down into a neat North versus South pattern. The Ormsbys' lawyer cited cases from New York, Massachusetts, Maine, and Indiana for the proposition of imputed negligence, and Connecticut, Missouri, Minnesota, Tennessee, Vermont, Pennsylvania, Ohio, Illinois, and England for the contrary rule, which was in accordance with a recent ruling of the U.S. Supreme Court[7] (VSCL file #1212: 27–8). What was notably absent, as it had been absent from the arguments in *Trout*, was any reference to Virginia precedent.

In 1878, two years after *Ormsby*, Virginia finally announced its formal adoption of a general principle of contributory negligence in a pair of cases involving collisions with persons, *Baltimore & Ohio R.R. Co. v. Sherman's adm'r*, 30 Vir. 602 (1878), and *Baltimore & Ohio R.R. Co. v. Whittington's adm'r*, 30 Vir. 805 (1878). Both cases were filed as actions in "trespass on the case," the old English writ, rather than as a claim for "negligence" in the newfangled American manner. Together, these cases signaled the Virginia Supreme Court's final, grudging acceptance of American common law, in a form imported whole from alien jurisdictions and unconnected either to local understanding and immemorial custom or to the equation of technological progress with *salus populi*. When Virginia finally put new wine into its legal bottles, it was a flavorless vintage, pressed from grapes grown elsewhere.

Sherman arose when a man who habitually walked along railroad tracks on his way home from work was struck and killed. Six of the cars at the end of the train had become detached from the rest. Their

---

[7] "In Illinois, says Mr. Wharton, there has been some fluctuation" (VSCL file #1212: 46). The Supreme Court case in question was *Sioux City & Pacific Railroad Co. v. Stout*, 84 U.S. (17 Wall) 657 (1873), which established the "attractive nuisance" doctrine in the context of a child injured while playing on a railroad turntable. The phrase "attractive nuisance" first appeared in *Keffe v. Milwaukee & St. Paul Railway Co.*, 21 Minn. 207 (1875) (cited at VSCL file #1212: 30–1).

momentum continued to carry them forward, but a gap of thirty yards developed between the cars still being towed under power and the detached cars running behind. Sherman stepped off the tracks to allow the train to pass, then stepped back on and continued on his way. At that point the track was on a downward grade and described a broad curve. Thus Sherman had little or no chance to see the cars, running free of any locomotive, that struck and killed him a few moments later. Sherman's estate sued under Virginia's 1870 wrongful death statute, which provided that a corporation could be sued for a tortious act causing the death of a person. The complaint contained duplicate counts that described the area through which the tracks ran as, alternatively, running through Shenandoah County and through "the corporate limits of the town of Edinburgh." The case was tried in December 1875, resulting in a judgment for the plaintiff for $3,000 (*Sherman*, 603–4, 606).

The key question was one of speed. It was agreed that the fact of the uncoupling of the cars was not itself evidence of negligence, as such accidents were "of very frequent occurrence on railroads, and . . . no means have yet been discovered or devised to prevent it." On the other hand, if the train was going too fast at the point where the cars came uncoupled, then the rear brakeman would not have had time to put on the brakes before the free-running cars struck Sherman. The plaintiffs contended that the train was running faster than the railroad company's own regulations would permit. This fact, however, did not impress Justice Burks:

These regulations are adopted for the convenience and safety of the defendant and of those who travel upon the road as passengers in the cars of the defendant, or those who cross the road at a place where they have a legal right to cross it, and not of those who may choose to walk upon the road for their own convenience or pleasure, and without any legal right so to use it.

Burks thus put the negligence case back into terms of property rights and private duties. The question of "undue speed" was not a matter of defining a general standard of conduct, but a condition of the legal relations between private parties based on their right to occupy property (*Sherman*, 624, 626).

Having dispensed with the possibility of the railroad's negligence, Justice Burks announced a principle somewhere between contributory negligence and assumption of risk: "Sherman knew that trains traveled the railroad many times every day, and might travel it at unexpected times . . . a person who chose to walk on the track . . . must do so at his own risk, and must take care to look out for and avoid danger by stepping off the track in time." Having assumed the risk of being on the tracks, Sherman was required to display minimal prudence: "The instinct of self-preservation seemed therefore to require that Sherman should use incessantly, while he was walking upon the track, both his eyes and his ears to discover any signs of danger whether approaching from behind or before. Had he heeded this plain admonition he would certainly have escaped all danger" (*Sherman*, 627, 629).

The announcement of the rule in *Sherman* is not surprising in light of the state of American tort law by that time, although the formulation of the rule was still couched much more in the traditional terms of property-based private duties than the Illinois version of the same rule. The most striking sentence in the opinion, however, came in its final paragraph: "We have not referred to any books or cases (with a single exception) in the foregoing opinion. The law on the subject, so far as material, can be found in *Sherman & Redfield on Negligence* . . . [and] *Wharton on Negligence*" (*Sherman*, 630). Here was an explicit disavowal of any attempt by the Virginia Supreme Court to fashion its own common law doctrine. Instead, in the late 1870s the project of Virginia's high court was the wholesale importation of doctrines as they had been worked out by northern courts in the 1850s.

The companion case to *Sherman* was *Baltimore & Ohio R.R. Co. v. Whittington's adm'r*. *Whittington* involved an employee of the railroad who was struck and killed by a passing B&O train. At trial, the judge instructed the jury to the effect that the company would be liable if the train had been running other than in the usual time and manner and the company had not given notice of the fact to its employees: "[I]t was the duty of the said railroad company to give such notice, and their failure to do so is the negligence of the said company, for which said company is responsible in damages" (*Whittington*, 30 Vir. at 808). On appeal, the verdict for the plaintiff was overturned in an opinion authored by Justice Waller R. Staples.

The ruling in *Whittington*, however, did not turn on the question of contributory negligence but on defects in the plaintiff's pleading. The issue was not, as it would have been in Illinois, the plaintiff's failure to plead his own lack of negligence. Instead, the problem was that the plaintiff had failed to specify the relationship between the parties, so that no duty of care could be determined at all:

Now, whether the plaintiff's intestate was at the time a passenger on the train and received his injuries as such, or whether he was an employee of the company and was injured while engaged in their service, or whether he was a stranger crossing the track of the company's road, or whether he was on the track at all, or in the cars, or at a station, or in what manner he was injured, the declaration does not inform us (*Whittington*, 809–10).

This was an absolutely explicit statement that the idea of a general action for negligence, by now well established in the northern states such as Illinois, had no place in Virginia's courts.

In fact, Staples was being not only hypertechnical but disingenuous, as the pleadings and argument at trial made it perfectly clear that Whittington had been a railroad employee, and that he had been killed while walking beside the tracks belonging to his employer. Staples' analysis, in fact, overlooked the argument that the trial court had relied on in crafting the preceding quoted instruction. Whittington's position was based on his specific expertise as a railroad worker. Hearing a train approaching, Whittington, it seems, had withdrawn from the tracks "a sufficient distance to be entirely safe, if the train had been running at its usual speed and with its usual cars." On this occasion, however, the train was pulling a Pullman car – which was wider than the usual cars – and was running unusually fast. As a result, when the train rounded a curve just before the point where Whittington and his fellow employees were working, "the increased speed of travel imparted to it a vibratory or oscillatory motion, and by reason of this motion and the greater width of the Pullman car, the deceased was struck by the iron step attached to that car" (*Whittington*, 810–11).

Confronted by this argument, Staples put the burden of special knowledge squarely on the employee:

[A] man who stands near enough to a railroad track to be struck by a train, if perchance there should be an increase of speed, or a change of cars, is simply guilty of the greatest imprudence and negligence.... [E]very person upon the approach of a train shall retire far enough to avoid injury, whatever may be the speed of the train or the width of the cars. He must at his peril place himself where he cannot be struck by the train so long as it continues upon its track.

Furthermore, in this case Whittington should have been particularly on his guard because the train was late: "He knew, or ought to have known, the train was considerably behind its usual time that day, and was, therefore, necessarily running at an increased speed" (*Whittington*, 813). Finally, reversing the earlier pattern of imposing special duties of vigilance on corporations, Staples declared Virginia's adoption of the Illinois pattern of imposing on employees a duty to be familiar with the operation of the railroad business:

These principles of law apply with peculiar force to employees of a railroad company, who are in a relation of privity with their principals, have every opportunity of becoming well acquainted with the business, and are presumed to know and understand something of the risks and dangers incident to that business. From such persons a greater degree of caution in avoiding dangers ought to be required than from passengers and others having no privity with the company and no especial acquaintance with the operations of the road (*Whittington*, 815).

This was a hopelessly mixed argument. Staples had gone from stating that the duty of care could not be calculated because the pleading did not specify the relationship between the parties, to saying that as a matter of law the nature of that relationship precluded liability. He had done so, moreover, by reversing the traditional Virginia pattern of imposing a duty of vigilance on corporate employers, instead burdening employees with an exceptionally demanding version of the Duty to Get Out of the Way. On the other hand, the reference to privity pointed to a purely traditional argument that duties of care arose out of private relationships between the parties. Furthermore, there was no suggestion here of adopting an Illinois-style universal rule that would have required passengers and cattle-owners to be familiar with the operations of trains, only railroad employees. Yet the rule of contributory negligence was a general one, and Staples had earlier relieved corporations of their duty to exercise vigilance over their employees on the grounds that they were *not* like traditional, pre-industrial employers:

When it is considered that upon many of the railroads there are hundreds and even thousands of laborers daily and hourly employed all along the line, and not unfrequently twenty and even fifty trains a day, this proposition that a company is under obligation to give notice to each of its employees of every change of schedule, and of every alteration in the width of its coaches, involves consequences of the greatest magnitude (*Whittington*, 812–13).

Staples' holding, then, was an admixture of modern and traditional elements. No general, universal duty of prudence was established for workers as a class, but a special duty of prudence would be imposed on industrial employees as the consequence of the nature of that work.

The outcome in *Whittington* was, if anything, a stricter bar to employee recovery than that imposed in Illinois. But while the outcome was one that might have been reached by an Illinois court, it was based on a very different mode of reasoning. The crucial element that was entirely missing was the expansive language of public interest and technological progress. In Staples' view, the conditions of the modern economy had only created new versions of traditional, privity-based relationships of competing private rights. The articulation of those rights still demanded specific pleading of the parties' relationships, but not any of the new demands of affirmative pleading that characterized the universal duties contained in the theory of general and contributory negligence.

The traditional elements in *Whittington*, especially the retention of different duties for different classes of persons, were next addressed in a case involving a passenger, *Richmond & Danville R.R. Co. v. Morris*, 31 Vir. 200 (1878). As the story emerged in trial testimony, Moses Morris had been working as a manual laborer on the plantation of Dr. Coleman. On the day of the accident, after a full day's work, he was ordered to travel four miles to a nearby town to get additional hands. He went to the station that evening and discovered that he was too late to catch a passenger train but that he might still ride on a caboose attached to a freight train due in an hour later. During the intervening hour, he bought a small bottle of whiskey for one of the hands, and had two drinks himself. He boarded the train at the instructions of the station agent and fell asleep. When the train reached South Boston, the conductor woke him up and told him to get off. A few moments later the conductor, observing that he had not moved, shook him again (VSCL file #1629: 1–2). The only light sources were the conductor's hand-held lantern and a second lantern carried by the local station agent. Morris arose, collected his belongings, and proceeded to the back of the caboose. In the dark, he failed to turn to his left onto the platform, instead stepping straight out onto the end of the car. At that moment the cars were jolted by being coupled to a new locomotive on the front end. Morris was thrown onto the tracks, then run over by the wheels of the caboose, suffering severe injuries.

Morris sued, claiming that the railroad had failed in its duty to use "due and proper care that the plaintiff should be safely and securely carried and conveyed." After a jury trial, a verdict was entered in his favor, with a judgment of $1,500 plus interest, and the railroad appealed. At trial, witnesses who carried him from the tracks to a nearby shack testified that the bottle of whiskey he was carrying was unopened and that he was sober. In addition, the conductor testified that after leaving the train he had taken up a position on the platform, with his lantern, a few feet beyond the end of the caboose and that the train was behind in its time. He also testified that there was no chain across the back of the caboose, "and if there had been the plaintiff could not have walked off the car;

but it was not customary to have chains across the platforms of caboose car[s]" (VSCL file #1629: 1–2, 5–6, 6–7).

The railroad's argument was another attempt to get the Virginia Supreme Court to adopt a general rule of contributory negligence: "The plaintiff was in fault in leaping from the car whilst it was in motion, and did not exercise ordinary care." In response, Morris' counsel argued that any rule of contributory negligence should be understood as an element added onto the traditional system of evaluating each case in accordance with its particular circumstances: "[T]here are many qualifications of the rule.... One of these qualifications is, that the care exercised by the plaintiff must be only such as prudent persons would be reasonably expected to exercise *under his particular circumstances.*" The phrase "particular circumstances" carried a huge amount of baggage in the context of the case. Morris' lawyers argued that Morris had acted in response to the instructions of a railroad employee. That fact, in turn, took on special urgency from a second, exceptionally important "circumstance": Morris was black. "It was a dark night; the negro was asleep; he is waked up by one whom he recognized as the person having authority to direct him, and he is told to '*get off*'. Was he to take it on himself to determine whether the order was a proper one? He was, indeed, exercising all reasonable care, in submitting himself, without question or hesitation, to the direction of the conductor of the train" (VSCL file #1629: 1–3, emphasis in the original).

To argue that the law recognized differences between children and adults was one thing. From a northern perspective, even the distinction between married women and other categories of adults carried some weight, as the public sphere was, indeed, the masculine preserve of independent adults. But Morris' lawyers were arguing something quite different: that ancient orders of citizenship had survived the abolition of slavery. This argument comprised a conception of "circumstances" quite different from that used in the North. In Illinois, the starting point for the analysis of a case involved an evaluation of "circumstances" that included the specific events and physical surroundings. These were infinitely variable, while the persons involved were, in the first instance, imagined to be fungible. Specific differences in legal status – for example, that of married women – entered into the equation only at a second stage, to adjust an existing set of expectations. The suggestion here, by contrast, was that in Virginia the character of the persons involved was the starting point for the evaluation of the circumstances of the case. In other words, the argument was precisely directed at a rejection of the idea of universal, uniform duties of care toward the public good in favor of older notions of specific relational duties deriving from the character of, and relationships between, the actors.

Justice Burks gave the clearest articulation yet of Virginia's version of contributory negligence, defined in terms distinctly different from those that were accepted in Illinois. In a case of mutual negligence, he ruled, there were two questions:

> 1. Whether damage was occasioned entirely by the negligence or improper conduct of the defendant; or, 2. Whether plaintiff himself so far contributed to the misfortune by his own negligence or want of ordinary care and caution that but for such negligence or want of ordinary care and caution on his part the misfortune would not have happened (*Morris*, 203).

For his authority, Burks cited a United States Supreme Court case, *Railroad Co. v. Jones*, 95 U.S. 439 (1877), and, from England, *Butterfield v. Forrester*, 11 East 60 (1809). Virginia would have contributory negligence, but on the English model of causation, not the American model of fault allocation. The result was a rule harsher in its effects than that which had by this time become prevalent in most northern jurisdictions.[8] By this analytical route, Burks arrived at the perfect statement of Virginia's version of the duty to avoid injury: "If there be any man who does not know that such leaps are dangerous, especially when taken in the dark, his friends should see that he does not travel on a railroad." The judgment was reversed, and the case remanded for retrial[9] (*Morris*, 209–10).

Gone was Justice Joynes' valorization of Trout's property rights, or Justice Moncure's sympathy for the situation of the Ormsbys. But absent, too, was any of the effort at balancing interests and allocating burdens that during the 1850s led the Illinois Supreme Court from the "clean hands" rule to the gross/slight balancing rule and finally to a standard of comparative negligence. Virginia's rule of contributory negligence, after 1878, embraced a sterile, formalistic declaration of legal equality. Was it a coincidence that Burks, an ex-member of the Confederate legislature, reached this conclusion when confronted by the proposition that the traditional solicitude for property owners over railroad corporations would now have to extend to ex-slaves as well as to ex-slaveowners?

---

[8] A northern exception was Pennsylvania, and Burks quoted a Pennsylvania Supreme Court use of phrases that echo with unintended irony: "It has been a rule of law from time immemorial, and is not likely to be changed in all time to come, that there can be no recovery for an injury caused by the mutual fault of both parties" (*Morris*, 204).

[9] I have been unable to determine the outcome of this case on retrial, despite the best efforts of the reference staffs at the Library of the Virginia Supreme Court and the Library of Virginia.

In the 1870s and beyond, Virginia's courts were confronted with claims brought by plaintiffs who did not have the virtues of antebellum "citizens." To make the railroads and other businesses of the state liable to these plaintiffs would not protect the traditional prerogatives of propertied elites. To the contrary, with the abolition of slavery, social and economic capital were likely to be found in the corporate business sector; the social valencies attached to railroads and their passengers were thus essentially the reverse of what they had been in the earlier era. If Morris was liable to be injured from obeying the instructions of train conductors, then "his friends" – those like him – had best keep Mr. Morris from riding trains at all, because Virginia's courts would not protect him.

Corporations Public and Private

Among the most revealing lines of cases considered by the postbellum Virginia Supreme Court were those that raised the question of the differences between private and municipal corporations. In the 1850s, all "corporations," regardless of their functions, were treated as private actors possessed of traditional property rights, and that pattern continued through the 1870s. In *Sawyer v. Corse*, 17 Vir. 230 (1867), the court insisted that a Virginia city was a private citizen, just like a business corporation or an individual, for purposes of determining liability for negligence. Sawyer was a contractor who had been hired by the county to deliver mail, and he in turn had hired Fleming as a rider. When some money sent by Corse was lost from Fleming's saddlebag, Corse sued both Fleming and Sawyer. At trial, the jury awarded a verdict for Corse on the theory that Sawyer was a common carrier and Fleming his agent. Although the original trial was in 1854, Sawyer's appeal did not reach the Virginia Supreme Court until after the Civil War. The case was a set-piece, a perfect articulation by Justice Joynes of a traditional legal taxonomy of "public" and "private" actors, responding to arguments by an eminent attorney lately returned to private practice, William Daniel.

Arguing for Sawyer, Daniel asserted first that he ought not to have the strict liability of a common carrier on the grounds that he had not promised to provide a public service: "He made no contract with the public; receives no pay from the public; and made no warranty to the public." This was a strikingly narrow definition of common carrier, one based entirely on the terms of contractual agreements and markedly different from the northern notion that one who profits from the needs of the public was bound by special obligations regardless of issues of privity or technical status. Daniel further argued that Sawyer and his employee were "public officers, each liable for his own acts, but not for the acts of the other," under a form of sovereign immunity. Finally, he proposed that there should be no liability on grounds of public policy, "[t]hat no one would contract for carrying the mails if he was to be held bound for all the misfeasances or malfeasances of his agents" (*Sawyer*, 235).

Daniel's last argument, in particular, makes hash of a simplistic analysis that would describe Virginia as imposing extensive duties on public entities and few on private individuals. The point is that the language of English common law was not primarily a language of "duties" at all. Rather, it was a language of private claims allowed or disallowed in litigation. Public officials, in this reasoning, had no liabilities to members of the public because they had no contractual relationship with them. So Daniel argued that his clients should be treated as public officials to shield them from liability because no private person would willingly contract to provide this essential service. The argument was that "common carriers" defined one set of contractual rights and obligations, and "public officials" defined another. In response, the attorney for the plaintiff argued that Sawyer and his employee were ordinary private actors, subject to ordinary liability (*Sawyer*, 236–7). Thus on both sides of the argument the either/or distinction between categories of public and private actor was the starting point for the analysis.

Justice Joynes immediately changed the terms of the argument by introducing the idea of extracontractual duties: "[T]he fact that Sawyer's obligation to carry the mail arose under a contract with the government, and that he made no contract with Corse, is no answer to the present action, which is not founded on the contract, but on the breach of duty." At the same time, discussing the idea that Sawyer was immune from private liability as a public officer, Joynes drew a sharp limit to the ability of corporations of any kind to claim for themselves the mantle of public purpose. Essentially, Joynes declared that no corporation – municipal or business – could be considered "public" unless it was an eleemosynary enterprise:

The effort has been made, both in England and the United States, to extend the application of this principle of exemption so as to embrace every case of a municipal corporation. . . . [W]here the authority, though for the accomplishment of objects of a public nature and for the benefit of the public, is one *from the exercise of which the corporation derives a profit*, or where the duty, though of a public nature and for the public benefit, may fairly be presumed to have been enjoined upon the corporation in consideration of privileges granted to and accepted by it, the exemption does not apply (*Sawyer*, 238–9, 241–2, emphasis added).

In other words, regardless of the project that a municipality or business corporation might undertake, it could not claim the immunities of a public office unless it was, in modern terms, a nonprofit entity.

As for Daniel's dire warnings that a flood of litigation would drive mail carriers out of business, Joynes was not impressed:

[A] just regard for the interest of the public requires that the contractor should be held responsible. . . . [S]uch liability will greatly increase the security of the public, not only by preventing collusion between contractors and their carriers, but by rendering the former more circumspect in their choice, more watchful over their agents, and more attentive to taking bonds for their faithful conduct.

Here were Illinois doctrines turned on their heads. To support his ruling, Joynes was appealing to the desirability of inculcating vigilance on the part of corporate actors, not their customers or employees, and protecting the private interests of individual citizens rather than looking to a corporatist model of collective good (*Sawyer*, 246–7).

At the same time, the outcome in Virginia was not as bad for carriers, and for corporations generally, as it might have been. There was good news for business in the high court's refusal to unify the schema of legal duties. Since the matter was being argued in negligence, rather than on the basis of contractual duties, the strict liability of a bailee for hire did not apply. (In Illinois, it will be remembered, the expansion of the bailments scheme of duties had been accompanied by a relaxation of the strict liability rule [*Sawyer*, 247–8].) On this basis, the case was remanded for a full trial on the question of negligence.

The issue of common carrier liability came up again in *Southern Express Co. v. McVeigh*, 20 Vir. 264 (1871). William McVeigh had shipped what he said was $200,000 worth of cotton by the Southern Express Company from Charlotte to Richmond. While stored in a warehouse in Charlotte, the cotton was destroyed by fire. The jury returned a verdict for $3,621.92, casting considerable doubt on McVeigh's original valuation, and the express company appealed. The case exemplified the antiquity of Virginia's laws regarding common carriers. The railroad company's lawyers used old pleading rules to argue that the claims could not be heard together on the grounds that they encompassed different forms of action: "assumpsit" and "trespass on the case," a tort. The difference was that a claim in assumpsit "counts upon the breach of contract implied from the undertaking, and does not rely upon a breach of duty resulting from the relation." As for the claim in case, it could not be heard, "for no duty imposed by law was violated. The responsibility and duty of a carrier does not begin until the goods are delivered to him, or to his proper servant" (*McVeigh*, 271, 273). The railroad company thus made its case in terms of preserving the old system of pleading and the analytical framework that it invoked.

McVeigh's lawyers argued from the same grounds, focusing on technical distinctions between types of common carriers and relying on the same digests that had been cited by Southern Express to argue that none of the claims depended on contractual arrangements. The plaintiff's complaint, they said, "merely sets up the contract as . . . inducement, not as the gravamen of the action . . . the true principle underlying all the cases, is, that the liability arises from negligence. This applied to all cases, common carriers and all others" (*McVeigh*, 280, 281).

In his opinion, Justice Francis T. Anderson was careful to extend the idea of generalizable duties of care only to "public employment": "[W]here there is a public employment, from which arises a common law duty, an action may be brought in tort, although the breach of duty assigned is the doing or not doing of something, contrary to an agreement made in the course of such employment, by the party on whom such general duty is imposed" (*McVeigh*, 284). The reason common carriers had been burdened with special duties, in the old common law system, was that they served a public function. Now Anderson was making it clear that those "special" duties would not extend beyond that public function. The issue then would turn entirely on the classification of Southern Express Company as a private or public enterprise. Once again, the Virginia Supreme Court was clinging to the public/private status distinction that had been the first element of traditional categories to fall in Illinois.

Concluding that the Southern Express Company was, in fact, a common carrier, the question that was left was the kind of technical common law conundrum, where the meaning of terms depended on the status and real or fictional relationships of parties, that had long been the bête noire of legal reformers. The goods in question had been delivered to a warehouse. Did this constitute "delivery" to the express company "*in their public character* of carriers?" "When a common carrier is also a warehouseman, questions of difficulty may often arise, in which *character* he received the goods." Justice Anderson concluded that railroads and express companies were primarily carriers: "And it is a fact of public notoriety, that express companies have their warehouses or offices." Based on this parsing of the taxonomy of bailees, Anderson concluded that

Southern Express was, indeed, strictly liable as an "insurer" of the goods independent of any contractual obligation, "and consequently the action against them is properly conceived in case" (*McVeigh*, 286–8, 290). Thus, finally, the rule of *McVeigh* was that a common carrier was liable as an insurer when it was subject to duty in tort as a public servant, but not when it was sued in assumpsit on the basis of private agreement. This was an outcome quite different from Illinois' abolition of strict tort liability for railroads, based on the idea that shippers and passengers had public duties reciprocal to those of carriers.

In 1875, the Virginia high court took up the continuing dispute between the City of Richmond and the RF&P Railroad that was discussed in the previous chapter. In 1873, Richmond had enacted a law that prohibited the operation of steam engines on Broad Street. The railroad sued, arguing, as it had before, that the regulation interfered with the railroad's vested property rights under its corporate charter, which had been renewed in 1870. The circuit court judge found that the regulation did not violate the company's contractual rights and upheld the ordinance, and the railroad appealed.

The railroad's first argument was about political authority. The legislature, counsel asserted, could not delegate its sovereign authority over the corporation's charter to the city: "The use which the company now makes of the street. . . . is a liberty granted by the sovereign to its subjects, in which the latter cannot now be disturbed except by the sovereign power" ("Petition of RF&P": 6–7). Second, the railroad argued that the city owed it contractual obligations. The 1870 charter had given the City of Richmond authority to determine the routes and regulate the operations of trains "provided no contract may thereby be violated" (*Richmond, Fredericksburg & Potomac R.R. Co. v. City of Richmond*, 26 Vir. 83, 85–6, 1875). The railroad seized on the last phrase to assert the supremacy of its vested contract rights over claims of public good:

Whatever may be the just influence of the maxim, "*salus populi, suprema lex*," the proper extent of the so called police power, it is denied that private corporations, such as this company, can be in any degree affected by a law passed for the sole purpose of promoting the convenience of the public generally, or any citizens or classes of citizens, in contravention of provisions in the charters of such private corporations respectively.

A contrary rule would be "a new and easy mode by which the constitutional security of private property and privileges may be broken down" ("Petition of RF&P": 7–8).

In his opinion, Justice Joseph Christian went through the familiar arguments about charters and contractual obligations, adopting the positions that the Richmond Common Council's special committee had articulated thirty years earlier. The city's grant to the railroad contained a clause reserving municipal regulatory authority over the use of particular forms of machinery[10]; a chartered city, unlike a county, had its own ownership rights granted by the legislature that limited the railroad's property rights[11]; and changes in conditions over fifty years permitted reevaluation of the relationship between the city and the corporation.[12] Having declared the city the victor in a straight contest between property rights claims, however, Christian moved to a broader consideration of the nature of corporations. He interpreted the phrase "provided no contract will be thereby violated" in the 1870 city charter as an appeal to common law principles of resolution: "The only fair and legitimate inference... is that the legislature, aware of the controversy between the city authorities and the railroad company on this subject, left it as an open question for the courts to decide" (*Richmond*, 93). The question was thus squarely put as an exploration of American common law principles and their relationship to the political economy of railroad corporations.

[10] These included an absolute and entire control over the streets of the city, excepting only the privilege to the railroad company *of constructing and connecting* their road with the depot on Broad street. Not a syllable is recorded about the mode or manner of transportation, whether by horse-power or steam, the entire regulation of that subject being reserved to the corporation with the rest of its chartered powers (*Richmond*, 90–1).

[11] [C]ounties have no chartered rights and privileges; and in these counties the railroad company acquired not only a right of way, but an absolute right of property in their road, and necessary property acquired in those counties, because, as empowered by their charter, they condemned the lands of individuals for these purposes, and paid them an equivalent in money. But... [w]ithin the limits of the city of Richmond all the right which the company acquired was the right of way over the street.... *subject to* the right inherent in the municipal authorities to control the use of the streets, and to protect the safety, comfort and general welfare of the citizens of the municipality (*Richmond*, 91–2, emphasis in original).

[12] The railroad, Christian wrote, claimed that "by its charter it has the right by *contract forever*, and under all circumstances, to run its cars *by steam* through the whole length of Broad Street":

> This company was chartered more than fifty years ago. At that time much of what is now known as Broad street was a mere turnpike, neither graded nor paved, with, scattered here and there, houses on each side. It is now one of the most attractive and populous streets in the city.... It is not therefore "unreasonable" that the city council, should, under this change of circumstances, prohibit the use of steam engines on this street" (*Richmond*, 86, 97–8).

The issue was not one to be determined on the basis of particular contractual negotiations or the terms of specific charters, but rather turned on the question of a city's authority to regulate the activities of its citizens:

> The general police power existing in the legislature, is transferred to every municipal corporation to be exercised by it, for the protection of the safety and general welfare of the citizens of such corporation.... It must *of course* be within the range of legislative action to define the mode and manner in which every one may so use his own as not to injure others.

And what was true of individual citizens, he wrote, citing Isaac Redfield's digest, was at least as true of corporations: "[I]t cannot be doubted that these artificial beings or persons, the creations of the law, are equally subject to legislative control and in the same particulars precisely as natural persons." The fact of public authority over the use of private property answered the original argument of the railroad to the effect that it was being deprived of its rights to property. A regulation was not a compensable taking, Christian said, and in enacting its laws, "the city council have not appropriated for the public use one dollar of the property of the company." Further, stated Christian, "If he suffers injury it is either *damnum absque injuria* or in the theory of the law he is compensated for it by sharing in the general benefits which the regulations are intended and calculated to secure.... These regulations rest on another maxim, *salus populi suprema est lex*" (*Richmond*, 99–100, 102).[13] Virginia thus steadfastly refused to follow Illinois into the brave new world of corporate *salus populi*. "Public" meant politically sovereign. Private corporations could not claim the authority of acting in the public good; their interests were a matter to be worked out in litigation through competing property rights claims.[14] The distinction between private rights and public duties remained intact.

---

[13] Quoting *Thorpe v. R. & B.R. Co.*, 27 Vermont 140, 149 (1854), Redfield's *Law of Railways*, and Chief Justice Lemuel Shaw in *Commonwealth v. Alger*, 61 Mass. (7 Cush) 53 (1851).

[14] The Virginia Supreme Court's decision upholding the city ordinances was itself appealed to the U.S. Supreme Court. Again, the railroad argued for the supremacy of property rights and the sanctity of contract. Chief Justice Morrison R. Waite made short work of the argument, using the traditional language of common law property rights: "The power to govern implies the power to ordain and establish suitable police regulations.... Such prohibitions clearly rest upon the maxim *sic utere tuo ut alienum non laedas*, which lies at the foundation of the police power..." (*Railroad Co. v. Richmond*, 96 U.S., 6 Otto, 521, 528, 1877). That Waite employed this traditional language is not surprising. Given a choice, when upholding a verdict, the Supreme Court will usually accept the reasoning of the lower court rather than engaging in extraneous adjustments to legal doctrine. It is noteworthy, for instance, that in the same year, the same Court decided *Munn v. Illinois*, 94 U.S. (4 Otto) 113 (1877), upholding Illinois' regulation of rates charged by the operators of grain elevators on the ground that such enterprises were "clothed with a

In 1877, the Virginia Supreme Court again found an opportunity to emphasize the point that everyone – individual, corporation, public agency, or city – was to be treated as a private rights–holding property owner for purposes of determining liability. In *City of Petersburg v. Applegarth's adm'r*, 28 Vir. 321 (1877), the owner of a sailboat sued when his ship was damaged while tied to the Petersburg dock. The damage was caused by an underwater stump – a "stob" – and Applegarth insisted that the city had been negligent in failing to clear the obstruction. The jury agreed and awarded a judgment for the plaintiff. On appeal, the city's position was that the trial judge had erred in delivering an instruction that described the city as liable for the negligence of its port warden "upon *the same principle*, and to *the same extent*, as a *private individual* is held responsible for the acts and omissions of his servant." Instead, Petersburg's lawyers tried to appeal to the principle of sovereign immunity to which Daniel had appealed in *Sawyer*, arguing that "municipal corporations are not liable at all for the misconduct, negligence or omissions of the agents employed by them in the exercise of their *political, discretionary* and *legislative* authority." The plaintiff agreed, but argued that when it acted outside its regulatory capacity, a city was an "'artificial person' like a business corporation," and therefore "liable to the same extent as private persons or corporations" (VSCL file #1302: 2, 4–5, quoting Sherman and Redfield, 1869: §119).

The plaintiff's lawyers' argument, again, reversed the pattern that was observed in Illinois during the 1850s. There, the model of the individual was "corporatized," that is, made subject to the special public duties and abstract standards that had previously applied only to artificial entities. Here, municipal corporations were being made subject to the full range of traditional private law doctrine. The court adopted this argument in its entirety. Justice Moncure reviewed the trial court's actions solely in terms of the competing private duties owed between the shipowner and the city by virtue of their contractual interactions, and consequently upheld the trial court's verdict against the City of Petersburg. Indeed, the only nod to modern modes of analysis that appeared in Moncure's opinion was his observation that contributory negligence, a theory that had not been raised in either party's written briefs, did *not* appear in the case.[15]

---

public purpose." An interesting implication of this fact is that the body of Supreme Court precedents may have helped to maintain the division between northern and southern legal cultures.

[15]   [T]he owner of the dock does not insure vessels against injury in it, and, if he has taken all the care that can reasonably be expected of him, he is not liable for damage done to a vessel by an obstruction in the dock. The master of a

The explanation for the differences between postbellum Virginia common law and that of Illinois was the difference in the political context in which the new rules were adopted. Lacking an underlying political language of progress and abstract public interests, the Virginia Supreme Court applied rules such as contributory negligence in the same black-and-white, formalistic manner of earlier rules that had led to opposite outcomes. With no process of working out legal principles, and no connection between legal doctrines and underlying concepts of political legitimation, Virginia's adoption of modern legal doctrine appears as the imposition of an external system of ready-made rules found in digests published in northern cities. Far from making the new regime more revolutionary, this denatured the system, rendering the new doctrines nothing more than rules for adjudication of individual cases. This was the step that permitted Virginia's conservative elites to preserve their political ideology in the face of doctrinal change. By divorcing legal duties from standards of social and political citizenship, Virginia could simultaneously preserve its fundamental commitment to the identification of different classes of citizens and, at the same time, put in place the legal rules that had drawn their initial coherence from the standardization of virtues. The result, ironically, was that when new rules appeared in Virginia, they were applied with savage absoluteness, since there were essentially no underlying norms to which parties could appeal to establish limiting principles. This, truly, was the triumph of sterile formalism.

In the end, Virginia adopted a version of England's common law regime, couched in terms of modern American pleading language. Even where a new rule was adopted, the starting point of the analysis and the analytical path involved in the adjudication of cases remained the old, traditional comparative evaluation of property-based rights and private, relational duties. What construction of the virtues of citizenship, then, emerges from the version of American common law that Virginia finally adopted in the 1870s? The answer is, none in particular. Virginia's version of modern American legal doctrines did not appear as an element of a larger political project of defining universal standards for participation in public life. Stripped of its connections to the primacy of property and the system of hierarchical social order, the law no longer transmitted any

---

vessel has a right to presume that all parts of a dock are safe, and is not guilty of contributory negligence by taking a place which might, under other circumstances, not anticipated by him, be less safe than another (*Applegarth* 340, quoting Sherman and Redfield, 1869).

underlying set of ontological commitments embedded in elite political culture. As a result, the political function of the law remained limited. The common law in Virginia continued to be conceived of as nothing more than the rules for competition between private, interested parties. In the end, Virginia's laws were like its railroads: primarily imposed from without, with no local "branches" – or roots – to connect the state to a national system it had neither played a part in creating nor particularly welcomed.

9

The South

Georgia, North Carolina, and Kentucky

In the decade before the Civil War, just as the states of the North demonstrated variations on Illinois' theme of forming new doctrines around an expanded conception of public duties, the states of the South displayed versions of Virginia's resistance to change in the name of preserving the order of slave society. The review that follows of Georgia, North Carolina, and Kentucky cases illustrates both the points of difference and the underlying unity in the pattern of antebellum southern common law development. Similarly, in the years following the war, these states followed versions of Virginia's pattern of first resisting, and then finally adopting, rules imported from outside sources without significant efforts at explanation and without grounding in the political culture or conditions of the time and place. One point of difference among southern states was whether railroad cases were, or were not, initially seen as driving the development of other doctrines. Regardless of the significance that was attached to railroad cases, however, the consistent pattern that emerges is one of resisting any unification in common law doctrines by making the facts of rail expansion fit, however awkwardly, into traditional analytical categories.

Damage to Property: Stock and Slaves

Above all, what provoked conflicts in Georgia's system of jurisprudence in the 1850s was the simultaneous existence of railroads and slaves. In 1850, a slave named Jacob boarded a train operated by the Macon & Western line, "for the ordinary fare for negroes, from Macon to the eight mile post above." When the train neared his stop, and was proceeding "about as fast as a man can walk," Jacob jumped off, fell, and broke his leg so severely that it had to be amputated. Jacob's owner sued for damages to compensate him for the loss in the slave's value.

What was needed, said Justice Eugenius A. Nisbet, were not new rules, only the determination of the meaning of old rules in new contexts:

> I do not consider that the decision of this question depends upon any new principles. We have determined it upon principles of the Common Law, long settled and familiar to the jurisprudence of Great Britain and of our own States. The interest of the question springs out of the application of those principles to a class of statutory persons, to wit: railroad corporations, unknown to the Courts of either country until within a very recent period, and to a class of subjects (negro slaves) not recognised as property in England.

But these new classes of "statutory persons" raised a host of questions. While traveling under a general pass issued by his owner, was Jacob a "passenger"? Certainly not in any ordinary sense, which led Justice Nisbet to raise the issue of public duties right at the outset: "It is made the duty of the owner, by law, not to permit his slave to leave his plantation without a ticket" (*The Macon & Western R.R. Co. v. Holt*, 8 Ga. 157, 160–1, 159–60, 1850). Then what was the relationship between Jacob, his owner, and the railroad? The law of bailments could not apply, since a contract would be required and there had been no privity between the owner and the railroad, and a slave could not make a contract. Above all, it was imperative that nothing be said that would alter Jacob's status as property and nothing more: "I need scarcely remark, that the slave could make no contract to bind his master.... The slave must be considered in the light of property, and in no other." Therefore the case was neither one about contracts, nor about equitable bailments. In fact, the case was not about a contract at all, it was about the unlawful conversion of property: "[The case] does not belong to the Law of Bailment.... The company converted the slave to their use, for profit – they are tort feasors, and liable as such; that is to say, they are liable for all injuries, whether they result from negligence or otherwise" (*Holt*, 162–3, 165).

The tort of conversion of property, however, unlike the traditional rules governing bailees, had a scienter element; that is, the railroad had to be shown to have *known* that the person being transported was a slave. "The black color of the African race," said the judge, "is presumptive evidence of slavery," but the railroad would be able to present a defense on the facts (*Holt*, 165–6). And on that basis, in 1860, the idea of a general standard of negligence applicable to Georgia railroads in the act of transporting slaves was born. So long as it exercised ordinary care, a railroad could not be liable for transporting a *light-skinned* slave: "To prescribe any more stringent rules in such cases would be to enjoin upon railroad conductors the duty of questioning as to the social status of every white passenger having a dark complexion, and refusing to give him conveyance unless he could prove his descent from Caucasian parents" (*Wallace v. Spullock*, 32 Ga. 488, 492, 1860).

The coexistence of railroads and slaves again provoked a consideration of new principles of negligence in *Macon & Western R.R. v. Davis*, 13 Ga. 68 (1853). An 1847 statute made "the several Railroad Companies of this State...liable in law for any damage done to live stock or other property." The plaintiff, whose slave had been struck and killed by a train, argued that this was in essence a strict liability statute, while the railroad argued that it should not apply to slaves: "It is argued, and with some plausibility, that the Legislature did not mean to place...property of the dignity and importance of slaves, who are reasoning and willing agents, upon the same footing with live stock, such as horses, cattle, or hogs.... The words, however, embrace all property, and of course include slaves." So long as the issue of slaves was resolved, however, the court was quite willing to consider the public interest in railroads and thus dismiss the argument that the statute created a basis for strict liability: "Such legislation would be a reproach to the civilization of the age.... Besides its oppressive injustice, it would be grossly inexpedient, inasmuch as it would deny to the public the incalculable benefits of Railroads, for no company would long exercise franchises thus encumbered." The conclusion was that the statute had essentially done nothing: "The Legislature did not intend to create a new liability, but to declare the liability of Railroads to the old Common Law rule" (*Davis*, 85–7). The door was thus opened to consideration of common law doctrines of what constituted "gross negligence" in a given case.

At the same time that the rules governing the relative duties of railroads and slaveowners were being worked out, a parallel line of Georgia cases was defining the same issues in the context of animals. *Branan v. May*, 17 Ga. 136, (1855), involved two mules that drowned when they were driven across a ditch dug by Branan. In his defense, Branan argued that May had been negligent in accepting his driver's advice that the mules could safely cross the water. Justice Joseph Lumpkin rejected this argument on the grounds that "the practice of the country" was the governing standard of conduct: "Is it not the universal custom, in pursuing a journey, when an obstruction occurs, to consult the driver, and to act upon his opinion? And if this be the common practice, Mr. May could not be said to be wanting in ordinary care in following it." On the other hand, citing *Butterfield v. Forrester* and nothing else, Lumpkin acknowledged the possibility that in a proper case, contributory negligence might be a defense. The rule would not be applied as a "clean hands" principle, however: "[N]otwithstanding the defendant be in fault, it does not dispense with another's using ordinary care and caution for himself" (*Branan*, 138). How the rule of contributory negligence would apply in Georgia, however, Justice Lumpkin did not explain.

The next year, in 1856, the Georgia Supreme Court considered a stock case, this time involving mules struck by a train. The railroad requested an instruction that, while other animals might be permitted to roam, "mules, being of a peculiar nature, should be kept up by the owner." This instruction was refused. Justice Henry L. Benning quoted the rule from *Davis*, that "if by the exercise of ordinary care [the railroad] could have prevented a collision, it is liable for the loss occasioned by the collision, even although the person sustaining the loss may have been, on his side, also guilty of the want of some degree of care." He went on, however, to describe the relative duties of stock owners and railroads in pure property law terms of the sort that had not been available in describing the conduct of the slave Jacob in *Holt*:

> The owner of the mules was guilty of some degree of negligence in letting them run at large in the vicinity of the uninclosed rail road track...that made him, I think, a trespasser against the rail road company. He had no right to have his mules on that track. But then, on the other hand, the company had no right to kill the mules merely for being there.

This was not a principle of contributory or comparative negligence or anything else of the sort, it was a statement of the traditional rule governing the conduct of landowners whose fields were invaded by wandering animals. This point was emphasized by the court's reference to Georgia's 1759 fencing statute that said that farmers who failed to enclose their fields could not recover damages for harm done to their crops by roaming animals (*The Central R.R. and Banking Co. v. Davis*, 19 Ga. 437, 438–9, 1856).

In 1860, in a case involving the death of a horse, Justice Linton Stephens repeated the principle that when the issue involved collisions between railroad and wandering stock, there was no issue of negligence or the defense of contributory negligence, there was only the need to consider the relative rights of property owners under traditional common law rules:

> But it was said, whatever may have been the negligence of the engineer, the owner of the horse was *in pari delictu*, in allowing his horse to go at large; that he, through

his horse, was a trespasser on the road. Such law as this would require a revolution in our people's habits of thought and action. A man could not walk across his neighbor's unenclosed land, nor allow his horse or his hog, or his cow, to range in the woods nor to graze on the old fields, or the 'wire grass,' without subjecting himself to damages for a trespass. Our whole people, with their present habits, would be converted into a set of trespassers. We do not think that such is the law.

What is striking in the analysis is the effort to hear an argument of contributory negligence as though it were an argument brought under the writ of trespass. If the owner of the horse had failed a duty of care, it must mean that the horse was a trespasser, and the generalization of that principle would go too far in light of the established habits and immemorial customs of the land. That railroads posed a new and special problem was their lookout; there was nothing here of duties owed by stock owners to passengers or the public's Need for Speed. Far from a presumption that the existence of railroad technology imposed universal standards of conduct on those who dealt with them, the Georgia Supreme Court relied on the older principle that conduct should at all times be governed by local custom: "Every man consents to what is universal in the country where he is, until he expresses his dissent in a form to give notice of it to the public, and where there is a mode prescribed he must pursue that mode" (*Macon & Western R.R. Co. v. Lester*, 30 Ga. 911, 913–14, 1860).

1860 was also the year that the Georgia Supreme Court returned to consideration of the question of the degree of care a railroad was bound to show in transporting slaves. Daniel Mitchell, his wife, and ten slaves boarded a train in Atlanta bound for Kingston. One of the slaves was injured by falling from a platform to which he had exited the train during a stop. Mitchell had paid second-class fares for each of the slaves traveling with him. The jury returned a verdict for the defendant, from which the plaintiff appealed. Justice Richard F. Lyon ruled that the duties of the railroad to safeguard slaves were its duties toward passengers rather than freight: "The carrier has not, and can not have, the same absolute control over [a slave] that he has over inanimate matter.... He is, in fact, a passenger, paid for as a passenger and so treated and held, not only by defendant, but by plaintiff." As a result, the railroad would not be strictly liable for the injury to the slave; instead it would be the plaintiff's burden of proof to show that the railroad's negligence had led to the injury in question. This was a general statement of the negligence principle, "no liability without fault," but there was not one word in the formulation of these standards that identified them as elements of a general theory of negligence. Nor was there any mention in the case of contributory negligence, either on the part of the slave for being on the platform where he did not belong or on the part of the slaveowner for failing to supervise his property adequately (*Mitchell v. Western & Atlantic R.R.*, 30 Ga. 22, 27, 1860).

In North Carolina, railroad cases involving damage to property began to appear as early as 1842, with *Garris v. The Portsmouth & Roanoke R.R. Co.*, 24 N.C. 324 (1842). The trial judge in that case ordered the jury that the railroad was liable for the killing of a steer at night, despite testimony that the engineer had ordered the brakes put on and the engines reversed as soon as he saw cattle on the tracks. Justice Joseph J. Daniel used the case to announce the principle of no liability without fault as a matter of the rules of "accidental trespass": "If in the prosecution of a lawful act an accident, which is purely so, arises, no action can be supported for an injury arising therefrom" (*Garris*, 325–6). The announcement of the rule in *Garris* did not signal the beginning of a jurisprudence built around stock cases, however, as similar rulings had done in northern states. In fact, the North Carolina Supreme Court did not consider a second significant stock case until 1858. In *Aycock v. Wilmington & Weldon R.R. Co.*, 51 N.C. 231 (1858), testimony established that cows grazing near a track wandered onto it, and that as the train approached them, its engineer did not blow the train's whistle although this was the "usual mode of driving stock from the road." Justice Richmond Pearson also noted that the train had not slackened its speed. "Extra speed of itself, may not constitute negligence, but where cattle are near the road, on each side, and some crossing, a due regard for human life and property, requires that the speed should be reduced, so as to prepare for an emergency, and be able to stop, if necessary, until the danger is passed" (*Aycock*, 233). There is, needless to say, no hint here of the idea that railroads must be free to determine their own best rate of speed, that speed is a social good in itself, or that the owners of cattle owe any duty to keep them from becoming obstructions to progress.

The last stock collision case from North Carolina before the Civil War was in 1860. The railroad in that case owned the track and land for one hundred feet on either side, and the owner of the cow that was killed did not own an adjacent property. The railroad argued that it should not be held responsible for the death of the cow because the railroad had been engaged in a lawful activity and the plaintiff "was a trespasser, in the first instance, by suffering his cow to get upon the road of the defendant." This was a statement of the property law doctrine that we have seen as the beginning of contributory negligence in other courts, but this court was having none of it. The English rule of enclosure, wrote Justice William H. Battle, was not in place in North Carolina: "Here, only a very small part of the lands, that is, such as were actually in cultivation were enclosed.... [F]locks and herds were, therefore, allowed to go at large, and, as early as the year 1777." Since the owner of the cow was entitled to permit her to roam, he had no obligation to prevent her from wandering onto a railroad track. As a result, the only question was whether there was evidence of negligence on the part of the railroad: "Had it appeared that the engineer employed the usual mode for driving cattle from the track of the road, by means of the steam whistle, then the defendant might have been excused under the authority of the case of *Aycock*.... But in the absence of such proof we must hold the defendant liable for the damage caused by the negligence of its servants" (*Laws v. The North Carolina R.R. Co.*, 52 N.C. 468, 469, 1860).

Injuries to slaves in antebellum North Carolina were governed by essentially the same rules of negligence, without countervailing principles of contribution, but some of the work of a contribution defense was done by legally mandated presumptions of fact. In *Herring v. The Wilmington & Raleigh R.R. Co.*, 32 N.C. 402 (1849), a train running at twenty miles an hour at two o'clock in the afternoon ran over two slaves who were sleeping on or next to the tracks, under a bridge. The railroad insisted that it was relieved from liability by the conduct of the slaves. The problem was that such negligence would have to be imputed to the slaveowner to have any effect, a possibility that Justice Pearson rejected: "No fault is imputable to the owner for not preventing his negroes from going about on Sunday and lying down where they please, nor is the amount of care required of the defendants thereby 'diminished'" (*Herring*, 408). (It is also possible that the court was considering the likelihood that the slaves in question may have committed suicide.)

The conduct of the slaves came into play, instead, in determining what constituted a reasonable response by the engineer to the discovery that there were men lying on the tracks:

If there had been a log of wood on the track, running over it would amount to negligence.... If there had been a cow on the track, the case would not be so clear, for the animal has both the instinct of self-preservation and the power of locomotion.... But as the negroes were reasonable beings, endowed with intelligence, as well as the instinct of self-preservation and the power of locomotion, it was a natural and reasonable supposition, that they would get out of the way, and the engineer was not guilty of negligence, because he did not act upon the presumption that they had lost their faculties by being drunk or asleep. If a deaf mute, while walking on the track, be unfortunately run over, it would certainly not be negligence, unless it was proven; that the engineer knew the man and was aware of his infirmity.

The progression, from a log to a cow to a slave to a deaf free person, demonstrates the progression of expectations, and the maintenance of categories, that is the hallmark of southern antebellum common law. The degree to which the railroad or a property owner would be charged with negligence would depend on where along that scale the "property" at issue fell. For the railroad to be asked to avoid injury to slaves would be impracticable, given the propensities of that particular species of property: "[A] knowledge of this impunity would be an inducement to obstruct the highway and render it impossible for the company to discharge their duty to the public, as common carriers" (*Herring*, 408–9). The desirability of railroads required that the law encourage people to stay out of the way; the existence of slavery required that the law not meddle with the order of property rights in doing so.

Slaves continued to create problems for the categories of legal duties in North Carolina through the 1850s. In 1850, a case arose out of a contract whereby a slave was hired out to work making turpentine. The party that hired the slave gave him a pass to take a train to a nearby city, but on the way the slave got hold of some liquor. He was found severely injured and drunk, after having apparently fallen from the moving train. The question on appeal was whether the employer of the slave had been negligent in giving him a pass to ride on a train, knowing that he had a tendency toward drunkenness. Justice Pearson said that there had been no negligence:

To allow a slave to be carried as a passenger on a railroad, certainly does not amount to negligence, and the circumstance that the negro is addicted to getting drunk, does not make it so in the absence of proof, that he was drunk and helpless when he was allowed to get on the train, otherwise it would be necessary to confine negroes of that description, which would prove that they were not fit to be hired out (*George v. Smith*, 51 N.C. 273, 275, 1850).

Hiring out slaves was a traditional element of North Carolina's economy. Industrial work, and in particular transportation by railroad, had drastically increased the risks associated with the practice, and just as they had in Virginia, the courts wrestled with the problem of accommodating traditional practices in a slave economy with the dangers to property and person that accompanied a new form of production. In *Herring*, Justice Pearson had said that slaveowners, like the owners of stock, were not responsible for ensuring the safety of the rails; now he conversely declared that railroads and those who used them for their business were not responsible for ensuring the safety of others' slaves. Either new rule would have interfered with the operation of the traditional economy of slavery, which depended heavily on slaves acting without direct supervision and for hire and yet at all times retaining the status of an intermediate category on the scale from a log of wood to a free white citizen. A slave was a uniquely unruly, uncontrollable kind of creature, and slaveowners were on notice of this fact. Quoting an earlier Georgia case, Pearson analogized the tendency toward drink with the equally unfortunate tendency to sneak across state lines:

It is said ... it will not do to say that under ordinary circumstances, one who hires a slave near the border of the State, must guard him by day and imprison, or chain, him by night, to prevent him from fleeing across the line. This applies to our case; the only difference being that, here, the slave was addicted to getting drunk – there, the danger to be apprehended, was the facility of escaping out of the State (*George*, 276).

In 1861, the North Carolina Supreme Court considered a case in which a train struck and killed a slave who was, in fact, deaf. Justice Battle ruled that in the absence of knowledge to the contrary, the engineer "had the right to presume that the slave had the ordinary faculties of hearing and sight, and that he was endowed with ... an instinct of self-preservation." There is nothing remotely surprising about this outcome, but it is important to recognize what did *not* appear in Justice Battle's brief statement of the rule. The analysis of the engineer's expectations of the slave was presented solely in the context of determining the standard for negligence on the railroad's part. There was nothing of contributory negligence, nor any commentary on whether the slave's knowledge of his own deafness pointed to any conclusions about his own conduct. The reason, in a property case, was clear. Any rule of contributory negligence in the context of property damage would require the imputation of the careless or even self-destructive actions of slaves to their owners (*Poole v. The North Carolina R.R. Co.*, 53 N.C. 340, 341, 1861). Slaves were a uniquely uncontrollable form of property, but that fact could not be allowed to cast doubt on the virtues of the class of their owners. Slaveowners might have to bear the loss of the value of their own property, but they could not be liable for the destruction that slaves might create. What makes this particularly interesting is that owners of animals and employers of free workers both were traditionally subject to vicarious liability for the actions of their property or workers; slaves, and slaveowners, were a unique intermediate case that precluded the unification of different common law doctrines into a single system of duties.

The treatment of cases involving damage to property in Kentucky paralleled that seen in Virginia and Georgia, although with an interesting twist in 1851. *King v. Shanks*, 51 Ky. 410 (1851), involved a slave who accepted an offer of 25 cents to drive a horse across a deep pond even though he could not swim, and was drowned in the attempt. Justice Thomas A. Marshall used the case as an opportunity to review a whole series of cases involving liability for causing harms to slaves. What is intriguing is that, throughout, the question is one of "conversion" – that is, the attempt to exercise control over property belonging to another – without any hint of a general negligence theory. In this context, the defendant would basically be subject to strict liability: "It is not necessary that the death of the slave, which was the damage to the plaintiff, should have proceeded immediately or necessarily from the inducement held out by the defendant for the undertaking of the slave." Justice Marshall reviewed similar rulings from South Carolina and Louisiana finding strict liability for a defendant who exercised unauthorized authority over the slave of another: "In such a case...it is in vain to say that the slave was a moral agent capable of wrong as well as of right action, and that he killed himself by jumping off when he ought not" (*King*, 415–16, 418–19).

The outcome and mode of analysis in *King* can be explained either by the need to preserve the status of slaves as nonhuman property, or as an effort to protect the traditional prerogatives of slaveowners to hire out their slaves without thereby assuming any and all risk of loss. The adoption of modern negligence doctrine would have made it nearly impossible for slaveowners to recover damages from those who employed their slaves, because slaves could always be argued to have contributed to their own injuries. The extent to which this was a form of analysis uniquely designed around slavery was demonstrated with the first real Kentucky railroad case involving damage to property – indeed, essentially the only antebellum railroad case decided by the Kentucky Supreme Court on any issue.

Louisville and Frankfort R.R. Company vs. Ballard, 59 Ky. 177 (1859), was a stock case, in which a mare was killed by a train while running across and in front of the locomotive. Remarkably, the Kentucky Supreme Court abandoned the southern jurisprudential pattern of the time and embraced the idea of contributory negligence on the part of stock owners. Justice Henry C. Wood began by observing that railroad personnel owed their

highest duties to their passengers, with whom they were in privity of
contract. And what of the duty to the property of others? The language
may ring familiar:

Speed in the transit, and exact punctuality in the arrivals and departures of trains
and their various connections, are imperatively required in this mode of conveyance. They are lawful, and the vital interests of the public require that they
shall not be interfered with. . . . In order to promote and preserve these essential
characteristics of railroad management, and to insure, as far as human prudence
can insure, the safety of the persons who may be passengers upon trains of railway
cars, it is necessary that the tracks of such ways be kept free from obstructions
of all sorts. There is a peculiar obligation upon the owners of cattle to keep them
off the tracks of railways. . . . [C]ompanies are not to be held liable for injuries
inflicted under such circumstances, unless it is proved that the conduct of the
companies or their agents has been reckless, wanton, and willful (*Ballard*, 184,
181–3).

The cases cited in support of this proposition are familiar: *Patchin*,
Thompson, and *Rockafellow* from Illinois; *Munger* and *Clark* from New
York; *Skinner* from Pennsylvania; *Elliott* from Ohio; and, not least,
Vermont Chief Justice Isaac Redfield's digest of railway law. Not a single
southern case was cited, nor any case involving slaves.

Justice Wood's departure from his own court's precedents is an exception that proves the rule of southern jurisprudence. As far as damages to
property were concerned, there was no hint of adoption of the modern
doctrines of general negligence in connection with stock cases in Georgia,
North Carolina, or Kentucky up until 1859, and nothing of contributory negligence with regard to slaves (with the very specific exception
in Georgia of cases involving the transport of light-skinned slaves without authorization). Across all these cases, as in the cases decided by the
Virginia Supreme Court in the same period, the law governing property
damages could not be modernized, because slaves were property and modernization of the categories of legal analysis challenged the logic of the
slave-driven system at numerous levels. Where cases involved injuries to
free, white citizens, however, the story was quite different, as we will see
in the discussion of crossing cases in the next section.

Injuries to Persons: Crossing Cases

Georgia in the 1850s heard two important crossing cases, both arising
out of a single incident. Mrs. Winn and her four children were riding in a
wagon being driven by one of the family's slaves. When they approached

a railroad crossing, Mrs. Winn ordered the slave (who is not named in the record) to stop, but he insisted that he could make it across before the train arrived. The mules balked while on the tracks, and the train struck the wagon. The driver and three of the children were killed, the wagon was destroyed, and Mrs. Winn was injured and disfigured. The railroad argued that if the driver had not recklessly tried to make it across the track before the train arrived, there could have been no accident, a straightforward assertion of the principle of contributory negligence.

The Georgia Supreme Court first heard this case in 1855, on an appeal from a suit by Mrs. Winn. There were three jury instructions at issue: "that if the carriage of plaintiff... was voluntarily stopped, and blocked up that portion of the road crossed by the rail road, then it was not rightfully on the road"; "that the conductors and engineers are bound to use the utmost skill and diligence to prevent accidents at crossings"; and "that in view of the great danger attending the running of cars and engines, the care and skill in conducting them must be in proportion to the danger." Justice Lumpkin found all these instructions to be in error. First, railroads were only required to exercise "reasonable care and diligence," a rule that "commends itself, as well on account of its simplicity as the universality of its application and... is the only one which can be prescribed by the Courts. They have tried in vain to be more definite and to classify the degrees of diligence; but the attempt has been abandoned as impracticable." What would constitute reasonable care would vary with the facts, but the rule was universal. As for the contributory negligence rule of *Butterfield v. Forester*, Lumpkin preferred to be guided by a version drawn from later cases: "[I]t ought to be left to the Jury to say whether, notwithstanding the imprudence of the plaintiff's servant, the defendants could not, in the exercise of reasonable diligence, have prevented the collision," he wrote, citing cases from Connecticut and Vermont (*The Macon & Western R.R. Co. v. Davis*, 18 Ga. 679, 680, 684, 686–7, 1855, citing *Robinson v. Cone*, 22 Vt. 213, 1850, discussed in Chapter 5).

The second case that arose out of the incident was a suit filed by the Winns' daughter, Malinda. This case reached the Georgia Supreme Court in 1856, with a new question: "[T]he proposition is now made for the first time; suppose the plaintiff, in the exercise of ordinary diligence, could have avoided the casualty, conceding there is fault on both sides, can there be a recovery?" Justice Lumpkin returned to the rule in *Branan v. May* (discussed earlier in this chapter), that "the plaintiff was not entitled to recover, if, in the exercise of ordinary diligence, he could have avoided the injury." But was there a conflict between the rule announced earlier in

Mrs. Winn's case and the rule of *Branan*? "Instead of repugnance, we see nothing but harmony . . . [I]f both parties are equally at fault, or neither are guilty, there can be no action; and that the right to sue lies between these two hypotheses. . . . He who is most negligent, can never ask a Court for compensation; he who is least so, may or may not, according to the facts and circumstances of the case" (*The Macon & Western R.R. Co. v. Winn*, 19 Ga. 440, 442, 445–6, 1856).

This looked a great deal like a comparative version of the contributory negligence rule. Unlike versions of this rule announced in northern cases, however, Lumpkin's derivation of principles was based on the proposition that railroads were *not* a special case, let alone one requiring reconsideration of other cases:

> How is a collision of this sort distinguishable, in principle, from those which happen daily in our towns and cities, and upon our great thoroughfares? Two gentlemen in buggies having the same right to the use of the street or highway, strive to take the best track from the other, and one or both of them are overturned. Would the party who was the greatest sufferer, consider himself entitled to redress?

The authority of custom, once again, was the fundamental legitimating principle for the law. Lumpkin's commitment to preserving the traditional rules that governed "two gentlemen in buggies" was not founded on any hostility toward internal improvements. Lumpkin, in fact, was well known in his state as a railroad booster and a legal and social reformer, and he made his feelings known in his opinion: "Our State is, unquestionably, mainly indebted to rail roads, for the proud pre-eminence which she occupies in the Union. And the patriotic and public-spirited men who built these roads, have sacrificed too much already to be made the victims of a blind and vindictive policy" (*Winn*, 446–7). But Lumpkin was also profoundly committed to the system of slavery, and the social order that it sustained (Huebner, 1999: 71–4, 81–7). The rule for free white travelers might be one of comparative negligence, but those rules would not extend to property to become unifying principles for the system of Georgia's common law.

Georgia, then, ended up with different rules for different contexts. In crossing cases, a principle of contributory negligence, modified by a comparative causation element, was drawn directly from northern precedents and adapted to fit the customs of the state. The justification for this principle, too, was rooted in local experience, drawn from Georgia's political culture. Instead of the overriding public Need for Speed that informed Illinois and other northern cases, the justification for the adoption of the new principles of negligence law in Georgia was the preservation of the customary prerogatives of gentlemen. Most important, there could be no hint of a rule of contributory or comparative negligence in cases involving stock, where there was no rule of contributory negligence of any kind, nor those involving harm to slaves, where the issue was transformed into one of conversion of property. Novel doctrines might be adopted, drawn from northern precedents, but the scope of those rules would be narrowly confined to fit the justifying principles that were appropriate to the social and political order of the antebellum South. Anything more far-reaching than that ran headlong into the fundamental need to ensure that slaves be kept cleanly in the intermediate category between gentleman and mule, a unique form of property that anchored a system of property law even while other parts of the system began to give way under the challenges of railroads and the need for prudence that they imposed on passersby.

North Carolina's highest court did not hear a single case involving injuries to free persons by trains between 1850 and 1861, nor did the Kentucky Supreme Court. Their silence may be taken as evidence that there was no great felt need to revise the state of legal doctrine in this area. Virginia and Georgia both similarly made the facts of railroad collisions with persons fit into the preexisting molds of traditional custom, based on an ideal model of "two gentlemen in buggies having the same right to use the street."

Contractual Relationships

The last category of antebellum southern cases consists of those that involved contractual obligations between a railroad and the plaintiff. To the extent that these cases less obviously pointed toward the basic premises of the slave economy, they were more open to considerations of a connection between the public good and the needs of railroads. Georgia, for example, began the 1850s with a case involving the meaning of "baggage" that incorporated the fraud principle that we saw in Illinois. Quoting the commentaries of Joseph Story and a New York case, Justice Nisbet stated that "a reasonable amount of baggage, by custom or the courtesy of the carrier, is considered as included in the fare for the person." If the value of the contents of baggage was excessive, "[t]he liability in such a case, would be wholly disproportioned to the compensation which he is presumed to derive from the fare of passengers.... [I]t is a fraud upon him to subject him to so great a hazard, without warning him of its existence." The problem, however, could not be reduced to a rule, but must be left to a jury's local knowledge of the character of the traveler: "The quantity and character of baggage must depend very much upon the condition in life of the traveler – his calling, his habits, his tastes, the length or shortness of his journey, and whether he travels alone, or with a family" (*Dibble v. Brown & Harris*, 12 Ga. 217, 225–8, 1852). Once again, specific modern rules of adjudication might be adopted, but the mode of analysis would remain traditional: case by case, grounded in local custom, based on the relationships between the parties and their status in the community.

The path of development of Georgia's employment law shows the same pattern. In *Scudder v. Woodbridge*, decided in 1846, the owner of a slave killed while working for hire on a steamboat sued. The boat owner cited the fellow-servant rule as it had been announced in railroad cases from Massachusetts and England. Justice Lumpkin was not impressed. Referring to the argument that the fellow-servant rule would promote vigilance, Lumpkin refused to consider any analysis that would blur the distinction between slaves and other classes of employees: "No two conditions can be more different than these two classes of agents: namely, slaves and free white citizens; and it would be strange and extraordinary indeed if the same principle should apply to both." Above all, the rule could not be extended to slaves lest the system of hiring out become a trap for slaveowners:

Once let it be promulgated that the owner of negroes hired to the numerous navigation, railroad, mining and manufacturing companies which dot the whole country, and are rapidly increasing – I repeat, that for any injury done to this species of property, let it be understood and settled that the employer is not liable, but that the owner must look for compensation to the coservant who occasioned the mischief, and I hesitate not to affirm, that the life of no hired slave would be safe. As it is, the guards thrown around this class of our population are sufficiently few and feeble. We are altogether disinclined to lessen their number or weaken their force (*Scudder v. Woodbridge*, 1 Ga. 195, 200, 1846).

Industrialization would have to accommodate itself to the situation.

The fellow-servant rule came under fire in the legislature, and in 1856 a law was passed abolishing the rule for "railroad companies." That fact did not keep the court from considering the question further, however, as in 1857 it ruled that the Western & Atlantic Railroad was not a "railroad company" at all because it was owned and operated by the State of Georgia[1] (*Walker v. Spullock*, 23 Ga. 436, 1857). In 1860, the Western &

---

[1] That decision was reversed by a statutory enactment in 1863, which provided that the 1856 law applied to the Western & Atlantic in the same way that it applied to

Atlantic was involved in a case that extended the *Scudder* analysis from slaves to free workers. The rule, wrote Justice Stephens, was grounded in public policy, "to secure to the public a more faithful service from employees on railroads, steamboats and other branches of business wherein the safety and property of the public are involved, by making it the interest of each one of such employees to look after and encourage the carefulness and fidelity of all the rest." In *Scudder*, the court had found that these policies did not apply in the case of slaves: "Nor can it be extended to other employees who from any cause are not in a situation to exert such an influence on their fellows" (*Cooper v. Mullins*, 30 Ga. 146, 150–1, 1860). The rule would not apply to slaves, nor to employees of "railroad companies," and it would apply only narrowly to free workers employed by the Western & Atlantic line.

North Carolina's high court began its consideration of the implications of rail expansion for the duties owed between parties to a contract with an analysis of the rules of agency and vicarious liability (when an employer will be liable for the acts of an employee) in *Wiswall v. Brinson*, 32 N.C. 554 (1849). In the process of moving a house from one side of a street to another, a contractor left a hole in the middle of the road into which the plaintiff's horse stepped. The owner of the horse sued the homeowner who had hired the contractor, and the question was whether in that situation liability could attach to the principal rather than to the contractor. The case did not involve railroads, nor pose new problems, but railroads and their nature provided the context for Justice Pearson's analysis.

The basic principle was the rule of vicarious liability for the acts of employees, *respondeat superior*: "The rule is founded upon justice, and exceptions to it should be allowed with caution, and only to the extent called for by public convenience" (*Wiswall*, 555). As the last phrase suggests, however, there was "an exception to the generality of the rule, made necessary by public convenience and general usage," and railroads were its defining exemplar. Applied literally, after all, such a rule would seem to make passengers liable to other passengers for the negligence of conductors and engineers: "When one enters a railroad car, the engineer and hands serve him – do work for him – carry him and his goods. But he is not liable for their negligence or want of skill.... [H]e did not make the selection, and although in a large sense they are his servants, yet they are the servants of the company." These principles were discussed only by

all other railroad lines. This latter statute, in turn, was interpreted to have retroactive effect.

way of contrast, as *Wiswall* did not involve analogous facts: "He selected his man; the work was done for his benefit.... There is no principle of public convenience, which calls for the exception." As a result, the home-owner was liable for the contractor's actions. In dissent, Justice Thomas Ruffin argued that property owners who employed contractors should not be liable for acts that they committed while not under the owner's direct control, because the two did not occupy the positions of master and servant (*Wiswall*, 555, 562, 565, 570). Both the majority and dissenting opinions are long and detailed. Both go through dozens of English cases without mentioning a single American case – and without ever mentioning slaves.

North Carolina's antebellum consideration of the fellow-servant rule took place in *Ponton v. Wilmington & Weldon R.R. Co.*, 51 N.C. 245 (1858). Justice Ruffin described the question of the rule as "raised now, for the first time, in the courts of this State," stating that the rule "owes its origin, or rather prevalence, probably, to the great number of servants needed and employed on the steamboats and railroads, which, have come so much into use in our times, and on which so many casualties or injuries from negligence happen." In general, and with some overstatement of the uniformity of its application, Ruffin found the rule to be universally accepted (*Ponton*, 246–7).

As noted previously, however, in southern courts the fellow-servant rule ran into the complication of slavery. In Georgia, a rule excepting slaves from the operation of the rule had extended to cover free workers who did not exercise mutual control over one another's actions. Ruffin, recognizing the same analytical connection, reached the opposite substantive conclusion:

The distinction was put upon the difference between a hired freeman and a slave.... But the distinction does not seem sound. It might be, if the slave were the person to be benefitted, by the recovery. But the action is by the owner for his benefit.... In the cases in the courts of the Southern States, already alluded to, the injury was generally to slaves, and both in those in which the decisions were for, or against the employers, such a distinction was disregarded, or, rather, not noticed. It would be singular, if the owner of a slave could recover for damage sustained by a slave, when upon the same state of facts, the slave, if he had been a freeman, could not have recovered (*Ponton*, 247–8).

The key sentence is the last one. As had been in the case in Virginia, extending special consideration to the interests of slaveowners had the result, in practice, of providing greater protections to employed slaves than to free workers.

The problem was that the law of employment and the law of property were completely separate, so that the obligations of employers toward employees working side by side were defined completely differently. But to rationalize this system would have meant the creation of universally applicable standards that made no distinction between freeman and slave, precisely the sort of standards that were providing the mechanism for the unification and standardization of legal duties in northern courts. The new forms of work and management that accompanied industrialization, and the concerns of traditional property rights, pushed the North Carolina Supreme Court in opposite directions. In *Wiswall*, Ruffin had dissented from the majority opinion based on his strenuous argument that one who has no control over the acts of his employee should not be liable for the harms that the employee causes. Now, writing for the majority in *Ponton*, Ruffin concluded that the fact that a slave and another employee exercised no control over one another had *nothing* to do with the applicability of the fellow-servant rule.

One way to read *Wiswall* and *Ponton* together is based purely on outcome: the employer/defendant always wins. In that case, we would see North Carolina's treatment as directly opposed to that of the Georgia Supreme Court, which labored to find exceptions to the rule precluding liability. But that reading overlooks the similarities in the two states' treatment of the issues involved. Both confronted the problem of mixed slave and free labor, both ended up defining a rule that applied to slaves and free workers alike, and both faced the question in the context of railroads. And, by opposite analytical paths, both started from the problem of slave labor and reached the same conclusion. Confronted by the challenge of corporate employment, both restricted the fellow-servant rule to the scope of traditional master-servant relations. The reason for the common solution was that these were two different strategies aimed at the same goal: to prevent the logic of railroad employment, and new models of industrial organization, from undermining the system of political economy that took as its starting point the supremacy of the private property rights of slaveowners.

North Carolina did not have any antebellum cases explaining the railroads' duties with respect to freight or baggage. There were two cases, however, that considered the question of a railroad's duty to care for hired slaves, and these were treated as property cases governed by the law of bailments. The rule that resulted was simply that railroads were required to follow custom. In *Slocumb v. Washington*, 51 N.C. 357 (1858), a railroad was found to have acted with "the degree of care generally practiced by the persons engaged in making railroad embankments and excavations," in respect to the lodging of their own slaves, employed in the work." By contrast, in *Lane v. Burdick*, 53 N.C. 248 (1860), where several slaves died of exposure due to the inadequacy of the shelter provided for them, a verdict against the railroad was upheld on the grounds that the shelter was less than that which was customarily supplied to rail workers.

Kentucky's treatment of cases involving contractual relationships began with an 1847 non-railroad case.[2] *Swigert v. Graham*, 46 Ky. 661 (1847), involved a slave hired out to work on a boat, but the case was analyzed in terms of trespass on property, not breach of contract. "The rule," said Chief Justice Marshall, was "that the bailee on hire, is bound to ordinary diligence. . . . that degree of care, or attention, or exertion, which under the actual circumstances, a man of ordinary prudence and discretion would use in reference to the particular thing were it his own property, or in doing the particular thing were it his own concern." Applying this rule to the case of a hired slave, the court ruled that everything would depend on circumstances: "It might be necessary in sending him to the bottom of a deep well or to the eave of a steep roof, to tie a rope around his waist. But if he were possessed of ordinary intelligence, it could not be required that in sending him across a wide bridge, he should even be cautioned not to jump or fall from it." In the absence of actual notice to the defendant that the slave was not "possessed of ordinary intelligence," the defendant's duty would be based on reasonable presumptions about the vulnerability of the property at issue. The case was different from the conversion analysis proffered in 1851 in *King v. Shanks* (discussed previously), said Marshall, because *Swigert* involved the lawful exercise of authority over another person's slave, which took the case out of the realm of trespass on property rights and into the negligence-like area of bailments. As a result, "the owners of the boat were responsible only for misconduct or culpable negligence" (*Swigert*, 664).

The only antebellum Kentucky case concerning baggage was a non-railroad case. *Steamboat Crystal Palace vs. Vanderpool*, 55 Ky. 302 (1855), involved a passenger who complained to a steward that the lock on his door was not functional. The passenger then went to sleep, and awoke later to find his watch and wallet missing. He sued on the theory that the

---

[2] An even earlier case, involving a railroad and an injury to a slave in the course of transport, was analyzed purely in terms of the traditional elements of trover and conversion (*The Lexington and Ohio R.R. Co. v. Kidd*, 37 Ky. 245, 1838).

boat's owners were bailees of his personal effects as a form of "baggage." Justice B. Mills Crenshaw conceded the validity of the argument as a matter of public policy, but overruled the lower court's verdict for the plaintiff: "[W]e know of no principle of the common law which will authorize a recovery in this case, and we have no statute upon the subject. *Salus populi* is a principle of legislative authority, not of common law interpretation." Crenshaw's insistence that invocations of the public good could not alter a rule of common law reflects perfectly both the conservatism of the southern legal tradition and the sharp contrast between that tradition and the emergence of a new system of uniquely American common law in the northern states (*Vanderpool*, 307–8).

The Postbellum South: The Adoption of Modern Doctrines in Georgia, North Carolina, and Kentucky

It would be too much to expect that with the abolition of slavery judges like Justice Lumpkin, in Georgia, should suddenly begin to give their modernizing impulses free rein in the adoption of common law principles, and yet that appears to be precisely what occurred. In *Rowland v. Cannon*, 35 Ga. 105, 107 (1866), Lumpkin read the statute excepting railroad companies from the operation of the fellow-servant rule in a way that turned it into a statement of a special case of a general, common law rule of contributory negligence. By this back door, he introduced modern negligence doctrine into Georgia's law.

The relevant statutory language said that, with regard to railroad corporations, "[i]f the person injured is himself an employee of the Company, and the damage was caused by another employee, and without fault or negligence on the part of the person injured, his employment by the company shall be no bar to the recovery." Instead of reading this to mean, straightforwardly, that the fellow-servant rule did not apply to railroads, Lumpkin read the phrase, "without fault or negligence," "negatively, that it would constitute a bar if fault or negligence be imputable to him." In other words, Lumpkin determined that *even in* the case of railroads, a general principle of contributory negligence, which had never been recognized in Georgia in the first instance, continued to apply: "[A]nd it is not promotive of goods thus to interpret the Code? The strictest fidelity should be exacted of all agents; and to allow one to hold the Road liable, when he himself contributed in part to the injury, seems to be wrong to the Road and the people generally, who are indirectly, but deeply interested in the fidelity of the employees" (*Rowland*, 107).

Thereafter, Lumpkin's name disappears from among the cases that defined Georgia's common law. The formal declaration of an adoption of the general rule of contributory negligence would wait until 1868. There was a revealing contrast in the way that the court handled two cases heard that term. The first, arising out of events occurring before the war, involved the death of a slave who was struck by a train while crossing the tracks "on a part of the track used very much by foot passengers to make a short cut from one to another of the public roads." Justice Dawson A. Walker decided that case in favor of the defendant on straightforward property law grounds in the same manner as the earlier cases: "The negro was on the road of the defendant, at a point where he had no right to be. It was at the hour of midnight.... The facts, all taken together, as they appear in the record, show the exercise of all ordinary and reasonable care and diligence, on the part of the agents of the Railroad Company" (*Holmes v. The Central R.R. and Banking Co.*, 37 Ga. 593, 597, 1868).

The second case, however, involved an injury to a passenger that took place after the war, and Justice Henry K. McCay used this case to announce Georgia's formal adoption of the rule of contributory negligence. Citing a national digest, *Pearce's American Railway Law*, McCay stated the rule that "[t]he man who neglects ordinary care to avoid an injury, has no just right to seek redress ... and we see nothing in the character of a railroad company which should subject it to damages for an injury caused by the neglect of its agents, where the person injured might, by the exercise of ordinary care, have avoided the consequences to himself" (*Macon & Western R.R. Co. v. Johnson*, 38 Ga. 409, 431–2, 1868). Disingenuously, perhaps, McCay also stated that this rule was in accordance with the earlier statement in *Macon & Western R.R. Co. v. Winn*, 19 Ga. 440 (1856) (discussed previously), the case that Justice Lumpkin had decided by drawing an analogy between trains and gentlemen riding in carriages.

In 1869, Georgia adopted a statutory code that included both a rule of contributory negligence and a renewal of the 1856 law limiting the applicability of the fellow-servant rule in cases involving railroad companies. That latter law, however, incorporated the exception to its limitation that Justice Lumpkin had read into the law in *Rowland v. Cannon*, 35 Ga. 105 (1866). Justice McCay summarized the law concerning contributory negligence, the fellow-servant rule, and the effect of admissions by agents in the context of railroad companies in *East Tenn., Vir., and Ga. R.R. Co. v. Duggan*, 51 Ga. 212 (1874): "An employee is, by the express terms of the Code, section 3036, only entitled to recover for damage caused by the negligence of another employee, in the running of cars, when the injured employee is without fault himself." In the particular case, the injured employee, Duggan, was contributorily negligent by virtue of having followed the instructions of the conductor to speed up in order to make up lost time: "He should have refused to disobey the known rules of the road. He was an old hand, and if such was the rule, he will be presumed to have known it" (*Duggan*, 213).

As for an admission by Duggan's supervisor that "the company felt it to be its duty to support the plaintiff for life," this was not binding on the railroad corporation: "No authority is shown for any such statement. It was not within the natural scope of the agent's employment. . . . " Finally, McCay declared the new function of the southern common law courts, to protect industry against anticorporate populism:

A railroad company, though it be a corporation wealthy and powerful, has rights before the courts which the conscience of judges is bound to respect. . . . Let us take care, and let the juries take care, that in their desire to protect the weak against the strong they do not forget that unfairness and injustice are without excuse even when the victim is strong; that even the devil is entitled to his due, and that a juror who fails wilfully to give it, violates his oath" (*Duggan*, 214).

The North Carolina Supreme Court took its first look at a contributory negligence doctrine in 1869. The case involved the nineteenth century version of a toxic waste dump, an abandoned saltpetre manufacturing facility that had been left with an inadequate fence. A statute required that while in operation, saltpetre manufacturers were required to maintain adequate fences. Some cattle wandered onto the property, drank from a trough full of poisonous waste, and died. Justice Robert P. Dick announced the adoption of the rule of contributory negligence without fanfare:

In all cases where a person, in the lawful use of his own property, causes injury to another, the party injured, before he can recover damages at law, must show that he has exercised proper care and is free from blame in regard to the matter. If it appears that the party injured has, by any act of omission or commission on his part, contributed to the injury complained of, it is generally damnum absque injuria.

The two authorities that Dick cited for this rule were an English case and a case from Connecticut. Beyond the announcement of the rule, the rest of the opinion concerned the rights of landowners to make lawful use of their property, under a theory of trespass:

His cattle were pasturing on the common, and ordinary prudence ought to have prompted him to keep an eye on the enclosure of the saltpetre works. The defendants were not required to keep up the enclosure except while engaged in their operations. The plaintiff's cattle were trespassing on the lands of the defendants at the time they were killed" (*Morrison v. Cornelius*, 63 N.C. 346, 350–1, 1869).

The limitation of the principle of contributory negligence in stock cases was tested in *Jones v. The North Carolina R.R. Co.*, a case that came up in 1872 and again in 1874. The first time, Justice William B. Rodman connected the case to the rule in *Herring* by weakening the distinction between animals and humans:

In *Herring v. W. & W. R. R. Co.* . . . it was held, that it was not the duty of the engineer to stop or slacken his train, when he saw a human being on the track ahead of him, unless he knew that the man was drunk or asleep, or otherwise put out of the general rule. . . . The same reasoning will apply, though with somewhat less force, to horses and other animals; they also have the instinct of self-preservation, though combined with less intelligence, and the power of locomotion. It would seem not to be a duty of the engineer to stop or slacken his train, whenever he sees an animal on the track. To do so would greatly impair the usefulness of the road, without a corresponding advantage to any one. But it is admitted to be clearly his duty to blow the whistle, for the purpose of frightening the animal (*Jones v. The North Carolina R.R. Co.*, 67 N.C. 122, 125, 1872).

On the second hearing of the case, after a retrial with new jury instructions, Justice Edwin G. Reade upheld a verdict for the plaintiff on the facts (*Jones v. The North Carolina R.R. Co.*, 70 N.C. 626, 1874). And just like that, a rule that had been carefully established to deal with the special case of slaves was expanded, without explanation, into a general principle raising the bar for proof of negligence in stock cases.

The ruling in *Jones* was not yet an announcement of a full-fledged rule of contributory negligence, however. That rule was announced in 1872, in a case that arose when a passenger attempted to jump to a platform from a train moving between two and four miles per hour. Justice Dick began by noting the railroad's duties: "The policy of the law which is ever solicitous for the protection of human life, requires common-carriers, who have charge of the safety of passengers to use a high degree of care to guard against probable injury." Having declared that primary duty, however, Dick immediately qualified it: "The act of the intestate in jumping off the cars while they were in motion at the rate of from two to four miles per hour, was the proximate cause of the injury, and the question is whether he exercised ordinary care under the circumstances." A lack of ordinary care on the part of the plaintiff would preclude recovery even from a common carrier engaged in the transport of passengers. But the details of the rule remained to be worked out: "[I]t is not necessary for us to express an opinion as to the rights of the parties, if the jury should find that the testimony of the conductor gives the truth of the transaction" (*Lambeth v. North Carolina R.R. Co.*, 66 N.C. 494, 498–9, 500, 1872).

The issue came up again without significant discussion in 1874,[3] and then came *Manly v. Wilmington & Weldon R.R. Co.*, 74 N.C. 655 (1876). A train running on a downhill grade at 3:30 P.M. ran over and killed "a colored girl, the child of the plaintiff, then about ten years old, who, together with her sister, some fifteen years old, was on the track asleep." The engineer testified that he had attempted to avoid running over the child:

At first he supposed the objects were small hogs, and blew his whistle. That so soon as he discovered the objects to be human beings he reversed his engine, threw the whole force of the steam upon the wheels and blew the whistle rapidly, but could not stop the engine until it had run over one of the girls, and passed about one hundred yards beyond. That when he first blew the whistle, one of the girls sprang up, endeavored to drag the other off, but was unable to do so, and escaped from the track (*Manly*, 656).

In Virginia, the rule of contributory negligence had been discovered when free black plaintiffs, rather than respectable white families, attempted to recover damages from railroads. In North Carolina, whether by coincidence or design, the pattern was exactly the same.

It is important to remember that up to this point, in North Carolina, the idea of contributory negligence had been introduced in the context of an injury to a passenger. The rule had yet to be employed in a case involving damage to property (stock). How would this case be described? The answer was that *Manly* introduced contributory negligence to North Carolina as a repetition of *Herring* without the element of slavery. "The facts here," wrote Justice William P. Bynum, "are so strikingly like those in the case of *Herring v. Railroad* ... that it is sufficient to refer to that case for a full discussion of the principles involved in this. The doctrine of contributory negligence ... is further well illustrated in the cases of *Morrison v. Cornelius*, 63 N.C. 346, and *Murphy v. Railroad*, 70 N.C. 437." He went on to cite cases from Massachusetts, Illinois, and Ohio.

Justice Bynum's invocation of earlier North Carolina cases was pure legerdemain. *Herring v. The Wilmington & Raliegh R.R. Co*, 32 N.C. 402 (1849) (discussed previously), was the case involving a train that ran over two slaves lying on the track. As we have seen, *Herring* did not contain a rule of contributory negligence. *Morrison v. Cornelius*, 63 N.C. 346, 350–1 (1869), a stock case, was decided by defining the wandering

---

[3] *Murphy v. Wilmington & Weldon R.R. Co.*, 70 N.C. 437 (1874).

cows as "trespassers," invoking the traditional question of duties owed by landowners to trespassers without any consideration of contributory negligence. And *Murphy*, in 1874, treated the issue in a single sentence, in the context of a case that was trivial on its facts (a wagon that was parked in a rail yard too close to the tracks was struck by an arriving train). The entire support for the rule in *Manly* came from earlier northern railroad cases, and the rule was a familiar one: "[When] the parties are mutually in fault, the negligence of both being the immediate and proximate cause of the injury, a recovery is denied upon the ground that the injured party must be taken to have brought the injury upon himself" (*Manly*, 658, 660).

In a different case, said Bynum, there might have been room to apply a comparative apportionment of damages, but not here:

As the capacity of the two is not disclosed in the case, we are to assume that they were of ordinary intelligence and physical activity. The mind of one was near the period of maturity for females. The other, though younger and more immature, was yet of sufficient age and discretion, under the control of her sister, or even without it, to be subject to the laws of ordinary care and diligence. If by the proposition of the counsel of the plaintiff, that "If there was negligence on the part of the children, it is not imputable to the parent, who is the plaintiff," is meant that the plaintiff is entitled to recover, notwithstanding any degree of negligence on the part of the children, we cannot assent to the proposition. It has no foundation in reason, and would be disastrous to commercial life.

On the other hand, the railroad had not been shown to have been negligent at all. The engineer, seeing the children, had taken them to be hogs and acted accordingly:

The engineer did not know, and was not bound to know, they were human beings. Their irrational conduct in lying still upon the track when the train was rapidly approaching at its usual time repelled the idea that they were intelligent beings. As soon as a nearer approach enabled him to see that they were human beings he seems to have made every possible effort to avert the disaster, but without success" (*Manly*, 660–1, 662).

The specific facts of the case aside, the rule in *Manly* announced North Carolina's adoption of a principle taken from northern cases: that a railroad has the right to expect and assume that persons would act rationally, and that persons who failed to get out of the way of oncoming trains had no right to recover damages for their injuries. North Carolina had discovered the Duty to Get Out of the Way.

The doctrines of contributory negligence were finally worked out in North Carolina in a pair of cases brought by John Doggett against the

Richmond & Danville Railroad. The first involved a fire started when sparks from a passing engine ignited a pile of cross-ties, destroying a fence belonging to one Chilcutt, and from there moving on to consume part of Doggett's fence. Doggett was not a black child mistaken for a hog, he was a white property owner asserting a claim that by English tradition would have subjected the railroad to strict liability.

Justice Bynum began by observing that the intervening landowner, Chilcutt, had been contributorily negligent in failing to keep his fence in repair, but he ruled that Chilcutt's negligence could not diminish Doggett's right of recovery: "If the plaintiff's negligence contributed directly to the injury, it is well settled that he cannot recover, but it is equally well settled that when he is only remotely and unconsciously negligent he is entitled to redress for all injuries inflicted by another, when by the latter the injuries could have been avoided by reasonable diligence" (*Doggett v. The Richmond & Danville R.R. Co.*, 78 N.C. 305, 307, 1878 [*Doggett I*]).

But Bynum was far from finished. He used the case as a reason to announce the adoption of two additional rules. First, North Carolina would hereafter follow two Pennsylvania cases in holding that a railroad that caused a fire was only liable for the first property that was damaged as a result, and not for harms to other properties caused by the spread of the fire:

There is a possibility of carrying an admittedly correct principle too far. It may be extended so as to reach the reductio ad absurdum so far as it applies to the practical business of life.... The defendant had the right to expect the destruction of Chilcutt's fence, because that was the natural and probable result of the fire; but the defendant had no right to expect the destruction of the other fences, nor is there any evidence that they would have been destroyed had each been disconnected and surrounding the premises of its owner (*Doggett I*, 308).

It is impossible to conceive of a rule more distant from the traditional liability of landowners for fires, or the general rule of *sic utere*, or the principle that the degree of hazard involved in a lawful activity determines the scope of liability.

But this new rule was not, as Bynum said, the basis for reversing the verdict in favor of the plaintiff. The real ground for the decision was another newly announced principle of North Carolina common law, the rule of the intervening cause: "The facts do not constitute such a continuous succession of events so linked together as to become a natural whole, which would make it a case of proximate damages." And this reasoning, in turn, brought the court back to the question of contributory negligence:

The danger was imminent, and the law imposes the burden upon the plaintiff of showing that he was not negligent. If either his family, servants, or the owners of the preceding fences stood at their plow handles and beheld the destruction of their property when timely exertions would have saved it, the law will not suffer them to throw the loss resulting from their own apathy upon the defendant (*Doggett I*, 308–9, 311).

The first *Doggett* opinion was a *tour de force*, and articulated a wholesale adoption of northern negligence doctrines in complete abrogation of North Carolina's common law traditions. Through the whole opinion, with the exception of a single citation to an unnamed Missouri case, Bynum relied on precedents from Pennsylvania, New York, Massachusetts, Wisconsin, and two national digests. The second *Doggett* opinion, in 1879, made those new doctrines the state's own, manufacturing a tradition out of whole cloth and finally announcing the applicability of the principle of contributory negligence to stock cases.

    The law of 1857, still in force, stated that where cattle were struck by railroads, the fact of the collision was *prima facie* evidence of the railroad's negligence, shifting the burden of proof to the defense. Prior to this case, a railroad in a stock case had not been able to meet that burden by appealing to the plaintiff's failure to control his cattle. In the key section of his opinion, Chief Justice William N.H. Smith cited only one source, Isaac Redfield's digest of railway law:

If the owner permits his cattle to stray off and get upon the track, and they are killed or hurt, the company is not liable unless the company were carelessly running the train.... [T]he company is not required to abate the usual and safe speed of their trains, lest there may be cattle on the road which may be killed or injured; and if a proper look-out is kept up, and all reasonable efforts made when the obstruction is seen, to avoid the accident, the company is exempt from responsibility, and the injury is ascribed to the contributory negligence of the plaintiff, in permitting his stock to roam about and get on the road (*Doggett v. The Richmond & Danville R.R. Co.*, 81 N.C. 459, 462–3, 1879 [*Doggett II*]).

    Smith then reviewed a whole series of North Carolina cases – including *Herring, Aycock,* and *Jones* (all discussed previously) – that had turned not on the question of contributory negligence, but rather on the question of what facts would suffice to establish the railroad's negligence in the first place. Based on his review of these cases, Smith declared that the new rule did not conflict with "our own reasonable construction of the act, and . . . is calculated to secure all its intended benefits to those whose property is destroyed or injured in their absence by railway trains, without doing injustice to the company" (*Doggett II*, 467).

Turning to employment relations, the 1870s also saw the North Carolina Supreme Court's adoption of the fellow-servant rule, even in railroad cases. As was the case in the contributory negligence cases, the first case in the series was only indirectly relevant. A railroad employee was killed when the train on which he was riding struck a section of washed-out track and plunged into a ravine. Justice Reade noted that the fellow-servant rule had been debated during the requests for jury instructions, but ruled that the issue was not relevant to the case: "These and other questions were fully considered. But the question upon which the case turns is outside of all these. Concede everything in the defendant's favor but this: was it not his duty to have some one at the break in the road to stop the train? Unquestionably it was. Nothing else but that could have prevented the catastrophe, and that would have prevented it" (*Hardy v. The North Carolina Central R.R. Co.*, 74 N.C. 745, 747, 1876).

Another opportunity to explore the issue of the fellow-servant rule, and another occasion on which the court balked, was *Crutchfield v. The Richmond & Danville R.R. Co.*, yet another case that came up twice, in 1877 and 1878. Crutchfield, a brakeman on the defendant's line, was crippled when a train on which he was working derailed due to defects in the track and rail bed. On the first hearing, the case was remanded with the instruction that the trial judge deliver instructions concerning contributory negligence, in distinction from assumption of risk:

Suppose then it were true . . . that the plaintiff either from the general nature of his employment on the defendant's road or by express contract, assumed the risk of all accidents, yet it would not follow that he would not be entitled to recover. He would still be entitled to recover if his injury resulted not from accident but from the negligence of the defendant. . . . But suppose the plaintiff as an employee on the road knew that the road and the engine were out of order, could he recover? It would seem that if an engineer whose peculiar duty it is to know the condition of the engine and to give notice of any fault in order that it may be repaired, runs the engine out of order without giving such notice and is injured, he is guilty of at least contributory negligence and could not recover (*Crutchfield v. The Richmond & Danville R.R. Co.*, 76 N.C. 320, 322, 1877).

After retrial, the case was again appealed to the Supreme Court, and again the fellow-servant rule was hinted at, but not formally adopted. Justice Bynum made it clear that the case had not resolved the question of the applicability of the fellow-servant rule previously: "[I]f it is supposed that the point now insisted on was decided in that case, a careful reading of the case and opinion will show otherwise." Then he declared that the question would remain a simple one of contributory negligence: "Did the plaintiff so far contribute to his injuries by his own negligence or want of proper care and caution, as but for such negligence or want of proper care and caution on his part, the accident would not have happened?" (*Crutchfield v. The Richmond & Danville R.R. Co.*, 78 N.C. 300, 303–4, 1878). The same thing happened when *Hardy* was appealed again. The only reference to the fellow-servant rule was a single sentence in a list of legal rules that the court said it had previously considered (*Hardy v. The North Carolina Central R.R. Co.*, 76 N.C. 5, 8, 1877).

Finally, in 1879, Justice Thomas S. Ashe authored an opinion that established the North Carolina fellow-servant rule:

Where the relation of fellow-servants or co-laborers is found to subsist, it is well established by the English as well as American authorities, and is conceded in the argument of this case, that the master is not responsible for an injury to one of his servants occasioned by the negligence of a fellow-servant engaged in the same business or employment. This principle has been so universally recognized by the Courts, that it may be regarded as a general rule of law.

The rationales cited by Ashe were that the employee agreed to assume "all the ordinary risks of the service, which includes the risk of the negligence of his fellow-servants." The rule, however, would not apply in a case where the negligence in question was that of a supervisor who had authority over the injured plaintiff: "Such an agent is what is known as a 'middle man,' who, as well as the laborer, is the servant of the master, and although he may work with the laborer in furthering the common business of the master, he is yet not a "fellow-servant" in the sense of that term as used by the Courts." And the source for this rule? Ashe cited cases from New York, Pennsylvania, Michigan, Indiana, and Missouri (*Dobbin v. The Richmond & Danville R.R. Co.*, 81 N.C. 446, 448–9, 1879).

Kentucky reached the same conclusions about the fellow-servant rule as did North Carolina, but Kentucky got there in 1865. Collins, a day laborer, was employed by the railroad digging and hauling gravel. He was working under the supervision of an engineer one day when the train sitting on the track next to him lurched forward, cutting off one of his legs. Attempting to help him, the engineer reversed the engine, cutting off Collins' other leg. Collins sued, and the railroad asserted the fellow-servant rule as a defense. Calling the issue "a new and unsettled question," Judge George Robertson ruled that an engineer who is supervising a day laborer is not the fellow servant of that laborer so as to preclude a recovery. Robertson went further, however, taking the opportunity to make a number of observations about the principles of negligence and contributory negligence. He ruled, for example, without citation to authority, that even where a plaintiff has been negligent, he may still recover in the event that the defendant is proved to have been grossly negligent, the gross/slight rule familiar from northern cases. He described the duties of care that railroads owe to strangers, adopting the principle that the degree of care required was proportional to "a motive power so tremendous and destructive as unregulated or carelessly or unskillfully regulated steam": "[A]s in every class of cases of bailment or trust, the requisite care is proportioned to the danger of neglect and the difficulty of conservative management; ordinary care in many classes of cases might be ordinary neglect, and ordinary neglect might be gross neglect in steam operations on a railway" (*Louisville and Nashville R.R. Co. v. Collins*, 63 Ky. 114, 116, 1865).

Having introduced a modern and distinctly northern scheme of calculation in negligence cases, Robertson returned to the fellow-servant rule, and based on the review of basic principles, he distinctly limited its application in Kentucky: "[T]his anomalous rule, even as sometimes qualified, is, in our opinion, inconsistent with principle, analogy, and public policy, and is unsupported by any good or consistent reason." The rule might make sense if the two employees occupied the same rank, since in that case neither could be said to be acting as the agent of the railway, "but beyond this, [the rule] is baseless of any other support than a falsely assumed public policy or implied contract." In addition, there had to be a limit to the level of risk that employees could be said to assume: "The corporation, being under an implied obligation to provide sound and safe cars and engines, and a competent and faithful engineer, his subordinates cannot reasonably be presumed to expect or to hazard his gross negligence, which borders on fraud and crime" (*Collins*, 117).

Furthermore, whatever the applicability of the fellow-servant rule, it could not apply on policy grounds to workers involved in different areas of employment: "In their employment, having nothing to do with the cars or the running of them, they, like the corporation's mere woodchoppers, are comparative strangers to the engineer and his running operations, and seem to be entitled to all the security of strangers.... They are, therefore, not, in the essential sense of contradistinctive classification, 'in the same service' with the engineer." Thus the rule could not apply except to workers of equal rank involved in the same activities, and it could not apply to limit an employer's liability in a case of gross negligence:

This is the only doctrine we can recognize as consistent with the enlightened and homogeneous jurisprudence of this clearer day of its ripening maturity; and, looking through the mist of the adjudged cases and elementary dicta, we can see no other fundamental principle which can mould them into a consistent or abiding form. That principle is the only safe clue to lead the bewildered explorer to the light which shows the sure way of right, and proves the true doctrine of American law (*Collins*, 118–19, 120).

The opinion is absolutely remarkable. In 1859, the Kentucky Supreme Court had pointed toward an abandonment of its established common law traditions in favor of a wholesale adoption of modern theories of contributory negligence, citing cases from Illinois and New York (*Louisville and Frankfort Railroad Company vs. Ballard*, 59 Ky. 177, 1859, discussed previously). In 1865, Justice Robertson described an entire new system of rules defining the liability of employers for injuries to employees *without citation to a single authority*. Not a case, not a treatise, is cited in the entire opinion that created a whole new system of duties of care that brought employment relations under the same aegis as the general principles of negligence that governed the duties of care between strangers. The principles of liability are drawn from the law of bailments, as they had been in Illinois a decade earlier, and the limitation of the fellow-servant rule is held out as "the true doctrine" of "*American* common law."

The fellow-servant rule was revisited in 1868, and again Justice Robertson worked to bring employment relations within the general terms of negligence doctrine. In *Louisville and Nashville R.R. Co. v. Robinson*, 67 Ky. 507 (1868), the plaintiff was a brakeman who claimed that he was injured due to the negligence of the engineer on the train on which he was riding. Robertson reaffirmed the *Collins* rules, and found that brakemen and engineers were engaged in the same activity and at the same level. Robertson then turned his attention to the gross/slight rule of contributory negligence:

[I]f the party complaining of hurt, by his own negligence contributed to it, he cannot recover damages from the company unless its co-operating agent, charged with gross neglect, could have avoided the impending damage by the observance of ordinary diligence, notwithstanding the neglect of the complaining party. These are the principles recognized in Collins' case; and the court below, in giving and overruling instructions, tried to conform to them. But they were not so defined as to enable the jury to apply the law to the facts with reasonable certainty (*Robinson*, 509).

This time Robertson cited one authority: his own opinion in *Collins*.

That same year, 1868, Robertson took on the question of contributory negligence in the conduct of a sixty-five-year-old passenger injured when he tried to step from a slowly moving train onto the platform. Reviewing the applicable law, Robertson repeated the three-part rule that he had described in *Robinson*:

1. If the damage to the appellee resulted solely from the negligence of the appellant's agents, it is liable for compensatory damages. 2. If it resulted solely from the negligence or temerity of the appellee himself, he is entitled to nothing. 3. If it was a compound result of negligence on both sides, then, as the appellee's own fault was contributory to it, he can recover nothing, unless the managing agents saw his perilous condition, and might, by ordinary diligence, have prevented his fall (*Kentucky Central Railroad Co. v. Dills*, 67 Ky. 593, 595–6, 1868).

The lawyers for the plaintiff cited a number of cases, including *Yarwood* from Illinois; counsel for the railroad cited only Redfield's digest of railway law and *Collins*. Robertson, in his opinion, cited no authorities at all.

The next year, the court revisited both the fellow-servant rule and the principle of contributory negligence as it applied to passengers. This time, Justice Mordecai R. Hardin authored the opinion in the case involving the fellow-servant rule, *Louisville and Nashville R. R. Co. v. Filbern's adm'x*, 69 Ky. 574 (1869). Filbern was the engineer on a train that struck a downed tree and derailed, killing him. His widow sued, and in its defense the railroad argued that the accident had been caused by Filbern's contributory negligence, or else that of the conductor, his fellow servant. The railroad cited authorities from Indiana, New York, and Massachusetts in support of its position. Hardin, however, merely cited *Collins* and *Robinson*: "Adhering to the law as thus expounded by this court," he wrote, "we are of the opinion that the court did not err in rejecting the rule contended for, as recognized in some of the English and American cases to which we have been referred" (*Filbern's adm'x*, 579–80).

As for the passenger case, the facts in *Louisville and Nashville R.R. Co. v. Sickings*, 68 Ky. 1 (1869), were familiar (compare *Holbrook v. The Utica and Schenectady Railroad Company*, 12 N.Y. 236, 1855, discussed in Chapter 5). The plaintiff was injured when a train passing up against the one in which he was riding struck his elbow, breaking his arm in two places. Chief Justice Rufus K. Williams, who wrote the opinion, took a very different approach than had Justice Robertson. He cited several treatises, as well as case law from Pennsylvania, Massachusetts, New York, Indiana, and New Jersey, in support of his conclusion that the passenger had been contributorily negligent and therefore could not recover unless the railroad had been grossly negligent or could have avoided the injury by due care. And when it came to determining the standard of that care, said Williams, it was important to recognize that Kentucky, too, had a Need for Speed:

> The increased speed of travel is not only an object with the corporation, but also with the passengers; and with this increased power of steam and the vast weight of the trains comes increased danger, and reason for more care and diligence; yet this increased speed is made legal by the various charters granted to such companies; and the demands of the traveling community for rapid and cheap transition makes all unnecessary delay onerous to both the corporation and customers. The mode of propulsion, the means of travel, the usual course of business, and common objects of the carrier, are all considerations entering into the question of diligence.

The plaintiff, moreover, had been not merely negligent, but in fact grossly negligent, in permitting his elbow to protrude out the window where it might become an obstacle to fast-moving trains passing within inches of his own conveyance:

> [A]s it is perfectly apparent in this case, had the appellee properly occupied his seat, and committed no gross negligence by unthoughtedly and unnecessarily placing his arm in the window, with his elbow protruding outside the car, no accident or injury would have befallen him.... [H]e not only contributed to his own injury, but may be said to have mainly, if not entirely, produced it" (*Sickings*, 8–9).

And that was that. Justice Robertson's remarkable experiment at devising a native Kentucky version of negligence doctrine was gone, replaced by the wholesale adoption of the principles worked out in northern cases in the decade before the Civil War.[4] Kentucky finally fit the same model of southern legal development as Virginia, Georgia, and North Carolina: resistance to modernization in the antebellum period based on the preservation of the social order of slave society; a period of resistance to wholesale change accompanied by selective incorporation of new rules in the years following the Civil War; and, finally, direct importation of modern doctrines from northern sources.

---

[4] The limiting principles that Robertson had worked out were not forgotten, however. In 1870, Justice Hardin concluded that at least actual willful negligence by a supervisor would not be subject to the bar of the fellow-servant rule (*Louisville, Cincinnati and Lexington R.R. Co. v. Mahony's adm'x.*, 70 Ky. 235, 1870).

10

Legal Change and Social Order

The argument of this book has been that the creation of the American system of common law in the antebellum North, exemplified by Illinois in the 1850s, expressed a shift in the dominant conception of American citizenship. An emerging model of citizenship was translated into law by judicial elites with ties to both the emerging political economy and the political systems in their states. That conceptual shift was itself the product of a confluence of technological developments, the political economy that they engendered, and a political culture receptive to the idea of change. A drastic expansion in the scope of the traditional legal concept of *salus populi* invested the pursuit of private interests with profound public consequences, leading to the creation of duties owed by everyone – farmers, industrial workers, travelers, shippers of goods – to a universal, collective interest in technology-driven progress. These universal, uniform duties were the legal articulation of standards for conduct and virtue that defined a model of citizenship suited to the needs of the railroad economy.

In Virginia, as in the South generally, none of these factors was present prior to the Civil War. Both legal and political institutions were dominated by conservative elites committed to preserving an essentially pre-industrial economy based on slavery, and the political and social order that had given them power. Political elites prevented incursions by interstate railroads, thereby limiting the challenge that new economic forms posed for the established order. This set of relations was reiterated on the bench, where appellate judges resisted pressures for reform from lawyers and lower court judges. Among dominant conservative elites, the political culture of Virginia moved in near perfect opposition to that of Illinois between 1820 and 1860. Preservation of a hierarchical social order required that the law articulate the differential standards of duty and conduct applicable to different classes of persons, and preserve the primacy of private relations as the determinants of legal obligations. Where Illinois' Supreme Court used law to extend the transformation of the state's political economy into a new conception of citizenship, Virginia's high court used law to protect old conceptions of a virtuous social order against the threat of transformation.

The unity of purpose and conception within each of the two national regions was not an accident, but rather was itself also one of the identifying themes in the creation of an American body of common law. Indeed, it might be more accurate, when speaking of the antebellum period, to describe the development of two distinct systems of American common law, only one of which survived to become nationally dominant in the decades following the war. The experiments that different states undertook were closely watched by judges in other states within each region, carried by published case reports, the growing prevalence of university-based legal education, and the appearance of national digests. The project of rationalization and standardization in the law was the work, in the words of John Phillip Reid, of judges whose "driving passion was to establish uniform theories to govern adjudication, rather than 'fragmentary rules or disorganizing exceptions'" (Reid, 1965: 407, quoting *Kendall v. Brownson*, 47 N.H. 186, 196, 1886, dissenting opinion).

Thus there were two distinct American common law systems in place by the end of the 1850s, of which Illinois and Virginia stand as respective exemplary cases. During that period, Illinois and Virginia, despite reaching substantively opposite outcomes, engaged in processes of legal development that bore marked similarities. Both states' high courts found themselves compelled to think hard about the meaning of their respective common law systems in response to the challenge of the railroads. Both adopted approaches that made law the vocabulary for articulating political models of citizenship in ways that had not been elements of common law courts' traditional functions. When William Blackstone and other English and early American writers spoke of the connection between English political virtue and the common law, they meant that the law provided a bedrock on which the society might be constructed, a distinct layer of rights separately developed by historical custom and separate from the public affairs of state. The arguments in the 1850s in both North and South made quite a different claim: that the law was imminently present in debates over the direction of public affairs.

To reiterate, the unity of purpose in northern and southern development reflected the fact that each legal regime carried, at its core, a political and social construction of "citizenship," conceived as the set of virtues that would be required for full membership in society, measured by access to common law courts. In Illinois and the North, the questions of the duties of corporations and the duties of stock owners, and the duties of the owners of chattels, and the duties of common carriers, finally became the question of the duties of everybody, and those universal duties became the unifying principles for the construction of new legal doctrines. That project was driven and ultimately justified by an ideology of Jacksonian leveling, the inevitability and desirability of change, and the ever-widening web of connections that bound together the future welfare of distant strangers.

The fundamental characteristic of the new model of citizenship was a norm of standardization, the replacement of old distinctions by uniformity. The political economy of speed and expansion promised everything and demanded everything. To feed the furnace of that vast machine, old systems would be chopped up into kindling. To smooth the tracks required evenly sized and spaced cross-ties, straight and parallel rails, and securely fastened connections between the pieces of the manufactured road. And what was required of the machines was equally required of those who rode on them and the society they served. It was not merely the case that rationalization served progress – rationalization *was* progress, in every sphere. This was more than a set of preferences or a political style; it was in essence a worldview. Old contradictions were resolved as unities, old identities were turned into contradictions that were then resolved by the adoption of uniform standards.

Northern courts embraced the new model and remade their system of laws around its normative requirements. To be a freeholder sharing in the use of public land had been the epitome of Illinois citizenship; in the eyes of the law, that same activity was transformed into an obstacle to public progress. The duty to watch over one's own property to avoid injury to others became, instead, the duty to be vigilant to avoid being harmed by others' actions. In the conception of the public good, the shared quiet enjoyment of a village green was replaced by the shared Need for Speed. The law, in this conception, was a means for the re-creation of society in novel and exceptional forms, driven by the wheels of technological progress and carrying the promise of a new kind of society for a new and exceptional kind of citizen.

The antebellum South, by contrast, reacted to the challenge of the railroads by making the law an instrument of resistance to change, preserving old rules in the face of new conditions. In some ways, this approach itself represented a departure from English tradition. The writ system of common law pleading had been highly complex, strictly formal, and nearly ritualistic in its specificity. When conditions required the law to accommodate new facts of social life, however, those writs could often be made flexible in practice. Formal conservatism was accompanied by substantive liberality in the formulation of legal fictions and the expansion of doctrines. This, for centuries, had been the pattern by means of which English common law had evolved, albeit slowly, a pattern propounded and legitimated by the "historical jurisprudence" of Edward Coke, Matthew Hale, and Blackstone (Berman, 1994: 1651).

Southern courts, by contrast, chose a course that was the opposite of the combination of formal strictness and informal flexibility that characterized traditional common law development. Virginia permitted considerable modernization in its pleading practices while freezing and even restricting the scope of remedies that were offered in its substantive doctrines. The potential for flexibility, however, was lost by virtue of the fact that social and economic relations were changing at the same time that the state's high court was preventing common law doctrines from evolving in response to those changes. That politically conservative mission deprived the common law of its capacity for growth and change, turning it instead into a statement about static social conditions. As such, the law took on a new, prescriptive function that it did not have in the English tradition of historical jurisprudence.

Like Illinois, Virginia diverged from ancient common law traditions by linking the formulation of legal rules with a particular construction of political citizenship. In Virginia's case, the model of citizenship was one that above all depended on innate distinctions between classes of persons. True political conservatives in Virginia rejected the appeal to a universally shared set of public interests in favor of a nearly feudal regime of vested private rights that in some ways predated the common law itself. In Virginia and the South, the insistence was that corporations and cities, slaveowners and chattel owners, employers and common carriers, all were ultimately and irreducibly private actors bound only by the duties that arose out of a particular set of relationships with other private actors. The law, by this understanding, was not a tool for redesigning the order of society in the pursuit of collective benefit, but rather a shield preserving social and political relationships against wild theories and abstract notions of *salus populi* that threatened to reverse the order of priority between property rights and tort duties.

Finally, in the 1870s and 1880s, southern courts adopted much of the common law scheme that had been characteristically "northern" in the 1850s. The rules that these courts adopted, however, lacked much of the underlying philosophical content and doctrinal flexibility that was displayed in the northern versions of the same rules. When the Virginia Supreme Court wanted a precedent to cite in announcing the rule of contributory negligence, it used the Illinois case *Aurora v. Grimes*, ignoring the half-dozen subsequent cases that had modified the rule in the intervening period. Southern courts did not go through the process of developing and working out their own particular versions of the new doctrines, nor did the principles of American common law express the legitimating claims of southern elites. Thus even after the national adoption of the system of American common law, there remained characterizable differences between the North and South in the formulation of doctrines and in the relationship between the dominant legal regime and the social and political orders.

The fact of railroad development alone did not dictate the course of legal change; conversely, the significance of slavery was not merely that it stood in the way of industrial development. It was not the case that support for railroads directly or necessarily equated with support for new political and legal ideas. And similarly, it was not the case that there was a simple opposition of economic interests between slaveowners and industrial manufacturers. Instead, the issues that were raised in each case were complex expressions of the challenges that the construction and operation of railroads posed for the legitimating principles of older forms of economy and society. To construct causal explanations for the path of American law requires an engagement of the relationships between legal doctrines, social order, and the interests of the participants in the process, and an understanding of the institutional settings in which those relationships were worked out.

Two additional questions arise at this point. First, how should changes in legal doctrine be understood in the broader context of societal development? And second, what does the development of American legal reasoning in the mid-nineteenth century tell us about American citizenship and its relationship to law? In the context of the developing political economy of the mid-nineteenth century, these become questions about modernization. That is, what is the relationship between the tendency toward rationalization and uniformity in the economy and the social and political functions of a legal system? These inquiries begin with the difficult and rather subtle question of the meaning of "change" in the law.

Changes in American Legal Doctrine: The Case of Third-Party Beneficiary Contracts

Changes in nineteenth century legal doctrine not only altered the rules of adjudication, they reflected changes in what society asked its laws to do. This is a historical development that may be difficult to see if one focuses purely on specific elements of legal doctrines. Legal historians have found various elements of modern common law doctrines in earlier rules, ranging from the general fault principle to particular principles of employment law and rules governing the liability of corporations (Donnelly, 1967: 742; Orren, 1991: 110–11; Karsten, 1997: 98–101, 299–300). As Peter Karsten has put the argument, "one can find doctrines in Roman or medieval law that are alleged to have been the products of the antebellum commercial-industrial revolution" (Karsten, 1997: 300).

On closer examination, however, it may appear that these arguments fail to pay sufficient attention to changes in the *meaning* of words. Karsten's comment was made in the course of an argument that it is wrong to see the rules enforcing third-party beneficiary contracts as novel nineteenth century creations. The point is an important one for this book. Like the law of bailments, the law of third-party beneficiary contracts pointed to a much larger set of issues. Earlier, it was pointed out that one of the truly transformative effects of the creation of the Chicago grain markets was the ability of farmers and grain merchants to sell futures contracts and thus escape the cyclical economic risks of the harvest. To create a market for these contracts, however, required the possibility of dealing in increasingly complex forms of interests in future harvests. Third-party contracts enabled distant capitalists to invest in local markets. If a farmer failed to sell grain to a merchant at an agreed-upon price, the merchant could sue. The capitalist who had invested money in the merchant's enterprise, however, would be out of luck if he were not able to bring suit based on the claim that he had a cognizable interest in the deal. Those were third-party beneficiary claims, and they were among the most basic elements in the scheme of legal prerogatives that emerged from a non-local economy. They are also usually thought of as quintessentially modern elements of contract law.

Karsten's point is that in the nineteenth century, English and European courts moved away from traditional rules that recognized the enforceability of third-party contracts, while American courts retained the old rule despite potential problems of conflicting jurisdiction and multiple actions. Thus from a formal, doctrinal perspective, the innovation that occurred was on the part of the Europeans. One of the examples cited by Karsten is an opinion by Justice Sidney Breese of Illinois: "Breese made note of the new trend away from the older rule in England, but he said of *Dutton v. Poole*, one of the leading examples of the older rule, that it represented 'the substratum of all the ruling of the British courts on the question up to this time'" (Karsten, 1991: 344).

As we have seen before, however, Breese made a positive habit out of cloaking radical innovation in the language of timeless custom, and in particular in language that claimed to discover the "real" meaning of common law rules. In this case, Breese's traditional language masked the fact that there had been a profound change in the circumstances of third-party contracts, such that an apparently static rule in fact demonstrated a significant shift in the public role of the law of private contractual obligations. In an earlier era, the rule of third-party beneficiary contracts had helped to preserve the existing social order by enforcing the economic order, permitting landlords to collect rents owed them from recalcitrant bailiffs, and family members to enforce promises, as when a father promised money to an older son on condition that it be used for the support of a sibling (Karsten, 1991: 333–5). With modernization, the preservation of those same social relations would have required the law to oppose the direction of economic development. That is, to continue to give legal force to the unwritten obligations that arose out of highly personalized interactions would no longer reflect the patterns of interaction that characterized economic activity, but would instead appear as an anachronistic relic of ancient tradition. In the late eighteenth and early nineteenth centuries, with the increase in the use of negotiable written instruments, there was a growing emphasis on formal, written records, which would provide a basis for a suit without appeal to third-party beneficiary claims.

By the mid-nineteenth century, the situation had changed. At that point, third-party beneficiary contracts were not artifacts of an earlier era of social and economic relations, they were elements of the most modern and most radical forms of capital exchange. For English law to have continued to enforce third-party obligations would have made English law an instrument of economic development rather than a guardian of social, economic, and legal orthodoxy. The rules of privity and consideration (i.e., that an obligation that is not supported by a mutual exchange of value cannot be enforced) were the legal tradition in the 1800s, and the English courts were not interested in unsettling that tradition regardless of any ancient precedents for the right being sought (Karsten, 1991: 338–9).

Antebellum Virginia, following England, did not permit third-party suits (Karsten, 1991: 375). Breese, by contrast, was eager to make precisely the analytical move that English jurists were resisting. By appealing to "tradition," he in fact permitted the direction of economic development to utterly transform the social practice of commerce. In other words, a radical change in the function of law was accomplished precisely by a (possibly disingenuous) insistence on preserving its letter. The implication of the analysis here is that the question of legal change cannot be restricted to whether a rule was retained or changed. Rather, the inquiry must be framed in functional as well as formal terms, asking, for instance, whether or not the law continued to protect existing social relations, or whether the law enforced or countered the effects of economic relations. The decision to retain a rule whose significance had radically changed was an affirmative move just as much as the decision to adopt a new rule was a check on change.

The focus on the meaning of "change" directs our attention to the question of the degree to which the law and the courts can be described as autonomous systems. One way of describing Virginia's antebellum legal conservatism is in terms of the control of the courts by social and economic elites who were able to resist pressures for reform by their control over the institution. The later importation of a national system of common law rules appears as a case of the courts acting with almost complete autonomy, or at a minimum as the instruments of non-local elites (and hence as autonomous agents vis-à-vis those elites). One suggestion, then, is that courts appear as autonomous agents during periods of change, and as nonautonomous during periods of legal stability. This, of course, may be read one of two ways: as indicating that relative autonomy is a precondition for change, or as indicating that one consequence of change in the law is an increase in the autonomy of the courts.

In this book, we have seen a high degree of consistency in the presence of traditional planter elites in Virginia's postbellum high court, and consistency in the membership of Illinois' high court across periods of both continuity and radical change. These facts suggest that the courts took on the roles of autonomous rule-makers in response to the desire to enact legal change. In other words, court autonomy does not appear as a structural condition of the system, but as a contingent effect of extra-institutional forces that create the impetus and conditions for change.

With regard to legal doctrine, the question of autonomy becomes the question of the relationship between law, language, and social practice. The law has an existence separate from the courts that enforce and define it, as an element of public discourse, a source of authority, and an important vocabulary for the assertion of ideological commitments. Even if one were to suppose, for example, that as a matter of personal biography individual justices carefully calculate particular efficiencies in economic outcome, the language with which that outcome is described, imposed, and defended will define the meaning of the case for future cases. This fact of common law reasoning simultaneously empowers language and limits judges' freedom of action. In ordinary times, that which a judge cannot say in legal language, he or she cannot do.[1] During periods of great change, judges are free to redefine boundaries of legitimate action, but even in those periods judges must use the language of legal reasoning to express themselves or risk undermining the institutions that give them their authority. *Salus populi* and *sic utere* were not replaced in the 1850s, they were redefined in terms of an extralegal political vocabulary.

Thus, with regard to language, legal reasoning is inherently conservative, but the conservatism of legal language is not necessarily the same thing as legal conservatism. As we have seen, legal words and phrases – "corporation," "duty," "contract" – can be redefined in accordance with changing demands. At times, however, the vocabulary of the law itself undergoes a process of revision and reformulation. Such radical changes in legal doctrine demonstrate points at which the accommodation of legal vocabularies to extralegal developments becomes either impossible or undesirable, and those external pressures dislodge an established system of legal reasoning. This occurs when the formal discourse of the law becomes incommensurate with the vocabulary of the social and political functions law is called upon to serve. The invention of American common law, in other words, could only have occurred at a historical moment of truly extraordinary contingency. This was precisely the moment that was observed in Illinois. It was also precisely what was not to be found in antebellum Virginia, where contingency was a rare commodity indeed. Without the confluence of interests, ideology, and institutions that worked

---

[1] The limitations that the inherent conservatism of legal discourse imposes on doctrinal change are discussed in Harry S. Scheiber, "Public Rights and the Rule of Law in American History," *California Law Review* 72 (1984): 217. See also Lucy Salyer, "Captives of Law: Judicial Enforcement of the Chinese Exclusion Laws, 1891–1905," *Journal of American History* 76 (1989): 91–117, arguing that in the context of immigration law, racist judges were prevented from imposing extreme outcomes by the constraints of legal rules.

to create Illinois' new way of thinking, change was not only not inevitable, it was nearly impossible.

The law's inherent resistance to change also means that reversal of change is just as difficult as the initial process of revision, and that without the same conditions of extraordinary contingency, such a reversal will be impossible. That is why the language of "timelessness" so easily lends itself to a new orthodoxy within moments of its creation. The instant a doctrine is announced, it becomes "orthodox," in the crucial sense of being implicitly reinforced by the language of legal discourse. As a result, *revanchisme* faces the same barriers as radical progressivism. In times of no more than ordinary change, the system of legal reasoning maintains a degree of autonomy that limits the intrusion of ideological commitments that cannot be easily expressed in the language of that system. Courts can provide an opportunity for revision – in personnel, in internalistic pressures for reform, in institutional arrangements – but ordinarily they do not, of themselves, give rise to change. The inherent conservatism that the role of formal language imposes on systems of legal thought thus requires us to look to extralegal conditions of contingency and determination in order to understand the implications of change in the law.[2]

The Nature of Legal Citizenship

Throughout this discussion, I have used the concept of citizenship as the linchpin for connecting legal doctrine, political ideology, and the requirements of modernization. I will begin these closing observations by repeating two quotations from the first chapter. The first is T. H. Marshall's definition of citizenship: "a kind of basic human equality associated with the concept of full membership in a community ... which is not inconsistent with the inequalities which distinguish the various economic levels in the society" (Marshall, 1964: 70). The second statement is Oliver Wendell Holmes' description of "standards of external conduct, which every man is *presumed and required to know*" (Holmes, 1881: 259). The argument of this book is, ultimately, that the two statements ultimately became synonymous.

The broad focus on the political construction of identity and the societal function of law has been a hallmark of several recent studies of

---

[2] These observations suggest a basis for the reexamination of attitudinal models of judicial behavior, which arguably fail to capture the sense of the process of judging cases, and hence may miss crucial points of consistency and difference in the creation of legal rules.

antebellum American law. Christopher Tomlins, far from treating labor law solely as a discrete and separate area of the law, employs that area of the law as a lens through which to examine central ideological elements in American thought (Tomlins, 1993). Greg Alexander similarly employs a close study of the development of nineteenth century property doctrines to illuminate the kinds of norms of social conduct and status that I describe here as standards of citizenship (Alexander, 1997). William Novak describes the common law tradition of local regulation as a kind of "nonconstitutional public law" (Novak, 1996: 12).[3] And Barbara Welke and Patricia Minter have explored the way in which the transportation industry, precisely by virtue of its inherent power to blur the lines between public and private space, became a central arena for the legal articulation of social norms based on class, race, and gender, and the process of working out conflicts among them (Welke, 1995; Minter, 1995). These works are reminders of the evident fact that universalist liberal norms are exclusionary at the same time that they are egalitarian (Mehta, 1990: 428–30). The articulation of a universal, minimum standard for public behavior leaves no room for those who cannot meet the requirements of that standard. As I have tried to show, the combination of universal duties and novel pleading requirements did not merely disfavor nonconforming plaintiffs, it erased them from legal view.

Like the meaning of legal doctrine, the meaning of legal citizenship is closely tied to an understanding of the conditions under which that meaning is subject to change, and the relationship between changes in that meaning and the larger societal environment. Marshall's characterization of citizenship was an essentially liberal conception, in which citizenship comprises a set of universal rights and specific associated obligations, formally defined, universally guaranteed, and publicly known. Marshall, in fact, was describing the idea of citizenship as an element of modernization theory, the more or less deterministic idea that the concept of formal rights to participate equally in society was a necessary antecedent to the development of a modern political economy, an argument that echoes

---

[3] Novak views the displacement of the traditional, local conception of *salus populi* as an event of the postbellum era. For Novak, this represented an abandonment of the idea of common law in favor of the modern state: "Common first implied localism. In contrast to the modern ideal of the state as centralized bureaucracy, the well-regulated society emphasized local control and autonomy" (Novak, 1996: 237, 240–1). For a discussion of other meanings of "common," see ibid, 41. In my reading, on the other hand, the common law was not so much displaced as reconfigured to serve the very process of modernization that Novak describes, a process that took place a decade before the Civil War.

those of Samuel Huntington (Huntington, 1968). Other writers on the meaning of citizenship have challenged Marshall's and Huntington's determinism, focusing variously on the actions of social movements or elite actors as causal events in the creation of new ways of thinking about national identity.[4]

Among more current writers, there tends to be an acceptance of the idea that citizenship begins with the recognition of legal or political rights, and that the focus on these formal rights is the basic premise of liberalism:

> Although there are a few basic obligations to obey the laws (generally to pay taxes, refrain from assault and rebellion, and to serve in the nation's armed forces), liberalism places the clear weight of its ethical and moral theory behind individual and negative rights. Legal and political rights, especially civil liberties and property rights, come first and are balanced by only a few obligations (Janoski, 1998: 15).

This assumption may be modified by a recognition of obligations associated in contractarian terms with the exercise of those rights (Janoski, 1998: 9–10), and the idea that the exercise of rights presupposes a standard of competence (Turner, 1993: 2). In general, however, liberalism is conceived of as a system of thought designed, in Robert Putnam's words, "to make democracy safe for the unvirtuous" (Putnam, 1993: 87).

As we have seen, these descriptions represent the reversal of the order of reasoning that was displayed in the formative period of American common law. This is an observation that casts doubt on the characterization of the nature and social functions of law in nineteenth century liberalism. The idea that American liberalism was the creation of an individualistic model of private property owners bound only by the most vestigial restrictions imposed by law or government is a myth. In William Novak's words, "Nineteenth-century America was a *public* society in ways hard to imagine after the invention of twentieth-century privacy. . . . Government and society were not created to protect preexisting private rights, but to further the welfare of the whole people and community" (Novak, 1996: 9). Prior to the 1850s, that community was defined locally, and the fact that property rights were the product of historical tradition conclusively established their public utility. The 1850s, in the North, saw the expansion of the

---

[4] Bryan Turner, considering Marshall's thesis, proposes that citizenship rights are "the outcome of social movements that either aim to expand or defend the definition of social membership" (Turner, 1986: 92). Richard Bensel, responding to Huntington, argues that the development of the American state was the response of "influential elements of the national elite" to the imperatives of increases in social complexity and inter- and intraclass conflict (Bensel, 1990: 6).

scope of "public" and a marked change in the meaning of its "welfare," but the basic political calculation remained the same.

The model of citizenship that is described in this book is very different from that which often appears in the legal historical literature. Reviewing the historiographical literature, Theodore J. Lowi sums up this traditional understanding as follows:

> [T]here is one very clear pattern in all of this, and that pattern is *individualism*. To state the matter as clearly and starkly as possible: *The one ethical principle that cuts through all the doctrines governing the disposition of injury cases is individual blame and fault in the allocation of responsibility* (Lowi, 1986: 204, emphasis in original).

The emphasis that Lowi sees in the literature on "individual blame and fault" invokes the idea of "responsible individualism" (Gold, 1990: 85). This may tell us more, however, about the normative preferences that have been imposed on the construction of legal historiography than about the organizing concepts that were most importantly at work in nineteenth century thought. The model of citizenship that appeared in the early creation of American common law is one that *reduced* the importance of the individual in favor of a corporatist model of conformity to standards of mass behavior in public.[5]

One way of reading this apparent contradiction is to observe that Jacksonian leveling was also an ideology of uniformity. Americans might speak of rugged individualism and the self-made man, but the reality of social practice was something quite different. Nineteenth century European travelers such as Harriet Martineau and Alexis de Tocqueville repeatedly commented on the emphasis on conformity that they observed in American social life.[6] By this reading, the arrival of technologies of transportation and communication extended an existing impulse toward conformity. The construction of uniform standards of citizenship in the law

---

[5] This reading helps to explain a fact that Novak finds puzzling: "One of the oddest things about the legal centralization of state power in late nineteenth-century America was that it was accompanied not by the expected enhancement of salus populi, common good rhetoric, but by its repudiation, and an offering in its stead of a heightened regard for *individual* rights and liberties" (Novak, 1996: 244). Instead of an emphasis on individuals, I find an emphasis on a different, more abstract, sense of "public" entirely consistent with the formation of a centralized national state.

[6] The American embrace of homogeneity was in sharp contrast to the fears of French writers across the political spectrum. Pierre-Joseph Proudhon, Charles Montesquieu, Alexis de Tocqueville, and Joseph Marie de Maistre all expressed fear of the social uniformity that they saw arriving with the expansion of the national state (Vernon, 1986: 82–93).

was a step toward the unification of social, political, and legal ideals into a coherent model of American citizenship.

A model of citizenship is simultaneously a standard for inclusion and a model of legitimation for both institutional and individual conduct. In the law, citizenship is the prerequisite for a legitimate claim on public institutions for the protection of private interests. Law is also the language of mediation between institutions, and between legally recognized categories of social actors, the point of necessary overlap that permits their interaction in any kind of ordered system. As such, and unsurprisingly, the formal analytical categories of legal language reflect a community's prevalent norms. This is the reason that a change in the categories of legal thought matters even if there is no great corresponding change in the patterns of winners and losers. In the nineteenth century, a change in the function of courts accompanied the transformation of "private" law into an instrument for the rationalization of American public life. In the process, American courts took on the role of defining a model of public citizenship through their creation of American common law.

Index of Cases

Kentucky

New York

North Carolina

Ohio

Bibliography

An Act of the General Assembly Concerning the Richmond and Danville Railroad Company. Richmond, VA, 1858.

Adams, Charles Francis. "The Railroad System." *North American Review* 104 (1867): 476–511.

Adlow, Elijah. "Chief Justice Lemuel Shaw and the Law of Negligence." *Massachusetts Law Quarterly* 42 (1957): 55–74.

Alexander, Greg. *Commodity and Propriety: Competing Visions of Property in American Legal Thought.* Chicago, 1997.

———. " 'Liberality' vs. 'Technicality': Statutory Revision of Land Law in the Jacksonian Age." Unpublished manuscript.

"American Genius and Enterprise." *Scientific American* 2 (1847): 397.

Angle, Paul M., ed. *Prairie State: Impressions of Illinois, 1673–1967, by Travelers and Other Observers.* Chicago, 1968.

Appleby, Joyce. *Capitalism and a New Social Order: The Republican Vision of the 1790s.* New York, 1984.

———. *Liberalism and Republicanism in the Historical Imagination.* Cambridge, MA, 1992.

Appleton, Nathan. "Labor, Its Relations, in Europe and the United States, Compared." *Hunt's Merchants' Magazine* 11 (1844): 217–23.

Ashworth, John. *Slavery, Capitalism, and Politics in the Antebellum Republic.* New York, 1995.

Atiyah, Patrick S. *The Rise and Fall of Freedom of Contract.* New York, 1979.

Avery, Dianne, and Alfred S. Konefsky. "The Daughters of Job: Property Rights and Women's Lives in Mid-Nineteenth-Century Massachusetts." *Law and History Review* 10 (1992): 323–56.

Baker, John H. *Introduction to English Legal History*, 3d ed. London, 1990.

Baltzell, E. Digby. *Philadelphia Gentlemen: The Making of a National Upper Class.* Glencoe, IL, 1958.

Barnard, D. D. "The President and His Administration." *American Whig Review* 7 (1848): 437–50.

Bensel, Richard. *Yankee Leviathan: The Origins of Central State Authority in America, 1859–1877.* New York, 1990.

Berlin, Ira, and Herbert G. Gutman. "Natives and Immigrants, Free Men and Slaves: Urban Workingmen in the Antebellum American South." *American Historical Review* 88 (1983): 1175–1200.

Berman, Harold J. "The Origins of Historical Jurisprudence: Coke, Selden, Hale." *Yale Law Journal* 103 (May, 1994): 1651–1738.

Berman, Harold J., and Charles J. Reid, Jr. "The Transformation of English Legal Science: From Hale to Blackstone." *Emory Law Journal* 45 (Spring 1996): 437–522.

Bigelow, Jacob. *Elements of Technology: Taken Chiefly from a Course of Lectures Delivered at Cambridge on the Application of the Sciences to the Useful Arts, Now Published for the Use of Seminaries and Students.* Boston, 1829.

Birkbeck, Morris. "Notes on a Journey in America, from the Coast of Virginia to the Territory of Illinois with Proposals for the Establishment of a Colony of English" (1817). Reprinted in *Prairie State: Impressions of Illinois, 1673–1967, by Travelers and Other Observers,* ed. Paul M. Angle, 62–7. Chicago, 1968.

Bishop, Joel Prentiss. *Commentaries on the Law of Married Women under the Statutes of the Several States, and at Common Law and in Equity.* 2 vols. Boston, 1873–5.

Bishop, William G. *Register of the Debates of the Proceedings of the Virginia Reform Convention.* Richmond, VA, 1851.

Blackstone, William. *Commentaries on the Laws of England* (1765–1769). 4 vols. Chicago, 1979.

———. "A Discourse on the Study of the Law," (1758). Reprinted in *The Gladsome Light of Jurisprudence: Learning the Law in England and the United States in the 18th and 19th Centuries,* ed. Michael H. Hoeflich, 53–73. New York, 1989 (page numbers in citations refer to reprinted edition).

Bloomfield, Maxwell. "Law Versus Politics: The Self-Image of the American Bar (1830–1860)." *The American Journal of Legal History* 12 (1968): 306–23.

Boorstin, Daniel J. *The National Experience.* New York, 1965.

Bowman, Shearer Davis. *Masters and Lords: Mid-19th Century U.S. Planters and Prussian Junkers.* New York, 1993.

"Brief of Railroad Company to the Supreme Court of Appeals of Virginia," filed August 31, 1874. Collection of the Virginia Historical Society.

Brophy, Alfred L. "Humanity, Utility, and Logic in Southern Legal Thought: Harriet Beecher Stowe's Vision in *Dred: A Tale of the Great Dismal Swamp.*" *Boston University Law Review* 78 (October 1998): 1114–1161.

Brown, John Howard, ed. *Lamb's Biographical Dictionary of the U.S.* Boston, 1903.

Bruce, Dickson D., Jr. *The Rhetoric of Conservatism: The Virginia Convention of 1829–30 and the Conservative Tradition in the South.* San Marino, CA, 1982.

Bruchey, Stuart. *Enterprise: The Dynamic Economy of a Free People.* Cambridge, MA, 1990.

Bryant, William Cullen. "Letters of a Traveller, or, Notes of Things Seen in Europe and America" (1850). Reprinted in *Prairie State: Impressions of Illinois, 1673–1967, by Travelers and Other Observers,* ed. Paul M. Angle, 100–108. Chicago, 1968 (page numbers in citations refer to reprinted edition).

Bryson, William Hamilton. "The Abolition of Forms of Action in Virginia." *University of Richmond Law Review* 17 (1983): 273–84.

———. "The History of Legal Education in Virginia." *University of Richmond Law Review* 14 (1979): 155–210.

———. *Legal Education in Virginia, 1779–1979: A Biographical Approach.* Charlottesville, VA, 1982.

Caldwell, Charles. "Thoughts on the Moral and Other Indirect Influences of Rail-Roads." *New England Magazine* 2 (April 1832): 288–300.

Carrington, Paul D. "The Revolutionary Idea of Legal Education." *William and Mary Law Review* 31 (Spring 1990): 527–74.

Chamallas, Martha, and Linda K. Kerber "Women and the Law of Fright: A History." *Michigan Law Review* 88 (1990): 814–64.

Chandler, Alfred D., ed. *The Railroads: The Nation's First Big Business.* New York, 1965.

———. *Visible Hand: The Managerial Revolution in American Business.* Cambridge, MA, 1977.

Chandler, Julian A. C. *The History of Suffrage in Virginia.* Baltimore, 1901.

Christian, George L. "Edward C. Burks." *Virginia Law Register* 3 (1897): 323–36.

Clayton, John. *Illinois Fact Book and Historical Almanac, 1673–1968.* Carbondale, IL, 1970.

Cobb, Thomas R. *An Inquiry into the Law of Negro Slavery in the United States of America.* New York, 1968.

Cogan, Neil H. "'Standing' before the Constitution: Membership in the Community." *Law and History Review* 7 (Spring 1989): 1–21.

Cole, Arthur Charles. *The Centennial History of Illinois, Volume III: The Era of the Civil War, 1848–1870.* Springfield, IL, 1917.

———, ed. *The Constitutional Debates of 1847.* Springfield, IL, 1919.

———. *The Whig Party in the South* (1813). Gloucester, MA, 1962 (page numbers in citations refer to reprint edition).

"Committee Majority Report to the [Richmond] Common Council," 1839. Collection of the Virginia Historical Society.

"Common Law Procedure Acts." *Quarterly Law Journal* 1 (1856): 6–10.

Conover, Pamela Johnston, Ivor Crewe, and Donald Searing. "Conceptions of Citizenship among British and American Publics: An Exploratory Analysis." *Essex Papers in Politics and Government* 73. Essex, UK, 1990.

Cook, Charles M. *The American Codification Movement: A Study of Antebellum Legal Reform.* Westport, CT, 1981.

Cronon, William B. *Nature's Metropolis: Chicago and the Great West.* New York, 1991.

Curtiss, Daniel S. "Western Portraiture and Emigrant's Guide: A Description of Wisconsin, Illinois, & Iowa" (1852). Reprinted in *Prairie State: Impressions of Illinois, 1673–1967, by Travelers and Other Observers*, ed. Paul M. Angle, 262–77. Chicago, 1968.

D.H.B. "Our Times." *Democratic Review* 16 (1845): 235–42.

Dabney, Virginius. *Virginia: The New Dominion.* New York, 1971.

Dagger, Richard. *Civic Virtues: Rights, Citizenship, and Republican Liberalism.* New York, 1997.

"Dane's Abridgement." *American Jurist and Law Magazine* 4 (1830): 63–86.

Davidson, Alexander, and Bernard Stuve. *A Complete History of Illinois from 1673 to 1873, Embracing the Physical Features of the Country; Its Early Explorations; Aboriginal Inhabitants; French and British Occupation; Conquest by Virginia; Territorial Condition and the Subsequent Civil, Military and Political Events of the State.* Springfield, IL, 1877.

Davis, David Brion. *The Slave Power Conspiracy and the Paranoid Style.* Baton Rouge, LA, 1969.

Dickens, Charles. "The Looking Glass Prairie" (1842). Reprinted in *The Prairie State: A Documentary History of Illinois,* ed. Robert P. Sutton, 233–40. Grand Rapids, MI, 1976.

Dixon, S. F. "Codification and Reform of the Common Law." *American Jurist and Law Magazine* 14 (1835): 280–302.

Donald, David Herbert. *Lincoln.* London, 1995.

Donnelly, Samuel J. M. "The Fault Principle: A Sketch of Its Development in Tort Law during the Nineteenth Century." *Syracuse University Law Review* 18 (Summer 1967): 728–50.

Durfee, Job. "The Influence of Scientific Discovery and Invention on Social and Political Progress" (1843). Reprinted in *The Annals of America,* vol. 7, 128–32. Chicago, 1968.

Eighty Years' Progress of the United States, from the Revolutionary War to the Great Rebellion: 1781 to 1861. Chicago, 1864.

Einhorn, Robin L. *Property Rules: Political Economy in Chicago, 1833–1872.* Chicago, 1991.

Ely, James W., Jr., and David J. Bodenhamer. "Regionalism and American Legal History: The Southern Experience." *Vanderbilt Law Review* 39 (1986), 539–67.

Ely, John Hart. *Democracy and Distrust: A Theory of Judicial Review.* Cambridge, MA, 1980.

Ernst, Daniel R. "Legal Positivism, Abolitionist Litigation, and the New Jersey Slave Case of 1845." *Law and History Review* 4 (1986): 337–65.

Ernst, Ferdinand. "Travels in Illinois in 1819," (1819). Reprinted in *The Prairie State: A Documentary History of Illinois, Colonial Years to 1860,* ed. Robert P. Sutton, 198–213. Grand Rapids, MI, 1976 (page numbers in citations refer to reprinted edition).

Farmer, James Oscar, Jr. *The Metaphysical Confederacy: James Henley Thornwell and the Synthesis of Southern Values.* Macon, GA, 1986.

Ferguson, Robert A. *Law and Letters in American Culture.* Cambridge, MA, 1984.

Field, David Dudley, and John F. Dillon. "Law Reform: Report of the Special Committee of the American Bar Association, upon the Delay and Uncertainty in Judicial Administration." *Virginia Law Journal* 9 (1885): 542–606.

Finkleman, Paul. "Exploring Southern Legal History." *North Carolina Law Review* 64 (1985): 77–116.

———. *An Imperfect Union: Slavery, Federalism, and Comity.* Chapel Hill, NC, 1981.

———. "Slaves as Fellow Servants: Ideology, Law and Industrialization." *American Journal of Legal History* 31 (1987): 269–305.

Fisher, William W., III. "Ideology and Imagery in the Law of Slavery." *Chicago-Kent Law Review* 68 (1993): 1051–83.

Foner, Eric. *Free Soil, Free Labor, Free Men: The Ideology of the Republican Party before the Civil War.* New York, 1995.

_____. *Reconstruction: America's Unfinished Revolution, 1863–1877.* New York, 1988.

Forbath, William E. *Law and the Shaping of the American Labor Movement.* Cambridge, MA, 1991.

Ford, Thomas. *A History of Illinois: From Its Commencement as a State in 1818 to 1847.* Urbana, IL, 1995.

Freehling, Alison Goodyear. *Drift toward Dissolution: The Virginia Slavery Debate of 1831–1832.* Baton Rouge, LA, 1982.

Freehling, William W. *The Road to Disunion, 1776–1854: Secessionists at Bay.* New York, 1990.

Freeman, William W. *Freeman's Illinois Digest.* Chicago, 1856.

Friedman, Lawrence M. *A History of American Law,* 2d ed. New York, 1985.

Gates, Paul Wallace. *The Illinois Central Railroad and Its Colonization Work.* Cambridge, MA, 1934.

Gawalt, Gerard W. "Sources of Anti-Lawyer Sentiment in Massachusetts, 1740–1840." *American Journal of Legal History* 14 (1970): 223–32.

Genovese, Eugene. *Roll, Jordan, Roll: The World the Slaves Made.* New York, 1974.

_____. "The Significance of the Slave Plantation for Southern Economic Development." *Journal of Southern History* 28 (1962): 422–37.

_____. *The Slaveholders' Dilemma: Freedom and Progress in Southern Conservative Thought, 1820–1860.* Columbia, SC, 1992.

Gold, David. *The Shaping of Nineteenth-Century Law: John Appleton and Responsible Individualism.* Westport, CT, 1990.

Goldin, Claudia Dale. "An Explanation for the Relative Decline of Urban Slavery: 1820–1860." In *Without Consent or Contract, The Rise and Fall of American Slavery, Markets and Production: Technical Papers Volume I,* eds. Robert William Fogel and Stanley L. Engerman. New York, 1991.

_____. "Urbanization and Slavery: The Issue of Compatibility." In *The New Urban History,* ed. Leo Schnore, 231–46. Princeton, NJ, 1975.

Goodwyn, Lawrence. *Democratic Promise: The Populist Movement in America.* New York, 1976.

Gordon, Sarah H. *Passage to Union: How the Railroads Transformed American Life, 1829–1929.* Chicago, 1996.

Greenleaf, Simon. *A Discourse Pronounced at the Inauguration of the Author as Royall Professor of Law in Harvard University.* Cambridge, MA, 1834.

Grigsby, Hugh Blair. *Journal.* Collection of the Virginia Historical Society, 1829.

Gross, Ariela. "Pandora's Box: Slave Character on Trial in the Antebellum Deep South." *Yale Journal of Law and Humanities* 7 (1994): 267–316.

Grossberg, Michael H. *Governing the Hearth: Law and the Family in Nineteenth-Century America.* Chapel Hill, NC, 1985.

Habermas, Jurgen. *Knowledge and Human Interests.* Boston, 1971.

Hall, James. "Letters from the West; Containing Sketches of Scenery, Manners, and Customs, and Anecdotes Connected with the First Settlements of the

Western Sections of the United States" (1828). Reprinted in *Prairie State: Impressions of Illinois, 1673–1967, by Travelers and Other Observers,* ed. Paul M. Angle, 88–93. Chicago, 1968.

Halsey, Don. P., Jr. "William Daniel." *Virginia Law Register* 7 (1901): 1–14.

Hamburger, Philip A. "The Development of the Nineteenth-Century Consensus Theory of Contract." *Law and History Review* 7 (1989): 241–329.

Hartog, Hendrik. *Law in the American Revolution and the Revolution in the Law.* New York, 1981.

Haskell, Thomas. "Capitalism and the Origins of the Humanitarian Sensibility, Part I." *American Historical Review* 90 (1985): 339–61.

Hawke, G. R. *Railways and Economic Growth in England and Wales, 1840–1870.* Oxford, 1970.

Hilliard, Francis. *The Elements of the Law; Being a Comprehensive Summary of American Civil Jurisprudence.* Boston, 1835.

———. *The Law of Torts or Private Wrongs.* Boston, 1859.

Hirschfield, Charles. "The Great Railroad Conspiracy." *Michigan History* 36 (1952): 97–219.

Hoeflich, Michael H. "The Americanization of English Legal Education." *Journal of Legal History* 8 (1987): 244–59.

———. *The Gladsome Light of Jurisprudence: Learning the Law in England and the United States in the Eighteenth and Nineteenth Centuries.* Westport, CT, 1989.

———. "Law & Geometry: Legal Science from Leibniz to Langdell." *American Journal of Legal History* 30 (1986): 95–121.

Holmes, Oliver Wendell. *The Common Law* (1881). Ed. Mark DeWolfe Howe, Boston, 1963 (page numbers in citations are from reprinted edition).

Holt, Michael F. *The Rise and Fall of the American Whig Party: Jacksonian Politics and the Onset of the Civil War.* New York, 1999.

Horwitz, Morton J. *The Transformation of American Law, 1780–1870.* New York, 1992a.

———. *The Transformation of American Law, 1870–1960: The Crisis of Legal Orthodoxy.* New York, 1992b.

Howard, Robert P. *Illinois, a History of the Prairie State.* Grand Rapids, MI, 1972.

Huebner, Timothy S. *The Southern Judicial Tradition: State Judges and Sectional Distinctiveness, 1790–1890.* Athens, GA, 1999.

Hunt, James Logan. "Ensuring the Incalculable Benefits of Railroads: the Origins of Liability for Negligence in Georgia." *Southern California Interdisciplinary Law Journal* 7 (1998): 375–425.

———. "Note: Private Law and Public Policy: Negligence Law and Political Change in Nineteenth-Century North Carolina." *North Carolina Law Review* 66 (1988): 421–42.

Huntington, Samuel. *Political Order in Changing Societies.* New Haven, CT, 1968.

Hurst, James Willard. *Law and the Conditions of Freedom in the Nineteenth-Century United States,* 2d ed. Madison, WI, 1964.

"Improved Hay-Maker." *Scientific American* new series 2 (1860): 216.

J.C.L. "Some Anecdotes of Judge Moncure." *Virginia Law Journal* 9 (1885): 449–52.

James, Mary Ann. "Engineering an Environment for Change: Bigelow, Peirce, and Early Nineteenth-Century Practical Education at Harvard." In *Science at Harvard University*, eds. Clark A. Elliott and Margaret W. Rossiter, 55–75. Bethlehem, PA, 1992.

Janoski, Thomas. *Citizenship and Civil Society: A Framework of Rights and Obligations in Liberal, Traditional, and Social Democratic Regimes.* New York, 1998.

Johnson, Allen. "Illinois in the Democratic Movement of the Century." In *Transactions of the Illinois Historical Society*. Springfield, IL, 1918.

Johnson, Donald Bruce, ed. *National Party Platforms*. Urbana, IL, 1978.

Jones, Alan. "Republicanism, Railroads, and Nineteenth-Century Midwestern Constitutionalism." In *Liberty, Property and Government: Constitutional Interpretation before the New Deal*, eds. Ellen Franklin Paul and Howard Dickman, 239–65. Albany, NY, 1989.

Jordan, Robert Paul. "Illinois: The City and the Plain." *National Geographic* 131 (1967): 545–97.

Karsten, Peter. "The 'Discovery' of Law by English and American Jurists of the Seventeenth, Eighteenth, and Nineteenth Centuries: Third-Party Beneficiary Contracts as a Test Case." *Law and History Review* 9 (1991): 327–81.

_____. *Heart versus Head: Judge-Made Law in Nineteenth-Century America.* Chapel Hill, NC, 1997.

Kasson, John F. *Civilizing the Machine: Technology and Republican Values in America, 1776–1900.* New York, 1976.

Keating, William H. "Narrative of an Expedition to the Source of St. Peter's River" (1824). Reprinted in *Prairie State: Impressions of Illinois, 1673–1967, by Travelers and Other Observers*, ed. Paul M. Angle, 84–87. Chicago, 1968.

Kennedy, Duncan. "Toward an Historical Understanding of Legal Consciousness: The Case of Classical Legal Thought in America, 1850–1940." *Research in Law and Sociology* 3 (1980): 3–24.

Kent, James. *Commentaries on American Law*, 7th ed., 4 vols. New York: 1851.

Kerber, Linda. *No Constitutional Right to Be Ladies: Women and the Obligations of Citizenship.* New York, 1998.

_____. *Women of the Republic: Intellect and Ideology in Revolutionary America.* Chapel Hill, NC, 1980.

Kettner, James H. *The Development of American Citizenship, 1608–1870.* Chapel Hill, NC, 1978.

King, Andrew. "Constructing Gender: Sexual Slander in Nineteenth-Century America." *Law and History Review* 13 (1995): 63–5.

Klafter, Craig Evan. *Reason over Precedents*. Westport, CT, 1993.

Klingberg, Frank. *The Anti-Slavery Movement in England.* New Haven, CT, 1926.

Kloppenberg, James T. "The Virtues of Liberalism: Christianity, Republicanism, and Ethics in Early American Political Discourse." *Journal of American History* 74 (June 1987): 9–33.

Kolchin, Peter. *American Slavery, 1619–1877.* New York, 1993.

Kostal, Rande W. *The Law and English Railway Capitalism, 1825–1875.* Oxford, 1994.

Kozol, Michael. "The Agony and Romance of the American Left." *American Historical Review* 100 (1995): 1488–1511.

Kramnick, Isaac. "The Great National Discussion." *William and Mary Quarterly* 45 (1988): 3–32.

Kutler, Stanley I. *Privilege and Creative Destruction: The Charles River Bridge Case.* Philadelphia, 1971.

Lenman, James H. "Railroads of the United States." *Hunt's Merchants' Magazine* 3 (1840): 273–95.

Levy, Leonard W. *The Law of the Commonwealth and Chief Justice Shaw.* New York, 1957.

Lewis, R. W. B. *The American Adam: Innocence, Tragedy and Tradition in the Nineteenth Century.* Chicago, 1955.

Lewis, Ronald L. *Coal, Iron and Slaves: Industrial Slavery in Maryland and Virginia, 1715–1865.* Westport, CT, 1979.

"Liability of Railroad Companies for Injuries, &c." *Quarterly Law Journal* 1 (1856): 289–98.

Licht, Walter. *Industrializing America: The Nineteenth Century.* Baltimore, 1995.

———. *Working on the Railroad: The Organization of Work in the Nineteenth Century.* Princeton, NJ, 1983.

Lincoln, Abraham. "Annual Address before the Wisconsin State Agricultural Society, at Milwaukee, September 30, 1859." Reprinted in *The Annals of America*, vol. 9, 121–6. Chicago, 1968 (page numbers in citations refer to reprinted edition).

———. "Emancipation Proclamation, 1862." Reprinted in *The Annals of America*, vol. 9, 398–9. Chicago, 1968 (page numbers in citations refer to reprinted edition).

———. "First Inaugural Address (1861)." Reprinted in *The Annals of America*, vol. 9, 250–5. Chicago, 1968 (page numbers in citations refer to reprinted edition).

———. "Second Inaugural Address (1865)." Reprinted in *The Annals of America*, vol. 9, 555–7. Chicago, 1968 (page numbers in citations refer to reprinted edition).

———. "Special Message to Congress, March 6, 1862." Reprinted in *The Annals of America*, vol. 9, 328–9. Chicago, 1968 (page numbers in citations refer to reprinted edition).

Locke, John. *Two Treatises on Government*, ed. W. S. Carpenter. London, 1975.

Lowi, Theodore J. *The End of Liberalism: The Second Republic of the United States.* New York, 1979.

———. "The Welfare State: Ethical Foundations and Constitutional Remedies." *Political Science Quarterly* 101 (1986): 197–220.

Luraghi, Raimondo. "The Civil War and the Modernization of American Society." *Civil War History* 18 (1972): 230–50.

Lurie, Edward. "Louis Agassiz and the Races of Man." *Isis* 45 (1954): 227–42.

Lutz, Donald S. "The Relative Influence of European Writers on Late Eighteenth-Century American Political Thought." *American Political Science Review* 78 (1986): 189–97.

Malone, Dumas, ed. *Dictionary of American Biography.* New York, 1934.

Malone, Wes X. *Essays on Torts.* Baton Rouge, LA, 1986.

Marshall, T. H. [Thomas Humphrey]. *Class, Citizenship and Social Development.* Garden City, NY, 1964.

Martin, Albro. *Railroads Triumphant: The Growth, Rejection, and Rebirth of a Vital American Force.* New York, 1992.

Marx, Leo. *The Machine in the Garden: Technology and the Pastoral Ideal in America.* New York, 1964.

McGraw, Thomas K. *Prophets of Regulation.* Cambridge, MA, 1984.

Mehta, Uday S. "Liberal Strategies of Exclusion." *Politics and Society* 18 (1990): 427–54.

Mensel, Robert E. "'Privilege against Public Right': A Reappraisal of the Charles River Bridge Case." *Duquesne Law Review* 33 (1994): 1–38.

Miller, Perry. *The Life of the Mind in America: From the Revolution to the Civil War.* New York, 1965.

Millson, John S. *Speech of Hon. John S. Millson, of Virginia, on the Wheeling Bridge Case, Delivered in the House of Representatives, August 14, 1852.* Collection of the Virginia Historical Society.

Minter, Patricia Hagler. "The Failure of Freedom: Class, Gender, and the Evolution of Segregated Transit Law in the Nineteenth-Century South." *Chicago-Kent Law Review* 70 (1995): 993–1009.

Moger, Allen W. "Railroad Practices and Policies in Virginia after the Civil War." *Virginia Magazine of History and Biography* 59 (1952): 423–57.

Monroe, Elizabeth Brand. *The Wheeling Bridge Case: Its Significance in American Law and Technology.* Boston, 1992.

Montgomery, David. *The Fall of the House of Labor.* New York, 1991.

Moore, Barrington, Jr. *Social Origins of Dictatorship and Democracy: Lord and Peasant in the Making of the Modern World.* Boston, 1967.

Morris, Thomas D. *Southern Slavery and the Law, 1610–1860.* Chapel Hill, NC, 1996.

Morris, Thomas R. *The Virginia Supreme Court, an Institutional and Political Analysis.* Charlottesville, VA, 1975.

Morton, Samuel George. *Crania Americana.* Philadelphia, 1839.

Moses, John. *Illinois, Historical and Statistical, Comprising the Essential Facts of Its Planting and Growth as a Province, County, Territory, and State.* Chicago, 1892.

Nash, Gary B. "The Philadelphia Bench and Bar." *Comparative Studies in Society and History* 7 (1965): 203–20.

National Cyclopaedia of American Biography. New York, 1904.

Nedelsky, Jennifer. *Private Property and the Limits of American Constitutionalism: The Madisonian Framework and Its Legacy.* Chicago, 1990.

Neuman, Gerald L. *Strangers to the Constitution: Immigrants, Borders, and Fundamental Rights.* Princeton, NJ, 1996.

Nock, O. S. *Railways of the USA.* New York, 1979.

Nolan, Dennis R. "The Effect of the Revolution on the Bar: The Maryland Experience." *Virginia Law Review* 62 (1976): 969–97.

Nott, Josiah S., and George R. Gliddon. *Indigenous Races of the Earth.* Philadelphia, 1854.

Novak, William J. *The People's Welfare: Law and Regulation in Nineteenth-Century America.* Chapel Hill, NC, 1996.

Oakes, James. *Slavery and Freedom: An Interpretation of the Old South.* New York, 1990.

O'Brien, David A., ed. *Judges on Judging: Views from the Bench.* Chatham, NJ, 1997.

O'Brien, John T. "Factory, Church, and Community: Blacks in Antebellum Richmond." *Journal of Southern History* 44 (November 1978): 509–36.

"On the Plan and Objects of the American Jurist and Law Magazine." *American Jurist and Law Magazine* 19 (1838): 1–3.

Orren, Karen. *Belated Feudalism.* New York, 1991.

Orser, Charles E., Jr. *The Material Basis of the Postbellum Tenant Plantation.* Athens, GA, 1988.

Ould, Robert. "Address in Honor of the Memory of Judge Moncure." *Virginia Law Journal* 7 (January 1883): 1–4.

Overton, Richard C. *Burlington West: A Colonization History of the Burlington Railroad.* New York, 1967.

Parsons, Talcott. Introduction, *The Theory of Social and Economic Organization,* by Max Weber. New York, 1947.

Peterson, Merrill D. *Democracy, Liberty, and Property: The State Constitutional Conventions of the 1820s.* Indianapolis, 1966.

Pickering, John. "A Lecture on the Alleged Uncertainty of Law; Delivered before the Boston Society for the Diffusion of Useful Knowledge, March 5, 1830." *American Jurist and Law Magazine* 12 (1834): 285–311.

Piott, Steven L. *The Anti-Monopoly Persuasion: Popular Resistance to the Rise of Big Business in the Midwest.* Westport, CT, 1985.

Pocock, J. G. A. *The Machiavellian Moment: Florentine Political Thought and the Atlantic Republican Tradition.* Princeton, NJ, 1975.

————. *Virtue, Commerce and History: Essays on Political Thought and History.* New York, 1985.

Posner, Richard A., ed. *The Essential Holmes.* Chicago, 1992.

Putnam, Robert D. *Making Democracy Work: Civic Traditions in Modern Italy.* Princeton, NJ, 1993.

Quenzel, Carol H. "The Manufacture of Locomotives and Cars in Alexandria in the 1850s." *Virginia Magazine of History and Biography* 62 (1954): 181–9.

R.B.H. "Liability of Hirer." *Quarterly Law Review* 6 (new series, 2) (1861): 1–9.

Rabin, Robert L. "The Historical Development of the Fault Principle: A Reinterpretation." *Georgia Law Review* 15 (1981): 926–61.

Ransom, Roger L., and Richard Sutch. *One Kind of Freedom.* New York, 1977.

Redfield, Isaac F. *The Law of Railways: Embracing Corporations, Eminent Domain, Contracts, Common Carriers of Goods and Passengers, Constitutional Law, Investments, &c., &c., Telegraph Companies.* Boston, 1867.

Reid, John Phillip. "Experience or Reason: The Tort Theories of Holmes and Doe." *Vanderbilt Law Review* 18 (1965): 405–36.

————. *Law for the Elephant: Property and Social Behavior on the Overland Trail.* San Marino, CA, 1980.

Reid, Thomas. *An Inquiry into the Human Mind on the Principles of Common Sense* (1813). Chicago, 1970.

Robert, Joseph C. *The Road from Monticello: A Study of the Virginia Slavery Debate of 1832.* New York, 1965.

Rose, Carol M. *Property and Persuasion: Essays on the History, Theory, and Rhetoric of Ownership.* Boulder, CO, 1994.

Rosenfeld, Richard N. *American Aurora: A Democrat-Republican Returns.* New York, 1997.

Ross, Dorothy. *The Origins of American Social Science.* New York, 1991.

Ross, Richard. "The Memorial Culture of Early Modern English Lawyers: Memory as Keyword, Shelter, and Identity, 1560–1640." *Yale Journal of Law and the Humanities* 10 (1998): 229–326.

"Rules of Decision of the Supreme Court of Appeals of Virginia, in the Exercise of Appellate Jurisdiction, in Certain Classes of Cases." *Virginia Law Journal* 9 (1885): 257–62.

Russell, William. "My Diary North and South" (London 1863). Reprinted in *Prairie State: Impressions of Illinois, 1673–1967, by Travelers and Other Observers,* ed. Paul M. Angle, 334–42. Chicago, 1968.

Salmon, Marylynn. *Women and the Law of Property in Early America.* Chapel Hill, NC, 1986.

Salvatore, Nick. "Response to 'Against Exceptionalism: Class Consciousness and the American Labor Movement, 1790–1920.'" *International Labor and Working Class History* 26 (1984): 25–30.

Salyer, Lucy. "Captives of Law: Judicial Enforcement of the Chinese Exclusion Laws, 1891–1905." *Journal of American History* 76 (1989): 91–117.

Scheiber, Harry S. "Public Rights and the Rule of Law in American History." *California Law Review* 72 (1984): 217–51.

Schumpeter, Joseph. *Capitalism, Socialism, and Democracy.* New York, 1975.

Schwartz, Gary. "Tort Law and the Economy in Nineteenth Century America: A Reinterpretation." *Yale Law Journal* 90 (1981): 1717–75.

Schwartz, Michael. *Radical Protest and Social Structure: The Southern Farmers' Alliance and Cotton Tenancy, 1880–1890.* London, 1979.

Schweber, Howard. "The 'Science' in Legal Science: The Model of the Natural Sciences in Nineteenth Century American Legal Education." *Law and History Review* 17 (1999): 421–66.

Seward, William. "Civilization: American and European." *American Whig Review* 3 (1846): 611–24.

Shade, William G. *Banks or No Banks: The Money Issue in Western Politics, 1832–1865.* Detroit, 1976.

_____. *Democratizing the Old Dominion: Virginia and the Second Party System, 1824–1861.* Charlottesville, VA, 1996.

Shepard, E. Lee. "George Wythe." In *Legal Education in Virginia, 1779–1979: A Biographical Approach,* ed. W. Hamilton Bryson, 749–55. Charlottesville, VA, 1982.

Shepherd, Samuel, ed. *Proceedings and Debates of the Virginia State Convention of 1829–30. To Which Are Subjoined, the New Constitution of Virginia, and the Votes of the People.* Richmond, VA, 1830.

Sherman, Thomas G., and Amansa Redfield. *A Treatise on the Law of Negligence.* New York, 1869.

Shurtleff, Nathaniell B., ed. *Records of the Governor and Company of the Massachusetts Bay in New England.* 2 vols. Boston, 1853.

Silbey, Joel H. *The American Political Nation, 1838–1893.* Stanford, CA, 1991.

Sinopoli, Richard C. *The Foundations of American Citizenship: Liberalism, the Constitution, and Civic Virtue.* New York, 1992.

Siracusa, Carl. *A Mechanical People: Perceptions of the Industrial Order in Massachusetts, 1815–1880.* Middletown, CT, 1979.

Skowronek, Stephen. *Building a New American State: The Expansion of National Administrative Capacities, 1877–1920.* New York, 1982.

Smith, Rogers. *Civic Ideals: Conflicting Visions of Citizenship in U.S. History.* New Haven, CT, 1997.

Starobin, Robert S. "The Economics of Industrial Slavery in the Old South." *Business History Review* 44 (1970a): 131–74.

———. *Industrial Slavery in the Old South.* New York, 1970b.

Stover, John F. *American Railroads,* 2d ed. Chicago, 1997.

Stuart, James. "Three Years in North America" (1833). Reprinted in *Prairie State: Impressions of Illinois, 1673–1967, by Travelers and Other Observers,* ed. Paul M. Angle, 94–9. Chicago, 1968 (page numbers in citations refer to reprinted edition).

"Subjecting Land to the Debts of the Deceased." *American Jurist and Law Magazine* 10 (1833): 457–60.

Sumner, Charles. "Resolutions on Secession and Reconstruction." Reprinted in *The Annals of America,* vol. 9, 323–5. Chicago, 1968.

Sumner, Charles, George Hilliard, and Luther Cushing. "On the Plan and Objects of the American Jurist and Law Magazine." *American Jurist and Law Magazine* 19 (1838): 8–10.

———. "Revisions of the Laws in Massachusetts." *American Jurist and Law Magazine* 13 (1834): 344–5.

Sutton, Robert P. *The Prairie State: A Documentary History of Illinois, Colonial Years to 1860.* Grand Rapids, MI, 1976.

———. *Revolution to Secession: Constitution Making in the Old Dominion.* Charlottesville, VA, 1989.

Swift, Elaine. *The Making of an American Senate: Reconstitutive Change in Congress, 1787–1841.* Ann Arbor, MI, 1996.

Thomas, Emory. *The Confederate Nation: 1861–1865.* New York, 1979.

Thoreau, Henry David. *Walden.* Princeton, NJ, 1971.

Thornwell, James Henley. "A Southern Christian View of Slavery." In *Minutes of the General Assembly of the Presbyterian Church in the Confederate States of America,* Appendix, 55–9. Augusta, GA, 1861.

Tomlins, Christopher L. *Law, Labor, and Ideology in the Early American Republic.* New York, 1993.

Tribe, Laurence H. *American Constitutional Law.* Mineola, NY, 1988.

Trollope, Anthony. *North America* (1862), 2 vols. New York, 1986 (page numbers in citations refer to the reprint edition).

Tucker, Nathan Beverly. "Lecture on the Study of the Law; Being an Introduction to a Course of Lectures on That Subject in the College of William and Mary." *Southern Literary Messenger* 1 (1834): 145–54.

Turner, Bryan. *Citizenship and Capitalism: The Debate over Reformism.* Boston, 1986.

_____. *Citizenship and Social Theory.* Newbury Park, CA, 1993.

Tushnet, Mark V. *The American Law of Slavery, 1810–1860: Considerations of Humanity and Interest.* Princeton, NJ, 1981.

Tyler, Lyon Gardiner, ed. *Encyclopedia of Virginia Biography.* New York, 1915.

Ulrich, Laurel Thatcher. *Good Wives: Image and Reality in the Lives of Women in Northern New England, 1650–1750.* New York, 1982.

Unger, Irwin. *The Greenback Era: A Social and Political History of American Finance, 1865–1879.* Princeton, NJ, 1964.

Unonius, Gustaf. "Chicago, 1857." Reprinted in *The Prairie State: A Documentary History of Illinois,* ed. Bruce P. Sutton, 361–7. Grand Rapids, MI, 1976.

"Usury Laws." *American Jurist and Law Magazine* 6 (1831): 282–309.

"The Utility and Pleasures of Science." *Scientific American* 2 (1847): 381.

Van Schreeven, William James. *The Conventions and Constitutions of Virginia, 1776–1966.* Richmond, VA, 1967.

Vernon, Richard. *Citizenship and Order: Studies in French Political Thought.* Toronto, 1986.

Ver Steeg, Clarence L., and Richard Hofstadter. *Great Issues in American History,* 2 vols. New York, 1969.

Wahl, Jenny Bourne. *The Bondsman's Burden: An Economic Analysis of the Common Law of Southern Slavery.* New York, 1998.

Warden, G. B. "Law Reform in England and New England." *William and Mary Quarterly* 35 (1978): 668–90.

Warren, Charles. *A History of the American Bar.* New York, 1966.

Webster, Daniel. *Writings and Speeches,* 18 vols. Boston, 1903.

Webster, George W. "The Sacredness of Death Is But the Sacredness of Life, Embalmed in Memory, a Sermon, Preached to the First Independent Congregational Society at Wheeling, Va." *Wheeling Gazette* (1851). Collection of the Virginia Historical Society.

Welke, Barbara Y. "Unreasonable Women: Gender and the Law of Accidental Injury, 1870–1920," *Law and Social Inquiry* 19 (1994): 369–403.

_____. "When All the Women Were White, and All the Blacks Were Men: Gender, Class, Race and the Road to Plessy, 1855–1914." *Law and History Review* 13 (1995): 261–316.

Welter, Barbara. "The Cult of True Womanhood: 1820–1860." *American Quarterly* 18 (1966): 151–74.

Wertenbaker, Thomas J. *Norfolk, Historic Southern Port.* Durham, NC, 1962.

Wertheim, Frederick. "Slavery and the Fellow Servant Rule: An Antebellum Dilemma." *New York University Law Review* 61 (1986): 1112–48.

Wharton, Francis. "Liability of Railroad Companies for Remote Fires." *Southern Law Review* 1 (1876): 729–47.

White, G. Edward. *The Marshall Court and Cultural Change.* New York, 1988.

White, Lawrence H., ed. *Democratick Editorials: Essays in Jacksonian Political Economy by William Leggett*. Indianapolis, 1984.

Wiecek, William M. *The Lost World of Classical Legal Thought: Law and Ideology in America, 1886–1937*. New York, 1998.

Wilentz, Sean. "Against Exceptionalism: Class Consciousness and the American Labor Movement, 1790–1920." *International Labor and Working Class History*, 26 (1984b): 1–24.

————. *Chants Democratic: New York City and the Rise of the American Working Class, 1788–1850*. New York, 1984a.

Wilson, Major L. *Space, Time and Freedom: The Quest for Nationality and the Irrepressible Conflict, 1815–1861*. Westport, CT, 1974.

————. "What Whigs and Democrats Meant by Freedom," in *The Many-Faceted Jacksonian Era*, ed. Edward G. Pessen, 177–91. Westport, CT, 1977.

Wolcher, Louis. "The Privilege of Idleness: A Case Study of Capitalism and the Common Law in Nineteenth Century America." *American Journal of Legal History* 36 (1992): 237–325.

Wood, Charles H., and Joseph D. Long. *Digest of the Illinois Reports*. Chicago, 1882.

Wood, Gordon S. *The Creation of the American Republic, 1776–1787*. New York, 1969.

Woods, John. "Two Years' Residence in the Settlement on the English Prairie, in the Illinois Country . . . with an Account of Its Animal and Vegetable Productions, Agriculture &c., &c., a Description of the Principal Towns, Villages, &c., &c., with the Habits and Customs of the Backwoodsmen" (1822). Reprinted in *Prairie State: Impressions of Illinois, 1673–1967, by Travelers and Other Observers*, ed. Paul M. Angle, 76–83. Chicago, 1968 (page numbers in citations refer to reprinted edition).

Wooster, Ralph A. *Politicians, Planters and Plain Folk: Courthouse and Statehouse in the Upper South, 1850–1860*. Knoxville, TN, 1975.

Wright, Gavin. *The Political Economy of the Cotton South: Households, Markets, and Wealth in the Nineteenth Century*. New York, 1978.

Zochert, Donald. "Science and the Common Man in Ante-Bellum America." *Isis* 65 (1974): 448–73.

Zweiben, Beverly. *How Blackstone Lost the Colonies: English Law, Colonial Lawyers, and the American Revolution*. New York, 1990.

Index